MEDIATING TRAVEL WRITING, MEDIATED CHINA

The Middle Kingdom in Travel Books and Blogs

Stefano Calzati

MEDIATING TRAVEL WRITING, MEDIATED CHINA

The Middle Kingdom in Travel Books and Blogs

Stefano Calzati

COMMON GROUND RESEARCH NETWORKS 2018

First published in 2018
as part of the New Directions in the Humanities Book Imprint
http://doi.org/10.18848/978-1-61229-981-5/CGP (Full Book)

Common Ground Research Networks
2001 South First Street, Suite 202
University of Illinois Research Park
Champaign, IL
61820

Library of Congress Cataloging-in-Publication Data

Names: Calzati, Stefano, author.
Title: Mediating travel writing, mediated China : the Middle Kingdom in
   travel books and blogs / Stefano Calzati.
Description: Champaign, IL : Common Ground Research Networks, 2018. | "First
   published in 2018 as part of the New Directions in the Humanities Book
   Imprint"--Title page verso. | Includes bibliographical references.
Identifiers: LCCN 2018018898 (print) | LCCN 2018032273 (ebook) | ISBN
   9781612299815 (pdf) | ISBN 9781612299792 | ISBN 9781612299792 (hardback
   : alk. paper) | ISBN 9781612299808 (paperback : alk. paper)
Subjects: LCSH: Travel writing--China--History. | Travelers'
   writings--History and criticism. | China--Description and travel.
Classification: LCC DS712 (ebook) | LCC DS712 .C345 2018 (print) | DDC
   915.104--dc23
LC record available at https://lccn.loc.gov/2018018898

Cover Photo Credit: Mónica O'Doherty López-Varela
Logo for CompLit InterArt book series Credit: Mónica O'Doherty López-Varela

Table of Contents

ACKNOWLEDGEMENTS

This thesis benefitted from the influence of many people who I sincerely feel the need to thank here. I owe my gratitude to my supervisors, Dr. Claudia Sternberg and Dr. Diane Morgan, for guiding my writing, dissipating my doubts, and compelling me to critically reflect upon my ideas.

Over these years, I have built links with scholars in the field of postcolonial studies and literature, cultural studies, and digital humanities. I would like to express my gratitude to the scholars I met in Hong Kong during the fieldwork: Prof. David Huddard and Prof. Julia Kuehn, for sharing their ideas on postcolonial literature and contemporary travel writing; Prof. Roberto Simanowski and Dr. Luciana Gattass, with whom I had illuminating conversations about the effects of social media on our lives. I also thank Prof. Simona Cigliana, who has tirelessly encouraged me to write and publish.

This thesis would not exist without the kind contribution of the writers I interviewed and the people who helped me to translate from Chinese the extracts quoted in the thesis. I also would like to mention the financial support I received during these three years: the Stanley Burton scholarship of the University of Leeds, which fully funded my PhD, and also the two grants, respectively from the Worldwide University Network (WUN) and the Universities' China Committee in London (UCCL), without which the fieldwork would have never seen the light.

Many other PhD students and friends accompanied my writing. They were an essential support against (and a refreshing distraction from) the blind alleys of the PhD. To mention them all would be too long, but this, I hope, does not diminish how thankful and honored I was to encounter them.

I am immensely grateful to my parents: wherever I go, whatever choice I make, they always back me, and this means a lot to me.

Last, my thoughts go silently to a person who is no longer by my side, but whose presence was crucial for the genesis of this work and her inspiration continues to be so for me today.

Introduction

You conduct a meeting in which the object participates, so that, together, object and
methods can become a new, not firmly delineated, field.

Mieke Bal, *Travelling Concepts*

To make your fortune, as the genre of the picaresque has long shown us, you have to
leave home and, often, to travel a long way.

Jonathan Culler, *Philosophy and Literature: The Fortune of the Performative*

This study is primarily concerned with establishing relations among its varied objects
of study: travel writing and China, printed and online travelogues, Western and
Chinese-authored texts, contemporary oeuvres as well as older ones. This work makes
travel books and travel blogs about China its center of interest and the lenses through
which addressing wider issues, such as the current status of the travel writing genre,
the kind of knowledge and social (dis)empowerment that travelogues in different
medial formats[1] may produce for readers and writers, and the confrontation between
authors from diverse literary and cultural backgrounds. Due to the intrinsic cross-
disciplinarity of the work, from literary and postcolonial studies to media ecology and
electronic literature, some concepts such as "paratext," "hypertextuality," and
"chronotope" are sometimes used outside of their native theoretical milieu (Mieke
Bal's quote in excerpt echoes) and other voices, that is, those of travel writers[2],
accompany the analysis in order to move from within the text *per se* toward an
exteriority that helps to think of travel books and blogs not merely as documents, but
as cultural artifacts and the outcomes of an endless negotiation between travelling and
writing. In doing so, the research is also led to interrogate its own analytical conduct
and, with it, the (supposed) theoretical divide between printed and digital texts, verbal
and visual modes, the West[3] and China, contemporary and "classic"[4] travel writing.
Method and objects, then, interpenetrate, collaborate, challenge each other, up to the
point where the present work becomes a *mise en abyme* of (and about) travel writing,

---

[1] The "book" and the "blog" are referred to here as "medial formats." While books and blogs are more than
mere "supports," such as a piece of paper, they cannot straightforwardly be regarded as media (e.g., the
radio, TV, and cinema). "Medial format," then, is a label that aims at finding a terminological compromise
to this in-between condition.
[2] In this work, the term "writers" encompasses both the authors of printed travel books and travel bloggers.
[3] According to the Oxford English Dictionary, the "West" chiefly refers to Europe and North America. Such
a definition is valid for the present work (with the sole exception of travel author Nathan Gray, who is from
New Zealand). However, as will emerge during the analysis of the interviews in Chapter 3, today the term
is more and more disjoined from a precise geographical frame and is increasingly charged with a political
connotation that comes to include all those areas of the globe that have entered the later stage of
industrialization.
[4] The term "classic" refers here to late 19th century/early 20th century texts.

insofar as it tests its own findings by reflecting upon the results of the three-month fieldwork in Hong Kong and China in which I was involved as both a scholar and a travel blogger (it is in this respect that Jonathan Culler's statement unfolds its full significance). All these issues will be hopefully expounded here, in the Introduction, whose function, more than elsewhere, is not so much to inform the reader about what s/he will find in the following pages, but to clarify the unifying principle for the upcoming analysis.

***

Travel writing is currently one of the most appealing genres in literature from both a commercial and an academic point of view. It is evident, even from a cursory survey of bookstores' shelves, that travel writing enjoys a popularity that is at odds with all the Cassandras announcing the imminent death of "real" travel and testifies, instead, to the genre's resilience and flexibility. On the other hand, to mention travel writing within an academic environment cannot but trigger a whole series of cultural, political, and epistemological[5] issues that have fueled the debate on this genre since what Grzegorz Moroz and Jolanta Sztachelska (2010: ix) have called "'the turn to theory' in Anglophone literary criticism." From an object of study, travel writing has gradually evolved into a field of enquiry of its own, attracting interventions from a variety of approaches and disciplines (see Hooper and Youngs 2004). The present work owes much to these studies – postcolonial studies *in primis* – as well as to the critical milieu – post-structuralism – from which they derive. Indeed, these investigations have drawn attention to a genre that was canonically considered "minor literature" and have done so by dislocating travel writing outside of stringently literary circles and unpacking its political and cultural implications variously bound to issues of privilege, mobility, and ideology (see, among others: Said 1978; Hulme 1986; Ashcroft, Griffiths, and Tiffin 1989; Pratt 1992; Spurr 1993; Lisle 2006; Douglas 2009; Huggan 2009).

At the same time, this work moves beyond the critical framework provided by these studies in that it also looks at travel writing on the Web. Thus, travel blogs are regarded as an instance of electronic literature and, specifically, a form of digitally based storytelling that variously re-enacts the journey and the encounter between Self and Other. According to Convertkit (2017) report on the state of the blogosphere, "travel" is permanently in the top 10 of the most popular blogs – seventh position – and the corresponding tag is ranked among the 30 most popular. Since the first decade of the new millennium, academic literature on blogs has witnessed an exponential blossoming. Methodologies adopted to study blogs include, among others, content analysis (Herring, Scheidt, Kouper, and Wright 2007; Papacharissi 2007; Bonsagit, McCabe, and Hibbert 2009), rhetorical analysis (Miller and Shepherd 2004), and ethnographic analysis (Nardi, Schiano, Gumbrecht, and Swartz 2004). These studies

---

[5] "Epistemology" is used in its broad (Anglo-Saxon) meaning of knowledge, thus transcending its narrower reference to "scientific knowledge" usually adopted in continental philosophy.

are significant insofar as they provide valuable data about features of blogs and blogging strategies. For instance, they show, contrary to commonly held assumptions, that blogs are mainly composed of written language and present a low frequency of links and comments (Herring, Scheidt, Kouper, and Wright 2007). Findings also reveal that blogs are mainly conceived as single-authored, personal diaries (Herring, Scheidt, Kouper, and Wright 2007; Papacharissi 2007), rather than as collaborative endeavors. The major limit of these studies is that they all conceive of blogs exclusively as a new kind of communicative genre: a conception that leads to blogs being considered in isolation from the medial, cultural, and literary background that informs them. In doing so, these studies overlook the complex interrelation of rhetorical[6] and medial features of blogs, as well as their epistemological and social underpinnings. Furthermore, not only are these studies a decade old by now, which is a significant time span when it comes to the exploration of the Web, but they are transversal in scope, that is, they do not focus on any specific themes. Hence, it becomes interesting to understand the extent to which the findings of these works may also apply to the specific case of more recent travel blogs.

Despite the consistency of literature on blogs, studies that concentrate on travel blogs are still limited (Pan, MacLaurin, and Crotts 2007; Carson and Schmallegger 2008; Pühringer and Taylor 2008; Wenger 2008). Carson and Schmallegger (2008: 101) define travel blogs as "personal webpages from travellers who publish their personal stories and recommendations." However formally correct this definition may be, it remains silent with respect to all those rhetorical and medial aspects that characterize travel blogs (not last concerning the encounter between the traveler and the host culture). Nonetheless, the definition's deficiency is at least indicative of the functional purposes underpinning much research on travel blogs: indeed, all the above-mentioned studies adopt a quantitative approach in the attempt to extract marketing information about tourists' behavior, rather than addressing travel blogs as texts (exceptions are Angé and Deseilligny 2009; Tang and Chao 2010). In this respect, Banyai and Grover (2012: 268) write that "although travel blogs offer destination marketers a window into tourists' travel experiences, research analysing the content of online travel diaries is still in its infancy." It is this statement that represents the starting point of the present study.

BETWEEN BOOKS AND BLOGS: TRAVEL WRITING AND TRANSMEDIALITY

While placing travel writing at the center of the analysis, this study travels in its turn. In order to avoid the risks of techno-determinism that a focus solely on travel blogs (or travel books) may imply, the analysis is grounded on a comparative approach: more precisely, a transmedial comparative approach. The underlying assumption of this work is that travel books and travel blogs represent two "intermedial transpositions" (Wolf 2008) that realize the same generic matrix: travel writing. "Intermedial transposition" is a phrase whose conceptual validity must be assessed in

---

[6] See further below for a definition of "rhetorical."

relation to two related terms: "transmediality" and "remediation." The former, coined by Henry Jenkins (2006: 6), acknowledges "the flow of content through multiple media platforms"; in other words, transmediality accounts for, and investigates, the redistribution of texts (broadly defined) on various media. The latter term was introduced by David Bolter and Richard Grusin (1998) in order to define how a given text is affected when passing from one medium to another. While Jenkins largely considers transmediality as one consequence of the hybridization among media and sees the Web as the medium that promotes this hybridization the most, Bolter and Grusin focus more on the effects that the process of medial transposition has on a given text, passing from a rendition of "immediacy," when the re-mediated text is as faithful as possible to the source, to "hypermediacy" when the text is deeply modified, according to the features of the new medium. The shared premise that links these terms is that all processes of transposition affect how a text is conceived, produced, and received. Here, however, the departing point is slightly different from that of Jenkins and Bolter and Grusin, insofar as it concentrates on the various realizations that a whole genre – travel writing – can take. So, the notion of "intermedial transposition" is best suited, as it fosters the idea of different occurrences on different medial formats that refer to the same generic matrix.[7] At this point, then, it is necessary to provide an operative definition of travel writing.

Despite the increasing attention to travel writing within academia since the 1970s, the elaboration of a commonly accepted definition of this object/field of study leaves scholars quite far from agreement. Problems are of a semantic, formalistic, and medial nature. According to Paul Fussell's (1980: 203) seminal definition, travel books are "a sub-species of memoir in which the autobiographical narrative arises from the speaker's encounter with distant or unfamiliar data, and in which the narrative unlike that in a novel or a romance claims literal validity by constant reference to actuality." Notwithstanding the hierarchization of "memoir" and "biography," which is left unexplained, from a transmedial point of view the main problem with Fussell's definition is to be found in the conflation between travel writing (as a genre) and the travel book (as a medial format). Carl Thompson (2011: 19) writes that "difficulties arise with any suggestion that we can equate travel writing in its entirety with the form Fussell calls the travel book." More broadly, the travel writing genre seems refractory to any definition that does not also take into account the format that "carries" the text, as the labels "travel book" and "travel blog" attest.[8] Therefore, the transmedial comparison advanced here results particularly fruitful in linking what is written in the texts to the analysis of the medial formats' features. Conceptually speaking, this is no novelty, after all, if only one thinks of Marshall McLuhan's ([1964] 1996) widely acknowledged idea that "the medium is the message." In fact, the present work is grounded on the assumption not only that the medium plays a role in the definition of genres, but more radically that the medium is

---

[7] The terms "transmediality" and "remediation" will be used interchangeably whenever the process of transposition from one medial format to the other will be discussed.
[8] This also happens in French and Italian: "récit de voyage," "blog de voyage"; "libro di viaggio," "blog di viaggio."

consubstantial to genre. Put differently, any text can be defined as the coalescence of generic and medial features, that is, what could be named a "*genium*" (genre + medium). Since no intermedial transposition is a neutral process, the book and the blog do have a significant influence on how the travel narrative is conceived and the genre eventually "interpreted" by and within these medial formats (Calzati 2013b). Based on this premise, to conduct a transmedial comparison between travel books and travel blogs (and also among them) means to acknowledge the specific "affordances" (Gibson 1977) of a given medial format and understand how these affect what is told in the texts. This is particularly pertinent when realizing that travel books and travel blogs are often enriched by a variety of visual elements – pictures, drawings, maps – which make of them multimodal texts (and, in the case of blogs, interactive ones). To consider all these elements as complementary to the written text or to overlook them altogether would be both reductive and misleading. Hence, this work aims to organically include them into the analysis by thinking of each text as a medially, generically, and culturally shaped artifact. This idea also echoes Asuncion López-Varela's (2016) prescription (and auspice) for literary and media studies to "move beyond the linearity of analogue models, to the semiotically complex narratives, prefigured in the navigable interactive spaces of online narrative phenomena" in order to effectively consider texts (here travel writings) as the constantly temporary instances stemming out of broader cultural practices.

Concerning the formal aspect of travel writing, Patrick Holland and Graham Huggan (1998: 14) overcome Fussell's hierarchization between autobiography and memoir by arguing that travel writing is a mix of the two: "like other autobiographies," they contend, "[travel writing] seeks to make retrospective sense out of discrete experiences"; however, in contradistinction to autobiographies, "travel narratives are less concerned with recuperating, or reinventing, a single self, than with following the trajectory of a series of selves in transit. In this sense, travel writing is more closely affiliated with memoir." On this same issue, Jonathan Raban (1988: 253-4) is even more inclusive when he famously claims that "as a literary form, travel writing is a notoriously raffish open house. It freely mixes narrative and discursive writing." Pushing this reasoning to the extreme, the most radical position is that of Jan Borm (2004: 13), according to whom "the point to determine is whether travel writing is really a genre at all. I shall argue here that it is not a genre, but a collective term for a variety of texts both predominantly fictional and non-fictional, whose main theme is travel." Eventually, it seems, the point is not so much to broaden or restrict the field that travel writing embraces, but to look at it from a different perspective. More specifically, the difficulty of elaborating a commonly accepted definition of travel writing can be disentangled by recalling Carolyn Miller's (1984: 151) words on genre: "an understanding of genre," she notes, "can help us account for the way we encounter, interpret, react to, and create particular texts." Put differently, according to Miller the notion of genre can (and should) tell us something about *how* texts work. Starting from here, it is contended that travel writing can be best understood when regarding it as a *rhetorical praxis*. The adjective "rhetorical" encompasses, in Miller's spirit, the ensemble of semantic, formal, and pragmatic features of the texts.[9] The first term – semantic – refers to what travelers recount – places visited, people encountered, historical and biographical anecdotes, etc. – as well as the strategies they resort to in order to represent and convey their experiences, such as figures of speech, stereotypes, visual elements, etc. In terms of form, this work is primarily concerned with first-person (either singular or plural) narratives. The stress on the presence in the texts of a clear narrating subject has one main motive: all those texts that keep at their core the "theme of travel" (as noted by Borm), but are predominantly informative, non-narrative texts, such as travel guides, will not be taken into account. As Stacy Burton (2014: 17) points out in her study *Travel Narrative and the End of Modernity*, the notion of narrative "puts into the foreground a crucial aspect of travel texts that has become more pronounced as they present themselves not as documentary studies but as stories, as narrator's accounts of their own subjective experiences." Great attention is then devoted to how travel writers decide to personally shape their stories and how they inscribe themselves in the text, what they decide to tell and, presumably, what they overlook. It must also be noted that, far from being congenital to the genre, the emergence in travel writing of an overt narrator mainly characterizes late-modern and contemporary texts. In early modern British travelogues, for instance, it was the rule for travelers – rather than the exception – to mask their observation behind a constructed neutrality that had to convey a sense of objectivity and reliability (see Thompson 2011).

A further issue concerning the form of travel writing has to do with the distinction between factual and fictional modes of narration. Holland and Huggan (1998) advance a valid argument when they state that any neat separation between these two modes is theoretically preposterous, since all accounts are, to a degree, fictitious; as a consequence, they talk of travel writings (quoting Hayden White) as "fictions of factual representation" (10). Although this position can be shared from a formalistic point of view, it is still inadequate, as it remains silent on one crucial point about travel writing, namely the relation to truth that these texts (pretend to) construct (Thompson 2011). This is strictly bound, on the one hand, to the way in which a given culture shapes its own concepts of truth, reliability, and accuracy, and, on the other hand, to what kind of information is expected from travel writing. Chapter 2 will be dedicated to this issue; here, it suffices to suggest that travel accounts, independently from their degree of fictionality, have to be plausible, thus describing experiences that really happened or are likely to have happened (on this point see also Hulme and Youngs 2007). The criterion of "plausibility" is propaedeutic to the exclusion from the realm of travel writing of more or less imaginary texts.

The last point to address is the extent to which travel writing can be considered as a pragmatic genre. In this respect, it is illuminating to remind ourselves of the opening words of Casey Blanton's (2002: 3) *Travel Writing: The Self and the World,* in which the author states that travelogues are texts "whose main purpose is to introduce us to

---

[9] In the present work, "rhetorical" comes closer to the notion of "genre." However, while the former stresses the various (semantic, formal, and pragmatic) characteristics of the text, the latter points to the relation between these characteristics as a whole and a given medial format.

the other and that typically demonstrate an engagement between the Self and the world." Travel writing constitutes a *mise en abyme* – through words, illustrations, interactive elements – of an experience that approaches and conflates different individual and collective cultural universes. This means that travel writing not only (as a literary genre) is historically determined in that it "changes, evolves, and decays" (Miller 1984: 13); but, as a praxis, it is synchronically shaped by the dynamic interplay between travelling and writing, between discovering and reflecting, between present and past; a dynamic, then, that has to be intended as socially and culturally dependent. Michel Butor's words ([1974] 2001: 70) can be revealing: "I travel in order to write because to travel, or at least to travel in a certain way, is to write (first of all because to travel is to read) and to write is to travel." It is from this sentence that one needs to start for looking at travel writing and, more precisely, at travelling and writing from a different point of view. A bare definition of "travel" is that of a displacement through space (or, more imaginatively, time). However, from the outset, "travelling" means something more. It signifies to introduce oneself to the Other, by dramatizing the engagement between oneself and the world. When it comes to Butor's statement in parenthesis, in which the French philosopher specifies that "to travel is to read," two interpretations are possible. The first one relates to the literal meaning of the act of reading. In this sense, by arguing that "to travel is to read," Butor points to the accumulation of knowledge, through various acts of reading, that the traveler acquires (about the visited country) not only before but also during and after the journey. In this sense, then, reading is a concrete act that enriches and transcends the travel experience *per se*. At the same time, reading can have a more metaphorical meaning: insofar as a journey puts the traveler in contact with an alterity, s/he is asked to "negotiate" such an encounter (i.e., make sense of it). To do so means to (be able to) "read" the Other, that is, recognize and understand it. However one decides to interpret the statement, it is evident that according to Butor, reading becomes the *conditio sine qua non* of travelling and writing (or at least of these practices done "in a certain way"). If the traveler is unable to read the encounter with difference, then travelling and writing lose their force: they lack that "transforming power" Butor mentions later on. Travelling, writing and reading all embed a transforming power which is dependent firstly upon the kind of journey the traveler accomplishes – the places s/he visits, his/her attitude toward the experience, etc. – and consequently on how s/he writes about it (Butor specifies that the form of the account is strictly related to the kind of journey accomplished). Eventually, Butor's claim tells us something about travelling and writing, namely that they are two symmetrical practices of knowledge.[10] On the one hand, any journey fuels (and is triggered by) what Pierre Bourdieu (1990: 35) defines as the desire of "escaping one's inattentive familiarity." Put differently, travelling kindles an attentive (pre)disposition toward the encounter with (and recognition of) otherness (which can occur at all latitudes, although the contact discussed here between Western travelers and China is cross-culturally charged). On the other hand, writing is a gesture of unavoidable inscription in the text

---

[10] See also Calzati 2014, 2015a, 2015b.

of the writer's self. More precisely, writing is an always-subjective trace into which the writer can eventually re-trace something of him/herself. In so doing, writing reveals the presence of the self to itself by marking a spatial (on the page) and temporal (in the sequentiality of writing and reading) distance from it. It is, then, possible to contend that while travelling helps to get in contact with what is perceived as (socio-culturally) different, writing entails a form of (gnoseological) understanding of the self through the page. From here, travelling and writing can be regarded as two complementary practices of knowledge: two practices, indeed, whose fixation on different medial formats – here books and blogs – give birth to remediated storytelling forms that attest "the constitution, confirmation and modification of human experiences" (López-Varela and Sukla 2015: x).

WRITING CHINA: THE POLITICAL RELEVANCE OF LITERATURE AND NEW MEDIA

At this point, it seems both useful and necessary to explain the choice of China as the thematic focus of the texts. The first reason is purely operative. As the present work is largely founded on a transmedial comparison between two different kinds of genium, there was the need to find a common thread that could delimit the scope of the analysis and make it more incisive. Hence, the choice of China responds to a unifying principle that projects an overall coherence over the selected texts.

There are, however, other more poignant motives that make China a privileged object of interest. In the introduction to *Sinographies: Writing China*, Eric Hayot, Haun Saussy and Steven Yao (2007: x) contend that "set as far as possible from the interfering West, China stands in not simply for an authentic otherness but for the very possibility of authenticity itself." In other words, China has represented over the centuries the ultimate emblem of Otherness for Western travelers; as such, it makes the investigation of the encounter between traveler and visited-culture more relevant. Yet, the statement quoted above contains, at least to an extent, an ideologically inflated vision, whose main effect is to deny to China any historical and cultural contingency. The point is that, while it is certainly important to "acknowledge[s] the fact that China is written" (Hayot, Saussy, and Yao: xi), because any representation not only draws on reality but contributes to its shaping, it is also necessary to remember that there is a "real" China out there from which travel writers draw inspiration. This entails, in Nicholas Clifford's (2001: 14-15) words, that one must "get behind any notion that there has been a single 'essentialized' Orient or China in the mind of the West and must be concerned with heterogeneity, with the interplay between the subjective and the objective." What Clifford does is to warn against the risk of an excessive discursivization of China, which would negate any possibility of "knowing" the Middle Kingdom[11] through the eyes and the words of travel writers.

---

[11] The term "Middle Kingdom" is used as a synonym of China. It does not bear any cultural connotation. It simply refers to the linguistic translation of the term "Zhōngguó" (中国), which means "China" in Mandarin and can be literally translated as "middle territory."

Clifford's argument is also a reaction against an all-encompassing interpretation of Edward Said's (1978) *Orientalism*, which has deeply influenced studies on travel writing. On this point, Dennis Porter (1991: 4) wisely notes that if the Orientalization of the East is a totalitarian discursive project, then "a knowledge as opposed to an ideology of the Other is impossible." The hypothesis here is that one can get to know China through travel books and travel blogs, but, in order to weigh and assess such knowledge, texts must be contextualized through the study of their genesis, as well as of the cultural ethos that informs them.

An additional reason for China to be a significant object of study is that, despite its gradual overture to the world since the late 1970s, it seems to remain variously incomprehensible for Westerners. By retracing the genealogy of the encounter between the West and the East – in particular, China and India – John Clarke (1997: 4) notes that "even where there was respect for the East, often to the point of elevating it to a position high above the 'decadent' West, the otherness, even the strangeness, of the East has been emphasised." As the analysis will show, this trope is still widespread today: China is often perceived and represented in contradictory ways that crystallize around the (sublimated) idea of mysteriousness. By collating travel texts from different cultural contexts and of different medial natures, this study probes the possibility of deconstructing China's often-elusive representation. In so doing, the research aims at also pondering the potential of the Web as a channel where to find up-to-date information about the country, in comparison with mainstream media.

This latter point leads to explore the role of the Internet in relation to (and within) China. According to some scholars (see Herold 2013; MacKinnon 2013; Hockx 2015) the West has usually an overemphasized perception of the press's and the Web's censorship in China. However, it is undeniably true that Chinese people can still face difficulties when it comes to delivering messages which differ from the line tolerated by authorities. To support this is the bare fact that some of the Chinese travel writers interviewed for this research had their books and blogs banned in Mainland China (they were only available in Hong Kong or Taiwan). Although – or maybe because – China has now more than 560 million active Internet users (CNNIC 2012), constituting the greatest Net population in the world, "to maintain the CCP's legitimacy and to protect national interests, the Chinese government continues its efforts to build a national 'e-border', also known by some in the West as 'The Great Firewall of China'" (Yuan 2010: 493). The efficacy of the Chinese government in controlling the Web is debated; yet, as Wenli Yuan (2010: 493) notes, "even foreign Internet companies, such as Yahoo! and Microsoft, have cooperated with the Chinese government in monitoring and reporting inappropriate online activities." This means that, however weak the control of the Chinese government may be, when it comes to obtaining news about China, foreign audiences are usually confronted with filtered information.

To be sure, this filtering also concerns Western media to the extent to which news about China largely responds to a restricted agenda that revolves around political or economic issues. Michel Hockx (2015) draws attention to a similar bias by recollecting his experience when researching the Internet literature in China: "many times over the course of my research," he notes, "audiences [in the West] asked very political questions about Chinese literature, of the kind that they would never ask about, for instance, English literature" (9). The hypothesis to be tested here is that contemporary travel books and travel blogs, written by either Western or Chinese writers, could represent a valid alternative to this dominating perspective. As Clifford (2001: 8) makes clear, "above all, there is about the travel account a directness, even a physicality, that is lacking in the work of the expert or the journalist. For the experts are bound by their academic sources, which are alien to us while the journalists are trained to see tomorrow's story, which too quickly becomes yesterday's." Differently from other figures, then, travel writers are more flexible and open in their writing, mixing registers and styles, anecdotes and descriptions, personal reflections and historical facts. This seems to be particularly fitting in the case of blogs, which, as seen above, are commonly conceived as storytelling forms where bloggers tend to express their own opinions with immediacy and informality. The idea, then, is that readers of contemporary travel writing may get a representation of China that deviates from other authoritative but restricted discourse(s) and, in the specific case of blogs, one which can be constantly updated. In fact, starting from the premise, as López-Varela (2016) suggests, that online "virtual community members act simultaneously as observers, participants, producers and critics of the multi-networked content," this work aims at exploring the extent to which travel blogs may provide an updated representation of China as a result of the cooperation among online readers/bloggers.

Overall, the relevance of the present work for scholars concerned with travel writing, China, and transmedial studies lies in the reading and collation of differently mediated contemporary texts (with the exception of Chapter 4). While much research on travel writing focuses on travelogues spanning usually from the Middle Ages to the first decades of the 20th century, at present, as Burton (2014: 11) points out, "scholars have yet to examine thoroughly exactly how the genre of the travel narrative changed in the twentieth century, or to theorize why these changes occurred." In this respect, the specific case of China is no exception. Existing research has widely explored Western-authored travel accounts from the past (see: Clifford 2001; Kerr and Kuehn 2007; Clark and Smethurst 2008; Kerr 2008).[12] These studies are often inter-disciplinary in nature – from anthropology and ethnography to cultural, gender, and literary studies – and politically concerned (at least in a broad sense of the term). In this sense, they are no doubt a valuable resource, as they represent both a procedural guide and a critical frame for the present work. Nonetheless, stopping often at the first half of the 20th century, these studies need to be complemented with an analysis of contemporary texts that have been so far overlooked. Similarly, some research has been conducted on pre-modern and modern Chinese-authored travel writing (Strassberg 1994; Tian 2012), but to the best of my knowledge there is no study in English that concentrates on the most recent decades. Therefore, at present contemporary travel writing about China – Western- or Chinese-authored; in print or online – remains a largely unexplored terrain.

---

[12] For a comprehensive survey of the literature on this subject, please refer to Chapter 4.

CHAPTERS AND METHODOLOGY

The volume is divided into three parts. Chapters 1 to 3 – the bulk of the study – constitute the first part, which revolves around the transmedial comparison between contemporary Western-authored travel books and travel blogs. As the analysis urges to investigate generic and medial features of the texts in a mutual relation, the research necessitated a holistic approach to the texts, which, while building upon existing literature on travel writing and transmedial studies, could trace its own methodological path in the making of the analysis. Although Chapters 1 to 3 aim at addressing individually a precise feature of travel writing (semantic, formal, and pragmatic), in each chapter rhetorical and medial issues find themselves inevitably interconnected. Hence, if a degree of overlap across the chapters is to be remarked, it will hopefully strengthen the analysis by offering different perspectives on the common transmedial ground, rather than representing a mere repetition.

After a brief introduction that permits to elaborate some preliminary insights about where contemporary travel writers go in China and how they write about the experience, Chapters 1 and 2 propose a bridging approach (and methodology) between print and online travel accounts in order to analyze the semantic and formal features of the texts discussed. Chapter 1 realizes a double theoretical gesture, on the one hand, through the application of Gérard Genette's (1997) concept of "paratext" – coined in relation to written books – to travel blogs, and on the other hand, by resorting to the notion of "hypertext" – largely used in relation to online documents – for the study of printed travelogues. Using these two concepts outside of their theoretical milieu allows moving beyond the self-evident differences between analogue and digital realms and highlighting their commonalities. Thus, to be examined are the ways in which the various rhetorical and multimodal features of the texts work relationally to produce a precise narrative. Inspired by Genette (1980) and Bal's (2002) works on narrative discourse, the spectrum of literary forms that travel writing can take is explored, as well as the ideological underpinnings (and their consequences on the representation of China and the travelers) of the discursive strategies that authors and bloggers decide to adopt. Particular attention is dedicated to the "narrative" and "ideological" functions taken on by the narrator, which, according to Genette, signal shifts in the "mood" of the account, and to the reporting of dialogues, regarded as the textual terrain where the encounter between the traveler and the Chinese occurs.

Chapter 2 calls upon Mikhail Bakhtin's ([1937] 1981) work on the chronotope, and it questions how each genium remodels the basic chronotope of the travel writing genre as "a route covered in a certain amount of time during a specific trip" (Korte 2008: 29). In the conclusion to his work, Bakhtin opens up to the possibility of extending the concept of "chronotope" to the medium that "carries" the text. Elaborating on that, the chronotopicity of the "represented world" – China – is related to the temporal and topological coordinates that each medial format builds and promotes. In fact, it is contended that the book and the blog have their own unique medial chronotope, which also dictates how the travel narrative is shaped. Moreover, since texts are often enriched with pictures, the possibility of applying the concept of chronotope to photography will be also discussed. Eventually, when it comes to consider travel books and travel blogs as texts that can convey information about China, it is necessary to ask, in the first place, what kind of information is at stake – that is, its epistemological horizon – and what are the generic and medial conditions that frame such information. In other words, to compare travel books and blogs means to understand what happens to the practices of travelling and writing when they "land" on the book and the blog formats.

This last issue is at the center of Chapter 3, which looks at travelling and writing as practices and investigates the conditions that make contemporary travel (in China) and writing (about China) possible. Moving beyond a mere taxonomic definition of travel and tourism, the chapter looks at the pragmatic side of the genre and identifies the variety of journeys and writings accomplished by the chosen travel writers, as well as the composite self-representations that they provide of themselves. In order to do that, a number of interviews with authors and bloggers were conducted and they will be referred to[13] in order to build a triangulation between the analysis, the texts, and the writers' own voices. To be sure, the interviews are not regarded as the site where a supposed truth about the text or the author may be found, but are considered as documents too and, as such, subjected to a close reading. The goal is to highlight points of fracture between what the writers say and what is included in their travel accounts.[14]

For this study, interviews were accomplished in various ways: in person, via Skype, or emails (whenever it was not possible to arrange a meeting with the writer). Resorting to different modalities to conduct the interviews made the corpus potentially heterogeneous. Being aware of that does not represent, *per se*, a legitimation that frees these testimonies from methodological critique. Nonetheless, this work pleads for a degree of flexibility in that it does not pretend to be an ethnography in the first place, but rather a literary study that identifies in the interviews a useful source for establishing a dialectics with the texts and the analysis.

The second part of the volume is constituted by Chapter 4. Taking the findings of the first part as its starting point, the chapter takes a diachronic look at Western-authored travelogues from the end of the 19th century toward the 1980s. In this way,

---

[13] With the exception of author Rob Gifford and bloggers BitByTheTravelBug, Viagra8868, and Yǒu Gè A, all contemporary travel writers mentioned in the study were interviewed. The interviews revolved around three main themes: 1) (self)perception of the writer and motives of travel; 2) writing and editorial processes and differences between travel books and travel blogs; 3) representation of China. Departing from these three themes, each interview then followed a flexible path, depending on the writer's work and responses.

[14] At the same time, implementing a close reading of the texts with interviews helps to overcome one of the main criticisms that is usually directed toward text analysis and, in particular, discourse analysis, namely the lack of attention to the sphere of production of the text. For instance, in his review of three books dedicated to critical discourse analysis (Hodge and Kress 1993; Fairclough 1995; Caldas-Coulthard and Coulthard 1996), Henry Widdowson (1998: 138) argues that what is provided in these works "is not the systematic application of a theoretical model, but a rather less rigorous operation" and that "without such theoretical support, the particular analyses (no matter how ingenious and well-intentioned) reduce to random comment of an impressionistic kind." Similarly, John Bateman, Judy Delin, and Renate Henschel (2004: 66), starting from a socio-linguistic standpoint, call for "a much more rigorous empirical basis" when it comes to analyzing texts. Taking the interviews into account is one way to transcend the text and possibly validate (or problematize) the findings of the analysis.

the study reflects upon itself and analyses older texts from a renewed standpoint: one from which an eventual understanding of whether the representation of China and the modes of representation adopted have really changed over time may be gained. Specifically, the analysis builds on Clifford's *A Truthful Impression of the Country* (2001), which surveys Western travel writing about China from the late 19th century to 1949, and tests the findings of this study in light of the discussion about contemporary travel books.

The last chapter – part three – resorts again to a transmedial approach. This time, however, under analysis are a few Chinese-authored travel books and blogs. The corpus of texts is smaller than that of Western-authored travel accounts: the chapter, in this respect, does not aim to constitute an equal balance to the previous analysis. Yet, by exploring how the "represented others" (at least for the present work) look at themselves, the hope is to soften the potential allegation of ethnocentrism with which the study may be charged. Indirectly, also at stake are the features of the travel writing genre and the figure of the travel writer as they are conceived in today's China (and how these differ from pre-modern and modern Chinese travel writing). This chapter is the outcome of three months of fieldwork conducted first in Hong Kong, where I was a visiting scholar at the Chinese University of Hong Kong, and later in Mainland China. The fieldwork was vital to get acquainted with a number of Chinese-authored contemporary travel books and blogs, as well as with scholars in the field. Moreover, it was thanks to this experience that I was personally able to meet with authors and bloggers and interview them, as I did with Westerners.

In the Afterword, I shift the focus from the texts and their authors to myself. During my fieldwork, I kept a blog – www.stillwandering.net – on which I regularly updated posts about my stay at the Chinese University of Hong Kong; my encounters with scholars, writers, photographers, and artists; my reflections about China, as well as my wanderings around the country. One could say that this work, after having travelled so much on paper among concepts, disciplines, and histories has become a performative piece of work itself. Briefly said, I attempted to make theory work (while travelling); the extent to which I managed to do so is not my duty to assess. The most important thing, I would argue, is that research has kept in motion, constantly re-enacting the dialogue between theory and practice, methods and concepts.

Lastly, in the Appendix I have provided a brief synopsis of each contemporary travel book and travel blog analyzed. Far from representing a mere reference list, this section includes significant information concerning the historical and cultural context of each work and writer, and it is referred to various times throughout the volume.

On the Insert tab, the galleries include items that are designed to coordinate with the overall look of your document.

THE ARCHIVE

To conclude the Introduction, it is useful to explain the criteria followed for the selection of the texts. After a preliminary survey, travel books and travel blogs have been distinguished according to two major axes. With regard to travel books, the distinction concerns monomodal texts (composed only of words) and multimodal texts (composed of words and illustrations). As for travel blogs, the major difference is between those blogs that are hosted on platforms and those that have been built independently by the bloggers.

The Western travel books and travel blogs examined here are in three different languages: English (written either by British, US-American, or New Zealand authors), French, and Italian. As a general pattern, each chapter refers to books and blogs in all three languages. This linguistic choice brought with itself a set of issues: 1) it indirectly questioned the homogeneity of the concept of "West"; 2) it greatly enlarged the potential archive of texts; 3) it required translations into English whenever no English-language edition of the text was available. Concerning the first point, it is not my intention to advance any *a priori* assumption about possible cultural similarities and differences among the texts surveyed, nor does it pretend to delve into the complex articulations of the countries' colonial past. The decision to look at texts beyond the English language is mainly an attempt to destabilize the English-centeredness that affects the majority of studies on travel writing (either contemporary or classic) and on blogging. In fact, as Tim Youngs and Charles Forsdick (2012: 12) remark, "the development of the genuinely internationalized critical approach that travel writing merits remains more of an aspiration." At the same time, *a posteriori* one could infer fairly stable patterns in the way in which Western travel writers represent China. However, such a claim would certainly need to rely on a greater corpus of texts to be verified. Concerning the second point, in order to make the corpus of case studies as homogeneous as possible, those texts that recount a proper journey in China were favored. Accounts that derive from residential experiences, or those in which China only represents one among many destinations of a broader journey were excluded.[15] With regard to the third point, I personally translated all the quoted passages in French and Italian whenever the referred text was not available in English; the original versions of the quotations have been provided in footnotes. At the same time, because the medium does play a crucial role in how travel accounts are shaped, it must also be noted that, whenever possible, the first edition of each text was made the object of study. Surely, a comparative reading among the various editions and reprints of each text would have been of interest for understanding how certain editorial choices affect the *mise en forme* of the genium. However, extending the research toward this kind of textual criticism would have exceeded the scope of this work and its core enquiry.

The term "contemporaneity" refers to a period that spans from the mid-1980s, when the effects of opening China's frontiers to foreign people and capital started to be felt around the country, to the present. This frame pertains to travel books only because blogs did not exist back in the 1980s. On this point, it must be remarked that it is difficult to date with precision the origin of blogs, but many scholars converge on the suggestion that the term "weblog" was firstly coined by the writer Jorn Barger in

---

[15] The only two exceptions are Colin Thubron's *Shadow of the Silk Road* (2006) and Oliver Germain-Thomas's *Le Bénarès-Kyôto* (2007). See Chapter 2.

1997 (see Walker-Rettberg 2008). Yet, despite the existence of earlier examples, the blogs I surveyed cover a shorter period, namely from 2005 to the present. This reduction corresponds with an understanding of the history of the World Wide Web that is by now widely accepted. It distinguishes two phases: from the origins of the World Wide Web (early 1990s) to roughly 2004, we witness the development of static pages; from 2005 onwards, the so-called Web 2.0 emerges, characterized by the spreading of dynamic pages and User-Generated Content (UGC). These developments, as the analysis will show, have consequences for both the kind of online writing produced and the difficulty of retrieving and preserving Web documents. All travel blogs mentioned in this work were accessible until October 2016, the only exception being the older version of Becki's blog (www.backpackerbecki.com, which is still retrievable from <http://archive.org>). Lastly, due to the fact that the analysis is, first and foremost, a textual one, those travel blogs which showed consistency in terms of content (i.e., length of the posts) and regularity of the updates (i.e., usually a dozen of posts) were privileged.

As for older travelogues, the temporal frame covered here stretches back to the end of the 19th century and identifies in Isabella Bird's *The Yangtze River and Beyond* (1899) its oldest reference. Bird was by no means the sole Western woman to travel in China at that time, nor the only one to have published an account of her wanderings in the Middle Kingdom (see, for instance, Constance Gordon Cumming's *Wanderings in China*, dated 1886). However, the great popularity enjoyed by Bird's text makes it a good, if not seminal, starting point for the present analysis. Moreover, the last decade of the 19th century is important for another reason: it turns China – at least in the eyes of travelers from the West – into an increasingly alluring land to visit, to the point that Julia Kuehn (2008) speaks of those years as the time in which China becomes a tourist destination.

The selection of Chinese-authored travel books and blogs followed by and large the same criteria used for Western ones. The focus remained exclusively on contemporary texts, because to project the analysis onto the past would have extended the research too far. In this regard, Xiaofei Tian's (2012) *Visionary Journeys: Travel Writings from Early Medieval to Nineteenth-Century China* and Richard Strassberg's (1994) *Inscribed Landscapes: Travel Writing from Imperial China* are two scholarly works that already provide useful insights. Tian's study on Imperial China shows also that Chinese elites, differently from what is commonly argued, widely travelled to the West and reported their impressions to entertain readers at home; Strassberg, instead, retraces the genesis and evolution of Chinese travel writing from the 4th century toward the first half of the 19th century. Strassberg's findings about the rhetorical features of the genre are brought into dialogue with readings of contemporary texts and the interviews with Chinese writers (Chapter 5).

The word "Chinese" comes to encompass people who were born either in Mainland China or in Hong Kong and who have lived in the country for most of their lives. Excluded were, instead, writers from Taiwan and Macau. By no means do these choices want to deny the different histories of the people from Hong Kong and Mainland China, or to erase the complex relations that endure between Mainland China, Taiwan, Macau, and Hong Kong. In fact, these issues will emerge in the last chapter, through the interviews with writers. The reason behind the decision to focus on Hong Kong and Mainland China was primarily practical, as it is where I conducted the fieldwork.

***

This study has travelled a long way, in both a literal and a metaphorical sense. Bal's quotation reported in excerpt about the encounter between object and methods continues as follows: "This is where travel becomes the unstable ground of cultural analysis." I believe this sentence represents the trait d'union linking Bal's and Culler's perspectives, and I hope, indeed, that by travelling – as Culler suggests – this work has made its fortune. The truth is: "travel" – either as a concept or as an object of study; either as a practice or as an imagined endeavor – is always an unstable ground, as it bears in itself the uncertainty of motion; that same uncertainty that springs out from the writing of both the wanderer and the scholar, whose positions, identities, and knowledge are similar in that they are challenged at all times. At every step. By every word.

CHAPTER 1

Travel Narratives Re-Mediated

Accounts narrating the vicissitudes of Westerners who travelled eastward toward China date back at least to the Middle Ages. Venetian merchant Marco Polo (1254-1324) was the first European to leave a detailed account of his peregrinations in Asia and China. Together with his father, Niccolò, and his uncle, Maffeo, they set off from Constantinople in 1271, travelling for two decades in Asia – then ruled by the Mongols – and China, and returning to Venice only in 1294. Jailed during the war between Venice and Genoa, Polo dictated his travel memories to his fellow inmate Rustichello da Pisa. The manuscript *Book of the Marvels of the World*, also known as *The Travels of Marco Polo*, soon spread across Europe and enticed both a great interest in the Far Orient and new journeys.

If Polo's purposes were chiefly commercial, Italian priest Matteo Ricci (1552-1610) reached China at the end of the 16th century with the main goal to establish a permanent Jesuit mission in the Middle Kingdom. In fact, Ricci remained in China until his death, regularly reporting on China's culture, customs and discoveries and spreading within the country not only Catholicism, but also scientific knowledge from Europe, which eventually strengthened the mutual influences between China and the West. Since the Renaissance, journeys to China multiplied in forms and scope: religious, commercial, political, geographical, scientific. "The reports of the Jesuits," writes James Clarke (1997: 41) in his *Oriental Enlightenment*, "were soon followed by those of other travelers, and by the middle of the eighteen century a considerable body of literature on the great civilization of Asia had been built up." The increasing number of accounts opened the doors to Western readers to the long and complex Chinese civilization and generated both positive and negative responses. Philosophers such as Montaigne, Leibniz, and Voltaire "were fascinated by its philosophy, by the conduct of the state, and by its education system, and in all kinds of ways sought to hold it up as a mirror in which to examine the philosophical and institutional inadequacies of Europe" (Clarke 1997: 42). At the same time, other thinkers openly opposed China: "in 1776 Friedrich Grimm pronounced China-worship to be excessive and in bad taste, insisting too that China was an unenlightened despotism, a view which was encouraged by Montesquieu. The most powerful anti-Chinese voice, however, was undoubtedly that of Rousseau" (1997: 52). These polarized perceptions run through the centuries continuously enhancing (rather than diminishing) the interest of the West toward the country: "for the foreigner," Douglas Kerr and Julia Kuehn (2007: 2) write, "there was always more of China than could be travelled, sketched, subjugated, dealt or traded with, inventoried, lectured or marveled at; China was a mise-en-abîme." It is for these same reasons that China has represented an alluring tourist destination for Westerners up to the present. At the same time, by the end of the 19th century, with the peak of Europe's expansionist projects, China became the political target of a number of Western powers. In particular, the two Opium Wars against the British Empire (1839-43 and 1856-60)[16] led to the signing of treaties which forced the Middle Kingdom to open itself to trade with Western powers, establishing, mainly along the east coast and the Yangtze River, a number of ports and possessions.[17] Among other causes, the signing of these treaties and the advancements in transportation turned late 19th century China into a tourist destination, marking the beginning of what Julia Kuehn (2008) has defined as the "China Grand Tour." Specifically, according to Kuehn (2008: 115), it is the travel guidebook by American journalist Eliza Scidmore, *Westward to the Far East* (1900), which underwent several reprints over the last decade of the 19th century, that "marks a shift of emphasis from independent self-directed travel to and in China to a more systematic and prescriptive travel itinerary as part of a Chinese Grand Tour." In other words, at the dawn of the 20th century, the Middle Kingdom officially enters the map of Western tourism. At that time, the itineraries suggested chiefly followed China's east coast, where many of the British, American, French, and German possessions were located. From the already booming city of Shanghai, Scidmore suggests, for instance, to reach Hangzhou and then either to go south to Hong Kong, visiting Ningbo, Wenzhou, Fuzhou and Xiamen, or to go north up to Tianjin and Beijing. In fact, what she proposes are the paths that writers Constance Gordon Cummings (1837-1924) and Isabella Bird (1831-1904) followed in those years and described in their travelogues: *Wanderings in China* (1886) and *The Yangtze River and Beyond* (1899).[18]

Still today, many of these cities – Shanghai, Beijing, Hong Kong, Hangzhou, Tianjin, Xiamen – represent unavoidable stops on a journey to China. While in Beijing, I interviewed Zhang Mei, the founder and manager of the travel company *Wild China*. Zhang is not a travel writer stricto sensu; however, her words are illuminating for understanding where contemporary Western travelers go in China. She described as follows the idea at the base of her company:

> I come from Dali, in Yunnan. When I founded *Wild China* 15 years ago my goal was to sustainably promote cities like Dali as a tourist destination, because I felt that China could not be reduced to the classic itinerary Guilin-Hangzhou-Shanghai-Xian-Beijing. China is much more than that; it is much

---

[16] For a comprehensive account of China's history, see John Roberts's *A History of China* (2011).

[17] More broadly, the power relations between the West and China, as they emerge from the texts that Westerners wrote, indicate the atypical uniqueness of China: while not being systematically colonized by Western powers, China had been forced to accept the presence of Western possessions on its soil. Hence, although China remained fundamentally independent during the expansion of Western colonial enterprises (which reached its peak at the end of the 19th century), this does not mean that China was not the target of imperialistic projects and discourses. Rather, the analysis will reveal the extent to which China was considered a commercial objective and, as such, supposedly in need of foreign guidance.

[18] Bird's travelogue will represent the starting point of the analysis of 20th century travel books, which will be conducted in Chapter 4.

more composite and contradictory, although these destinations still remain on the list.[19]

Having in mind the image that the tourism industry has built of China over at least the last four decades, Zhang's goal is to help people to travel differently. This means, then, to offer alternative experiences to be juxtaposed with the "well-known" China. Zhang elaborated on the consolidated representation that some travelers have of China as follows: "many tourists think of China in terms of its imperial past; my goal is to show them that besides this legacy, China is something else nowadays."

By turning to the contemporary travel books and blogs analyzed in this work, a preliminary assessment of where travel authors and bloggers go in China (and whether their journeys follow those of their predecessors) is advanced. For this task, the summaries of each text provided in the Appendix are of great help. Overall, travel authors accomplish rather long journeys, usually from one to several months. The only exceptions, in this respect, are Sergio Ramazzotti, who stayed in China for a couple of weeks, and those writers who travelled during the 1950s, 1960s, and 1970s, when the itineraries and their duration were strictly dictated by the Chinese authorities (the experiences and works of these authors will be discussed in Chapter 4). Moreover, while many travel authors do visit the most celebrated cities and historical sites of China, they also tend to travel beyond the east coast and to move toward the western regions of the country, in particular the Tibetan plateau. Clara Arnaud, Constantin de Slizewicz, Nathan Gray, Colin Legerton and Jacob Rawson, Luc Richard, and Colin Thubron all delve into the less inhabited (by the Chinese) and frequented (by other travelers) regions of the Middle Kingdom. This means that today's itineraries comply to an extent with those of early 20th century travelers, although contemporary travelers are now exploring China's inland much more frequently. The ways of travelling of contemporary authors are also diversified: by air travel (e.g., Rob Gifford, Bamboo Hirst), public transport (e.g., Olivier Germain-Thomas, Legerton and Rawson, Thubron), private vehicles (e.g., Giorgio Bettinelli, de Slizewicz, Richard), on horseback or on foot (e.g., Arnaud and Gray). This suggests that, beyond visiting less popular areas, contemporary authors also strive for customizing their experience – for example, using uncommon means of transport and/or planning individually their trip, as we will see – in order to make it different, if not extravagant, when compared to that of mass tourists. Zhang's words clarify this idea well: "There are intrinsic human needs to cover the very basic famous sites. This part will never change. What you can change is the way you conceive your travel."[20]

By contrast, the synopses of travel blogs provided in the Appendix show that travel bloggers usually have less time at their disposal: their journeys last from a couple of weeks to roughly a month (Becki is the main exception). In terms of itineraries, a distinction can be identified: those bloggers who post their blogs on

---

[19] Mei Zhang, interview by Stefano Calzati, 11 June 2015, in person.
[20] Mei Zhang, interview.

platforms – such as Travelpod.com[21], Top-depart.com[22] or Turistipercaso.it – usually recount experiences that are limited to the most touristic places: Supermary58, BitByTheTravelBug, Flavia, Mathieu, Millycat all visited only the most popular attractions in China. The bloggers who set up their own online spaces, instead, do go to touristic places, but they also tend to visit less known areas (the main exception, in this regard, is Emil who, on his own blog, describes a fully-arranged touristic trip). Indeed, as bloggers entirely in control of their own online spaces, Becki, Gattosandro Viaggiatore, and Curieuse Voyageuse are also keen to plan their experiences and travel independently. All these points will be expounded in the following chapters; here it suffices to note that the way of travelling and the itineraries followed by the travel writers constitute markers of difference among the texts. For this reason, if it is true, as Michel Butor ([1974] 2001: 84) famously notes, that "the very form of the described trip cannot be completely separated from the form of its description or the effects it produces," it is necessary to investigate how each travel writer decides to recount his/her own experience. This is even more important for an analysis that aims at comparing different kinds of genium (i.e., travel books and travel blogs). In this first chapter, the emphasis lies on the discursive and hypertextual features of the narrative, in order to highlight the ideological underpinnings of the writers' textual choices and their uses of the medial formats.

***

By focusing on six contemporary travel books and six travel blogs, the aim here is to explore the formal features of the texts. A comparison between travel books and blogs, as "intermedial transpositions" of the same genre, requires addressing both how these geniums are modeled as artifacts, and how such modeling affects their affiliation to the "raffish open house" that travel writing represents. The analysis, then, focuses on two interconnected aspects. The first one investigates the way in which the specific affordances of each medial format stir the coming into being of the travelogues, that is, how the texts "appear" and the editorial choices underpinning them. The second aspect has mainly to do with how the narrative discourse is shaped and, consequently, the literary form each text takes. In the introduction to the volume *The Ekphrastic Turn*, which opens this book series, Asun López-Varela and Ananta Charan Sukla (2015: xiii) explain this issue very clearly when they address the necessity of

---

[21] After years of activity, the platform Travelpod.com was closed in mid-2017. Two blogs which were hosted on the platform are discussed in this volume: one by blogger Ataritouchme and the other by blogger Robjstaples. The former can be retrieved on http://archive.org (see also the Bibliography); the latter, unfortunately, has not been stored anywhere and can no longer be reached.

[22] The same fate of Travelpod.com also applies to the French platform Top-depart.com. The blog by Mathieu discussed here, which was on this platform, can also be retrieved on http://archive.org (see Bibliography). No doubt, these cases attest to the volatility and temporariness of online writing in comparison to printed publications. As we will see, this is one of the features of the medial format (online blogs) responsible for shaping travel accounts in a precise way, i.e. as texts to be parsed and surveyed quickly in search of travel tips, rather than enjoyed as a pleasurable reading that provides a clear and personal apprehension (by the traveller) of what s/he has experienced.

investigating "how narratological patterns may or may not operate, depending on the specificity of the medium, when expressed through the physicality of the book and electronic means." In fact, matters of technology and rhetoric can never be fully separated. In this respect, the chapter covers the whole spectrum of the different kinds of texts considered – travel blogs on platforms and individual ones, as well as multimodal and monomodal books – in order to provide a mapping of the whole archive. Moreover, insofar as the intent is to propose a bridging approach between these geniums and the print and online realms (rather than reinstating their differences), the analysis will move back and forth between the print and online realm, starting from travel blogs, going toward travel books, and eventually returning to travel blogs.

Concerning the study of online texts, much of the research in recent years has taken as its starting point printed texts (Shepherd and Watters 1998; Landow 2003; Bateman, Delin, and Henschel 2004; Askehave and Nielsen 2005). In doing so, online texts have been considered as emanating from the realm of print, thus leading to consolidate a one-way approach (Walker-Rettberg 2008), which inevitably highlights the differences between print and online texts and the uniqueness of the latter. In the present work, it is proposed to reverse the perspective and, in order to do that, a double symmetrical gesture is proposed. On the one hand, the notion of "paratext," coined by French scholar Gérard Genette (1997) exclusively in relation to written books, is applied to travel blogs. On the other hand, the concept of "hypertext," widely adopted in relation to online texts, is used for studying travel books. At this stage, the analysis focuses on travel books and blogs as a specific set of texts, but the discussion can be easily extended to other online and print texts.

Secondarily, in order to investigate the literary form of travel books and travel blogs a narratological approach, inspired by Genette's (1980) work on the narrative discourse, is favored. This is motivated by the nature itself of the texts under analysis, which are, in fact, first-person narratives. To study how the texts are shaped means to acknowledge how the writers decided to articulate the narrative, that is, the presence (or absence) of descriptions, personal reflections, dialogues with locals or other travelers, as well as pictures and other visual elements. Elaborating on Mieke Bal's (2002) critique of orthodox narratology, according to which we can never think of a narrative as fully a-ideological, the analysis wants to assess how the representation of Self and Other – of the traveler and China – are ideologically charged.

TRAVEL BOOKS AND BLOGS AS GENIUMS

Gérard Genette (1997: 41) notes in *Paratexts: Thresholds of Interpretation* that "the genre contract is constituted by the whole of the paratext and, more broadly, by the relation between text and paratext." Hence, he suggests that any genre is the result of a negotiation between the text *per se* and the variety of heterogeneous messages – the paratext – that "surround [the text] and extend it, precisely in order to *present* it" (1997: 1). To be precise, all those elements that are included within the book as a medial format – such as the publisher's typesetting choices, title(s) and subtitles, prefaces, introductions, afterwords, and dedications – are called "peritext," while those elements that accompany the book "at a more respectful (or prudent) distance" (1997: 4) – such as interviews with the author, commercials that promote the work, etc. – are defined as "epitext."

The concept of paratext and the theory that Genette built around it are extremely useful to the aims of the present chapter, because they provide a formal framework for the comparison of print and online travel writings. And yet, it is also important to remember that the French original of Genette's work, *Seuils*, dates back to a time – 1981 – when the Web was non-existent and analogue modes of writing, despite the increasing popularity of personal computers, were still dominant. This is possibly one of the reasons that guided Genette's attention to the paratext solely in relation to the book format and as a verbal realization. However, Genette himself acknowledges in his work the possibility of "other types of manifestation" (1997: 14) of the paratext, beyond the written language. In this sense, the comparison between travel books and travel blogs represents a fruitful case study to extend Genette's work to multimodality, as well as to test his findings within a transmedial context.

Multimodal online texts have been studied from a variety of perspectives. Semiotics and socio-linguistics are certainly the most prolific ones (Yates, Orlikowski, and Okamura 1999; Bateman, Delin, and Henschel 2004; Askehave and Nielsen 2005; Knox 2007; Bateman 2008). Günther Kress and Theo van Leeuwen (1996) elaborate a model for the analysis of multimodal texts that directly draws on Michael Halliday's (1978) Systemic Functional Linguistics (SFL). From here, they define a grammar of the possible visual choices that can be made when conceiving a multimodal text and the consequent meanings that these choices carry. Within what they call the "textual" meta-function, Kress and van Leeuwen define three main areas of meaning-making: "salience," "framing," and "information value." Concerning the latter, which is the most important for this chapter and the most debated one, Kress and van Leeuwen argue that the organization of written language and visual elements follows three main oppositions: "top-bottom," "left-right," and "center-margin." The top-bottom opposition realizes a distinction between "ideal" and "real": what is found at the top represents "the idealized or generalized essence of information" (Kress and van Leeuwen: 193), while what is found at the bottom is usually factual information. The opposition left-right produces a distinction between "given" and "new": the former "is something the reader already knows" (Kress and van Leeuwen: 189), whereas the latter "is something which is not yet known to the reader" (Kress and van Leeuwen: 189). The opposition center-margin represents a value distinction between what is "the nucleus of information" (Kress and van Leeuwen: 196) and those other elements that "are in some sense subservient" (Kress and van Leeuwen: 196).

John Knox (2007) has developed Kress and van Leeuwen's study – and specifically the area of "information value" – in order to apply it to webpages, notably newspaper homepages. Knox identifies the dichotomy "head-tail" along the vertical axis, where content on the top part of a webpage is deemed more relevant than that in the bottom part. As for the horizontal axis, Knox argues that content in the central column of the page is of primary importance, while that at the sides is secondary. Knox's study is relevant here in that it adapts Kress and van Leeuwen's work to the online realm. And yet, because his model dates back to the beginning of Web 2.0, when the emergence of dynamic webpages was still at the beginning, it is significant for the discussion developed here to test its validity on today's webpages also and, possibly, to extend it to texts other than online newspapers, namely travel blogs.

***

The analysis focuses first on those travel blogs that are hosted on platforms. The three main platforms discussed here are the Italian Turistipercaso.it[23], the French Top-depart.com[24], and the English Travelpod.com.[25] According to Google Rankings, when the analysis was conducted (2012-2014), these were the three most popular travel blog platforms in each of the three languages surveyed. Turistipercaso.it (Figure 1) is a platform founded in 1998 on the wave of the popularity enjoyed in Italy by the homonymous TV show (the title can be translated as "Tourists by Chance"). On the platform, which is free of charge, travelers and bloggers can find and exchange information about potentially any destination in the world. This is also why the homepage presents a very composite layout that establishes from the outset the richness of the content provided (Figure 1). Travel blogs, of which there are now more than 28,000[26], have a core role within the platform, attested by the fact that the link "Travel Dairies" found on the main navigational bar on the homepage is the second one from the left, just after "Home" (Figure 2). Nonetheless, the platform goes well beyond its function of travel blogs aggregator. Indeed, it includes a variety of other services and links, such as "Magazine," "Forum," "Photos," and "Videos." Therefore, the platform is conceived as a multi-service portal that inflects the theme of travel in many ways and interprets it as a leisure activity in a broad sense.

---

[23] http://www.turistipercaso.it.

[24] http://www.top-depart.com.

[25] http://www.travelpod.com.

[26] Data were found on the "About" section of the website.

Figure 1: The homepage of *Turistipercaso.it*

Figure 2: The main navigational bar of *Turistipercaso.it*

Top-depart.com (Figure 3) is a free French travel blog platform founded in 1997. Before the closure, it hosted more than 140,000 blogs.[27] The platform presents a simple layout: the logo "Top-Depart" occupies the top-left corner of the page, a navigation bar is shown just below, and users can find the most recent updates by scrolling down the page. The big link "Create My Free Blog," which is found on the right side of the homepage, reasserts the importance of the blogging community as one of the core aspects of the website. Yet, the links of the navigation bar on the homepage interpret the idea of travel according to various trajectories: "Travel Blogs," "Organize the Journey," "Travel Guide," and "Travel Forum." Hence, this

---

[27] Data found on the platform's homepage: http://www.top-depart.com.

platform is also meant to be a multifunctional portal in which travel blogs constitute only one of its many sections.

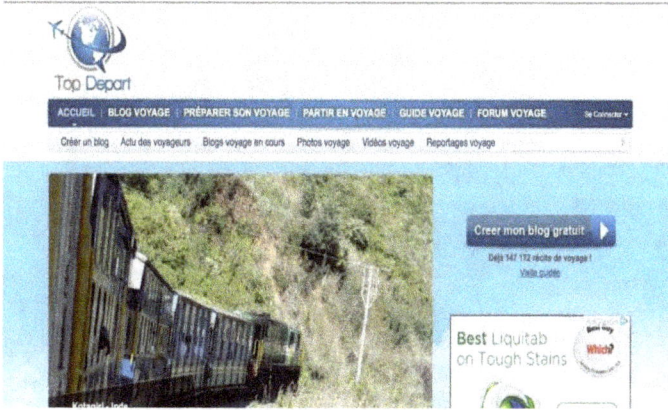
Figure 3: The homepage of Top-depart.com

Travelpod.com is a free English platform founded in 1997. It is the one that most stringently focuses on blogging in relation to travel, as the heading on the homepage "Blogging Built for Travellers" suggests (Figure 4). By scrolling down the page, users get a sense of how the platform works and the services it provides (Figure 5). For instance, bloggers have the chance to visualize their trips on a map, count the miles travelled, or, notably, turn their blogs into a book. In the second half of the homepage one also gets a glimpse of the platform's outreach, in terms of partner companies, number of travel blogs shared per week, and the most popular accounts.

Figure 4: The homepage of Travelpod.com

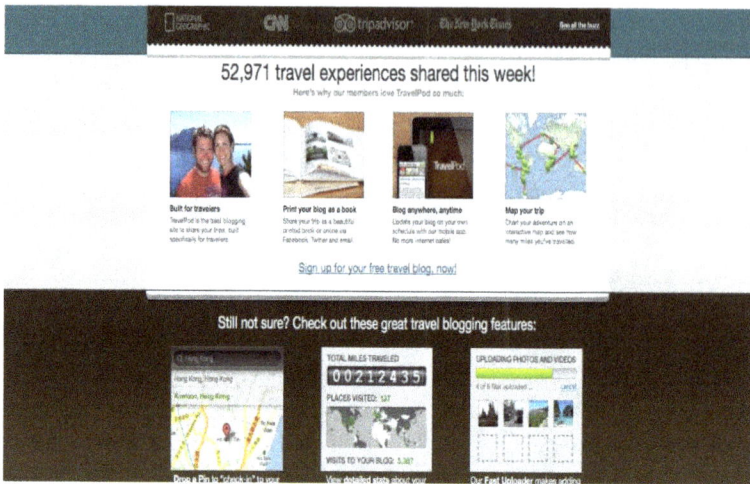

Figure 5: Services and outreach of the platform Travelpod.com

In order to assess the applicability of Knox's model to travel blogs, three case studies from these platforms are discussed: *Cina, nel regno di mezzo* (2012) by Supermary58, *Un peu partout en Chine* (2007) by Mathieu, and *All o'er China during Spring Festival Holiday* (2006) by Ataritouchme. Below are the screenshots of these travel blogs' homepages:

Figure 6: The homepage of Supermary58's blog

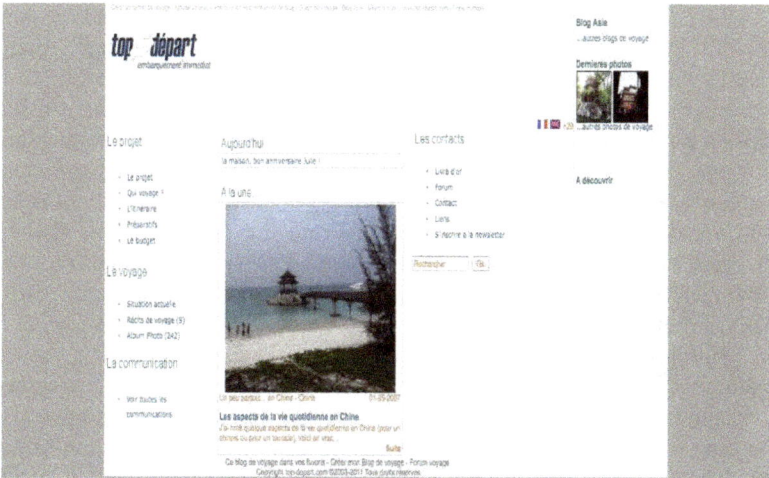

Figure 7: The homepage of Mathieu's blog

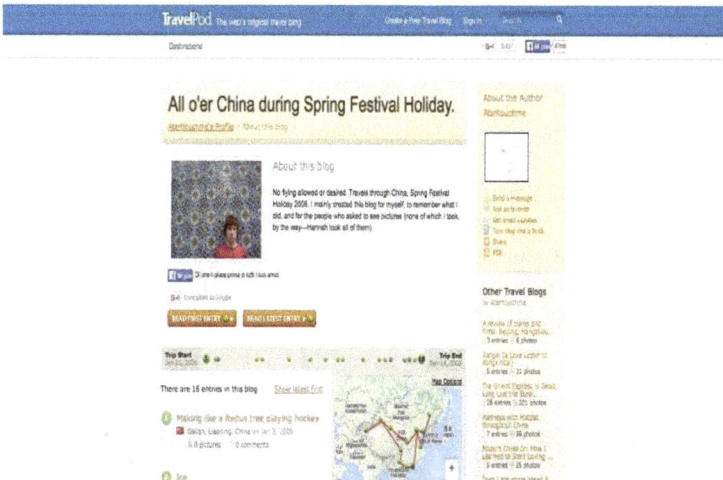

Figure 8: The homepage of Ataritouchme's blog

Figure 6 shows Supermary58's blog, hosted on Turistipercaso.it. As one can see, both the horizontal axis and the vertical axis identified by Knox are of problematic applicability. Indeed, the top part of the screenshot is heavily occupied by the platform's agency (i.e., the logo and all the partner companies that support it). Then below the platform's logo, one finds the heading of the blog, a sub-heading, and a small link to the blogger's personal page. In fact, it is only by scrolling down the page that one finds the blog's posts: according to Knox's model, then, the travel account *per se* occupies a secondary position with respect to the whole page.

Figure 7 refers to the French travel blog *Un peu partout en Chine*, hosted on Top-depart.com. The reader is confronted with a plain layout. The blog's homepage is composed of a wide central column with a picture and two narrower columns at the sides. On the left column is a list of links and details that revolve around the journey – such as: "Project," "Who is travelling?," "Itinerary," "Preparations," "Budget" – which are by no means already known to the reader; on the right column, other links allow readers to contact the blogger. Again, the layout of Mathieu's blog is difficult to frame within Knox's model. The top part of the screen is occupied by the platform's logo; however, it is on the left that one gets the most relevant information about the blog. Similarly, establishing contact with the blogger is possible only by browsing the links that are on the right side of the page. From the point of view of the travel account, these kinds of information are at least as important as the platform's logo or the central picture that introduces the blog.

Lastly, Figure 8 is taken from Ataritouchme's blog *All o'er China during Spring Festival Holidays* hosted on the platform Travelpod.com. The layout of Ataritouchme's blog is the most coherent within Knox's model. Travelpod.com's agency occupies the very top of the screen. Then the central part of the page is filled with the blog's heading, a blog summary, and a map of the trip. At the same time, however, what is found on the right – namely the blogger's profile – is again very much constitutive of the travel blog as a first-person account and it would be misleading to characterize it as a secondary piece of information. Moreover, it is only by scrolling down the page that one obtains information about all the stages of the journey.

***

The situation is more ambivalent when it comes to individual travel blogs. Below are the screenshots of three homepages of individual travel blogs, written, respectively, by Italian Gattosandro Viaggiatore (Figure 9), French Curieuse Voyageuse (Figure 10), and British Becki (both the old version of her blog [Figure 11] and the new one [Figure 12]).

Figure 9: The homepage of Gattosandro Viaggiatore's blog

Figure 10: The homepage of Curieuse Voyageuse's blog

Figure 11: The homepage of *Backpackerbecki.com*

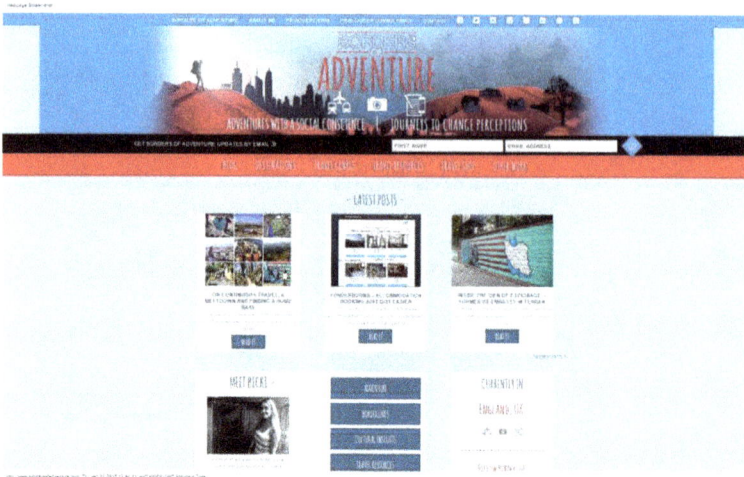

Figure 12: The homepage of *Bordersofadventure.com*

The three travel blogs comply with the conventional structure of blogs, described as "frequently updated websites consisting of dated entries arranged in reverse chronological order so the most recent post appears first" (Walker-Rettberg 2008: 19). In this respect, individual travel blogs tend to approximate Knox's axes, although some of their layout features still remain controversial to frame into his model.

Gattosandro Viaggiatore is an Italian blogger who decided to set up her own blog (active since 2010) using the Content Management System (CMS) Blogger.com. The blog opens with the heading in the top central part of the screen; then, just below, a navigational bar includes a few links: "About Me," "Travel Diaries," "My Drawings," "Contacts." Further below, it is possible to access at least the most recent posts, without the need to scroll the page down. The major issue in light of Knox's model concerns all those elements found on the right column of Gattosandro Viaggiatore's blog, namely the icons of social networks and the author's profile. These elements bear a strategic relevance for the conception of the travel blog as an online personal account and by no means can they be considered as secondary.

Curieuse Voyageuse's blog is a French blog active since 2009. Its layout is very similar to that of Gattosandro Viaggiatore. The greatest section of the screen is occupied by the heading of the blog. Above it, a narrow navigational bar contains the links to various destinations: "China," "Asia," "Africa," "Europe." In fact, the order of the links reasserts the centrality of the blogger's experiences in China, where she travelled and lived for a couple of years. One also finds the links "Art," "About" and "Press" which hint at the blogger's interests and personal contacts. Below the main heading, users can usually read a few lines of the latest post, after which they are required to scroll down the page. Then, on the right column one finds the icons of the major social networks, as well as a short biographic profile.

The case of British travel blogger Becki is very interesting because, having kept her blog *Backpackerbecki.com* since 2012, in 2014 she opted for a radical restyling of the blog, whose URL is now *Bordersofadventure.com*. Such a change can represent a very fruitful case study within the present discussion, because it sheds a light on how (fast) the appearance of blogs can change. From the screenshots of the two homepages, the first thing to note is that the latest version has lost, at least partially, the prototypical vertical blog structure, which characterizes the older version of Becki's blog. Indeed, the layout of *Bordersofadventure.com* follows a horizontal axis, which radically differs from the model elaborated by Knox. More specifically, the main heading is followed and anticipated by two navigation bars: the one above is dedicated to the promotion of the site with links such as "About Me," "PR/ Advertising," "PR/Blogger Consultancy" and "Contact"; while the one below classifies the content under various labels: "Blog," "Destinations," "Travel Genres," "Travel Resources," "Travel Shop" and "Other Work." Also, the distribution of the posts below the main bar follows a horizontal layout and the reader is confronted with the latest updates without the need to scroll down the page. While in the previous version of the site, the navigation bar mixed links about content and social promotion, the present version neatly distinguishes between the two. As a consequence, the reader is given the option of two different paths: one that leads to direct contact with the blogger and another that allows the exploration of Becki's work. Hence, the site turns out to be no longer (solely) a travel blog but a portal where readers can get diversified information on travels and destinations, as well as on the blogger's activities and experience. It is not by chance that Becki defined her website as "more of a storyboard"[28] than a simple travel blog.

More generally, the difficulty of using Knox's model for analyzing today's travel blogs (both on platforms and individual) can be attributed to a number of reasons, from the consolidation of the Web 2.0 and the evolution of CMSs, to the emergence of increasingly rich and dynamic pages and the changes in online reading practices. However, from a broader perspective it is possible to suggest that such difficulty is symptomatic of the fact that understanding how online texts are built and "make sense" is not so much a matter of dissecting them into layers or axes, which is what socio-linguistic approach often tend to do, but of investigating how their various elements work relationally.

A possible methodological alternative in the study of today's (travel) blogs is represented by Genette's work on the paratext. In an article dedicated to *Paratext and Digitalized Narrative*, Dorothee Birke and Birte Christ (2013) discuss the possibility of applying such a concept to online pages, but remain skeptical of the effective feasibility of the project. They note that "as long as a text is available in the form of a distinct physical object and is, as such, limited in its expanse, the concept of paratext can be applied productively" (80); however, once a text loses its physicality, this "leaves scholars at the impasse that Genette himself warned of, namely that of 'rashly proclaiming that all is paratext'. At that point, the concept loses its force of distinction." (80) Differently from Birke and Christ, it is contended here that the absence of physicality does not preclude looking at blogs through the lens of

---

[28] Becki, interview by Stefano Calzati, April 28, 2014, email.

paratextuality. However, it is necessary to preliminarily assess where the boundaries of a travel blog are to be traced.

In this regard, the distinction between travel blogs on platforms and individual travel blogs requires further elaboration. If such distinction seems easily discernable at first sight, it turns out to be more problematic once one looks at how websites are built and organized. In other words, the broader questions become: What is an online text? What are its boundaries? In the present context, an online text is a document that works through a "page metaphor" (Bateman 2008: 9). The page represents the lowest common principle of organization of any online text. Michalis Vafopoulos (2012: 413) technically speaks of online pages as "Web beings": "each Web being," he notes, "occupies a specific locus on the Web. The identification in Web space is given by the URI namespace." Problems arise when it comes to identifying the highest inclusive principle of a blog or website. Indeed, while in a book the pages are gathered together according to the principle of sequentiality (you can go back and forth or skip pages, but this does not affect the organization of the book), each page of a website is potentially linked to a galaxy of other pages. So, what are the outer boundaries of a travel blog? From the point of view of the medium, they coincide with the Web as a whole. However, once one adopts a rhetorical perspective, these boundaries can be narrowed. In the case of a travel blog, for instance, they can be represented by the blogosphere or by the blog platform – if this is the case – that hosts it. Ultimately, a travel blog can be considered as a website whose pages are denoted by a "rhetorically homogeneous" text and are imputable to a "single authorship."

"Rhetorical homogeneity" is a concept inspired by Karen Schriver's (1997: 343) "rhetorical cluster," which is defined as "a group of text elements designed to work together. They are comprised of visual and/or verbal elements that need to be grouped (or put in proximal relation) because, together, they help the reader interpret the content." In this spirit, the notion of rhetorical homogeneity applied to the travel blogs under examination aims at identifying the presence of a travel account that pertains specifically to a journey in China. It can happen, indeed, that either such an account is only one of many others written by the same blogger or that within each page a variety of visual and written elements that do not directly relate to the journey can be found (such as pictures of friends/readers, off-topic comments, etc.). As we will see, such heterogeneity affects how the blog's appearance and the narrative discourse are shaped. At the same time, it is often the case that bloggers are only directly responsible for some content on their blogs because a variety of other elements (such as commercial advertisements) are beyond their control. It is in this latter regard that the notion of single authorship is introduced, elaborating on that of "authorization" proposed by Genette (1997). Birke and Christ (2013) are right when they note that, in itself, the notion of authorization is problematic in Genette, because he uses it quite ambiguously, sometimes in order to refer to the choices of the (real) author, sometimes to indicate a more general and abstract legitimation over the text. Within the present discussion, single authorship stands for the writer's projected agency into the text and refers to all those features of the text that are at his/her discretion. To a degree, the notion of single authorship is not easily discernible, since travel blogs (but also books) are always the result of collective (and sometimes conflicting) cooperation among various actors. However, the stress here is placed not so much on identifying specific textual responsibilities but on the effects that the use of the medial format's affordances made by the bloggers have on the text.

Through the notions of rhetorical homogeneity and single authorship it becomes possible to apply the notion of paratext to travel blogs. For the sake of simplicity, the analysis focuses on the two travel blogs that represent, due to their features, the extreme examples under examination: Supermary58's blog on a platform (Figure 13) and Gattosandro Viaggiatore's individual blog (Figure 14).

Figure 13: Peritextual elements on Supermary58's blog

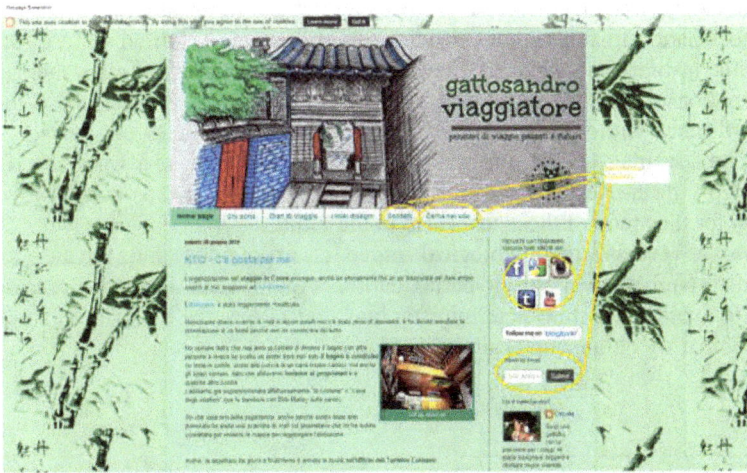

Figure 14: Peritextual elements on Gattosandro Viaggiatore's blog

Looking at the homepages as a whole, a radical difference in the way in which these blogs appear and how the content is organized is noticeable. Supermary58's page hosts a variety of elements: banners, companies' links, social networks' icons, promotional services. Even the background is filled with an advertisement. This variety of elements can be considered peritextual in two respects: 1) they do not depend upon the blogger's decision but on the Web agency that manages the platform (namely: the agency Master Advertising, to which we find a link at the very bottom of the platform's homepage), and 2) they enrich the page with elements that are rhetorically heterogeneous to the blogger's travel account because these elements do not specifically relate to China or even travel. On Gattosandro Viaggiatore's page we still find some of these peritexts – namely, the icons of social networks – but all other elements are excluded. Moreover, the peritextual elements that appear on the page, which fall in this case under the blogger's own control, tend to be arranged around the text – more in the spirit of books' peritexts – while on Supermary58's they are scattered around the whole page and into the text. It is then possible to argue that the peritextual elements on the blogs on platforms are more invasive than those on individual blogs. Indeed, in the former the peritext is not centrifugal to the travel account – as Genette suggests with regard to books, which is also what happens on Gattosandro Viaggiatore's blog – but centripetal[29] and, in being so, it brings into the space of the travel account a multiplicity of messages that threaten its recognizability, as well as the blogger's authorship. Hence, while classic publishers' intervention on a book's peritext is mainly denotative (i.e., it strives to conceal itself), the agencies behind the construction of Web platforms tend to make their intervention evident. As William Vesterman (2002: 444) notes, "the multiplying demand for credit is producing inflation in the medium of exchange – authorship – which is thereby diluted as a measure and store of value." The sole amendment to this argument is that credit, online, is not "demanded," but simply taken by those agencies that make the online space available to users. This implies not so much the "death of the author" (Barthes 1977), but the manifest proliferation of authorial simulacra on the page, which goes hand in hand with a hybridization of the overall formal features of online documents, insofar as the text *per se* tends to mix with a variety of other messages. To use the notion of paratext in relation to online texts allows us precisely to highlight these tendencies without the necessity to identify layers or axes of analysis, as seen above. The advantage is that the analysis considers the texts as a whole and remains disjoined by the fast evolving conditions of the Web and it thus constitutes a valid approach for the study of these texts also in the future.

Now, a reversal methodological move is expounded and travel books are analyzed through the lens of "hypertextuality." Again, such a reversal represents an attempt to avoid the techno-deterministic bias that affects the majority of studies that aim at comparing online and print texts.

---

[29] Ellen McCracken (2013) uses the same concept of "centripetality" in order to discuss the different pathways that readers follow when engaging with texts on digital devices. Here, the term "centripetal" acknowledges the collapsing into the (space of the) text of those peritextual elements that usually surround it in books.

HYPERTEXTUALITY IN PRINT

By investigating the specificities of electronic texts, Michael Shepherd and Carolyn Watters (1998: 97) argue that these texts differ from analogue ones in that they are characterized by "functionality," that is, by the "capabilities afforded by [the] new medium." From here, the two scholars coin the term "cybergenre" for defining all electronic texts that have such specific functionality. There are two main problems with this claim: the first one is that the notion of "functionality" is fundamentally tautological, insofar as it is said to be a prerogative of online texts only; the second one is that this term is not elaborated enough and encompasses too wide a series of aspects, from the dynamic content of online documents to their hypertextual characteristics.

Reversing Shepherd and Watters's perspective, one could ask: do print texts lack functionality? There are three possibilities. If functionality refers to the interfacing affordances supported by analogue and/or digital medial formats, then the answer is no. Indeed, each medial format possesses its own specificities: that is, one interfaces with books by holding them in our hands, turning pages, etc., while in order to interface with online texts one needs to click, type addresses, etc. If, however, by functionality one means to address dynamic and interactive content such as links, then this is a feature unique to online texts. Lastly, if functionality points to hypertextuality in the sense of the interconnectedness of a given document to others, then the specificity of online texts is contentious; or, rather, it is a matter of perspective. "Hypertext," writes Marie-Laure Ryan (2005: 290), "is a genre if we view it as a type of text, but it is a (sub)medium [that is, dependent upon the medium of the Web] if we regard it as an electronic tool for the organization of text." Hence, if one takes on a medial point of view and stresses the fact that online texts are connected to others via links, thus "making the entire field of interconnections obvious and easy to navigate" (Landow 2003: 4), then hypertextuality is applicable to online texts only. By contrast, if we adopt a rhetorical point of view, remarking that a given text is "caught up in a system of references to other books, to other texts, to other sentences: it is a node within a network" (Foucault 1972: 23), then both offline and online texts are hypertexts. Here, a rhetorical perspective is favored, a position that helps to bridge the divide between analogue and digital realms, revealing the extent to which online texts and print ones do share degrees of hypertextuality. Hence hypertextual texts are all those texts that overtly manifest the system of (cross)references that supports them. In this sense, the notion of hypertextuality comes close to that of intertextuality as defined by Roland Barthes (1977). The major difference is that while Barthes considers intertextuality as the underpinning discursive network in which the text is embedded, so that "the writer can only imitate a gesture that is always anterior, never original" (146), hypertextuality is regarded here as the effective surfacing in the text of such a network of references. In particular, this analysis looks at the presence in travel books and travel blogs of: 1) quotations; 2) illustrations (as a cross-reference to words); 3) links; and 4) notes (either as footnotes or endnotes).

***

Curieuse Voyageuse's (2009) blog represents a fruitful case study to begin with because it underwent a "remediation process" that led it to be also released as a book, *La Chine à fleur de peau* (2011). Blogger Curieuse Voyageuse started to keep her eponymous blog in 2009, when she moved to China. In 2011, she went back to France but, since then, has continued to write about her trips around the world. When Curieuse Voyageuse started blogging in 2009, she decided to begin narrating the trips she had previously taken to China, either for work or leisure, before her decision to effectively move there. The remediation process to which Curieuse Voyageuse's blog was subjected is, overall, one of "immediacy" (Bolter and Grusin 1998), that is, one that strives to remain as adherent as possible to the source text, trying to reduce the effects of the new medial format on the remediated text. The book contains a variety of pictures taken from the blog that are not interpolated into the text, as it happens online, but inserted into the middle of the book. In this sense, the relation text–image is affected in favor of a stronger division between the two modes and a greater hegemony of words over pictures. The printed text, however, is unaltered and it also mirrors the subdivision of the posts. This also means that any time the blogger quoted a passage from a different text or source, this same quotation also appears in the book. In this respect, as links could not be included, the writer compensated for this deficiency by expanding the corresponding text in the book with some of the information reachable online via the link. See the following example:

> *Blog*: We passed the nights in the Miao villages we visited. Miao are the fifth minority in terms of number of people, counting nine million members in 2000. This striking number and the extension of their geographic spreading can explain the diversity of costumes and idioms from one region to the other. This site gives plenty of information on this minority. In the villages we visited, some days are really busy and people try to catch the tourists' attention so that villagers can get some money out of their presence. I despised these dances accomplished with no enthusiasm, and I didn't see any entirely. Only the beauty of the costumes was really worth it…[30] (Curieuse Voyageuse 2009; author's translation)

> *Book*: For three days, I wandered around rice fields and villages inhabited by the Guizhou ethnic minority. These peoples have completely different ways of life, traditions and idioms from the Han, the Chinese majority. There are officially 56 ethnic minorities in China. Before today, I visited four villages: Matang, Ching'an, Langde and Xijiang, inhabited by Miao and Gejia. These

---

[30] "Nous avons passé quelques nuits dans les villages Miao que nous avons visités. Les Miao sont la cinquième minorité en nombre de personnes, 9 millions de Miao ont été recensés en 2000. Ce nombre important et l'étendue de leur répartition géographique expliquent la diversité des coutumes voire des langues d'une région à l'autre. Ce site donne de nombreuses informations sur cette minorité. Dans les villages visités, certaines journées sont très animées, pour plaire aux touristes de passage, ce qui permet aussi aux villageois de s'enrichir un peu. Ces danses faites sans enthousiasme m'ont guère plu, je n'en ai vu aucune dans son ensemble. Seule la beauté des costumes vaut vraiment le coût."

two ethnic minorities count several million people, being minorities on a Chinese scale! These cultures are recognized by the Chinese government, which grants them some more space and political power. However, these minorities are often folklorized, and it is not rare for celebrations and traditions usually devoted to crucial moments of life to be commercialized in favor of tourists. And whenever curiosity compels you to take a break, it is possible to discover a bit better such different ways of life. For example, how women carry their babies: here, they are kept on the back, in the African way. Idioms are very different too, but if you dedicate some time to people, you can exchange several smiles and a bunch of words. We passed several nights in the Miao villages we visited. Miao are the fifth minority in China, in terms of number of people, insofar as nine million were counted in 2000. This striking number and the extension of their geographic spreading can explain the diversity of their costumes and idioms from one region to the other. In the villages we visited, some days are mainly dedicated to entertaining activities in order to appeal to passing tourists so that villagers can get a small source of revenue. I despised these dances accomplished with no enthusiasm, and I didn't see any entirely. Only the beauty of the costumes – such as the traditional Miao costumes with a headdress, chest protection and silver shin guards – was really worth it...[31] (Croiziers 2011: 41; author's translation)

It is evident that the longer version published in the book is enriched with details that online are reachable only by clicking on the provided link. Drawing on Genette's (1997) terminology, it can be said that the online source represents a peritextual element with respect to the blog, as it is connected to it, while remaining at a certain distance (signaled by the access to another URL). By contrast, in print Croiziers co-

---

[31] "Depuis trois jours je me balade entre rizières et villages des minorités ethniques du Guizhou. Ces sont des groupes de populations ayant des modes de vie, des traditions, des langues qui diffèrent totalement de ceux des Han, chinois majoritaires. Il existe cinquante-six minorités ethniques reconnues en Chine. J'ai visité à ce jour quatre villages: Matang, Ching'an, Langde, et Xijiang, des ethnies Miao et Gejia. Il s'agit de deux groupes ethniques de plusieurs millions de personnes, les minorités étant ici à l'échelle chinoise! Ces cultures sont reconnues par l'Etat chinois, ce qui leur permet d'avoir un peu plus de place et de pouvoir dans les représentations politiques. Cependant ces minorités sont souvent folklorisées et il n'est pas rare de voir fêtes et traditions autrefois réservées aux grands moments de la vie, commercialisées pour les touristes de passage. N'empêche, si la curiosité pousse à prendre le temps, on peut découvrir un peu mieux ces manières de vivre si différentes. Ne serait-ce que par la façon de porter les bébés: ils sont ici 'attaches' dans le dos, à la manière africaine. Les langues diffèrent aussi, mais si on consacre un peu de temps aux gens, de nombreux sourires et quelques mots sont toujours échanges. Nous passons plusieurs nuits dans les villages Miao que nous visitons. Les Miao sont la cinquième minorité de Chine en nombre, neuf millions d'entre eux ayant été recensés en 2000. Ce nombre important et l'étendue de leur répartition géographique expliquent la diversité des coutumes voir des langues d'une région à l'autre. Dans les villages visites, certaines journées sont principalement occupées par des animations, pour plaire aux touristes de passage, ce qui permet aux villageois d'avoir une petite source de revenu. Les danses faites sans enthousiasme ne me plaisent guère, je n'en vois aucune dans son ensemble. Seule la beauté des costumes comme par exemple le costume traditionnel Miao avec la coiffe, la protection de poitrine et leurs jambières en argent vaut vraiment le coup"

opted the online source into the narrative, taking care to rephrase the information found on the Web and making it her own. The major difference between the book and the blog has to do with the fact that the former only refers to Curieuse Voyageuse's journeys and stay in the Middle Kingdom, without taking into account those posts that do not relate directly to China (such as the one in which she mentions to have been nominated for an annual blog award). In other words, from the book are excised all those episodes that are considered as rhetorically heterogeneous to the travel narrative, and that, as such, become epitextual to the travel book.

In general, it is possible to contend that *La Chine à Fleur de peau* is a book that presents a variety of hypertextual features – such as pictures, quotations – that try to mimic the online text as faithfully as possible. However, the book required also reshaping the travel account according to more rigid formal criteria that could present the text as a coherent narrative. The book tends to narrativize the travel experiences and to make it more easily recognizable in terms of genre, leading us to suggest that it is the book's physicality that projects onto Curieuse Voyageuse's experience a teleology and generic connotation that are completely absent from the blog. In the book, the knowledge of China is presented as a gradual, incessant discovery: it is a progressive scratching of layers from absolute ignorance to full appreciation made possible by the very fact of journeying. Such themes on the blog appear more disarticulated and, at best, deductible *a posteriori* when comparing among themselves the posts recounting the blogger's various journeys.[32]

Moving from a case of remediation of a French blog into a book, the analysis now concentrates on two multimodal travelogues – one in English and one in Italian – that have only appeared in a book format: *Invisible China: A Journey through Ethnic Borderlands* (2009) by US-American Colin Legerton and Jacob Rawson and *La Cina in Vespa* (2008) by Italian Giorgio Bettinelli. Later on, the case of three monomodal travel books (in English, French, and Italian) will also be taken into account. With this transition, the analysis also begins to focus more closely on the shaping of the narrative discourse and the literary forms of the texts. In the last part of the chapter, this same attention will be paid to travel blogs in order to assess the extent to which travel blogs also present the same formal hybridity usually credited to travel books.

THE LITERARY FORM OF TRAVEL BOOKS

According to Genette (1980), all narratives are a form of telling (diegesis): this means that they necessarily imply a narrator and ultimately can only provide the illusion of mimesis (i.e., the "showing" of the event compared to its telling). So, mimesis and diegesis are not two mutually exclusive modes; rather, the narrative presents variations in its "mood," that is, the distance of the diegesis to the (mimesis of the) event. In this section, particular attention is devoted to descriptions, personal

---

[32] Drawing on Bakhtin's ([1937] 1981) distinction between the chronotope of the novel and that of the epic, in the next chapter I will discuss the extent to which blogs' narrative tends to be "epicized," which means that its temporal and spatial coordinates are abstracted and lose their internal dynamicity, so that posts on a blog appear as standalone pieces that do not respond to an overreaching (chronotopic) narrative structure.

reflections, and dialogues (as the textual terrain where the encounter between Self and Other is best displayed). Genette argues that the ways in which dialogues are embedded in the narrative provide varying illusions of mimesis. For instance, "reported speech" creates a sense of mimesis and proximity to the event, because people's words are transcribed verbatim; on the contrary, "transposed speech" is embedded in the flux of the narration, thus keeping a greater distance from the episode recounted (171-3). The mood of the narrative is also influenced by the functions that the narrator can take (255-6). According to Genette's terminology, when the author maintains a basic "narrative function," for example through the descriptions of places or events, s/he tends to "disappear" from the text; by contrast, whenever s/he assumes an "ideological function," interrupting the narrative in order to provide comments, his stance fully manifests itself. The point is that, as Mieke Bal (2002) reminds us:

> Any description is modelled by an ideological vision. We need to question the idea of non-focalized, or zero-focalization description, theorized and defended by narratologists such as Genette. It can be either the plot or the description itself, it does not make any difference from the point of view of the ideological partiality that is embedded. [33] (Bal: 200-1; author's translation)

This means that all narratives are ideological and, according to Bal, there can only be varying degrees of effacement of the (ideological) function assumed by the narrator (who, in the case of travel narratives, is also – via a narratively constructed persona – the author). Bal limits her analysis to the use of language (adjectives, modal verbs, etc.). However, in the case of first-person travel narratives, the discussion can be extended to the shifting of the narrator's "I" between narrative and ideological functions, as well as to the way in which s/he decides to report dialogues. All these changes in the mood of the narrative have direct consequences on the literary form that the travel account takes and also on how Self and Other are represented.

***

The first travel book under examination is *Invisible China* (2009) by Colin Legerton and Jacob Rawson. Legerton and Rawson are two US-Americans who spent about five years in China completing their Master's degrees there while studying Mandarin. They undertook their travel at the end of their stay in China with the explicit intention to get in contact with ethnic minority "people in towns and villages all around the borderlands of China" (14). The book opens with a map of China in which all the ethnic minorities encountered by the authors are localized (Figure 15):

---

[33] "Qualsiasi descrizione è modellata da una visione ideologica. Occorre diffidare perciò dall'idea di una descrizione non focalizzata o a focalizzazione zero, teorizzata e difesa da narratologi come Genette. Che sia la trama o che sia invece proprio la descrizione non fa differenza dal punto di vista della parzialità ideologica che sta dietro."

Figure 15: The whole map of China at the beginning of *Invisible China*

What is notable is that the illustration is not a "proper" map but a drawing in which space and distances are distorted and no precise point of reference is given (except for Beijing). This drawing is responsible for creating a "subjective" spatial representation that is dependent, in the first place, on the ethnic minorities who inhabit it. Hence, the spatial dimension of the journey becomes functional to the localization of the peoples encountered by the travelers. This impression of space-through-ethnicity is reinforced throughout the text in two ways: on the one hand, the book is organized according to four regionally defined chapters – the Northeast, the Southwest, the Northwest, and the East – which follow the development of the journey. These chapters are introduced by maps in the same style as the first one, which show each region together with the names of the minorities, the main cities or towns, and the foreign bordering countries (Figure 16).

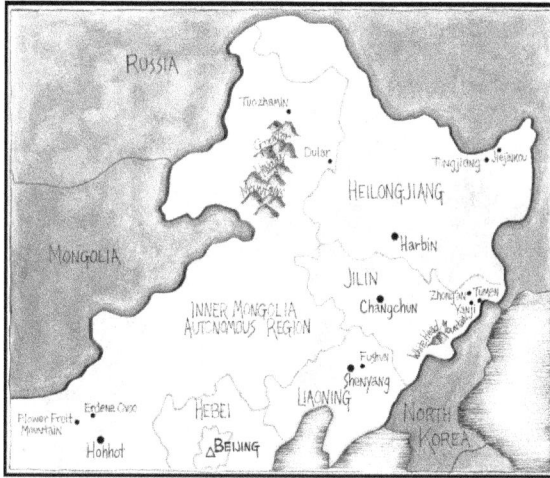

Figure 16: Map introducing a chapter in the book
Source: Polly Fossey and Jamie Northrup

On the other hand, very few and brief indications about the time of travel (such as the duration of the various legs of the journey), are given. In so doing, the authors freeze the spatially and ethnically dominated narrative of the journey into a temporal void that leaves the reader, so to speak, to confront a two-dimensional representation of the experience; a chartographic representation. The following is an example of how condensed the discursivization of the time of travel is:

> We left Tuozhamin the next morning. Our next destination was another village just a hundred miles downstream, but the tricky geography of the Hingans forced us to travel a roundabout path. A few days later, we arrived in Dular by the only possible means: a jerky three-hour bus ride down a one-lane dirt road stuck in the early stage of construction. (Legerton and Rawson: 23-4)

Maps are not the sole visual elements present in the book. The authors also inserted 50 pictures (Figures 17 and 18 are two examples) that are arranged following the development of the journey.

Figure 17: Colin Legerton among Uygur people

Figure 18: The authors of *Invisible China* playing with children
Source: Matt P. Jager

Being gathered together in the middle of the book, the photographs of *Invisible China* help to create the impression of a visual account that is autonomous, rather than merely supportive, of the written text. The majority of the pictures (34 out of 50) portray only local people in their milieu, while in others (9 out of 50) the authors also appear in the pictures and they are usually engaged *intra pares* with locals. These photographs then reassert Legerton and Rawson's purpose, stated in the opening of the book, to "learn directly from the minority people" (13), and they shape the text in the spirit of an ethnographic study of China's ethnic groups.

This consideration finds also proof in the way in which the narrative is modeled. To begin with, in terms of hypertextual features we find many quotations from other texts. Examples are the aphorisms and poems that are found either at the beginning of each chapter (as excerpts) or within the text (italics in original):

"It takes a great people to build a great wall. But it takes an even greater people to make the Chinese build a great wall" Mongolian saying. (Legerton and Rawson: 61)

A popular Chinese children's encyclopaedia defines ethnicity: *"Our great motherland is a unified country of many ethnic groups. The fifty-six ethnic groups that dwell in this vast and prosperous territory collectively created our long-standing history and glorious culture. In this large multi-ethnic family, the Han race occupies the majority, at more than 90 percent of the total population."* (Legerton and Rawson: 4)

"This is one of our most important songs." Clearing his throat he began to read the metric lyrics: *"Let us sit and speak of ancient days / Our fathers lived in Do Son, Vietnam / In the third year of King Hong Thuan's reign / Our kinsmen washed up on Chinese Fu'an / They lost their bearings on the tree-clad isle / A lonely home surrounded by blue seas / Quickly they began their exploration / And saw the White Dragon lurking in the east."* (Legerton and Rawson: 84)

By introducing other voices through direct quotations, the authors foreground local knowledge so that (Western) readers are put in contact with it in a mimetic way (i.e., with a minimal degree of filtering by the authors). These references, then, contribute to counterbalance the "We" of the authors upon which the narrative depends. Beyond that, Legerton and Rawson adopt two other narrative strategies to further soften their presence into the text. On the one hand, they completely omit biographical information about themselves and personal comments on what they witness. In fact, the authors' "We" maintains a narrative function that rarely transcends the flow of the diegesis. Moreover, the writing of dialogues follows a fixed pattern: these are in the form of reported speech when it is the autochthons who speak, while they are transposed speech when it is the authors' turn:

> We approached an older woman, like us an idle bystander, to find out if all these jellyfish were for local consumption. "Goodness no! They are far too expensive for us to eat. These are all for export." Now in conversation with the older woman, we determined to take advantage of the situation to learn how she felt the land reclamation of the 1960s that attached the three islands to the mainland had affected their fishing industry. "Land reclamation was great for our people. When Mao brought more land between our islands, we were all able to plough and grow our own food." (Legerton and Rawson: 88)

Through these strategies, Legerton and Rawson put minority people even more to the foreground, while their writers' simulacra fade into the background. For these reasons, it is possible to suggest that both the written narrative and the pictures conjure up to shape the travelogue in the form of an ethnography, in which what is most relevant is the representation of the Other, rather than the travelers'; it is more about letting readers know how China's ethnic minorities live, than recounting Legerton and Rawson's impressions along the road. The authors' words are a confirmation of this: "we felt it was important to take ourselves out of the frame to focus more on what we were actually seeing, so that us and the readers could gain even more from the experience."[34]

Moving now to a second multimodal book, the case of *La Cina in Vespa* (2008) by Giorgio Bettinelli is taken into account. Giorgio Bettinelli (1955-2008) was a popular Italian travel writer, whose peculiarity was to travel to the remotest regions of earth riding his Vespa. His wanderings are recounted in a number of travel books, among which: *In Vespa da Roma a Saigon* (1997; trans. *Riding a Vespa from Rome to Saigon*) and *Brum Brum. 254.000 chilometri in Vespa* (2002; trans. *Brum Brum: 254,000 kilometers on a Vespa*). In the travelogue *La Cina in Vespa*, Bettinelli recounts his journey around the Middle Kingdom, which, in his later years, had become his country of residence. In the author's own words, the goal of the journey is "to realize a trip on a Vespa that touches all the 34 geographic areas [of China]" (48). Far from simply detailing the stages of the journey, in this travelogue Bettinelli pours all sorts of reflections, from personal episodes to political critiques, passing through a variety of opinions on music, cinema, and literature. As a consequence, the thematic boundaries of the book transcend the travel *per se*[35] to encompass the author's whole vision of life, with respect to which his narrating persona keeps an overtly ideological stance. As a consequence, the idea of travel-as-leisure rapidly transcends into the idea of travel-as-necessity, so that Bettinelli's persona is, so to speak, romanticized and turned into the "eternal traveller," as he (somewhat proudly) admits:

> The person who leaves for a short trip leaves all behind and is concentrated only on the trip ahead. But the person who spends sixteen years of his life travelling must necessarily be concentrated on his life because what surrounds him is nothing but his life.[36] (Bettinelli, p. 57; author's translation)

Such self-representation is further strengthened by the fact that, beyond the heterogeneity of the themes treated, even when Bettinelli writes specifically about the journey, he usually links it to his many previous adventures. Hence *La Cina in Vespa* is inscribed into a long series of achievements as both a traveler and a writer:

> Needless to say, having decided to live in China for the next one or two years, while completing the travelogue about the 144,000 kilometres driven between 1997 and 2001, traversing 90 countries, from Ushuaia to Hobart, the

---

[34] Colin Legerton and Jacob Rawson, interview by Stefano Calzati, September 18, 2013, email.

[35] Emblematic is the fact that the "real" departure only occurs at page 60, being anticipated by a series of events (such as the death of Bettinelli's father) whose very function is to create the dramatic preconditions for the journey.

[36] "Chi parte per un viaggio breve lascia a casa tutto il resto ed è concentrato solo sul viaggio che ha davanti. Ma chi spende sedici anni di vita viaggiando per forza di cose deve essere concentrato anche sulla sua vita, perché quello che ha intorno non è nient'altro che la sua vita."

idea that I cannot ride a Vespa in my 'elected country' is much more annoying than a little stone in my shoe.[37] (Bettinelli: 39; author's translation)

To the extent to which *La Cina in Vespa* overtly focuses on Bettinelli's persona and his opinions on a variety of topics, the form of the text is best thought of as an autobiographic diary. At the same time, China and the Chinese tend to retreat to the background. This erasure is achieved in particular through two strategies. The first one concerns dialogues: these are reduced to a minimum throughout the text, despite the fact that, during a great part of the journey, Bettinelli is accompanied either by Ya Pei or by his Chinese lover, Manuelle, that is, two insiders who could easily negotiate between the author and the people they meet. This leads to a silencing of the Chinese and a representation of China as merely a space to be traversed in order to accomplish the endeavor. And yet, it is when looking at the pictures inserted in the book that the travelogue's egocentric nature emerges more vividly. There are 16 photographs in total, inserted in the middle of the book, and in 12 of them the author is photographed alone, directly looking at the camera.

Figure 19: Giorgio Bettinelli riding his Vespa

Figure 20: Giorgio Bettinelli near the Great Wall

---

[37] "Inutile dire che, avendo deciso di vivere in Cina per un anno o due in attesa di completare il racconto dei 144.000 km percorsi tra il '97 e il 2001 attraverso novanta paesi, da Ushuaia a Hobart, l'idea di non poter essere in sella e dare un colpo di acceleratore nel mio 'paese di elezione' mi dava fastidio più di un sassolino nella scarpa."

Figures 19 and 20 disclose very little of the places visited, or the people encountered by the author. Rather, they reinforce the image of Bettinelli as a solitary traveler (and one that stereotypically adheres to the idea of Italianness, as a mix of masculinity and Latin lover's attitude). In fact, the sole "relation" that the author entertains in these photographs is that with his beloved Vespa. The function of these pictures is to testify the author's accomplishment to ride a Vespa in China and visit all its 34 geographic areas. Only in two photographs a woman (very likely Ya Pei) appears, but the captions, which simply mention the place or the date – "Kashgar, old town" and "Yunnan, south of China, 2008" – are not helpful in clarifying who she is, thus requiring the reader to collate the text and the photographs in order to disentangle the dilemma. Overall, readers are confronted with a text that shows a good degree of hypertextuality, presenting pictures as well as cross-references to Bettinelli's other travelogues and his own travel diary. Differently from *Invisible China*, however, here these elements are self-centered, thus stressing the autobiographical nature of the account and overlooking an effective engagement with (and representation of) the Chinese.

***

To conclude the discussion concerning the hypertextuality of travel books and their formal features, the analysis focuses on three monomodal travelogues. The examples provided are: *Ivre de Chine: Voyages au coeur de l'Empire* (2010) by French author Constantin de Slizewicz, *La birra di Shaoshan* by Italian Sergio Ramazotti, and *China Road* (2007) by Briton Rob Gifford. Being monomodal texts, none of these texts are illustrated (*China Road* only presents a map of China at the very beginning). In this respect, they lack *a priori* one of the elements that make the accounts hypertextual. Nonetheless, these texts present some degrees of hypertextuality.

The travelogue by Constantin de Slizewicz is the most hypertextual of the three. At the age of 20, de Slizewicz left his studies and moved to Beijing. Since then he has been living, working, and travelling in China, contributing with reportages to both French magazines and Chinese newspapers. He traversed the whole Middle Kingdom many times: from Beijing to Kashgar, from Harbin to Lhasa. *Ivre de Chine* recounts the 2002 journey that de Slizewicz accomplished together with his friend Alexandre driving a sidecar from Beijing to Kunming. While narrating their vicissitudes on the road, de Slizewicz recollects in the book his past years in the country: the beginning in Beijing and the gradual shift toward the south-western remote regions of the country, allured by the traditions of Tibetan minorities. Given de Slizewicz's (and Alexandre's) deep acquaintance with China, the narrative presents a variety of encounters that the two have with Chinese friends, as well as a number of dialogues with local peoples, such as the following one with a policeman who patrols the road:

> [Policeman]: "Comrades, where are you from?" [De Slizewicz]: "Beijing"; [Policeman]: "You speak very good Chinese, where are you originally from?" [De Slizewicz]: "France." [Policeman]: "Where are you heading with your motorbike?" [De Slizewicz]: "Yunnan." A short silence, then he tells us

with his thumb up: *"Niubi! Niubi!* Super! Super!"[38] (De Slizewicz: 59; author's translation)

This dialogue reveals that de Slizewicz thinks of himself, in the first place, as a Beijing dweller, while the policeman seems more interested in knowing his country of origin. The author's insider position is also reasserted by his knowledge of Mandarin, which is transcribed in italics in many occurrences throughout the text. Concerning references and notes, the author fills the text with both direct quotations from other texts (including his own) and with endnotes, adding to his travelogue features that are proper to a scholarly text. These are a few examples:

"As long as we continue to think of pre-1950 Tibet as a utopia, XXI century Tibet will not exist." [1] Donald Lopez, *Fascination Tibétaine*, Autrement, 2003.[39] (De Slizewicz: 74; author's translation)

Despite the departure of missionaries and the persecutions during the Great Leap Forward and the Cultural Revolution, there still is a community of several thousand Tibetans, who pray every week in their stone-made churches. [1] I have recounted this first trip to Catholic Tibetan communities, as well as the epic journeys of French and Swiss missionaries to Tibet in my book *Les Peuples Oubliés du Tibet*, Perrin, 2007.[40] (De Slizewicz: 140; author's translation)

"The legs of women will dance in the air, run into the desert, rest beside the rivulets left by streams. And the world will be peaceful." [1] Some of these notes are taken from the introduction to Luo Xu's work, edited by the Xin Dong Cheng Space for Contemporary Art Gallery: www.chengxindong.com.[41] (De Slizewicz: 222; author's translation)

The widespread use of footnotes enriches the travel narrative with a multiplicity of (textual) voices that eventually corroborate de Slizewicz's personal reflections made on the road. In this way, not only does the author demonstrate being by now an insider

---

[38] "'Camarades, vous venez d'où?'; 'Pékin'; 'Tu parles bien chinois! Tu viens de quel pays?'; 'France'; 'Avec votre moto, vous allez où?'; 'Au Yunnan.' Un bref silence, puis il dit en nous montrant son pouce: '*Niubi! Niiubi!* Super! Super!'."

[39] "'Aussi longtemps que nous continuerons de faire du Tibet d'avant 1950 une utopie, le Tibet du XXI siècle ne pourrait exister.' [1] Donald Lopez, *Fascination tibétaine*, Autrement, 2003."

[40] "Malgré le départ des missionnaires et le persécutions subies durant le Grand Bond en Avant et la Révolution Culturelle subsiste toujours une communauté de plusieurs milliers de Tibétains, qui chaque semaine prient dans leurs églises en pierre. [1] Ce premier voyage chez les Tibétains catholiques et l'épopée des missionnaires français et suisses au Tibet, je les ai racontés dans mon livre *Les peuples oubliés du Tibet*, Perrin, 2007."

[41] "'Les jambes des femmes danseront dans l'air, courront dans le désert, se reposeront au bord des rigoles laissés par les ruisseaux, qu'il sera calme ce monde.' [1] Certaines de ces notes sont extraites de l'ouvrage de présentation de Luo Xu édité par la galerie Xin Ding Cheng Space for Contemporary Art, www.chengxindong.com"

in China, but of having acquired a profound understanding of the Tibetan region, due also to his years of research on the region's history and the publication of an essay to which he makes reference in the second quote. Hence the narrative of *Ivre di Chine*, despite being fundamentally an autobiographic travel narrative, gets closer to the essay. In fact, while de Slizewicz opts for elevating the accuracy and objectivity of his account by resorting to other sources, at the same time his "I" is free to assume an overt ideological stance throughout the text. The last quotation deserves particular attention, as it also presents a link within the footnote. What is at stake is not so much the obvious fact that this link lacks interactivity, but rather that de Slizewicz decided to add such a piece of information in the book, *despite* the impossibility of directly reaching the website. Hence, by creating a connection that ties the book to the Web, the print format forces – without crossing it – the medial boundary that separates online and offline texts.

The second monomodal travelogue to be examined is *La birra di Shaoshan* (2002) by Italian freelance journalist Ramazzotti. The book recounts Ramazzotti's ten-day stay in the city of Shaoshan, which is Mao Zedong's birthplace. Instead of wandering up and down the Middle Kingdom, Ramazzotti's goal is to dig into the Chinese culture by settling down in a specific place (i.e., a symbolic place in light of China's recent history). From the outset, the development of any spatial and temporal trajectories is annihilated. Time represents an ephemeral framework that does not connect places or crossings, but only articulates the passing of the author's writing. The following dialogue between the author and Celia, his Chinese interpreter, frames well Ramazzotti's stay and purpose in Shaoshan:

> [Ramazzotti]: "Actually, I'm also here to work," I said. She stared at me in bewilderment. [Celia]: "What kind of job?" [Ramazzotti]: "I tell stories. At least, I try." [Celia]: "For whom?" [Ramazzotti]: "For the people in my country." [Celia]: "And do they listen to them?" [Ramazzotti]: "Somebody does. Somebody."[42] (Ramazzotti: 20; author's translation)

This passage reveals the extent to which Ramazzotti thinks of his journey to Shaoshan as mainly related to his profession. Consequently, his goal is to provide (Italian) readers with an account of this experience that can shed some light on contemporary China. A few dialogues between Ramazzotti and Celia reveal, indeed, the author's struggle to understand China: "[Celia]: 'Do you really think that China is so contradictory?' [Ramazzotti]: "I only think it is a crazy country. But I want to stop thinking and take it for how it is, without objections."[43] (132; author's translation) Although (or maybe because) Ramazotti has difficulty understanding China, he does not seek an overt confrontation with it, but tends to center the narrative on his own

---

[42] [Ramazzotti]: "'A dire il vero io sono anche qui per lavorare' dissi. Lei sgranò gli occhi: [Celia]: 'Che tipo di lavoro?' [Ramazzotti]: 'Racconto storie. Almeno ci provo.' [Celia]: 'A chi?' [Ramazzotti]: 'Alla gente del mio paese.' [Celia]: 'E loro ascoltano?' [Ramazzotti]: 'Qualcuno sì. Qualcuno.'"
[43] [Celia] "Pensi davvero che la Cina sia così contraddittoria?" [Ramazzotti]: "Penso solo che sia una pazzia. Ma voglio smettere di pensare e prendere ciò che viene, senza obiezioni."

persona. In other words, the narrator maintains a self-centered focus and assumes an ideological function. This is done in two ways: in terms of hypertextuality, the author fills *La birra di Shaoshan* with references to his past travel experiences, thus strengthening his self-representation as a navigated traveler and reporter. In the following passage, for instance, he recounts to Celia why he keeps a diary in which he pastes beer labels from each country he has visited:

> "Beer labels are my travelling souvenirs. I paste them into a diary, a bit like a photo-book. Each beer label represents a meeting. I turn the pages of my album and I think: 'I drank this beer with Magdalena Gutierrez at the hotel Carrasco in Montevideo' and then: 'This one was the last one of a great drinking night with Luis Quintanal, the night that we missed our flight to Santiago by ten minutes and the plane crashed into a mountain just after take-off' and again: 'We drank this beer in Faya-Largeau, me and Jean-Marie Mamadou, who was 14 and told me he was tired of fighting a war that had already killed eight of his brothers and a sister.'"[44] (Ramazzotti: 59-60; author's translation)

By pouring into the text his past adventures, the author's persona gets close to the idea of "total traveller" as represented also by Bettinelli. Moreover, in doing so Ramazzotti surreptitiously ties *La birra di Shaoshan* to his previous works in which these same adventures are recounted, such as *Vado verso il Capo* (1996) and *Carne verde* (1999). Because of the dominant position that Ramazzotti occupies in the narrative, the relation between Ramazzotti and Celia is not built on a plane of equality. This unevenness is best witnessed in the reporting of dialogues (second strategy). It often happens that the author's turns are very long, while the replies of Celia are usually very short. This creates the impression of Ramazzotti keeping a position of superiority with respect to his guide, even though he needs to rely on her in all circumstances:

> [Celia]: "You have been to Shanghai. You have seen the skyscrapers." [Ramazzotti]: "Celia, I slept in the Jin Mao. The hotel begins on the 54th floor; the previous 53 are all empty." [Celia]: "The television didn't mention that." [Ramazzotti]: "No, but that's the truth. It is an empty crystal tower only good to shout to the world: 'Guys, look at us, we too are able to build skyscrapers. Why don't you invest money in our country?' And it also says to the Chinese: 'See? We were right. In Tiananmen Square, when we shot at

---

[44] "Le etichette di birra sono i miei ricordi di viaggio. Le incollo in un libro, come in un album di fotografie. Ogni etichetta è un incontro. Scorro le pagine e penso: 'Questa l'ho bevuta con Magdalena Gutierrez all'hotel Carrasco a Montevideo', e poi: 'Quest'altra è stata una sbronza colossale con Luís Quintanal la sera che avevamo perso per dieci minuti l'aereo di Santiago e l'aereo era esploso contro la montagna dopo il decollò e ancora: 'Questa la scolammo a Faya-Largeau io e Jean-Marie Mamadou che aveva quattordici anni e mi disse che era stanco di combattere una guerra che gli aveva portato via otto fratelli e una sorella.'"

your sons, we defended communism, and these are the results."' [Celia]: "But" she tried to reply.[45] (Ramazzotti: 170; author's translation)

The almost pedagogic function that the author occupies in this and other dialogues betrays the extent to which his approach to China is deeply influenced by what he already knows, or believes to know, about the country. Ramazzotti, in fact, rejects the very possibility of learning from Celia about China. It is as if his brief journey to Shaoshan is functional to reassert his already formed impressions. The following is an emblematic example of the author's projection over Celia of a stereotypical image that pertains more to his own ideas of how the Chinese are, or should be, than to how she effectively is:

> A pair of jeans was enough to make you become detestable because it revealed to me your desire, maybe concealed even to yourself, to be part of that same world that you condemned in words. I preferred when you were wearing a skirt to the calf – that length that's so silly, so *Chinese*.[46] (Ramazzotti: 50-1; author's translation)

In Ramazzotti's eyes, Celia does not conform to the idea of "Chineseness": an idea, of course, shaped by the distance that culturally and geographically separates China from Italy. Ultimately, more than with China, Ramazzotti is silently dialoguing with Italian readers, with whom he shares similar assumptions about the Middle Kingdom. The largely ideological function of the narrator and the fact that the few hypertextual features of the texts are self-directed tend, similarly to Bettinelli's text, to obfuscate China, which becomes an object of interest only insofar as it frames the author's writing-as-a-profession. Differently from Bettinelli, however, Ramazzotti does not expand the theme of the text beyond the journey; rather he sticks to his goal to provide Italian readers with an inside story about China. Hence, the text could be said to follow the journalistic reportage with influences coming from the diary, due to the repeated intromission of the author's "I" into the narrative. Many of these formal features are also detectable in *China Road*, the last travelogue analyzed in this chapter.

China Road (2007) was written by British journalist Rob Gifford, who "first came to China as a twenty-year-old student in 1987, to spend a year studying the Chinese language in Beijing" (xxii). After that, he was hired as a correspondent from China for National Public Radio. In 2006, he was asked to leave China for a new job,

---

[45] "[Celia]: 'Sei stato a Shanghai. Avrai visto i grattacieli.' [Ramazzotti]: 'Celia, ho dormito nel Jin Mao. L'albergo cominciava al cinquantaquattresimo piano. I primi cinquantatré erano tutti vuoti.' [Celia]: 'Questo la televisione non lo ha detto.' [Ramazzotti]: 'No, ma è così. Una torre di cristallo vuota giusto per poter dire al mondo: Ehy, guarda qui, anche noi siamo capaci di costruire grattacieli. Perché non vieni a investire un po' di soldi da noi? Inoltre serve anche a dire ai cinesi: Avete visto? Avevamo ragione noi. Sulla piazza Tian'An'Men, quando sparavamo addosso ai vostri figli, stavamo difendendo il comunismo, ed eccone qui i risultati' [Celia]. 'Ma...' tentò di dire Celia."
[46] "Un paio di jeans bastavano a renderti detestabile, perché mi rivelavano il tuo desiderio, nascosto forse anche a te stessa, di essere parte di quel mondo che a parole condannavi. Ti preferivo con la gonna a metà polpaccio – quella lunghezza così insulsa, così cinese."

and he decided to undertake a journey along Route 312 – sometimes described as the Chinese equivalent to Route 66 in the US – before leaving the country. From this initial self-representation, it is possible to suggest that Gifford bears an insider position in China insofar as, having spent several years in the country, he has acquired a fair understanding of internal dynamics, which linguistically emerges in the use of words in Chinese reported in italics throughout the text.

Gifford confesses his desire, along the way, to meet and talk with as many common people as possible, or what he calls – resorting to a Chinese formula – "*lao bai xing*" (trans. "old hundred names"): "truckers and hookers, yuppies and artists, the famer and the mobile-phone salesmen" (xxi). The stories of these "ordinary Chinese people caught up in an extraordinary moment in time" (xix) are then inscribed within the broader narrative of the Middle Kingdom. It is in this way that Western readers are directly connected to the image of China as a whole:

> I think the West needs to pay more attention to China's problems because I think there could well be a crunch coming in China. There is one big question in my own mind: which is it going to be for China, greatness or implosion? (Gifford: xix)

Despite Gifford's declared intention to engage with Chinese people from all over the country, the narrative is largely subservient to his goal to deliver, from an eminently Western point of view, his opinions about China:

> By the time I'd finished the journey I was wondering whether it would be better just to let the readers draw their own conclusions. However, my editor pointed out that if you, dear reader, have schlepped with me right across China, the least I owe you is a few suggestions as to how things might develop there in the future. (Gifford: 322)

In this passage, what is remarkable are both the author's willingness to provide personal notations about China, as well as the informality of his writing, which tightens the connections to his readers, with whom he shares the same cultural background. More broadly, the mirroring between the West and China constitutes the leitmotif of the whole book. Interestingly, such mirroring is projected not only onto the future, but also the past:

> If you want to trace the origins of the human rights eventually enjoyed in the West, the origins of the jury system and the idea that a monarch could be bound by law, it is no exaggeration to say that all roads lead through Runnymede. So, the question that has always troubled me is this: If China was so developed and so civilised and so advanced before its time, why was there no Chinese Runnymede? (Gifford: 105)

Gifford applies to China a whole series of concepts – such as "jury system," "individual freedom," "human rights," "monarch," etc. – which are drawn from the history of the West. The path itself that Gifford envisions for China is co-opted from a Western conception of progress:

> This for me is really the big question facing China now, at the start of the twenty-first century and perhaps the one that will decide whether the country goes on to greatness. Will it just follow the same cycle as every dynasty in Chinese history, or will it, *can* it, break the cycle and take a different path? There are several very important ways in which today's China is different from the past and which suggest that it *may*, just *may*, be able to avoid going the way of former dynasties and perhaps for the first time form an ongoing, progressive linear narrative to Chinese history. (Gifford: 323)

Gifford is aware of the risk of providing readers with a Manichean representation of China and he stresses that is not his intention to "criticize or condemn Chinese tradition, or to ask arrogantly why other cultures can't be like ours" (105). Yet, at the very moment in which he recognizes the risk, he reasserts the binary clash us/them, which is at the core of the whole narrative. His call for an engagement of the West with China's future is (already) made from a predominant position of the former over the latter. The uneven opposition West–China is reinforced by the fact that the text – which bears, indeed, a low degree of hypertextuality – does not present any references to other texts that may soften or challenge Gifford's point of view.

Moreover, the dualism West–China is reflected in dialogues. It is true that the book is rich in conversations, made possible by Gifford's fluency in Mandarin. Nonetheless it is often the case that these conversations, in the form of the direct speech, are overtly built on the dualism of we/you:

> "I know, you Westerners think that after capitalism, there will still be capitalism. We Chinese think that after this stage of capitalism, there might eventually be communism." I open my eyes wide. "Really? You really believe that?" She nods. (Gifford: 27)

This dialogue is built in such a way that the speakers are on a plane of equality. However, such equality is functional to re-establishing the diversity and distance between Self and Other, that is, between the traveler and the readers on the one hand, and the Chinese, on the other. More broadly, this dialogue shows the extent to which all narrative strategies are ideological, but it is not possible to attach to any of them a univocal ideological function *a priori* (Legerton and Rawson resorted to direct speech to foreground local people). Therefore, it is necessary to assess the ideological taintedness of narratives case by case, by contextualizing the form and meaning of what is recounted. Formally speaking, it could be said that all these features bring *China Road* close to the travel reportage and personal journal. In fact, Gifford conceives of his account not only as the tale of a journey, but also as a text that delivers an up-to-date representation of China, filtered through a precise, ideological stance.

To conclude this chapter, the analysis focuses once again on travel blogs, by specifically taking into account the posts that bloggers dedicate to China, in order to assess their degree of hypertextuality, as well as the generic form(s) with which they tend to comply.

HYPERTEXTUALITY IN TRAVEL BLOGS AND THE FORM OF THE NARRATIVE

We have seen that travel blogs' pages – both those on platforms and individual ones – present a high degree of hypertextuality, largely due to the insertion of a variety of peritextual elements, such as links, banners, pictures, social network icons. Yet, when it comes to delimit the analysis to the travel accounts *per se,* the situation is more controversial. The analysis addresses first the travel blogs on platforms.

***

Even from a cursory overview it is clear that the texts of all three of the travel blogs on platforms introduced beforehand manifest a very low degree of hypertextuality.

Figure 21: A post of Supermary58's blog on *Turistipercaso.it*

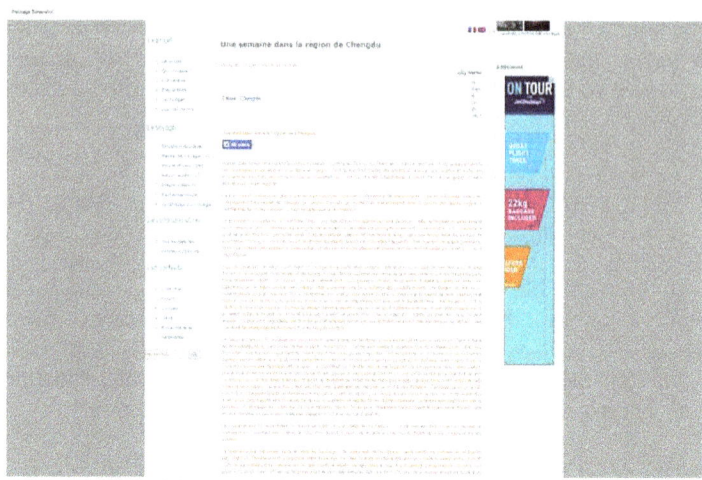

Figure 22: A post of Mathieu's blog on *Top-depart.com*

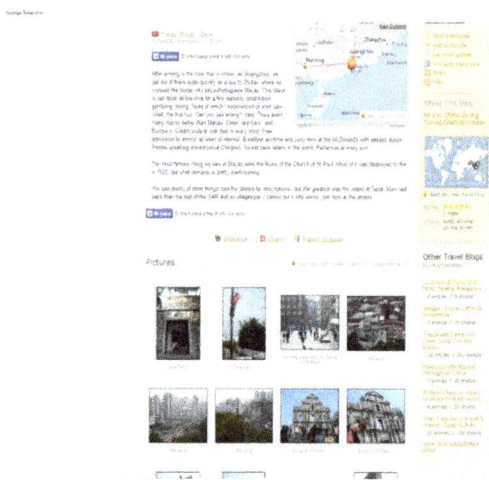

Figure 23: A post of Ataritouchme's blog on *Travelpod.com*

Supermary58 (Figure 21) went to China in 2012 for 17 days. She wrote ten posts about this experience: in none of them do we find links to other sources or references to other texts. Moreover, there are no pictures included in the posts because Turistipercaso.it urges bloggers to publish their photographs and videos in another dedicated section of the platform. Therefore, Supermary58's account is exclusively verbal, requiring users to browse the whole website if they want to get a visual representation of the places visited by the blogger. The main consequence of this policy of the platform is to strengthen the overall sense of community, while homogenizing the bloggers' contribution with that of other users. According to Supermary58, however, "it's not a problem if they [the pictures] are not in the blog, as far as they are posted somewhere."[47] This suggests that she does not seem to worry about the peculiar publishing procedure of the platform. Hence, Supermary58's persona tends to lose its singularity and appears more as just one blogger among many. This is also strengthened by the fact that once we access her profile page on the platform, neither a picture nor a short bio can be found (only her age and the date in which she joined Turistipercaso.it).

In narrative terms, in the posts we never find conversations, either with Chinese people, or with the companion with whom Supermary58 travels. The monologicity of the account is further enhanced by the fact that the blogger maintains an integrally narrative function throughout the text. The extract below attests to the extent to which the blogger adopts a "distanced" position from what she experiences by keeping a purely diegetic stance:

> Tiananmen square is at the heart of Beijing and we reach it very early in the day in order to avoid the crowd of tourists that visit it everyday. You can access it only through check-in points which are under surveillance by armed and attentive policemen. The square is surrounded by buildings and monuments, among which are the Monument to the People's Heroes, Mao's Mausoleum, the Great Hall of the People, and the National Museum of China.[48] (Supermary58 2012; author's translation)

Supermary58's "I" never assumes an ideological function by either commenting or "filtering" her description through a subjective point of view. This choice, in turn, leaves readers at a certain distance from China, the Chinese, and the events recounted, due to the fact that the narrative never mimetically represents the experience. Rather, what the blogger does is provide tips and information to would-be travelers in this way, complying with the writing that can be found in travel guides. This is in line with the blogger's own intents, as she claimed in the interview: "I have decided to keep an online travel diary in order to help those travellers who were planning a trip I had already made to follow my steps."[49]

A very similar case is constituted by Mathieu's blog (Figure 22). In 2007 Mathieu went to China with his wife for four weeks. The whole blog, which counts 10 posts, reads as a one-voiced account:

> Already a week since our departure, and still I haven't had the chance to update the blog… Indeed, we had a busy week going from a 48-hour visit to

---

[47] Supermary58, interview by Stefano Calzati, July 4, 2014, email.
[48] "Il cuore di Pechino è Piazza Tienanmen e noi ci arriviamo molto presto per cercare di evitare le folle di visitatori che ogni giorno la frequentano. Si accede solo attraverso metal-detector sorvegliati da poliziotti molto attenti. E' circondata da edifici e monumenti tra i quali il Monumento agli Eroi del Popolo con il Mausoleo di Mao, il Palazzo dell'Assemblea Nazionale del Popolo e il Museo di Storia Cinese."
[49] Supermary58, interview.

Beijing to rushing to Wuhan, in order to arrange our departure to Sanya, and then a visit to the dentist, a reunion with my love's family, etc. Beyond that, Internet access is not available everywhere, and often the connection runs very slowly (between 10 and 20 kb/s). So, this is a short summary of the events (sorry for the lack of historical and touristic details, but I do not have the guide with me at the moment).[50] (Mathieu 2007; author's translation)

The text consists of a homogeneous chain of notations composed of verbs, facts, and actions. Not only does the blogger avoid providing comments that would lead him to assume an ideological function, but the travelling personae never enter into dialogue with the Other, nor with each other. This is so despite the fact that Mathieu is travelling with a Chinese companion – his wife – who knows the country and the language, and likely did engage with locals. The lack of changes in the mood of the narrative is also strengthened by the fact that in none of the posts does Mathieu insert links or references to other sources, which would have opened the text to different points of views. Lastly, even though the platform gives the option to the blogger to include pictures within the account, there are none in the whole blog. Hence, what emerges is a writing that functions chiefly as a way to remember and to connect the blogger with those readers at home – like relatives and friends – who are following his experience, without however providing any deep insights as far as the representation of China is concerned. This consideration finds further proof in the lack of personal notes on the blogger's profile page, where it is possible to read nothing more than: "Mathieu: It's me :-) Tao: It's her." Clearly this is a piece of information that does little to build the blogger's persona and, instead, reveals the extent to which the blog is conceived for a readership that already knows the blogger.

Ataritouchme's blog *All o'er China during Spring Festival Holiday* (Figure 23) has 16 posts over a period of one and a half months. The main difference from the previous two blogs is that Ataritouchme included a great number of pictures in the blog (as the blogger writes at the beginning, however, these were not taken by him, but by his friend Hannah). In terms of narrative discourse, the whole account is composed of brief descriptions of the places visited and the things done. Posts are usually very short, bare in syntax, and sometimes filled with jargon:

No flying allowed or desired. Travels through China, Spring Festival Holiday 2006. I mainly created this blog for myself, to remember what I did, and for the people who asked to see pictures (none of which I took, by the way. Hannah took all of them). (Ataritouchme 2006)

---

[50] "Déjà une semaine qu'on est partis, et toujours pas de mise à jour du blog... En fait on a eu une semaine très chargée, entre Pékin à visiter en 48 h et les courses à Wuhan pour préparer le départ à Sanya, passer chez le dentiste, voir la belle famille etc. De plus, l'accès à Internet n'est pas présent dans tous les hôtels, et souvent pour un débit médiocre (entre 10 et 20 ko/s). Voici donc un petit résumé des évènements (désolé pour les détails historiques et touristiques, j'ai pas le guide du routard sous la main)."

Similarly to the other two bloggers, Ataritouchme's "I" maintains a narrative function that does not transcend into an overtly ideological role. Besides, he opts for not reporting dialogues, or other links to outer sources, thus simply creating an account in which the writing runs uninterrupted and unaffected in its mood. Again, the text has the goal of keeping memory of the events and sharing them with those who are willing to read, as the blogger himself pointed out: "for me a travel diary is primarily a record of events so I can recall them well." Furthermore, when asked why he chose Travelpod.com as a platform, he answers: "It was, I guess, the first one I came across. I really don't know any other travel blogs and don't care to experiment. It works well enough."[51] To emerge, then, is a rather naïf approach to the choice and use of the platform. Due to that, however (as well as to the kind of narrative produced), the blogger flattens out all that pertains to both the representation of himself and of China, producing a narrative that keeps readers aways from the events.

Overall, all three blogs are characterized by a low degree of hypertextuality, producing a narrative that keeps readers away from the events, and shaped as informal personal journals. "Personal," however, does not mean subjective: indeed, while the "I's" of the bloggers never abdicate their narrative function, the (self)representation of bloggers and of China are abstracted, neutralized. These findings confirm the validity of previous studies on blogs, which concluded that blogs are mainly single-authored diaries composed of written language and with a low frequency of links (Herring, Scheidt, Kouper, and Wright 2007).

***

The scenario appears more articulated in relation to individual travel blogs. Travel blogs by British Becki, French Curieuse Voyageuse, and Italian Gattosandro Viaggiatore all present a high degree of hypertextuality. Becki (2012) wrote 11 posts on China over a period of roughly two months. In each post, there are usually a couple of links, for example to the Web sources that are dedicated to the landmarks visited by the blogger (the text in Figure 24 contains a link to the Great Panda Breeding Base website). There are also plenty of pictures and these are included within the account, revealing the purpose to balance visual elements and words and to organize them in a mutually dependent relation (Figure 24). At the end of each post a note in bold usually sums up the whole post in the form of an off-the-record commentary (Figure 25).

---

[51] Ataritouchme, interview by Stefano Calzati, July 3, 2014, email.

Figure 24: A post on Becki's blog dedicated to Chengdu. Pictures and links are included

> Extreme cultural difference is what makes travel invigorating, to stop and see just how different we are and how we go about things. You just always have to stop and remember that we are just a strange and fascinating to others as we are in awe of them and, for me, that's what makes travel special. Fascination is education.

Have you been to China? What shocked you the most?

Figure 25: A footnote in a post dedicated to Beijing on Becki's blog

Concerning the narrative, the alternation between the descriptions of places, personal anecdotes, and reflections continuously rearticulates the mood of the discourse. Sometimes the blogger assumes a chiefly narrative function, as in the following passage:

> Seeing pandas in Chengdu is as popular as visiting the Great Wall of China in Beijing or the Terracotta Army in Xian. As soon as you arrive in the city you known you hit the land of pandas madness. Their adorable faces greet you from every street corner, appear on all manner of advertisement, and are even used to decorate taxi car bonnets. (Becki 2012)

It is remarkable that even in such a descriptive paragraph, the blogger opens her writing to the "you" of the reader marking the intention of overtly addressing, with her advice, a precise group of followers (i.e., potential tourists). At other times, Becki focuses on personal stories in line with her passion for "uncovering alternative angles to the well-established [destinations]" (Becki 2012), as she notes on her site. In so doing, the blogger's "I" also takes on an ideological function. Below, for instance, Becki recounts a humorous episode that occurred in a Chinese massage center:

As my friend's face turned a little white when I entered the room, she simply screamed at me: "OH MY GOD, what HAVE they done to your back?" Looking over my shoulder I couldn't see a thing, until I ran to the toilet and lifted up my top. I'd been tortured. After six hours of cycling, our arses hurt from the crappy bike seats and we were tired, dishevelled, sweaty and ready to wind down. The grand idea at this point was to spend the last hour or so of the day relaxing with some spa-like indulgence. Lying down, my back was cracked and the deep tissue massage took my breath away. It hurt like hell but it wasn't too different from what I've had at home, only harder. Except that, alongside the pressure of his knuckles, there was a slight scratching sensation. How and why was he scratching? When the ordeal was over I knew I'd just laugh about it over a few beers. In China, we had a funny story to tell almost every day and today would be mine. Except it wasn't funny at all. It turns out the scratching wasn't his fingers, but a plastic card used to bring blood to the surface of my skin in order to help release toxins, and this was the result. (Becki 2012)

Here the blogger mixes the tale of an episode in which she was directly involved with comments on her whole experience in China. The first few lines of the passage are also significant because Becki includes a dialogue with a friend in it, in the form of reported speech. Therefore, Becki's posts do present many variations in the narrative mood and these help to draw readers closer to the events by remodeling the diegesis.

In Curieuse Voyageuse's (2009) posts on China, the written text is often mixed with pictures (Figure 26). Sometimes, it can also happen that pictures are posted alone, thus representing the sole mode of narration. Moreover, it is common to find in each post links to other sources, which are either internal to the blog or directing to external sources (Figure 26). Then, at the end of each post, as a form of footnote, users always find a bunch of links that point to other similar posts (Figure 27).

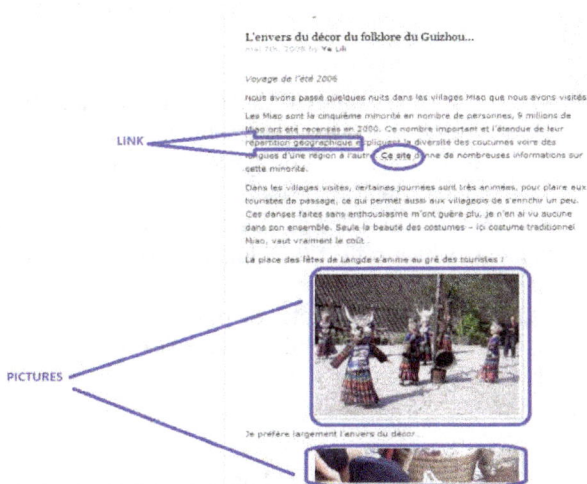

Figure 26: A post by Curieuse Voyageuse with pictures and links inside the text.

Figure 27: Links at the end of a post on Curieuse Voyageuse's blog

Quotations from other texts are also included: the following is an example taken from the post dedicated to Datong's caves, in which the blogger refers to the official UNESCO document about this ancient archaeological site:

> The caves are rightly described by UNESCO as "masterpieces of early Chinese Buddhist cave art," and they represent "the successful fusion of Buddhist religious symbolic art from south and central Asia with Chinese cultural traditions." Statues are well-preserved and the whole site is really amazing! (Curieuse Voyageuse 2009; author's translation)

The blogger also demonstrates her willingness to engage with locals. For instance, in a post dedicated to her visit to the Sky Temple in Beijing, she does not linger on a detailed description of the place; rather she recounts the encounter with an old lady who is practicing Tai Chi:

> We had a great time: she taught me some Tai Chi notions and positions. I made quite a few people laugh. I thought she was a really beautiful old lady. She told me she is there every day of the year. Indeed, I came back one year later and she was there, exactly on the same spot![52] (Curieuse Voyageuse 2009; author's translation)

In this passage, the conversation between Curieuse Voyageuse and the old lady is embedded into the narrative. Yet, readers can easily get a glimpse of a very intimate encounter. Similarly to Becki, Curieuse Voyageuse strives to find alternative ways of looking at China, dwelling on usually overlooked details or on the telling of personal anecdotes. The narrative, hence, is filled as much with descriptions as with subjective impressions and opinions, which reflect the blogger's passage from a narrative to an ideological function.

Gattosandro Viaggiatore (2012) wrote 24 posts about her (second) journey to China, which lasted approximately a month. Each post contains a variety of pictures

---

[52] "Nous avons partagé un bon moment: elle a voulu m'en apprendre plus et elle m'a appris quelques pas de Tai Chi. J'ai fait rire un bon nombre de passants. Je l'ai trouvée vraiment belle dans son grand âge. Elle m'a dit être là tous les jours de l'année. J'y suis revenue un an plus tard, elle était exactement au même endroit!"

interspersed in the text (Figure 28). There are also various links both within each post and at its end (Figure 28), where the blogger meticulously details all the places she visited, the means of transport used, the hostels booked, the costs sustained, etc. Then, it is not rare for the posts to be concluded by a note – usually in italics – that gives some extra information or provides a comment on the experience narrated (Figure 28).

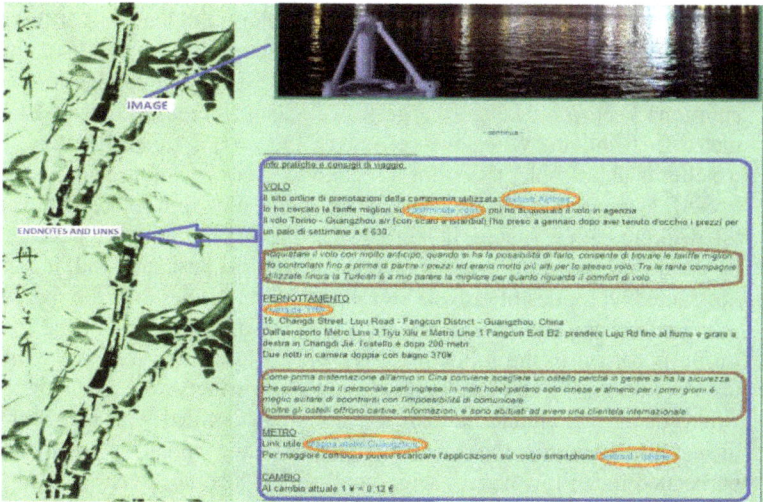

Figure 28: A picture, various links, and two endnotes in one of Gattosandro Viaggiatore's posts.

These features attest to a considerable confidence of the blogger with the publishing practices implied by the chosen CMS. In fact, she stated that "my blog is constantly evolving and I make all efforts to improve it."[53]

In terms of narrative discourse, it is illuminating to compare how Supermary58 and Gattosandro Viaggiatore recount the "same" episode, namely their arrival in Beijing:

> The Aeroflot flight lands on time in Beijing. It's roughly 10 am; we collect our baggage, we exchange some euros for yuan and we take the tube to DongSi stop, which is ten minutes away from our hostel. We check in and, because in our hostel there is a ticket office, we decide to book our next train transfers. For moving around the city, we will use a rechargeable card, which is sold in all metro stations. The first visit is to the Sky Temple.[54] (Supermary58 2012; author's translation)

---

[53] Gattosandro Viaggiatore, interview by Stefano Calzati, July 8, 2014, email.

[54] "Il volo Aeroflot atterra puntuale a Pechino. Sono circa le 10 del mattino ritiriamo i bagagli, cambiamo un po' di euro in yuan e prendiamo la metropolitana che in poco tempo ci porta alla fermata di Dong Si distante circa 10 minuti a piedi dal nostro ostello. Facciamo il check in e, visto che all'interno dell'ostello c'è un banco escursioni/biglietteria, ci premuriamo di prenotare i trasferimenti notturni in treno che faremo nei

After a roughly 20-hour journey (considering both the flight and the waiting for the transfers), we are finally in Beijing. We set the clock six hours ahead and, after a few minutes, we realize how big the airport is. After having attended to the bureaucracy at the Immigration Office, we go to collect our baggage. We follow the signs that tell us to go down the stairs and we find ourselves at a train station! It's amazing that in order to reach the baggage claim, we have to take a train, and it does take quite long to get there! Our baggage is already there when we arrive, so we pick it up and take a train to the city centre. Outside of the window, the sky is blue. I am tired, but emotions keep me awake. We get off at Dongzhimen Station and take the metro to Jishuitan. When we get out of the metro, we realize that the hot weather is unbearable. I stop for a second to check my notes and congratulate myself, as everything has run smoothly so far. The first impression is harsh: the walking path is ruined, in some places there is not even the pavement and in others we have to walk along the street because the walking path is obstructed with piles of gravel. Motorbikes and bicycles take the right of way over pedestrians and everything here is dusty and shabby. On the road, the traffic is heavy: in the following days, we will get used to horns, which are used continuously and randomly. Completely sweaty, we reach the hutong where our hostel should be. The narrow street is filled with restaurants that have an unhygienic look, but nonetheless they spread a good smell of barbecued meat; low houses with small rooms hosting seven or eight people seated around a table; some vendors of fruits and vegetables showing off cages in which a few cocks are segregated and about to be cooked. The hostel gives me a strange impression. Being hosted in a typical Chinese house with an internal court, the architecture is precious, but the roof that covers the whole area and all the decorations that hang from it make the ambient a bit oppressive. The rooms of the main hostel are divided across two floors, in which we meet a bunch of Western people. The lady at the reception desk speaks English and, having photocopied our passports, accompanies us to "our" hostel, which is located on a quiet street. What a joy! Our room is in a wonderful building at the centre of which there is a garden with plants, trees and a fountain. I like it straight away. We rest for a while and then decide to go out to get acquainted with the area, which appears as an intricate set of streets. And yet, we ultimately orientate ourselves easily.[55] (Gattosandro Viaggiatore 2012; author's translation)

---

prossimi giorni. Per gli spostamenti in città utilizzeremo una tessera ricaricabile in vendita presso le stazioni della metropolitana. La prima visita la facciamo al Tempio del Cielo."

[55] Dopo un viaggio durato una ventina di ore (tra volo e attese in aeroporto per lo scalo) siamo finalmente a Pechino! Mettiamo l'orologio 6 ore avanti e dopo pochi passi ci rendiamo conto di quanto è enorme questo aeroporto. Dopo le pratiche di immigrazione ci dirigiamo al ritiro bagagli. Seguiamo la freccia che ci dice di scendere le scale e... ci troviamo alla stazione di un treno. Pazzesco! Al ritiro bagagli ci si arriva col treno,

Two considerations can be made here. To a certain degree, the routines that Supermary58 and Gattosandro Viaggiatore account for are rather similar: the landing, the luggage collection, the metro, and the arrival at the hostel. It could be said that both texts reflect the point to which the preliminary stages of (almost) any travel have been commoditized. On the other hand, it is possible to note that Gattosandro Viaggiatore's text is much richer and tries to give an account of the arrival that goes beyond a mere descriptive plane. This means that Gattosandro Viaggiatore's "I" does not remain attached to its basic narrative function, but assumes in many circumstances an ideological role ("the hostel gives me a strange impression"; "What a joy!"; "I like it straight away"). Moreover, Gattosandro Viaggiatore tries to deliver an original and personal account that derives from continuous attempts to engage with locals, as the quotation below exemplifies:

> When we return to the hotel, a half-empty bottle of vodka on the reception desk tells us that there's a party going on organized by Mr Shi and his friends. When he sees us he makes two euphoric comments: he tells me that I'm beautiful while to Lore he tells something we cannot quite guess, but which provokes many laughs. We discreetly move away from them before finding ourselves involved in an all-night-long party with a glass in hand. We fix our meeting with Mr Shi tomorrow at 7am, let's say 7.30am, he specifies. What a character! [56] (Gattosandro Viaggiatore 2013; author's translation)

---

che non ci mette neanche poco! Le nostre valigie sono già lì che ci aspettano, così andiamo a prendere il treno che ci porterà in città. Dai finestrini Pechino ci saluta con un bel cielo azzurro, io sono stanca ma l'emozione mi tiene sveglia. Scendiamo alla stazione Dongzhimen e prendiamo la metropolitana per Jishuitan. Usciamo dalla metro e il caldo ci stende. Mi fermo un momento a controllare i miei appunti e a esultare un pochino per essere riusciti a fare tutto bene, almeno fino qui. L'impatto è un po' forte: il marciapiede per l'ostello è sconnesso, in alcuni punti non c'è la pavimentazione, in altri bisogna passare sulla strada perchè ci sono cumuli di terra. Motorini e biciclette (entrambi elettrici) si prendono la precedenza sui pedoni e in generale tutto quanto intorno a noi ha l'aspetto polveroso e trasandato. Sulla strada il traffico si fa sentire: nei prossimi giorni ci abitueremo ai clacson, suonati in continuazione anche senza motivo. Decisamente sudati arriviamo all'incrocio con l'hutong dell'ostello. Una via stretta, con ristoranti che hanno l'aspetto poco igienico ma che mandano un buon profumino di carne grigliata. Case basse, con stanze minuscole al cui interno si intravedono 7 o 8 persone attorno al tavolo. Qualche venditore ambulante di frutta e verdura, e una gabbia con qualche gallina viva pronta per essere spennata. L'ostello mi fa una strana impressione. L'architettura è carina, essendo una tipica casa cinese col cortile interno, ma il tetto che chiude tutta l'area che dovrebbe essere all'aperto e l'accozzaglia di decorazioni che pendono dal soffitto rendono l'ambiente un po' opprimente. Qui, su due piani, ci sono le stanze e le camerate dell'ostello principale, e ci sono una decina di ragazzi occidentali. La signorina della reception parla inglese, e dopo essersi fatta le fotocopie dei nostri passaporti ci fa accompagnare al "nostro" ostello, che si trova poco più avanti, in una via interna. Che meraviglia! Una bellissima costruzione bassa che gira intorno a un cortile delizioso con piante, alberi e una fontana. Mi piace all'istante. Ci riposiamo un po' e poi usciamo per prendere un po' di confidenza con la zona, che subito mi sembra un complicato intrico di vie ma ci orientiamo abbastanza facilmente."

[56] "Al nostro rientro in hotel la bottiglia mezza vuota di vodka sul bancone della reception ci suggerisce che è in corso un festino tra Mr Shi e i suoi amici. In preda all'euforia fa due commenti nei nostri confronti, a me dice che sono beautiful, a Lore una parola che non riusciamo a capire ma che provoca grasse risate da

The extract is taken from the post that Gattosandro Viaggiatore wrote about the city of Zhanjiajie. The title itself of the post – "It's only you who can do such a troublesome journey and call it a holiday!" – comes from a phone call that the blogger had with her mother. The title has the function to set the ironic tone of the whole post, while providing a preliminary interpretation of the experience through not so much the blogger's perspective but her mother's voice. Similarly, in the passage above, Gattosandro Viaggiatore recounts the tentative dialogue – half in English half in Chinese – that she had with the owner of the hotel, in this way including his own voice into the narrative. Overall, the blogger's posts present an articulated narrative in which shifts in the mood, signaled by the passage from a narrative to an ideological function, help the reader to get close to the scene.

Lastly, a note is required on the presence of comments in the blogs. Comments can be considered as a form of dialogue between bloggers and readers. These exchanges are extra-diegetic because they are not an integral part of the account, but remain external to it. Hence, they have to be regarded as peritextual elements. Interestingly, in none of the travel blogs on platforms analyzed so far do we find comments to the posts, a feature that strengthens the monologicity of these texts (and hints also to the limited readership of the blogs). By contrast, on individual blogs comments are quite numerous. The majority of the conversations between the blogger and the blogs' visitors are subservient to appraise what the blogger has written or done. It is the case, for instance, of the comments to Becki's blog on Pandas, which go from "I am so relieved to hear that the pandas are well cared for and have plenty of room to roam around" to "Adorables!!!!! Way too cute" (Becki 2012).

Beyond these complimentary comments, there are, however, some exceptions, such as the following one, always from Becki's blog:

> [Rob Hornby]: "Two tips for the park. 1. Buy a panda card from one of the local shops, which gets you cheaper entry and also allows for other local discounts. This helps with 2. Not openly advertised but on a tour we found a door through which you could meet a real panda face to face and will pose for a photo while sat on your lap. Sounds a bit odd but this is similar to holding a koala. Very expensive but does go toward the park. It's not advertised so keep your eye out." (Becki 2012)

> [Backpacker Becki]: "Thanks Rob I did mention the 'hold a panda' moment. Although I don't totally agree with it!" (Becki 2012)

This exchange, taken from the post that Becki dedicated to the Panda Reservoir in Chengdu, exemplifies the extent to which comments can also constructively become a means for completing or clarifying what the blogger has written. In this specific case,

---

cui ci defiliamo prima di trovarci con un bicchiere in mano a brindare con loro tutta la notte. Ci diamo appuntamento per domani mattina verso le sette, lui rilancia, facciamo sette e mezza. Che personaggio!"

because Becki feels that her reliability as a traveler and writer has been questioned, she is not afraid to correct what the reader mentions in his comment.

The complex articulation of the narrative of individual blogs, together with the presence of comments, differs substantially from what is witnessed in blogs on platforms and, consequently, with the findings of previous studies on blogs (as mentioned earlier). In this respect, although individual travel blogs can be said to approach the form of the personal journal, the way in which the narrative is shaped and the presence of hypertextual elements open the accounts to a hybridization of their form, mixing features from the travel guide, the multi-service portal, the tourism website, and the diary.

CONCLUSION

The aim of the first chapter was to provide a formal characterization of contemporary travel books and blogs. Being inscribed in the realm of transmediality, the analysis required addressing the form of the texts in relation to the medial formats that "carry" them. Eventually, this also led to some insights into how China and the Chinese are represented by authors and bloggers.

As a brief introduction, by drawing back onto early 20th century texts and on the interview with Chinese travel curator Zhang Mei, it was shown that the itineraries of today's travel writers partially overlap with those of "classic" travelers, while other areas have entered the tourism circuit later.

Subsequently, Genette's (1997) work on the paratext was applied to contemporary travel blogs. The choice to adopt this concept, coined initially in relation to written books, was fruitful to reverse the one-directedness of many studies that compare print and online texts. At the same time, it also evaluated the inefficacy of those models for the study of online pages, such as Knox's (2007), which identify axes or layers within each document and attempt a compositional analysis of the text. By using the notion of paratext, it was possible to maintain a holistic perspective over travel blogs and understand how they are built and "appear." While individual travel blogs present peritextual elements that are usually organized around the text similarly to printed books, on travel blogs on platforms these elements tend to invade the space of the text. Hence, particularly on platforms, the recognizability of the text is jeopardized by the inclusion of a multiplicity of peritexts that largely depend on the agencies behind the construction of the platforms. This, in turn, leads to a fragmentation of the authorial stances in charge of what appears on the screen.

In the second part of the chapter, the concept of hypertextuality, used mainly in connection with online texts, was extended to the study of contemporary travel books, with the intention, again, to bridge, rather than contrapose print and online realms. Such reversal led us to assess that travel books bear a higher degree of hypertextuality than travel blogs on platforms do, and a lower degree when compared to individual travel blogs. The kinds of hypertextual webs that offline and online texts weave are different. In books, references mention sources that are not physically there (apart from references internal to the text itself). This suggests that hypertextuality in books is mainly epitextual in the sense that references, although inscribed in the text, open the book to an exteriority that transcends its own physicality. In the case of blogs, instead, links allow the reader to retrieve sources while remaining within the same online environment. Hence, hypertextuality on the Web is coalescent: what happens is that on the Web the peritext tends simultaneously to occupy the space of the text and to extend toward the epitext's realm, eventually merging into it. At the same time, however, it would be hazardous to deny any applicability of Genette's study on paratexts to online texts, exclusively on the basis of the lack of physicality of Web documents. When approaching the Web, indeed, not all is paratext: there still remains a valid epitextual distinction to be made, namely between online and offline content, whenever online texts mention sources that can be accessed in their printed form only. The guiding principle of such a paratextual difference is no longer that of distance, as Genette (1997) suggests when discerning between peritext and epitext. Rather, it is a medial principle that is at stake, insofar as the analogue and digital realms are (still) incommensurable.

Thirdly, by combining the concept of hypertextuality with Genette's (1980) study on the mood of the narrative and the narrator's functions – narrative and ideological – the formal features of print and online travel accounts were characterized. The analysis confirmed the formal heterogeneity of travel books. Ethnography, diary, reportage, essay: all these forms have been found among the texts surveyed and some of them also coexist in the same text. Concerning travel blogs, a major distinction was detected. The accounts hosted on platforms chiefly comply with the diary form. Online, such form is characterized – due also to a low degree of hypertextuality – by a monologic narrative that rarely presents shifts in the mood. Hence, readers are confronted with texts that maintain a certain constant distance toward the events recounted; a distance that tends to flatten the representations of both the blogger and China. On the other hand, the accounts on individual travel blogs manifest – also in reason of their high degree of hypertextuality – a formal hybridization. Features that belong to the diary, the anecdotic account, the travel guide, the tourism portal all inform these accounts. While the findings concerning travel blogs on platforms confirmed those of previous studies on blogs, which were characterized as single-authored journals with usually a paucity of links (and comments), individual travel blogs differ quite radically from these conclusions. This can be due to a number of reasons – e.g. consolidation of the Web 2.0, emergence of customizable CMSs, changes in reading practices – for sure, however, this change is the sign that contemporary blogging has evolved (compared to ten years ago) and diversified (compared to platforms).

The emphasis on the formal features of the accounts will be further developed in the next chapter drawing on Mikhail Bakhtin's concept of "chronotope." In particular, the point to assess in more detail is the kind of information (and knowledge) about China that each genium (and writer) can deliver.

CHAPTER 2

Medial Chronotopes and Mediatized Representations of Travels in China

Mikhail Bakhtin's ([1937] 1981) concept of "chronotope" is very useful for the present transmedial comparison between travel books and blogs, because it allows looking at each genium as a site of negotiation between the "represented world" and its "modes of representation," so that it will be possible to shed some light on what we, as readers, can get to know about China when opting for one genium or the other.

Bakhtin defines the chronotope as "the intrinsic connectedness of temporal and spatial relationships that are artistically expressed in literature. The chronotope in literature has an intrinsic generic significance. It can even be said that it is precisely the chronotope that defines genre and generic distinctions" (1981: 258). Travel writing, in this regard, is a particularly fruitful object of analysis for at least two reasons. First, the unfolding of time and space is a crucial aspect of the genre, insofar as travel accounts are presupposed by a displacement in space and time that is both physical – the journey *per se* – and metaphorical, that is, the writing process.[57] As Barbara Korte (2008: 26) notes, "every piece of travel writing constructs a specific world and thus implies a 'chronotope' or 'time-space'." Elaborating this idea further on, Korte suggests that the concept of chronotope can find a reflection at both the thematic level of the text – if and how the space and time of the journey are thematized in the travelogue – and at the discursive level, that is, how the narrative creates its own temporal and spatial framework. Korte connects this latter level to the characteristics of the narrative discourse as identified by Genette (1980) and as they were discussed in Chapter 1. Here, to be taken into account will be primarily the thematization of the space and time of the travel, always keeping in mind the brief synopses for each text provided in the Appendix. The second reason that makes the relation between travel writing and chronotope highly productive is that, as discussed in the Introduction, we witness the tendency to identify travel writing in tight relation to the medial format that carries the text. On this point, Bakhtin argues that "there exists a special group of genres that play an especially significant role in structuring novels, sometimes by themselves even directly determining the structure of a novel as a whole. Examples of such genres would be confession, the diary, travel notes, biography..." (1981: 321). The purpose of this chapter is to move from the text

---

[57] This, of course, could also lead to the broader discussion about writing as an act, at once, of unavoidable inscription of the "I" on the page (see Benveniste's argument about the language's subjectivity [1971]) and of constant deferral of this same "I" to itself (Derrida 1976). However, the point stressed here is simpler, namely the parallelism between travelling and writing as two mirroring practices.

toward the medium in order to extend the notion of chronotope also to the book and blog as medial formats. Illuminating, in this sense, are Bakhtin's "concluding remarks" to his work. Here, the Russian intellectual pushes his reflection about the chronotope of the novel toward a broader horizon, arguing that "out of the actual chronotopes of our world (which serve as the source of representation) emerge the reflected and created chronotopes of the world represented in the work (in the text)" (1981: 255). In other words, Bakhtin seems to hint at the idea that the book, as a textual artefact binding together the representational and the represented world, is also chronotopic. In the same spirit, Asif Agha (2007: 321) affirms that "the novelistic chronotope connects the world of the author to the 'chronotopic situation' of diverse listeners-readers due to the physical materiality of its textual form." In this respect, the notion of genium, far from being only a descriptive term, comes to define a conceptual field of generic and medial negotiations, which, at once, internally dictate the chronotope of the text and externally guide its chronotopic interpretation. Bakhtin only refers to the book because this was (and still is) the most widely spread medium for literary novels. However, once we apply his argument to the comparison between travel books and travel blogs, we can attempt an investigation of the chronotopic features of the book and the blog as medial formats and consequently the different representations of the journey, as well as of the traveler and the China, which travel books and blogs promote. The idea that the book, as a medial format, has its own chronotopic principles has been tested indirectly by Polish writer Zenon Fajfer (2010), who coined the term "liberature" to define those literary works that expressly exploit the physicality of the book to make sense of the whole text.[58] Here, this idea is broadened, insofar as it is assumed that any medium has precise chronotopic principles and, as such, they inevitably affect the text, independently from the author's willingness to exploit them.

The chapter proposes first an intra-medial comparison between three pairs of travel books, moving from monomodal to multimodal ones. Secondly, the transition from the realm of print to the online space is constituted by the analysis of the pictorial book *Carnet di viaggio: Cina* (2005) by travel artist Stefano Faravelli. Thirdly, the intra-medial comparison will concern four travel blogs, two of which are hosted on platforms, while the others are independently built. In the conclusion, some considerations are drawn on the different kinds of chronotopes that each genium promotes and, consequently, the different kinds of information that readers are likely to find when reading them. Besides, insofar as travel books and travel blogs are (often) multimodal texts (and in Faravelli's case a "transmodal" one, see below), the chapter also contemplates the extent to which visual modes (i.e., photography and pictorial illustrations) can be read chronotopically, thus applying Bakhtin's concept beyond written language.

---

[58] A clarification of the concept and some examples of "liberature" can be found at: http://www.liberatura.pl/liberatura.html (site in Polish).

BEHIND THE WALL AND SHADOW OF THE SILK ROAD

The first pair of monomodal books under analysis is constituted by two travelogues authored by the renowned British travel writer Colin Thubron.

In 1987, Thubron published *Behind the Wall*, a text that recounts his journey across China at a time in which entering the country and moving around was still subjected to many restrictions. Mao had died only a decade before, the physical and psychological consequences of the Cultural Revolution were still painfully perceived, and China's opening toward the West was still in its infancy. Then, two decades later, Thubron went back to China in order to travel the whole length of the Silk Road, from Xian up to the Turkish coast. *Shadow of the Silk Road* (2006) came out from this experience: here China only constitutes the point of departure, while the majority of the chapters are dedicated to Middle Eastern countries such as Uzbekistan, Afghanistan, Iran and Turkey. While, 20 years later, entering and travelling in China became easier, the whole journey across Asia still presented difficulties and dangers, insofar as some of the regions Thubron went through were in a state of war (often against Western powers). These partially specular situations compel the author to specify in two notes at the beginning of each book, that "the identity of several people has been disguised, in case harsher times return" (Thubron 1987: ix) and "in the midst of political uncertainty, the identity of several people described in the narrative has been disguised" (Thubron 2006: introduction).[59] In both cases, then, the historical time in which the journeys were undertaken plays a major role in dictating how the experience is represented and, in particular, it requires Thubron to fictionalize the identities of the people encountered.

From the point of view of the present work, the comparison between these two texts is worthwhile in that China firstly represents the geographical frame of the whole travel experience, while two decades later its account is inscribed within a broader narrative. The aim, in this respect, is to understand the extent to which the passing of time and the different shaping of the narrative in the two books have affected the representation of China (and of the traveler). At the beginning of his first book, Thubron lets transpire a sense of alienation with respect to the Middle Kingdom and its people. The following passage is an example:

> I tried to talk to three old men who had set up a counter piled with second-hand books, but they stared back at me dumbly. When I joined a queue outside a milk-stall, the women I addressed only simpered and covered their mouths with their little blue residency permits. A suspicion that these people would remain forever inaccessible was filling me with suppressed alarm. Like an insecure child, I began to crave for any kind of contact, even abuse. (Thubron 1987: 6)

---

[59] From here, the path of the discussion could also lead to address the stringent political relevance of travel writing, but such an issue is beyond the scope of the present chapter. On this point, please refer to Calzati 2015a.

The very fact of being confronted with something new and incomprehensible, which leaks from this quotation, is what compels Thubron to travel in the first place, as he mentioned in the interview: "for me, travelling is the satisfaction of curiosity. All my travel books start with ignorance, with my not knowing or understanding a culture."[60] The preliminary impossibility of approaching locals occurs despite Thubron's pre-departure effort to learn Mandarin and acquire as much information as possible about China. To an extent, however, the feeling of alienation is gradually diluted with the passing of time. Meaningful, in this sense, is the author's encounter, toward the end of the journey, with a Sino-American couple: on this occasion, Thubron is more inclined to speak with the Chinese woman than with her US-American husband:

> In one shrine I came upon a young American and a Chinese girl whose fingers rested tentatively on his arm. She was statuesque, with proud Mongolian cheekbones. They had been married the year before, she said – he a teacher, she a Beijing student. The man clambered to a temple higher up, exclaiming at its beauty. But the girl stayed behind. "My family were appalled by our marriage," she said. "They told me I'd be bought and sold in the market as a prostitute. Literally." "Even my own friends thought he just wanted me as an oriental slave in the house." "Actually, I've always got my way. I am used to it." I laughed. "I thought you were." (Thubron 1987: 255)

Overall, although Thubron manages to reduce, in the long run, the cultural distance that separates him from China, he remains dissatisfied with his experience, to the point that in the interview he claimed that: "the Chinese have always been hard for me to understand; they have required of me a real effort in terms of adaptation, and then the language is very difficult." While this acknowledgment exceeds the boundary of the travelogue, arriving at a much later time (the interview was conducted in 2013), in the text, too, it is possible to retrace the enduring presence of a divide between the author and China. Despite having travelled around the country for months and having traversed it from north to south and from west to east, Thubron's acquaintance with China remains at a superficial level. This is why both the representation of China and the author's are anchored to well distinct worlds. In many occurrences Thubron appears as a Westerner of whom Chinese people can barely understand the provenance:

> At supper, I was regaled by workers from a plastic factory. They talked in bursts of boyish jokes which they translated for me into the school-taught Mandarin of the Cantonese south. They were in holiday mood, and plied me with questions. Only occasionally – when I told them that in Britain most people received a month's holiday (they received a week) and that we worked five days a week (they worked six) – did they lapse into perplexed or ruminative silence; and when I mentioned that Western governments were

---

[60] Colin Thubron, interview by Stefano Calzati, May 27, 2013, in person.

full of contending political parties instead of a single authority, the illusion of our togetherness was temporarily shattered, and the girls stared at me with big uncomprehending eyes, and the men murmured. Finally, when they heard I was travelling alone, I saw that I slid altogether out of their comprehension. All foreigners go everywhere in groups, they said. Always. And they go top class. (Thubron 1987: 173)

In other passages, it emerges how China, despite all Thubron's efforts, remains a world apart in which it is difficult to delve. Hence, if Thubron is led to think of himself as a typical Westerner, as the quotation above also betrays, China chiefly functions as a term of comparison; a mirror against which the author can reflect himself. In taking up this role, then, China rarely comes into focus in all its diversity. Sure, Thubron does encounter and talk with many Chinese, but these soon lose their individuality and become representative of a greater mass. So, for instance, readers come to know that Westerners and Chinese people are treated differently in 1980s China:

> Even in our obscure hotel, the barriers were not all down. I sat in a banqueting-hall sterilised by table-cloths and kitsch paintings, and settled to a meal which cost an extravagant 5 kwai – while he [Thubron's guide] vanished into another room and ate one for a twelfth as much. No, said the waitress, I could not eat in the common part of the restaurant. It was unorthodox. (Thubron 1987: 112)

Above all, the travelogue is revealing of the advantageous position that a Westerner, willingly or not, occupied in China still at the end of the 20th century. Meanwhile, the very possibility of approaching the Chinese beyond the curtain of formality was hindered. The historical time of the journey and the forms of privilege that travelling embeds affect the whole experience and it is according to such coordinates that the traveler's Western background and China come to belong to two separated realities, enticing that sense of frustration that permeates Thubron's experience.

***

In *Shadow of the Silk Road*, readers are confronted with a less polarized representation of the experience. Quintessential, in this respect, is Thubron's deconstruction of the space of the journey: he reasserts in many passages that the Silk Road is not a single path but many:

> Trying to comprehend the medley of voices and features around me, I was slipping into a river where nations lost their meaning. This, after all, was the road whose Chinese silk lay in the graves of Iron Age Germany. It had spread variousness, and a rich impurity. (Thubron 2006: 116)

The questioning of the linearity of the whole itinerary triggers, in turn, a more composite representation of China. The idea itself of China as a homogenous country is challenged:

> In the crowds, at either pole of life, went little girls in iridescent caps, like old-fashioned dolls, and widows under coarse brown veils. The air reeked of resin and coal dust, and filled with the quavering music of Arabia. No Chinese was in sight. Central Asia was suddenly close and palpable. Among the sheepskin hats and skull-caps of the Uighur went Kyrgyz herdsmen in white felt trilbies, and here and there were lean Tajiks from the Pakistan border, their women walking under high pillbox hats dripping with silver pendants. (Thubron 2006: 140)

In this passage, which narrates the author's stay in Kashgar, it is above all the varied ethnic composition of the whole "Chinese" population that makes Thubron realize that he is traversing a country whose geopolitical unity does not go hand in hand with cultural homogeneity. At the same time, China appears fragmented not only ethnically, but also by being dislocated on different temporal planes. In fact, the China of the past periodically comes to attend at the present time of the journey. Differently from *Behind the Wall*, which was very focused on the historical time of the journey (references to the past were mainly directed toward the recent Cultural Revolution), *Shadow of the Silk Road* manifests a constant alternation of temporalities, as the following passage attests:

> It was from Khotan, perhaps, or from the Chinese heartland, that the jealously guarded secrets of sericulture spread. Old legends tell of their betrayal. A spoilt Chinese princess, it is said – betrothed to the King of Khotan – smuggled the mulberry seeds and silkworms over the frontier in her headdresses, and the convent where she established them was still there in Xuanzang's time. More than a century after her, in about AD 552, silkworm eggs reached Constantinople concealed in the staffs of two Nestorian monks, travelling, it seems, from Khotan. And China's age-old monopoly was broken. For more than half a year the sky above the town was opaque muslin, dense with unseen sand, and the sun was only a white coin discarded there. (Thubron 2006: 126).

All this contributes to building a more articulated chronotope of the experience, that is, one that constantly redefines its own space-time frame. On the one hand, the space of the journey is decomposed and comes to encompass a whole continent; on the other, the time of the narrative shifts back and forth, intertwining past and present. These chronotopic variations go hand in hand with the fictionalization of the journey: stories become legends, encounters become phantoms (or shadows, as the title suggests). It is quite telling, for example, that the author inserts throughout the book – in italics – an imaginary dialogue he entertains with an old merchant of the Silk Road:

Why do you travel this way? It is the Sogdian merchant again. Will your book tell how many days' journey between trading towns and what markets are to be found there?

No, my markets are not yours. People create their own countries.

So, it is. When I took to trading copper and indigo, all cities turned to copper and indigo.

[Waits] *Only when you become old, and no longer move, the countries do not change. They sit in your head like artefacts.*

[Irritably] *It may not be like that.*

...Then, looking back, you will see the cities become a long procession leading to nothing. This is beautiful in its way, and was once enough to make you travel. Would you want this forever?

...I want to sleep... (Thubron 2006: 242)

Insofar as Thubron can no longer reflect himself against a single mirroring otherness (which was represented by China in the previous text), he creates the fictional character of the Sogdian merchant with whom to establish an interior dialogue (indeed, a monologue). Within the varied chronotopic articulation of the narrative, the boundary between fact and fiction is questioned, and in such interrogation, it is the author's subjectivity to play a pivotal role. Thubron explained this point well in the interview, claiming that travel writing is "a sort of postmodern collage, of which the sole consistent thread is the personality of the travel writer."[61] What is significant to remark is that the closer Thubron gets to the end of the journey, the more he feels at ease and among people who share with him a similar background (despite the fact that Thubron cannot speak any Arabic, nor is he an expert of Middle-Eastern countries). In this sense, it seems that the traversing of Central Asia, while allowing the author to provide a more kaleidoscopic image of China, distances the Middle Kingdom even more from the author's roots. Here is Thubron's own opinion:

When I came to China to start my journey along the Silk Road, I did feel I knew China better, although I was in a region of China – that of Xian, in the northwest – that is not typically Chinese but is inhabited by Uygur people, who are Muslims, and from that point of view I have to admit that, in a way, I felt it was easier to understand them than the Chinese. Then, as I told you, the closer I got to the Mediterranean, the more I had the impression that I

---

[61] Thubron, interview by Stefano Calzati, May 27, 2013, in person.

knew people better. I knew we shared more similarities, and these people, too, had a more specific perception of the West than the Chinese did.

The recognition of the various paths that compose the Silk Road mirrors the problematic homogeneous perception that the West has often (had) of China and the East. In the making of the experience – that is, in the unmaking of the Silk Road as a single chronotopic dimension – China and Asia's complexities get challenged. And yet, what this provokes, in the end, is the reassertion of the effective cultural distance that keeps the author (and Europe) away from China.

LA TRAVERSÉE DE LA CHINE À LA VITESSE DU PRINTEMPS AND *LE BÉNARÈS-KYÔTO*

The second pair of monomodal travel books discussed are *La traversée de la Chine à la vitesse du printemps* (2003) and *Le Bénarès-Kyôto* (2007) by French author Olivier Germain-Thomas. The first book is a brief recollection of the author's journey through China before reaching Japan (his final destination), and after having already visited India, Thailand, and Vietnam. In fact, what Germain-Thomas recounts in *La traversée* is only one leg of the broader journey from Varanasi to Kyoto which he later narrates in *Le Bénarès-Kyôto*. While Thubron wrote two travelogues that dealt with China over a span of two decades, Germain-Thomas recounts in two different ways – in the short span of four years – the same journey. Hence, it becomes interesting to investigate how the representation of his experience in China has changed when being transposed from one book to the other. Germain-Thomas spoke of this during the interview:

> I have to confess to you that nobody had really noticed that what I wrote in the two books refers to the same journey. As far as China is concerned, I wanted to write a book immediately after the end of the journey, when the memories were still fresh in my mind. So, I wrote *La traversée* very quickly. Then, I devoted myself to the writing of *Le Bénarès-Kyôto* and when it came to writing the chapter on China, I tried, for every episode, to describe it from a different perspective: a lightened perspective.[62]

The aim here is to understand, in terms of the chronotope of the narrative, what such a different perspective consists of and to connect it to a discussion of the book as a medial format. To begin with, it is possible to note that *La traversée* is filled, mainly in the first chapters, with a number of comparisons between India – which the author knows well – and China, a country completely unknown to him. Here is one example:

> I reach the 1,000 caves where I find, carved in the stone, the Greek face of Gautama, which came directly from Gandhara following the Silk Road.

---

[62] Olivier Germain-Thomas, interview by Stefano Calzati, January 22, 2015, Skype.

> Nobody bows. Everyone is attracted by souvenir shops. Have these people lost their sense of holiness, or has this always been a matter of appearance? In Lourdes, there are also plenty of souvenirs. Am I biased by India?[63] (Germain-Thomas 2003: 37-8; author's translation)

This quotation is emblematic of Germain-Thomas's need to represent China through India. As Anthony Pagden (1993) notes, travelers tend inevitably to frame the unknown in terms of the known, according to a "principle of attachment" that helps them to make sense of reality. As a matter of fact, Germain-Thomas confesses at the very beginning of the book that "I do not know China, although I am fairly acquainted with Asia"[64] (13; author's translation). More generally, the travelogue is configured as a personal research on China and, in particular, on its arts and spiritualism:

> While preparing this crossing, I tried, with the help of books and meetings, to approach Chinese thought. I was astonished to realize how much it resonated with the evolution of my quest to find a spiritual path that is not constrained by dogmas.[65] (Germain-Thomas 2003: 13; author's translation)

From this passage, the two most important threads of the book can be extrapolated. On the one hand, the author manifestly acknowledges that, because he did not know anything about China, he collected a lot of information before the departure. This effort finds proof in the book's many quotations from various sources – religious, philosophical, and historical – which, as seen in Chapter 1, strengthen the travelogue's hypertextuality. On the other hand, the passage above shows that the author's journey is largely conceived as an interior quest. The narrative, then, unfolds two complementary chronotopic trajectories: vertical and horizontal; internal (the traveler's personal quest) and external (the crossing of China). The title of the book helps to support this same idea: the journey, indeed, is presented as a movement through China, from south to north, while the time of travel, its duration, is not objectified, but a relative one, namely the spring blossom season. The title, then, configures from the outset a chronotopic frame that is a negotiation between the external world (China) and the internal self-discovery of the author; or better: the author looks at China from an intrinsically subjective temporal point of view. The important aspect to stress is that these two movements – vertical and horizontal – are not given or linear; rather, their development is constantly interrogated. The author's possibilities to understand something more about China, as well as about himself, are

---

[63] "Je me dirige vers la grotte des Mille Bouddhas où je retrouve, sculpté dans la pierre, le visage grec de Gautama venu du Gandhara à travers la Route de la Soie. Personne ne s'incline. On s'affaire devant les vendeurs des souvenirs. Ce peuple a-t-il perdu le sens du sacré ou ne l'a-t-il jamais eu qu'en surface? Les souvenirs aussi pullulent à Lourdes. Suis-je déformée par l'Inde?"

[64] "Je ne connais pas la Chine, alors que je connais assez bien l'Asie."

[65] "Préparant cette traversée, j'ai cherché, avec livres et rencontres, à aborder la pensée chinoise. J'ai été étonné de constater qu'elle était en résonance avec l'état de mon évolution à la recherche d'une voie spirituelle qui ne fut pas embrigadée par des dogmes."

repeatedly challenged. For example, at times, Germain-Thomas admits a certain uneasiness when travelling in the Middle Kingdom, because he feels disoriented:

> Differently from all the similar situations I went through since Varanasi, here, in this place, I feel transparent, but my spirit, unfortunately, is unable to derive from it a glimpse of that reality that the thickness of myself obstructs.[66] (Germain-Thomas 2003: 15; author's translation)

At other times, instead, he manifests a more positive attitude:

> I guess that a part of me (where is pride in this pleasure of the unknown?) is definitely not unhappy to cross China without the possibility of communicating. I enjoy the fall into a state of *wuwei*. To marry the movement of the train and that of the minutes that follow its rhythm.[67] (Germain-Thomas 2003: 78; author's translation)

Eventually, the conclusion of the book offers to the reader a sort of pagan agnosticism. Indeed, the author's interior quest and China's understanding reach a suspended state:

> I feel *at home* within India's foreignness, while here I cannot feel free, as if the ideograms and the hieratic statues of sanctuaries have sealed themselves and erected a barrier.[68] (Germain-Thomas 2003: 86; author's translation)

> I've tried my best to seize certain aspects of Chinese thought; I have found in it something to work on. Evidence: China changed me, but I wouldn't be able to say how.[69] (Germain-Thomas 2003: 122; author's translation)

More broadly, in what appears as a typical postmodern gesture, it is the possibility itself of knowing that is contested by Germain-Thomas. Any form of understanding of oneself and the Other can only be temporary and subjective; travelling and writing, as practices, can only trace potential paths of knowledge, or hint at viable interpretations, but never provide the traveler or the readers with certainties. This was Germain-Thomas's opinion in this respect:

---

[66] "Contrairement à toutes les situations semblables vécues depuis Bénarès là, sur cette place, je me sens d'une transparence dont mon esprit, hélas, n'a pas su profiter pour saisir cette réalité que l'épaisseur de moi obstrue."

[67] "Je divine qu'un part de moi (où est l'orgueil dans ce goût de l'inconnu?) n'est point trop mécontente de traverser la Chine sans pouvoir communiquer. Je m'amuse à me mettre dans un état de *wuwei*. Epouser le mouvement du train et des minutes égrenées à son rythme."

[68] "Je me sens chez moi au sein de l'étrangeté de l'Inde alors qu'ici je ne puis me laisser aller, comme si les idéogrammes et les statues hiératiques des sanctuaires refermées sur eux-mêmes dressaient un barrage."

[69] "J'ai essayé d'attraper le mieux que je pouvais certains aspects de la pensée de la Chine; j'y ai trouvé de quoi avancer. Une évidence: la Chine m'a changé, mais je ne saurais dire en quoi."

I could say that the journey is a mirror that tells me where I am in my life's evolution and also where my heart is. The interesting thing, however, would be to ask: is there anything that the journey has revealed to me about myself that I ignored? Well... I don't know, *non lo so...*

***

Four years later, Germain-Thomas published *Le Bénarès-Kyôto*, in which he narrates the whole journey through Asia. The author pointed out in the interview that, as far as the organization of the journey is concerned, "I simply bought a flight ticket Paris-India and another one from Japan to Paris. Then, I improvised." Overall, then, the journey was spatially and temporally pre-defined, but all that lay in between was left to chance, the only criterion being to always remain on the ground. Even from a cursory reading, it is easy to realize that the chapter dedicated to the Middle Kingdom contains the same episodes recounted in *La traversée*. And yet, the way in which they are narrated is very different. Let's take the two following passages about Suzhou as an example:

> The bike, a small café where to warm up with a soup, a grimace in front of a dish of duck skins, the birth of the night by the Wumen bridge that crosses the circular canal, the desert alleys of the hotel, a dream of the Kingdom of the dead, characterised by several abstracts shapes. On the packed train an old man with a Cistercian smile cuddles for several hours a fifteen months baby who is likely his nephew. He makes jokes, sings a song and repeatedly kisses his hand. In the carriage inspectors, sweepers, and sellers of socks or biscuits succeed one another dressed impeccably.[70] (Germain-Thomas 2003: 91-2; author's translation)

> Leaving Suzhou, I realized that, despite the rain, I was happy to ride my bike along the canals, to see the peonies blossoming, to be welcomed by tufts of bamboos, to follow a ray of light on the water until the stinky mud. The morning train is packed, the seats are uncomfortable, the landscape is flat. Where to get off? At what time? Wuxi, Changzhou, Nanjing (at 13h 42); the train remains empty.[71] (Germain-Thomas 2007: 149; author's translation)

---

[70] "Bicyclette, estaminet où se réchauffer avec une soupe, grimace devant un plat de peaux de canard, naissance de la nuit au-dessus du pont Wumen qui enjambe le canal circulaire, l'hôtel aux couloirs déserts, rêve du Royaume des morts habité d'une multitude de constructions abstraites. Dans le train bondé, pendant plusieurs heures, un homme âgé, avec un souris cistercien, câline un enfant d'une quinzaine de mois qui doit être son petit-fils. Il lui fait de farces, lui chante une chanson et sans cesse prend sa petite main pour l'embrasser. Dans la voiture se succèdent de contrôleurs, des balayeurs et des vendeurs de chaussettes ou de galettes dans des uniformes impeccables."
[71] "Quittant Suzhou, je me souviens que, malgré la pluie, j'ai été heureux de pédaler le long des canaux, de voir des pivoines éclore, d'être accueilli par des touffes de bambous, de suivre dans l'eau un rayon de

The first passage is characterized by a more subjective and possibly poetic representation of the visit to Suzhou; one in which dream and reality intermingle – a bit in the spirit of Thubron's imagined dialogues with the old merchant – and both space and people acquire an almost fairy, magical connotation. In his second travelogue, Germain-Thomas opts for a more factual recounting of the journey in terms of the places visited, the things done and the passing of time. The point to stress here is that such a change is due, at least to an extent, to the fact that the chapter on China is part of a greater travel experience (and narrativization): an experience, indeed, that où no longer solely evoked but is textually included within the book. The author explained this as follows in the interview:

> Overall, I believe it is a matter of the literary organization of what I wanted to say. I usually start with an idea in mind and try to find the best way to organize what I want to say. It is a matter of literary balance.

The balance of which Germain-Thomas talks is reflected, for instance, in the fact that the various comparisons between India and China, which characterized *La traversée*, are reduced to a few in *Le Bénarès-Kyôto*. Insofar as India is effectively described in the book, the author is no longer compelled to anchor his impressions about China to this more familiar country:

> In *La traversée*, which I wrote immediately after the end of the journey, I felt the need to insert some quotations, possibly because I also had more space at my disposal: you see, it is always a matter of balance. In *Le Bénarès-Kyoto*, instead, I tried to look at the time spent in China from a different perspective, as I said before. So, I effaced many quotes because I felt that they had lost their meaning, their literary function.

As the narration of the crossing of China is anticipated and followed by the tale of the other legs of the journey, both the internal quest and the subjective chronotope that framed *La traversée* lose much of their strength. For example, many of the quotations from religious and spiritual texts that enriched the first travelogue are eliminated. In *Le Bénarès-Kyoto*, the journey is presented as a sequential, linear experience. This means that the reconfiguration of the temporal axis triggers also a different representation of space. Firstly, in *Le Bénarès-Kyoto* the recounting of the crossing of China is no longer connected with the arrival of spring; rather it is punctuated by a south-north geographical trajectory. Hence, China is reconceived as the stage of the whole travel that stretches between Vietnam and Japan. Secondly, descriptions of the physical traversing become more prominent due to the erasure of those personal reflections which, in the former book, were mainly related to the interior quest of the author. Overall, then, *Le Bénarès-Kyoto* dispels the subjective/interiorized

---

lumière jusqu'à la boue nauséabonde. Le train matinal est bondé, les banquettes inconfortables, les paysages plats. Où descendre? A quelle heure? Wuxi, Changzhou, Nankin (à 13h 42), le train se vide."

chronotopic frame of *La traversée* in favor of a more factual representation of the experience, kindled, as the example above of the train schedule suggests, by an objectification of the time of travel. This, as the words by Germain-Thomas corroborate, is due at least in part to the re-inscription of the section dedicated to China into a broader narrative (and a thicker book) that clearly defines its point of departure and arrival in terms of both space and time.

IL MONDO OLTRE IL FIUME DEI PESCHI IN FIORE AND *CARTOLINE DA PECHINO*

The third comparison involves two Italian travelogues, written by Sino-Italian author Bamboo Hirst. The first one is *Il mondo oltre il fiume dei peschi in fiore*, it was published in 1989 and it contains several pictures; the second one is *Cartoline da Pechino*, it was published in 1998 and it is only composed of written text. Through this comparison the chapter starts addressing the possibility and consequences of extending the notion of chronotope to visual elements such as photographs. In order to do that, a brief theoretical excursus, which departs from Roland Barthes's (1981) *Camera Lucida* and moves toward Kress and van Leeuwen's (1996) *Reading Images*, is demanded.

***

In his famous *Camera Lucida*, Barthes argues that the "unicity" of photography lies in the fact that the referent (what is represented) comes to adhere to the reference (the form of photography). In other words, Barthes confers upon the technological apparatus of photography such a power (indeed, a power of transparency), whose force – its "punctum of intensity" (1981: 90) – is to eternally testify "that-has-been" (1981: 77). The main problem with such an argument is that Barthes seems to imply the uncontested presence of a referent to which photography smoothly applies: a referent that is there to be photographed and immortalized. However, as Jean Baudrillard (1994: 2), among others, has thoughtfully noted, photography can only give back a modeling of the grasped instant, not solely because there is no ur-referent to which photography may refer, but precisely because photography is a medium and, as such, cannot return but a mediated representation of what it frames. It is in this spirit that Jacques Rancière (2009: 15) affirms that "in order to preserve for photography the purity of an affect, Barthes erases the very genealogy of the *that was*." By hypostatizing the transparency of photography, Barthes turns the instant into an absolute, but in so doing, he overlooks that "that-has-been" always conceals a history of its own. Put differently, each photograph bears in itself the chronotopic conditions that "created" the referent for the camera and for the act of photographing. Barthes, then, is right when he states that each photograph has an "adventure" (1981: 19), noting, with regard to the picture of a schoolboy, that "it is possible that Ernest is still alive today (but where? How? What a novel!)" (1980: 84). Indeed, what a novel!

Unfortunately, however, Barthes does not develop this argument any further, as if "scared" by the depth and breadth that may open beyond the punctum.[72]

In *The Work of Mourning* (2001: 57), Jacques Derrida develops Barthes's argument, eventually acknowledging the fact that, because photography has a "*dynamis*," its punctum is "drawn into metonymy." Put differently, what Derrida suggests is that Barthes's punctum – which represents the unicity of each photograph – always stands for something else: it is a window opened onto a time-space that unfolds beyond itself. Derrida also argues that "remaining as attentive as possible to all the differences, one must be able to speak of a punctum in all signs, any discourse, whether literary or not" (2001: 53). Despite such a claim, it is remarkable that Derrida subsequently considers these differences between words and images to be incommensurable. Indeed, he claims that photography as a technological apparatus attests to "the failure, or at any rate the limit, of all that which, in language, literature and other arts seemed to permit grandiose theories on the general suspension of the Referent" (2001: 53). So, in photography, the referent cannot – out of necessity – be suspended but always shown and manifested. As seen, however, what photography performs is the illusion of presenting us with the referent. So, as soon as one acknowledges its deceptive effect and stresses, by contrast, its work of mediation between the eye and the world, then also the incommensurability of photography and literature tends to fade away. The differences, if any, lie rather in the (different) logics that literature and photography follow in order to "create" their own referents. Literature – here, semiotics can help to elucidate the point – relies on a syntagmatic logic, that is, on a progressive accumulation of words. In fact, it is this accumulation that makes the referent appear as constantly deferred (i.e., "suspended" according to Derrida). As Maurice Blanchot (1983: 9) magnificently contends, "the literary experience is an ordeal in which what we are able to do (for example, see) becomes our powerlessness; becomes, for instance, that terribly strange form of blindness which is the phantom, or the image, of the clear gaze – an incapacity to stop seeing what is not there to be seen." So, literature creates a referent that is not there; or, rather, one that is metonymically there but constantly postponed. Words do have a visual potential (i.e., they can be read paradigmatically, such as Chinese characters or futurist poetry), but their salience has often been standardized by the publishing apparatus, so that the referent can only be imagined (i.e., inferred through the endless accumulation of words) via the meaning of words. On the other hand, images work paradigmatically, in the sense that they display their signs spatially; they (superficially and apparently) spread the referent before our eyes. However, this does not mean that the referent is *already* there; rather, as Derrida (2001: 53) himself notes, "by the time – at the instant – that the punctum rends space, the reference and death are in it together." In other words, the (paradigmatic) visual spatialization of the referent sanctions its very disappearance. It is for this reason that it becomes crucial to recognize the chronotopicity of photography, as photography discloses the value of

---

[72] To be sure, at stake it is not much the writing of Ernest's novel, but the recognition of the punctum's depth, that is, the multiple possible novels that the picture can entice (see further below in the chapter).

"that-has-been" only in relation to its chronotopic frame (of both the technological apparatus and the represented world). On this same line, Henri van Lier (2007: 18) warns that "the photograph is made up of indices. Therefore, its unity of construction and reading is not the decision of the *trait*, which is characteristic of signs [i.e. painting], but of the *littoral*." What van Lier contends is that, similarly to written texts, photographs are also a "lazy machine" (Eco 1979: 24) that necessitates not only an observer but also an interpreter, in order to be decoded. Photographs should not only be looked at but also "scrutinized" (i.e., read syntagmatically), as Barthes (1981: 105) himself suggests. This latter idea is intended to be a visual close reading aimed at revealing the chronotope of the instant: a chronotope that relates to both what is represented and its mode of representation. "Photography," Rancière (2009: 11) argues, "exploits a double poetics: it refers to the legible testimony of a history written on faces and objects, and pure blocs of visibility, impervious to any narrativization." It is, then, the paradigmatic organization of the referent in photography that pushes its chronotope out of focus. In this respect, Gunther Kress and Theo van Leeuwen's (1996) *Grammar* for the analysis of multimodal texts is strategic here for investigating the syntagmaticity of photography. Specifically, it is the discussion on visual modality, intended as the representation of "people, places, and things as though they are real, as though they actually exist in this way, or as though they do not – as though they are imaginings, fantasies, caricatures, etc." (156), that will be followed as a guiding paradigm.

***

Bamboo Hirst was born to a Chinese woman and an Italian diplomat in Shanghai and lived in China until the age of 13, when she was obliged to leave the country due to political insecurity. She then moved to Italy, where she still lives and works. In 1988, after many years of absence from her native country, Hirst decided to take a journey around China: "Now that I am about to land [in China]," she notes in the preface to the first book, "many good and bad memories come back to my mind."[73] From the outset, then, the travelogue is configured as a journey *à rebours* on the track of the author's own memories. In fact, the presence throughout the text of a discourse of nostalgia, defined by Debbie Lisle (2006: 214) as the failing quest for (lost) authenticity, signals the difficulty for the author to recompose the fracture between the old China of her youth and the present China of her journey. The following passage, which recounts Hirst's hopeless search for the old Saint Joseph Convent in which she grew up, is emblematic:

> "This was your courtyard; there in the middle stood the Virgin Mary with Bernadette," says Father Jong. Despite these explanations, I cannot orient myself; everything seems displaced. I cannot locate with precision where

---

[73] "Ora che mancano solo pochi minuti al nostro appuntamento mi ritornano in mente, incalzanti, ricordi belli e brutti."

classrooms or the chapel were. I simply take some photos, hoping these and others will help me rebuild the puzzle of my memories.[74] (Hirst 1989: 137; author's translation)

This extract is also worthwhile in another respect: Hirst mentions that she took pictures of the places visited, supposedly to trigger her memories. As a matter of fact, several pictures enrich the whole book; however, these are not the ones actually taken by Hirst but rather by the well-known Italian photojournalist Giorgio Lotti, whose name also appears on the book cover. Interestingly, Hirst never refers to Lotti's presence during the journey or him working alongside her, so that readers do not know if Hirst and Lotti travelled together. In the interview, Lotti clarified the point, revealing that the photographs were taken on different occasions over a period of 16 years: "As a reporter for *Epoca* and *Panorama* [two popular Italian magazines] I went to China 12 times between 1974 and 1990."[75] This means that, although these photographs are roughly contemporary to the journey accomplished by Hirst, they nonetheless refer to another China; they recount another story and presuppose another chronotope. In this respect, it is possible to suggest how it is precisely the chronotopic discrepancy between Lotti's photographs and Hirst's journey that helps, among other visual choices (discussed below), to close the gap between the old China remembered by Hirst and the present China in which she travels. Indeed, as Lotti noted, "even if we had worked together, this would not have made any difference because Bamboo was writing about her journey to China, binding this experience to the memories of her childhood. My photos are more recent than the time of her childhood and older than the time of her journey. To be sure, I have been working in China at a time when progress had not transfigured cities yet, and this helps find a consonance with Bamboo's journey; however, the China I photographed during the 1980s is different from that of Bamboo's childhood." Such a chronotopic discrepancy is even more crucial in relation to China, which, as Lotti remarks, underwent radical socio-political and urban changes during the last two decades of the 20th century. Indeed, while Hirst recounts a journey that took place after the reopening of Chinese borders to visitors, Lotti's photographs relate to a China that was still inherently isolated from the rest of the world. From this point of view, if one considers the conditions that presupposed Lotti's activity, all his photographs acquire an even deeper documentary relevance insofar as the historical time that frames them was affected by an enforced limitation to access and move around China. Thus, it can be suggested that besides (and even beyond) Barthes's "that-has-been," these photographs testify above all to the very *possibility* for the photographer to be *there*.

Lotti also revealed that he let Hirst decide which photographs to insert in the book: "Although I am the author of all the photos, the decision about which ones to

---

[74] "'Questo era il vostro cortile, nel mezzo c'era la Madonna con Bernadette', dice padre Jiang. Nonostante queste spiegazioni non riesco comunque a orientarmi bene; adesso tutto mi sembra spostato, non riesco a localizzare con precisione le aule, la cappella. Mi rassegno allora a prendere delle foto, sperando che forse mi aiuteranno in seguito a ricostruire insieme alle altre il puzzle dei miei ricordi."

[75] Giorgio Lotti, interview by Stefano Calzati, February 17, 2014, Skype.

include could not be mine because I did not know what Bamboo wanted to write. As a consequence, I preferred to leave to her the choice of the photos. What I did was simply to make available to her a certain number of pictures. On that occasion, choosing good photos was not the only criterion; they also had to be appropriate." The notion of "aptness" is central here for a number of reasons. First of all, it hints at the idea that, although the book takes *de facto* the form of a collaboration between Lotti and Hirst, the photographs are, to a certain degree, functional to the writing. As a consequence, Hirst is considered as the sole person who could (try to) give a visual representation to both her travel experience and her memories. This, however, holds true only based on a theoretical plan. Indeed, when asked to provide some elucidations on the rationale that guided the selection of the photographs, Hirst noted: "It wasn't actually me who selected the pictures but the publisher and, to be frank, I was quite angry when I discovered that many scenes of which I write were not represented visually."[76] From such a declaration, the extent to which the photographs only indirectly refer to what Hirst wrote emerges more clearly (as well as the fact that a book is always the result of a cooperation between author and publisher).

From here, two lines of inquiry open. The first one interrogates the potential level of distortion, if not falsification, that photographs bear with respect to the text, in particular when their inclusion transcends the will of the author. The second one, which is deeply intertwined with the former, investigates how photographs and text relate and negotiate the chronotopic discrepancy discussed above. With regard to the first line of inquiry, it is useful to remember that contemporary travel writing is a genre intrinsically bound to both the necessity to be accurate toward actuality and the pretention to be trusted. Far from depending on universal parameters, the texts' reliability is determined by cultural values which can change over time and in space. In his *A Social History of Truth* (1994) Steven Shapin contends that each culture builds its own concepts of accuracy, credibility and reliability based on "the expectation that knowledge will be evaluated according to its appropriate place in practical, cultural and social action" (xxix). Here, it is argued that the discussion about travel writing's reliability requires being not only socio-historically contextualized but also connected to the use that the authors make of the medium. As seen above, pictures convey the illusion of an intrinsic veridicity: the irreplaceable witnessing of that-has-been. When it comes to travel writing, while it is true that pictures can be regarded as documentary proof of the accomplishment of the journey – here Bettinelli's case discussed in Chapter 1 is exemplary – they can also represent, in Jan Baetens' words (2005: 237), "a real menace to the ontological specificity of fiction," that is, to the syntagmatic construction of the referent performed through written language. In this sense, photographs seem less subjected to the control of the author, insofar as "in a single blow, that which is presented to us is so immediate, so non-mediated, that within the shock itself there is a *loss of mastery* [emphasis added]" (van Lier 2007: 29). This line of reasoning, however, holds true only if one considers the visual and the verbal as two incommensurable systems. By contrast, once one

---

[76] Bamboo Hirst, interview by Stefano Calzati, April 28, 2014, in person.

acknowledges the permeability of the paradigmatic and syntagmatic logics in the construction of the referent, thus advancing a more profound reading of visual elements (and language), then what photographs and words do is simply disclose different horizons of reliability. These horizons can diverge, but also be consonant, so that words and photographs cooperate in filling their respective gaps and voids (what Eco [1979] calls "white spaces").

So, the questions in relation to *Il mondo oltre il fiume del peschi in fiore* become: how do photographs and text relate? How do they negotiate the chronotopic discrepancy that affects them? First of all, it is notable that the pictures are quite numerous (49 out of 248 pages) and are interspersed throughout the whole book. In this sense, illustrations and words entertain a balanced relationship within the book in that neither of the two modes dominates the other. Moreover, the very decision to alternate words and pictures creates a strong relation between them and blurs any neat authorial distinction, *as if* the work were accomplished organically from the outset. In particular, this (deceptive) effect of (chronotopic) concordance is pursued in three ways. Firstly, captions are quotations taken from the text, so that what is described with words by Hirst seems simultaneously immortalized in pictures by Lotti. Secondly, Hirst rarely thematizes the time of travel. As Werner Wolf (2005: 433) reminds us, the visual options available to an image for rendering the passing of time are rather limited: "the reasons for the narrative 'deficiencies' of single pictures derive from the limitations of the pictorial medium as a whole. For instance, principles of causality and teleology can be only inferred." Hirst's vague notations on her movements around the country, in favor of a static, pictorial representation of the journey, help the words and pictures to find deeper assonance. For example, each chapter is dedicated to a city – Beijing, Suzhou, Qufu, Shanghai, etc. – while the narrative transitions from one chapter to the other – that is, the author's progression from one place to the other – are rather elliptical, and it is only at the very end that Hirst informs us that the journey lasted six weeks. One could say that the episodes recounted constitute still frames connected by the binding of the pages and onto which it is primarily the book (as a medial format) to impress an overarching coherence. Thirdly, the chronotopic concordance between words and images has to do with both what is represented in pictures and their mode of representation. To start with, all the pictures are in black and white. The effects that this choice has on what is portrayed are worth discussing. Kress and van Leeuwen (1996: 253) contend that "black and white" kindles a neutralization of affection, indicating "'what might be' rather than reality" (Kress and van Leeuwen: 159). While their analysis is certainly defendable, another – yet complementary – interpretation is possible. The black and white works here as a blurring of the chronotopic coordinates of what is represented, so that scenes are "epicized," so to speak: they are secured within a visual desaturation, which annihilates any temporal (and historical) precise anchorage. The notion of "epicization" is derived from Bakhtin ([1937] 1981). In his work, Bakhtin argues that the epic is a genre in which, differently from the novel, the chronotopic coordinates of narrative are fixed. Hence, the chronotopic world of the epic is immutable and its characters, who bear a highly symbolic meaning, are disjoined from any concrete evolution; they can only fulfill a destiny which is transcendent and beyond their will. On the contrary, in the novel the characters "take flesh," they are in control of their lives and through their actions they can evolve. This makes the chronotopic world they live in very specific and concrete.[77] From these premises, in the present context the term "epicization" refers to the rarefaction and freezing of the chronotopic coordinates internal to the "represented world" (be it verbally or visually represented). Put differently, scenes are "epicized" when they lack precise space-time coordinates, thus turning the scenes into bi-dimensional, static frames (Calzati 2013b). In Lotti's pictures, the recourse to the black and white contributes to the sense of space-time suspension that is typical of the epic. This acquires an even stronger relevance when thinking that, for Lotti, "it is through colours that we can recreate movements and evolution in photography." In order to better exemplify this point, it is fruitful to look at two examples. The first one is the following picture (Figure 29) found on pages 120-1 of Hirst's book:

Figure 29: A peasant

A standing young woman is immortalized while seeding a ploughed field by hand. She wears humble clothes. The figure of the woman and the earth under her feet are in focus, although it is not possible to identify her physiognomic traits due to her bent position. The rest of the field, both in the foreground and in the background (which takes up the majority of the photo's space), is out of focus. As Kress and van Leeuwen (1996: 161) affirm, "by being 'decontextualized', shown in a void, represented participants become generic, a 'typical' example'." In this sense, the

---

[77] On this issue, refer also to Georg Lukács's *The Theory of the Novel* (1971).

impossibility of recognizing the woman's traits and blurred surroundings confers upon the whole picture a highly symbolic (i.e., epic) connotation. The woman comes metonymically to stand for all the Chinese who are and have been peasants. However, because she is portrayed alone, the picture could also bear a counter-message, one that relates to China's recent history. Namely, the photograph could point to the progressive abandonment of the countryside, which happened in particular after 1978, when Prime Minister Deng Xiaoping opened China to "the socialist way to capitalism" (which also led to those deep architectonic changes in the cities mentioned by Lotti). Thirdly, if one relates the photograph to the text next to it, a further interpretation can be proposed. In the book, the picture is juxtaposed with Hirst's encounter with a woman called Blu Cielo ("Blue Sky"), who recounts to the traveler her hard times in the countryside during the Cultural Revolution when many people were "re-educated" through work in the countryside. The photo, then, comes to refer to a much more precise and traumatic event: the migration to the countryside that a whole generation of Chinese people was forced to experience in the 1960s. The point to stress is that, independently from the interpretation one decides to favor, all of them are *possible*, insofar as they are presupposed by the chronotopic horizon embedded either in what is represented, in its (epic) mode of representation, or in the relation between text and image.

A second example is useful to show how also other visual and compositional strategies beyond the black and white can be read chronotopically. The selected picture (Figure 30) is found on page 70:

Figure 30: The mosque in Xian

This picture is taken from an angled perspective and shows the close-up of an elderly man who is seated by the doorstep of an old mosque. In the foreground are four pairs of shoes, while in the back, past the figure of the man, is a second entrance to the mosque, in front of which nobody stands. The caption tells readers that the mosque is the one in Xian, thus providing a precise spatial settling. Concerning visual perspective, Kress and van Leeuwen (1996: 135) suggest that when a scene is framed from an oblique angle, it usually conveys a lack of participation of the photographer to the scene. In the present case, although it could be said that the perspective works as a form of respectful distance from the scene, another interpretation of its effect is advanced. Again, the difficulty with identifying the traits of the old man confers upon him a symbolic connotation: he stands not only for all Chinese Muslims but also for the millenarian history of Islam in China. This is, indeed, supported by the caption, which states: "the Great Mosque was built 1200 years ago," (Hirst 1989: 71). At this point, depending on whether one dwells upon what is represented *per se* or upon China's history, the photograph can convey two diverging messages. On the one hand, by focusing on the man's age, one could think that Islam, in China, is now followed by old people only and, at any rate, by a restricted number, because in the foreground only four pairs of shoes can be seen. On the other hand, if one contextualizes this image historically – that is, when it was taken: mid-1970s – it could also come to testify a fresh wave of Islam, at least in comparison to the years of the Cultural Revolution, during which all forms of religious belief were persecuted and many places of worship were destroyed. It is according to this latter interpretation that the use of the perspective acquires a specific chronotopic function. The photo's oblique angle drags the viewer's gaze from the old man down to the pairs of shoes in the foreground. Certainly, there are "only" four pairs of shoes, but more striking than the number is the absence that looms over them – the absence of the people who wear them. The presence of these shoes brings with itself the phantasmagorical absence of their owners, whose stories, it is argued, come to stand for the history of Islam in China. In fact, the oblique angle works as a *mise en abyme* of Islam's vicissitudes in the country: in the background, the absence of believers in front of the second door stands for China's forceful secularism during the Cultural Revolution; the old man in full shot witnesses today's rebirth of religious worshipping; while the shoes in the foreground attest to the strengthening of this renewal, leading to believe, from the point in time of the interpretant, that Islam has continued to grow. The caption corroborates this interpretation by stating that "The Great Mosque is currently under renovation but functions are being celebrated. An old Muslim tells us that devotees are a few hundred and during the Cultural Revolution the mosque was reconverted by the Red Guards into a farm."[78] More generally, what this second example reasserts is that each photograph, far from being a transparent impression of the instant, always embeds a chronotope that equally pertains to the subject represented and to its mode of representation. Photography, then, cannot help but mediate between the eye and the world, thus opening up a hermeneutical space that can be investigated following diverse chronotopic interpretations.

***

Now the analysis moves on to the second travelogue by Hirst. *Cartoline da Pechino* (1998) was published a decade later than *Il mondo oltre il fiume del peschi in fiore*

---

[78] "La Grande Moschea è attualmente in fase di restauro, ma può già accogliere i suoi fedeli. Un vecchio di fede musulmana ci racconta che i fedeli attualmente sono alcune centinaia e durante la Rivoluzione Culturale la moschea fu impiegata dalle Guardie Rosse come una fattoria."

and released by publisher Feltrinelli instead of Mondadori. According to these data, one might expect to read a different story, a different journey; yet it is possible to attest that the great majority of the episodes recounted in the two books are the same, though Hirst claimed to have undertaken a second journey to China.[79] So, where do the differences between the two travelogues lie? First of all, *Cartoline da Pechino* breaks with the representation of the journey as a quest to retrieve the author's childhood. The most evident example, in this respect, is that no mention of the old Convent Saint-Joseph Convent is provided. The discourse of nostalgia disappears and references to old China work as a vague historical background whose investigation does not constitute the personal stimulus for travelling.

Secondly, passing on the visual mode, *Cartoline da Pechino* does not present any photographs. When compared with the previous book, this exclusion has consequences for both the chronotope of the narrated experience and the structure of the whole book. In particular, the tendency in the previous book to avoid references to the passing of time and to present the journey as a collection of frames is here radicalized. Chapters are not only shorter, but are also titled after a theme, rather than a specific city: "The House of Tea," "The Trees' Doctor," "The Art of Living," "Around the Temple," etc. In this way, the space-time frame of the journey is further dissolved and readers are confronted with an even more abstracted representation of Hirst's experience: a representation that is chiefly a sequence of apercus – indeed, "postcards," as the title suggests – rather than the recounting of a "proper" travel. This interpretation is also supported by Hirst, who claimed in the interview that she wanted "to describe scenes rather than the unfolding of a journey." The narrative, then, takes on much of the epicization of the pictures: the overall experience is parceled into small episodes which are disconnected not only among them in space, but also from any precise temporal frame, either personal (Hirst's memories) or collective. More than in *Il mondo oltre il fiume del peschi in fiore*, it is the book, as a medial format, to provide the structuring coherence of the whole work, whose constitutive episodes would remain, otherwise, disconnected. The point is that, by keeping in mind the previous book, one cannot help but feel (i.e., see) the absence of Lotti's contribution among the pages that comprise *Cartoline da Pechino*. The pictures, indeed, not only offered the reader the chance to undertake a visual journey around China (and among the rubbles of Hirst's memories), but they linked the stories recounted between them and they filled the gaps of the narrative, by providing a visualization of the "represented world" that often worked as an allegory.

At this point, one could also wonder about the extent to which *Cartoline da Pechino* does constitute a travelogue. The answer is in the affirmative for two reasons. First of all, although the unfolding of the travel is rather ethereal, the reader can infer its development in various occurrences. In the following passage, for instance, Hirst condenses into a few lines her move from Suzhou to Shanghai:

---

[79] Hirst, interview.

The first houses of Suzhou appear close to the railway; soon the train slows down and passengers begin to gather in the hallways, pressing up against the doors. I know that Blue Sky will stay in the "Venice of China" only for a few days. I tell her that I would like to meet her again in Shanghai when she gets back. We organise our meeting at Cathay Hotel, at tea-time, the following week.

This time, at Cathay, our roles seem reversed...[80] (Hirst 1998: 36; author's translation)

The second reason comes from Hirst herself. When asked how she would define these books, she straightforwardly responded: "no doubt these are travelogues – they derive from two trips I took in China; the only difference is the way in which I have shaped the material at my disposal." To deny such generic affiliation, then, would be misleading. However, it remains controversial why the recounting of two different journeys coalesced into the same narrative and on this point Hirst did not provide further comments. From the point of view of the present work, however, what is striking is the impact that the conception of the book, as either a monomodal or multimodal work, can have on the chronotopic frame of the "represented world."

***

The first part of this chapter discussed how the chronotopes of travelogues change according to what is narratively included into the books (Germain-Thomas), the passing of time and the spatial extension of the journey (Thubron), and the decision of including (or not) pictures (Hirst). In all three cases, it was the physicality of the book that eventually dictated the organization of the narrative and constituted its outer boundary. This means that also the book, as a medial format, embeds a specific chronotope, and this is projected over the narrative, usually modeled as a linear, teleological work "with a beginning and an end" (Bakhtin: 255). Now the analysis moves toward travel blogs to investigate what the chronotope of this medial format is and how it shapes the (chronotope of the) travel narrative. However, as a form of transition between the two realms, attention is directed first to the peculiar case of *Carnet di viaggio: Cina* (2005) by Italian traveler and artist Stefano Faravelli.

As the title of the book suggests, *Carnet di viaggio: Cina* presents readers with a typical carnet de voyage: the format is that of a book, but printed on its pages are a number of watercolors, that have been transposed – reprinted – from the author's sketch book. Therefore, *Carnet di viaggio: Cina* is already the outcome of a remediation process. The paintings inserted in it are the result of a creative process in which the hand of the artist not only copied the scene but also recreated it, through an

---

[80] "Le prime case di Suzhou sfilano ai lati della ferrovia; ben presto il treno rallenta e i passeggeri cominciano a raccogliersi nei corridoi, ad ammassarsi attorno agli sportelli. So che Blu Cielo si fermerà solo pochi giorni nella 'Venezia della Cina' Le dico che mi farebbe piacere incontrarla di nuovo al suo rientro a Shanghai. Ci diamo appuntamento al Cathay Hotel per il tè, la domenica successiva. Questa volta al Cathay i ruoli mi sembrano invertiti."

artistic effort that is different from the mechanical system of reproduction at the base of photography. The extent to which these two realms are incommensurable is explained well by van Lier (2007: 18), who notes that "it is the minimal unit of the works they give birth to that is different: paintings are constituted by traits susceptible of being interpreted as signs, while photography is made of indices, that is, mere signifiers." In a similar vein, Sigfried Kracauer ([1927] 1993) expresses his point of view on the difference between photography and painting in these terms: "In the artwork the meaning of the object takes on spatial appearance, whereas in photography the spatial appearance of an object is its meaning." What he means is that, while the technological apparatus of photography makes everything that appears in a photograph significant, precisely for the very fact of being there regardless of the photographer's intervention, in painting it is the painter who decides which details to include (and exclude) in the artwork, independently from their being effectively real or present. In this sense, Faravelli's work is certainly closer to the artistic book than the literary travel book. However, his pictorial illustrations are also accompanied by handwritten words that either describe the images or recount episodes of the journey not represented visually (Figure 31).

Figure 31: A watercolor taken from Faravelli's carnet

Because of these features, the carnet offers the chance not only to explore the chronotope of an artistic travel book, but also to discuss the distinction between monomodal and multimodal books. In the previous chapter, it was shown that the distinction between blogs on platform and individual ones is more contested than one could expect from a cursory browsing of the Web, due to the interconnectedness of webpages. The same criticality also concerns monomodal and multimodal books.

Indeed, as soon as we get closer to the text, we are confronted with the need to characterize more neatly where the border between one mode and the other is traced. Bateman (2008: 104) argues, for instance, that "just as accounts of language, its graphological form, and punctuation can consider visual elements to function paralinguistically, we can also consider certain textual elements and formatting options to be paravisual." Pushing this reasoning further, it could be said that any written text is always, at the same time, verbal *and* visual, as writing is in itself a visually based act (see Mitchell 1994). The point is that, nowadays, the process of production for books has been highly standardized and the salience of paravisual elements has been brought, so to speak, to the margins of signification. This means that in printed books the visual appearance of letters and words does not carry any (extra)meaning. Yet, when one faces a book such as Faravelli's, the threshold separating verbal and visual modes is blurred. The figure above shows how in Faravelli's work the writing, which bears the subjective mark of the author's calligraphy, is at the same time an intelligibly discernible form of written language *and* a pictorial gesture.[81] Approaching (again) the writing to its graphological form, in which the composition of the signifier can be subjected to interpretation, Faravelli's work represents a reminder of the fact that the line between monomodality and multimodality has not always been that clear. This, as will be discussed shortly, also has consequences for the chronotopic frame built by the whole book and by the painting on each page.

To begin with, Faravelli's work is not a unicum, but, as he pointed out, "it follows the tradition of the 'carnet' in which, on the one hand, words and images intertwine, overlap, blur; while, on the other hand, there is, in each plate, a co-presence of objects and personal experiences."[82] Hence, here too there is the canonization of a series of rhetorical features and practices that, in a way, make of the carnet a subgenre in itself. The pages have lost their typographic standardization; yet, they cannot be fully considered as paintings either, insofar as the writing (and the reader's effort to decipher it) plays a major role in them. In a way, the carnet mimics Chinese books, because Faravelli's handwritten words have a meaning not only as signifieds, but also as signifiers. At the same time, because in each plate the author mixes calligraphy and drawings, the pages' meaning can no longer be derived from a paradigmatic reading and a collation between words and images. Rather it requires a more organic (syntagmatic) approach. The merging of these two modes produces what could be called a "synesthetic work," in which the pleasures of the visual contemplation and the reading can never be fully separated. Calligraphy regains its aura of uniqueness, and the watercolors find in the words that accompany them not only anchorage but also, more radically, fuel for their internal narrativity (thus bypassing the images' congenital limitedness in rendering the passing of time, as discussed above). From these premises, it is already possible to foresee different levels of reading of Faravelli's plates: at the macro level, there is the linear reading dictated by the succession of the book's pages. At the level of single pages, each

---

[81] It is in this respect that the book could be categorized more than multimodal as transmodal.
[82] Stefano Faravelli, interview by Stefano Calzati, April 15, 2014, in person.

plate "tells" a story that is quite autonomous from those that precede and follow it. It is as if readers were faced with an endogenous and an exogenous narrative – one that pertains to the medial format as a whole and one that pertains to the content of the single plate – and each one of them has its own chronotopic coordinates.

Remaining on the level of the single page, the reader/viewer is confronted with a "thickness of meaning" that is due to the mode of representation – watercolors – as well as to what is represented. First of all, Faravelli overtly acknowledged that his decision to paint watercolors was due to the fact that "I favour aestheticism over historicism and from here the choice of watercolour derives, a technique that tends to blur boundaries, so that the eye has no anchor bolts." Faravelli escapes from visual realism (which characterizes the greatest majority of travel photographs) and, in so doing, he obliges the reader to pause over each plate, to delve into it, and to traverse the variety of symbols and signs that are presented. At the same time, the author made clear that such technique disjoins the scenes from precise space-time coordinates with the overt intention "to frame the plates in a mythical space-time dimension." In other words, watercolors contribute to "epicize" the represented world, insofar as its chronotopic axes become ephemeral (it is notable, for instance, that borders are always faded). This effect is further strengthened by the lack of (verbal) notations regarding the time of travel and by the difficulty to retrace the whole itinerary that Faravelli followed in China. In fact, it is only the chapters' subdivision of the book that gives a general sense of the main places visited: "Beijing," "Urumqi," "Chengdu," "Yunnan," "Hong Kong." Even the map that opens the book (Figure 32) is a cartographic stylization of China that only conveys a general sense of the itineraries (emblematic is the use of the plural in the heading: "My Journeys in China"), without however providing a detailed temporal articulation of its stages:

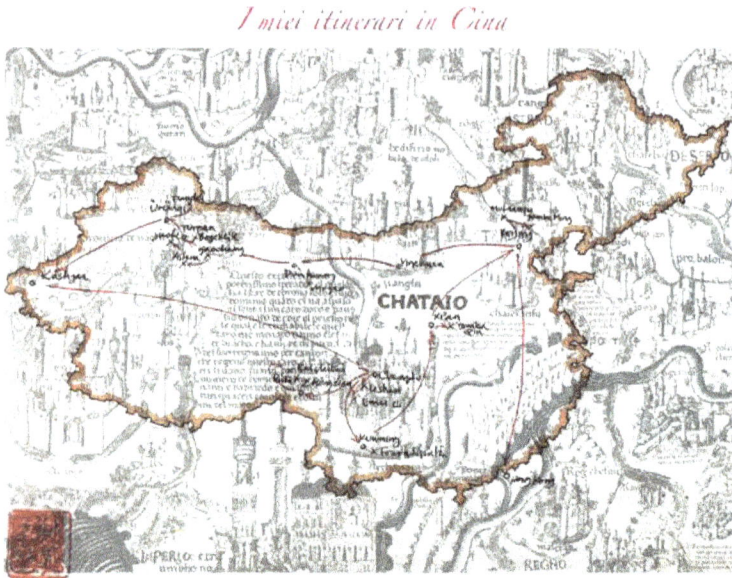

Figure 32: The opening map in Faravelli's carnet

In line with Faravelli's passion for medieval *mappae mundi*, China is not a space but it returns to be a place; symbolism dominates over (geographic) objectivism. Hence, all along the carnet readers are presented with self-standing scenes (i.e., disconnected amongst themselves) that are crammed with symbols – indeed "almost archetypes."[83] The problem, as the author himself acknowledged in the interview, is that by saturating the carnet with symbols – which are more easily recognizable by the readers but tend to provide a generalized image of China (e.g., the Great Wall, the Gobi Desert, and Hong Kong's skyline) – he risked reproducing a stereotyped vision of the country. It is in this respect that Faravelli specified that his plates, although painted while travelling, are nonetheless reworked during the journey and after its conclusion, by drawing upon a series of objects and other texts that go well beyond the travel experience: "it is in the assemblage, that is, in the gaze that I project onto the work as a whole, that lies, I believe, originality." In fact, it is such assemblage that the reader is required to disentangle. Often, visual elements are distributed randomly on the page: they follow convoluted, non-linear paths and the calligraphic writing that blends with them functions only partially as a guide – a reading principle – for their comprehension. So, not only is the calligraphy rather hard to decipher, but the whole page demands to be dwelled upon, investigated, explored. The reader is left to wander with the eyes and the mind around each page, performing a multi-trajectory, syntagmatic reading that builds connections among elements that are sometimes

---

[83] Faravelli, interview.

distant in space and time (i.e., the frame of the single page, the whole book, the time of the reading, and the internal time of the narrative). Without doing this, the reader would be "simply" staring at a painting, without understanding its internal story.

In order to provide an example, the analysis now dwells on the plate represented above (Figure 31). The painting was done in Baishitai, near the city of Zhongdian in the province of Yunnan (south-west of China). All these pieces of information have to be retrieved by going back in the book to the page that introduces the section dedicated to Yunnan. The plate in itself, indeed, does not contain geographic coordinates, so that the painting under examination is suspended in a sort of spatial void. The written text that contours the main central image helps to interpret what is depicted: "Baishitai means 'source of white water' and the source is really there! A magic corral, like the one of medieval fairy-tales, protects it. Trees are decorated with ashy scarfs and red ribbons that fluctuate in the wind" (Faravelli: 67, author's translation). The central image, in fact, represents a water source. Although the painting is rather detailed, its purposely unfinished contours, which intermingle and overlap with the writing, reinforce the sense of spatial and temporal suspension of the scene, enticing the connection with the remote Middle Ages mentioned in the writing. This sense of chronotopic eradication is also stressed by the fact that all the other details – such as the face of the man on the left-top corner – are depicted over a white background, which, as Kress and van Leeuwen (1996: 166) remark, is symptomatic of a minimal degree of contextualization. The most interesting and paradoxical thing, however, occurs when one realizes that certain details within the page remain, so to speak, unexplained. Their visual presence certainly fulfills a creative function, but not one of which readers can trivially understand the meaning. Faravelli explained this in the interview: "Sometimes, I also like to let the people I encountered along the journey impress their own mark upon the text, be it in the form of a signature, a seal, a drawing or a few words." This testimony projects a new light onto Faravelli's work. Beyond the fact that his work questions, in each page, the border between verbal and visual realms, through the interview it becomes clearer that his carnets also carry additional layers of meaning as material artifacts: "There is, in each plate, a co-presence of objects and personal experiences; in other words, the [watercolor] technique mixes together with some of the objects I have found during this and other journeys." This means that the creative assemblage does not exclusively pertain to each plate or journey, but it also involves the materiality of the carnet as a whole and extends toward Faravelli's many travels. The point is that such process cannot be easily sensed by reading/enjoying the carnets, but requires the ultimate intervention of the artist's voice. In the plate represented above, for instance, one can see that the bottom-right corner is occupied by a square within which some symbols are depicted. The writing surrounding the square explains that this is a poem donated to the author by an old shaman whom the author met (depicted in the top-left corner). And yet the writing on the page does not explain how to decode the symbols of the poem. Indeed, it was only when speaking with Faravelli that its meaning was fully explicated: it is a blessing to the author himself and his family (the stylized man on the left projects his power on the two figures on the right), as well as an auspice for wealth (the fish) and professional satisfaction (the symbols that surround the single figure at the center).

Ultimately, it appears that Faravelli is not afraid to reach the point in which the reading of his carnets becomes an always precarious practice; "understanding" his work, then, means to transcend the chronotopic horizon of each page and the whole carnet to get in contact – metaphorically and literally – with him. Through the conversation between the author and the reader, the journey continues to actualize itself beyond the physicality of the book, so that each travel experience projects its spell onto the real world and coincides, more generally, with a global vision on the practices of travelling and the artistic gesture of "writing" about it: from the reading of the text to the reading of the world, Bakhtin's concluding remarks about the possibility to think of the whole society in chronotopic terms finds here a realization.

THE CHRONOTOPE OF TRAVEL BLOGS

The analysis passes now to discuss the chronotopic features of travel blogs. Even before addressing a number of specific case studies, some preliminary considerations can be advanced concerning how the medial format affects the construction of the texts' space-time horizon. When it comes to investigating online travel narratives, it is necessary to acknowledge a double articulation. From a textual perspective, all the accounts analyzed recount journeys that have been already concluded. Hence, both the experience and its narrativization are finished. Nonetheless, from a medial perspective, the conditions of the narrative's existence are, so to speak, always temporary. This is so because the possibility to update or change the blogs' content continues to loom over them even once the travel experience is over. One could say, then, that the chronotopic coordinates of the blog format are always open-ended (at least *in potentia*, Calzati 2013a). Furthermore, because a blog can be updated, either by adding new entries or by modifying/erasing old ones, its chronotope is unstable at the level of both the single entry and the whole website. More precisely, blogs are not (and cannot be) conceived as fully accomplished works, precisely because their *raison d'être* is that of being temporary and constantly updatable. While the book's physical finitude frames the chronotopicity of the work as something comprehensive and coherent, blogs do not have physical outer boundaries, only nominal ones (i.e., the URL). This, as we will see, also requires readers to accomplish an extra (reading) effort in order to recompose the text beyond the way in which it is presented on the screen. Walker-Rettberg (2008: 115) explains this well when she notes that "each post makes sense in itself, but read together the posts tell a larger story. That story is usually partial and incomplete and does not form a narrative whole." In other words, what is narrated in blogs responds mainly, if not exclusively, to the chronotopic rhythm imposed by the medial format upon the writing process, rather than to an overarching (preliminary) conception of the work.

Some of these considerations find proof in the first travel blog under analysis, *China 2014* (2014) written by American blogger BitByTheTravelBug, and found on the popular platform Travelblog.org. In itself, the title of the blog already provides a chronotopic frame, however general it may be. Once we access the blog, such frame is further articulated: the blogger wrote seven posts about her two-week journey to China and each post reports the date and the place. So, we come to know that

BitByTheTravelBug stayed in China from the 18th of May to the 1st of June and she dwelled the whole time in Beijing where she took some Mandarin classes (indeed, the main goal of the journey).

Before delving into the blog, it is useful to provide a brief analysis of the whole platform. Travelblog.org is currently one of the biggest travel blog platforms on the Web.[84] As such, if one wants to read BitByTheTravelBug's blog, s/he must either browse the platform, according to a regional sub-division of travel destinations, or use the search box. In this sense, the platform – similarly to the others encountered – requires one to navigate through the variety of content provided and trace one's own reading path accordingly. As soon as one accesses the blogger's personal page (Figure 33), the platform provides a whole accountability of her activity. In the case of BitByTheTravelBug, the blogger only uploaded a picture of herself, while she left the space of the text blank. Then, on the right side of the page it is the platform that gives a set of data which concern, among others, the number of blogs written, the date in which the blogger joined the platform, her last access, her followers, and her forum points.

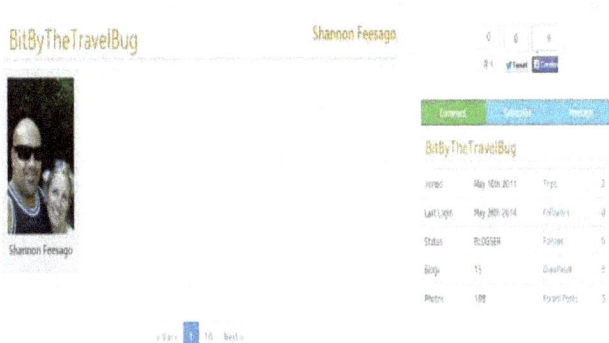

Figure 33: The "About" page of BitByTheTravelBug

Put differently, by publishing her own blog on a platform, BitByTheTravelBug agrees to partially delegate her self-representation to the platform. The way in which Travelblog.org does this is symptomatic of the "datafication" of the online experience as characterized by Morrison (2014), namely, as a shift from a "single-authored narrative understanding" of online writing toward "algorithmically-generated items." In fact, Travelblog.org provides a chiefly quantitative characterization of BitByTheTravelBug's activity and, in doing so, it conceives of her persona as chiefly a platform user (rather than a traveler and blogger). This means that, as far as travelling as a practice is concerned, very little is disclosed about the "quality" of the journeys she accomplished. For instance, we do not know either where she went, or

---

[84] From the "About" page it emerges that the platform counts more than 200,000 members and 700,000 blogs entries. According to Alexa Web analytics (www.alexa.com), the platform is among the 50,000 most visited sites on the Web, making it one of the most popular travel-related portals.

for how long. In other words, the chronotopic specificity of the blogger's travel experiences remains unexplained on the "About" page.

When focusing on the blog, it is possible to witness that the account complies with the typical (online) journal in that posts are organized according to a precise chronological sequentiality. At the same time, the basic chronotopic conception of the travel narrative, as a route covered in a certain amount of time (see Korte at the beginning of this chapter), is questioned. First of all, the account lacks an internal spatial trajectory, insofar as the experience is largely sedentary. Secondly, any thematization of the duration of the experience is lacking. Hence, the temporal framing is delegated to the posts' dates only. Each post recounts a specific episode that occurred in Beijing or in its close surroundings: the first day of class, the exploration of the capital's main landmarks, and a tour to the Great Wall. These episodes characterize the experience of BitByTheTravelBug as a touristic and educational one. Most importantly, the singling out of episodes-posts as self-enclosed, independent units (one to the other) strengthens the idea of an account-per-snapshot. Such an account does not present an overall narrative cohesion among its parts; rather, it is the (extradiegetic and platform-delegated) arrangement of the posts according to the objective time-date of the journal that dictates the chronotopic horizon of the experience. Emblematic, in this regard, is the fact that the blog opens and closes in a rather trenchant way:

> I made it to Beijing without any major hiccups. I did get a shoelace stuck in the people mover while my hands were full with coffee and an egg McMuffin. (BitByTheTravelBug 2014)

> The men tried to give us their noodles and baiju (strong Chinese liquor). We politely declined and waited for our own noodles. None of us got sick, but we found out the next day that 2 other students went there the day before and were sick for 2 days... guess we got lucky that time. (BitByTheTravelBug 2014)

The first few lines mention the blogger's arrival in Beijing, while the second quote constitutes the end of the blog. Both the beginning and conclusion of the blog are *in media res*. The blogger is not compelled to provide an introduction to the account, nor any concluding remarks, which could have helped the reader to contextualize the whole experience. The epicization of the narrative witnessed, in particular, in Hirst's second travelogue, is here strengthened. In fact, the episodes recounted can be enjoyed as stand-alone pieces and it is the readers who are asked to recompose, *a posteriori*, an overreaching narrative frame. This latter aspect, which is connected to the reading practice and depends on how blogs are built, is even more evident in the following blog analyzed.

Conoscere Pechino tra dinastie e imperatori (2013) is the heading of the first post dedicated to China by Italian blogger Flavia. The blogger has written a total of five posts about her trip to China – which according to the dates of the posts lasted roughly one and a half months, from 21st September to 5th November 2013 – and she published these posts on the platform Blogdiviaggi.com. As soon as one accesses the homepage, it is notable that the platform stresses the individuality of bloggers, urging them to provide a picture of themselves and a biographical note on the "About" page that gathers all contributors: "the beauty of this platform is that it is not a classical site or a travel guide," it is affirmed, "but it is OUR blog. It is made *by travelers for travelers*."[85] To support this statement, the platform offers two complementary reading paths to users: on the one hand, on the homepage it is possible to browse a world map and read all the posts about a given country. On the other hand, on the "About" page, one finds the profiles of all bloggers with a link that redirects to their travel experiences. Following this (latter) way, then, the browsing of the platform leads us to explore the website depending on the posts written by each individual blogger. What is most notable is that the posts published by each blogger – in this case Flavia – are not regrouped according to the travel destinations, but following merely a reversal chronological order (Figure 34). It could be said, then, that the "topos" of the posts is in function of the chronos of the journey(s) and this comes to coincide with the whole blogger's activity on the platform, in a way transcending any specific space-time frame of travel. On Flavia's page, for instance (Figure 34), the first post dedicated to China is preceded by an entry about Valley d'Itria in Italy, where she went roughly three months before, while China's last post is followed by a piece dedicated to Bavaria.

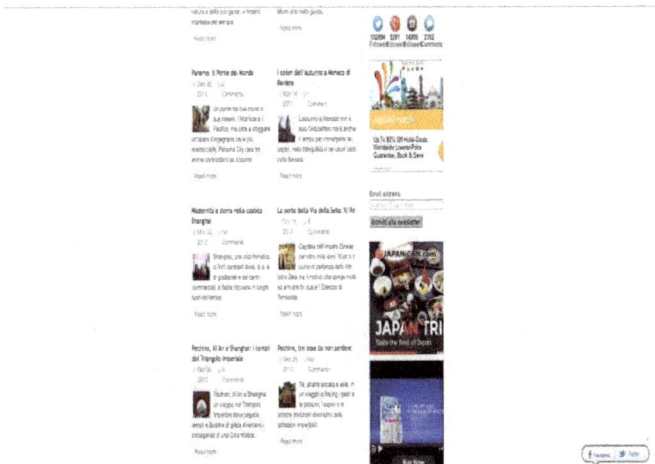

Figure 34: All the posts written by Flavia

The fact that Blogdiviaggi.com is dominated by the diachronic, objective flow of time strengthens the authorial role of the blogger and reduces the importance of the destination; to count, above all, is the very principle of travelling and writing.

---

[85] "Il bello di questo blog è che non è il classico sito o la guida di viaggi è il NOSTRO blog è un blog per noi viaggiatori da noi viaggiatori."

By reading Flavia's posts dedicated to China, it can be highlighted that these constitute brief apercus about the places visited and are connoted by concise information in the spirit of travel guides. The following are two quotations taken from Flavia's post dedicated to Beijing:

> The capital is home to 20 million people and 5 million cars. Our first visit is to **Tiananmen Square which, being 44 hectares wide, is the largest in the world**. In the middle are a war memorial and the flag of the CPR.[86] (Flavia 2013; author's translation)

> The Sky Temple in Beijing is surrounded by 276 hectares of vegetation. The buildings have round shapes to symbolize the sky; in turn, they are inscribed into squared shapes, which symbolize the earth, according to Taoism. To prevail is the blue of ceramics, also known as blue China, which connotes many buildings, as well as the number nine, which is recurrent in many buildings all around China. The number nine, indeed, stands for the emperor, so that, for instance, the number of steps to reach the building's entrance is nine; similarly, the number of tiles that compose the rounded floor is nine, and there are also nine ornaments surrounding the entrance and the exit.[87] (Flavia 2013; author's translation)

It is quite evident that these posts are largely composed of a series of objective information, or what Korte (2008: 35) calls "pauses": "In a pause," she notes, "we are presented with discourse, but not story; the most usual case is the descriptive pause." On Flavia's blog, the descriptiveness of the pause is characterized by factuality. In this regard, it is worth recalling Jan Blommaert and Jef Verschueren's (1998: 17-18) words concerning the construed discourse of "diversity" in the West: "the Other, always different and strange, exists timelessly and undisturbed, with their roots set firmly in one place, once and for all." Similarly, Edward Bruner (1991) contends that in tourism promotional materials travel destinations are usually presented as static. This aptly applies to Flavia's blog, where the rendition of Beijing is delegated and limited to a bare description of its landmarks and their features, as if they had to be consumed. Moreover, Flavia's persona is also abstracted, in that the posts lack any subjective commentary. In this sense, it could be said that the datafication of the online experience witnessed on the platform Travelblog.org (concerning the blogger's

---

[86] "La capitale ospita 20 milioni di abitanti e 5 milioni di automobili. Prima tappa della nostra visita alla città la Piazza Tian' An Men: con i suoi 44 ettari di estensione è la piazza più grande al mondo."

[87] "Il Tempio del Cielo di Pechino si trova all'interno di 276 ettari di verde. La zona monumentale è caratterizzata da strutture rotonde, che simboleggiano il cielo, inserite in strutture quadrate, che simboleggiano la terra, secondo quanto sostenuto dalla religione taoista. Ciò che prevale in questo Palazzo è il colore blu, detto poi anche blu Cina, delle ceramiche che ne rivestono alcuni tratti importanti, e il numero 9 che si trova ricorrente nei monumenti dell'intero paese. Il numero 9 infatti simboleggia l'Imperatore, ed ecco che il numero di gradini per raggiungere i palazzi è 9, il numero di pezzi di marmo utilizzati nel pavimento a cerchio è 9 e anche i paramenti posizionati sulle porte di entrata ed uscita dei templi sono 9."

personal page) is projected here onto the posts and the blogger's persona. This implies a further draining of the diegetic development of the account, which results in a fragmented patchwork of pieces related to an array of "visits." More than on BitByTheTravelBug's blog, in Flavia's the epicization of the narrative is subservient to deliver touristic tips that objectify what is recounted and makes the blogger's subjectivity recede to the background of the text, if not disappear. Here, Theodor Adorno's (1991) warning about the kind of information delivered by classic mass media finds an apocalyptic actualization:

> The curiosity which transforms the world into objects is not objective: it is not concerned with what is known but with the fact of knowing it, with having, with knowledge as a possession. This is precisely how the objects of information are organized today. Their indifferent character predestines their being and they are incapable of transcending the abstract fact through any immanent quality of their own. As facts they are arranged in such a way that they can be grasped as quickly and easily as possible. (Adorno: 85)

The kind of knowledge conveyed by Flavia's blog is chiefly abstract and emptied of any internal fueling force. As such, it is detached from its author and it acquires the status of a given. This idea will be further elaborated through the analysis of the next travel blog, written by US-American Emil.

Emil's Trip to China (2006) is an individual travel blog created relying on the CMS Blogger.co.uk. Emil went to China in 2006 with a group of colleagues: they journeyed around the country for a couple of weeks – from the 4th to the 20th of October – visiting the main touristic destinations. By scrolling the blog's homepage to the bottom, we come to know that the blog is built using the "dynamic views" template. It is this choice that makes it possible to permute the appearance of the blog according to various layouts, which are listed on the black bar just below the blog's heading: "Classic," "Flipcard" (default), "Magazine," "Mosaic," "Sidebar," "Snapshot" and "Timeline" (Figure 35).

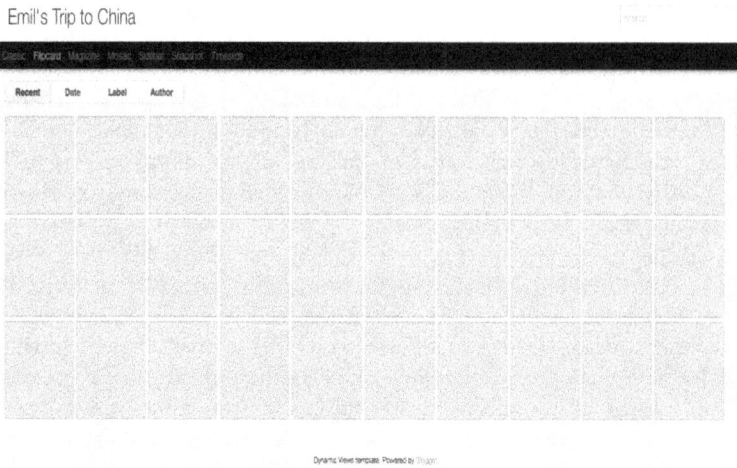

Figure 35: The homepage of Emil's blog

Then, further down, four more links – "Recent," "Date," "Label," and "Author" –
allow one to perform other arrangements of the content (although these do not really
produce sensible changes, because Emil has written only one blog and has not labeled
its posts). The possibility to change the layout of the blog is relevant within the
present discussion, because each one of them not only constitutes a stylistic choice,
but impresses a precise chronotope upon the experience. Apart from the "Classic"
design, which configures the typical central column filled with posts listed in reversal
chronological order, it is notable that none of the other layouts displays the verbal and
visual content of the entries. For example, the "Flipcard" design, which is the default
one, shows 30 cards turned upside down and when the cursor passes over them, they
reveal the date of the entry. However, nothing is disclosed about the content of the
experience. Hence, the "Flipcard" layout disjoins space from time – we know the date
of the entry but not the place – and, most importantly, its flipping feature is more
telling of the medial potentialities of the template to permute the appearance of the
blog, rather than being subservient to the chronotopic framing of the travel narrative.
In turn, these permutations also have consequences for the way in which the travel
blog can be read. By presenting all the entries/cards in one screenshot, the Flipcard
layout gives the possibility to the reader to choose how to "assemble" Emil's narrative,
that is, the spatial and temporal order of the reading. Put differently: it is the
(chronotope of the) reading that "creates" the (chronotope of the) travel blog. In this
regard, the homepage of Emil's blog represents an exemplary case of what Francisco
Varela, Evan Thompson, and Eleanor Rosch (1991) mean by "enaction," namely that
cognition and knowledge are prompted by action, rather than by predetermined
configurations of the world. To see an object does not mean to recognize it, but rather
to visually guide the action toward a goal (before and regardless of the meaning of the
object). It is this kind of effort that makes online reading (and the reading of Emil's
blog) more serendipitous and fragmented, that is, directed not much toward a classic
linear apprehension of the content, but rather to identify and isolate precise bits of text.

Katherine Hayles (2012) speaks in this respect of "hyper-reading," intended as a reading whose founding logic is not paradigmatic and linear, but guided by a constantly changing time-space frame (which can be the page, a window, a section of a website, etc.). In other words, in Emil's case the platform exposes its own medial potentialities to such an extent that it multiplies the possible reading paths and demands a syntagmatic effort from the reader.

For the sake of the analysis, the focus remains here on the Flipcard layout. By clicking on each card, a new window opens and presents readers with text, pictures, and comments. As each post is displayed within a different space (i.e., a new window opens), it is visually isolated from the rest of the blog. In the top-left corner of the new window, one finds two arrows that give the possibility of going back and forth between the entries, but one also simultaneously has the chance to change the design or to browse randomly the other posts that remain in the darker background (Figure 36).

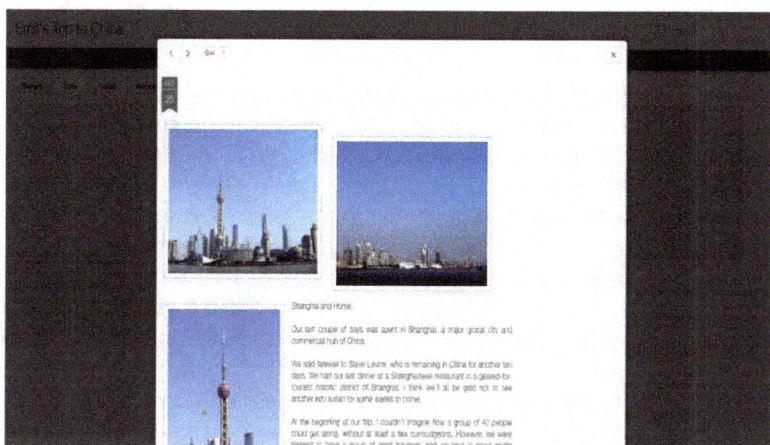

Figure 36: One post of Emil's blog with, in the background, its homepage

Hence, the blog offers the possibility to perform *both* a paradigmatic reading – the post – and a syntagmatic reading – the browsing of the platform. This reasserts the idea, already discussed in Chapter 1, that the whole blog is nothing but a heterogeneous collection of pages that 1) are opened to a galaxy of other pages; and 2) exist only when they are actually reached. Consequently, the chronotope of the blog format is spatially inhomogeneous (a web, indeed) and temporally durative, meaning that pages exist only at the time of the visit. Now, if we focus on the posts of Emil's blog, we can better understand how these features affect also what is told and shown. Here is the first post:

> Day 1 An uneventful flight. We flew from JFK to Beijing on Air China on a Boeing 747. The plane was the smallest 747 we'd ever seen, as it only had 37 rows. About half the plane was walled off to use for cargo. Here's our entire alumni group in Tiananmen Square, looking at Tiananmen Gate [see

picture below]. Our guides advised us against holding up our UNC banner, as police are more vigilant against perceived group protests with the presence of the Falun Gong. maybe at the Great Wall. (Emil 2006)

This post is significant in two respects. First, it has the function of introducing the whole blog and yet it does so in a very peculiar way, that is, by plunging the readers directly into the story. Time references are missing (apart from the mentioning of "Day 1"), while space – the route – is condensed into a few words that dictate the trajectory of the flight, from New York to Beijing. Emil tends to epicize the narration and marginalize its time and space coordinates both thematically and discursively in favor of a purely documentary account. This becomes even more prominent when considering that this one and also other posts are filled with everyday details that are considered, in Emil's own words, "uneventful." It is in this second respect that the quoted passage is also remarkable: by accounting for an "uneventful flight," the post overtly reveals the extent to which the chronotopic rhythm of the blog – its necessity of being constantly updated – affects the narrative, eventually turning "uneventfullness" into something relevant.

The pictures (and their chronotopic reading) also support these considerations. To begin with, Emil's pictures betray an amateur approach to photography: the pictures are often displayed without any rigorous logic on the page, so that their relation with the text appears to be arbitrary. Here, Susan Sontag's (1977: 9) claim that "travel becomes a strategy for accumulating photographs" fully resonates, insofar as Emil's primary intention seems to publish as many pictures as possible. Besides, both what is represented and its mode of representation convey the conventional use of the camera by the blogger and the commoditization of the medium. Sometimes, the subject represented is not correctly framed; other times, a whole set of photographs reproduce the same scene from very similar angles, thus suggesting a tendency to favor quantity over quality. Moreover, many pictures reproduce touristic landmarks (e.g., Tiananmen Square, the Potala, Shanghai's Bund). In fact, not only the reproduction of these landmarks reasserts their having become touristic places, but the way in which they have been photographed is telling of the objectification to which these places have been subjected. Emil usually photographs them from a frontal perspective, one that, by zeroing the possibility of a *mise en abyme* of the *regard*, presents the scene in a plain, bi-dimensional form. This mode of photographing conforms to what could be called a "touristic chronotope" of the image in that the internal space and time of the "represented world" tend to be erased, in order to show things "as they are"; or better, to show touristic places as everybody knows them. In his famous work on the *Tourist Gaze* ([1990] 2002) John Urry notes that photography has "constructed what is worth going to 'sightsee' and what images and memories should be brought back" (129). This clearly emerges from Emil's blog where photographs, far from "releas[ing] the body from tiring and daunting travelling," as Jonas Larsen (2006: 245) suggests in relation to tourism and photography, rather entice travels by showing precisely those places that "everybody" can (should) reach. More generally, all these aspects are indicative of the fact that the pictures bear here a predominantly repository function: they do not manifest a precise subjective gaze – the attempt to provide a personal rendering of what was experienced – on the contrary, they are posted to testify the accomplishment of the experience. The first picture (Figure 37) is particularly relevant in this sense, because it shows from a frontal perspective the group of people with whom Emil travelled. Everyone is staring at the camera, an occurrence that Kress and van Leeuwen (1996: 118) label as "demanding gaze" because it seems that the subjects ask the observer something.

Figure 37: A group picture on Emil's blog

So, what do they ask? One could say that this photograph (and the others portraying Emil and his colleagues) bear a strong self-referentiality: the time frame of what is shown is reduced to a single point in space, that is, China as a touristic place to be visited. The historical time of the pictures is flattened in favor of a time that is exclusively the time of Emil's experience in China. Such a chronotope is, indeed, typical of tourism, intended as a practice that entails visiting places in series: "In one ride," writes Emil (2006) toward the end, "we were able to experience tourist China, urban China, and rural china [sic]. I will never forget it." From this statement, it is not hazardous to infer that, first and foremost, what the photographs (and their subjects) implicitly ask the observer is to be looked at: "See who we are! See *where* we are!" but also: "See what *you* could enjoy one day!" If, according to Barthes, photography testifies "that-has-been," here we are in the presence of a sub-case that attests to the "having-been-there" of these people (who are typical short-term travelers). As a consequence, the whole experience is turned into a touristic performance: pictures portray landmarks; the contrast between urban and rural places – such as Shanghai's skyline and Guilin's inland – are the center of a fetishized attention; even ethnic minorities are considered as people to be gazed at rather than to be engaged with. Exemplary is the fact that in the pictures that portray, for instance, Tibetan people Emil never appears together with them, suggesting the retention of a distance between observer and observed. China and the Chinese, hence, become objects of representation: they are presented through a precise touristic imaginary that annihilates any internal chronotopic trajectory, any possible novel – time is a fixed one and space is bi-dimensional. This favors a conception of the whole journey as a leisure experience that does not demand a plunging into the country, but only an external look at it. Here, the meaning of Kylie Cardell and Kate Douglas's (2016) words concerning travel blogs as a commoditized form of contemporary travel writing finds its full explanation: "just as travel loses some of the philosophical potential of journey as self-discovery," they note, "and as once exotic routes become ever more well-worn and accessible, so the travel blog now enacts a pro forma stability that threatens some of the individuality such sites originally traded on" (306). The paring postulated by Butor ([1974] 2001) between how one travels and the kind of writing produced seems once more confirmed: a rushed look at China cannot but kindle a commoditized representation of it and of the whole experience.

As one last example, it is worth returning to blogger Becki, as the two versions (2012 and 2014) of her blog can highlight how changes in the conception of the travel blog as a genium can affect the chronotopic horizon of what is recounted. Both versions of Becki's blog are built upon a Wordpress Premium plan (i.e., they require an economic investment) that, by allowing the optimization of various options related to the blog's performance (e.g., easier traceability on search engines, the use of HTML5 design, etc.), has relevant consequences for the fruition of the blog and its enjoyment by the reader. For example, it is possible for the blogger to customize the blog's content fully – which would have been unthinkable if she relied on free-of-charge blog platforms – by inserting "heavy" materials in the form of high-resolution pictures and videos, or by integrating the blog with the on-going flow of her Facebook and Twitter updates. The presence of this multimodal and interactive content opens up the possibility of multiplying the ways and paths through which the site's content is effectively enjoyed. In other words, such a variety of content promotes (and possibly exacerbates) the hyper-reading already discussed in relation to Emil's blog. For instance, not only can readers, at any time, browse through all the sections of the blog (which are constantly found on the navigational bar), thus switching between a syntagmatic reading and a paradigmatic reading, but they can also click on Becki's Facebook or Twitter accounts and, in doing so, have access to her latest updates. These options, then, lead to repeatedly reconfiguring the chronotopic horizon of Becki's experience. An emblematic example, in this sense, is the fact that Twitter, by allowing very fast updates, conveys the idea of an ongoing flux of travel episodes that radicalizes more than the blog's posts the apparent eventfulness of the reporting (i.e., everything becomes crucial). By exploiting the connectivity granted by social networks, Becki pushes to the extreme the rhythm imposed by the blog format onto the travel narrative (which is ultimately broken down into minimal parts, i.e., tweets).

The fragmentation of the chronotope of Becki's journey(s) occurs both at the level of the whole website and when focusing on the posts dedicated to China. First of all, the homepage appears since the outset as a puzzle of different heterogeneous pieces. For instance, on the old version of the site, at the date of the 30th of April 2014, one could read an entry on London criminal spots, a review on Kensington Palace, four entries concerning German destinations (namely Erfurt, Weimar, Potsdam, and Berlin), an entry on the benefits of renting an apartment on vacation, and one with tips on snowboarding clothing. Similarly to what happens on Flavia's page, the chronotopic horizon of the blog comes to coincide with Becki's entire online activity, independently from where she goes and how long the journey takes. Moreover, similarly to BitByTheTravelBug, Becki's travel account dedicated to China is eventually dispersed into a variety of unrelated posts, so that if readers really want to follow Becki's peregrinations in China, they must browse the whole site, or use the search box. This is because Becki tends to present her travels as unbounded experiences in terms of both time and space: being a professional globetrotter, she can go where she wants whenever she wants. This (chronotopic) conception of travel is very different from the "normal" touristic trip, which usually has precise dates of beginning and end (or what is called the "loop home-away-home," which will be discussed in the next chapter). By contrast, Becki's experience seems governed by a (romantic) "free wandering lust" which echoes Bettinelli's self-representation as the eternal traveler. Hence, any effort to retrieve an overarching coherence among Becki's stories is doomed to fail, precisely because there is no second-order architecture (either on a rhetorical or medial level) that encompasses the posts of the blog, which emerge as fully autonomous pieces. In particular, such epicization of the travel narrative(s) is reinforced in two ways.

As seen in the previous chapter, the posts, rather than narrating the stages of her journey in China, contain episodes often concluded by an off-the-record commentary that seals them off from the others. Moreover, in the older version of the blog the posts were dated only by day and month, so that it was already quite difficult to retrace the whole itinerary followed by Becki in her "indefinite Round the World adventure," as one can read in the "About" page. This aspect, however, becomes even stronger in her new blog where posts' dates are erased. The stress is all on the present, but this dimension is not rooted, as Blanchot (1983: 29) mentions with reference to the literary journal, in the immanent and irreversible "movement of writing in time, in the humble succession of days whose dates preserve the routine." On the contrary, it is an absolute present: an ethereal time, disjoined by any rigid sequential logic, since we do not know when the episodes occurred, or when the writing was done.

Another aspect in which Becki differs greatly from other bloggers is the visual. The pictures uploaded within each of her posts are consonant with the blogger's effort to always provide an alternative look at the country she visits (as mentioned earlier). For instance, even when she goes to tourist places, such as Beijing, she tries to avoid major landmarks, as well as the typical tourist gaze, in favor of a more personalized point of view on China.

Figure 38: A picture of hutongs on Becki's blog

If Emil tended to represent China in a very axiomatic way – on one side the developed metropolis (such as Beijing and Shanghai) and on the other side the poorer regions (Tibet); on one side tourists, on the other locals – in Becki's case, instead, such a contrast is embedded within each photo: it is applied to the subject and its mode of representation and it is not the mere result of a juxtaposition. So, for instance, Beijing is symbolized by the hutongs (Figure 38) rather than by the Forbidden City or the Great Wall. Moreover, in the photograph that portrays the hutongs one can see the humbleness that characterizes these houses, but also – contrary to what one could suppose – the fact that middle-class people live in there; one sees old dwellings in front of which new motorbikes stand; and one sees garbage randomly thrown next to windows finely embellished with plants and flowers. The tension is internal to pictures and not created by the contraposition with what is missing. Besides, it must be noted that the majority of the pictures are devoted to the Other. The Chinese, indeed, dominate the scene, and when Becki appears in the photographs, she is often among locals. In this sense, the (touristic) "having-been-there," which connotes many of Emil's pictures, is here softened, showing a deeper engagement with people.

Finally, some notations can be made on the photographs' mode of representation. Pictures generally suggest a fair knowledge of the medium by Becki, insofar as they are all well-framed, have a good light balance, present a varied array of subjects, and match with the text. This means that 1) the blogger has not uploaded the pictures randomly, but took care while taking and selecting them; and 2) the display of the photographs does not respond to a mere logic of accumulation but to an organic arrangement alongside with words. Furthermore, it is possible to note that, although photographs adhere to the contemporary idea of visual "naturalism," conceived by Kress and van Leeuwen (1996: 158) as "how much correspondence there is between the visual representation of an object and what we normally see of that object," they nonetheless manifest a degree of appropriation and re-elaboration in the way in which the subjects are represented. The sporadic recourse to black and white, for example, far from conveying a neutralization of affect, as suggested by Kress and van Leeuwen (1996), or an epicization of the "represented world," as it was the case with Lotti's works, is symptomatic of Becki's attempt to produce the subject, rather than merely reproducing it. The blogger, then, does not hesitate to make use of the camera as a means of mediation of and toward the chosen subject, trying to escape the touristic chronotope and, in so doing, personalizing her *regard*.

CONCLUSION

Complementing the analysis in Chapter 1, the formal and semantic features of travel books and blogs were investigated here through the lens of Bakhtin's ([1937] 1981) chronotope. This concept was particularly well suited for two reasons. First of all, travel writing is a genre presupposed by a physical and metaphorical displacement (the journey and the writing). In this sense, travel books and blogs are geniums in which the coordinates of space and time belong to both the represented world and its mode of representation. Secondly, the Russian intellectual himself, in the last pages of his work, hinted at the possibility of extending the concept of chronotope beyond the texts and toward the medium that "carries" them. The chapter argued that the book and the blog, as different medial formats, present specific chronotopes. At the same time, the concept of chronotope was also applied to the visual realm, proposing the chronotopic analysis of pictures (multimodal books and blogs) and pictorial illustrations (Faravelli's carnet).

From here, the intra-medial and inter-medial analysis showed how travel books and travel blogs "interpret" the travel writing genre differently. The comparison between three pairs of travel books highlighted the role played by the book, as a physical artefact, in dictating not only what is included in the text, but also how the account is shaped. It emerged that, however rhapsodic the thematization of the chronos and topos of the journey may be, the book functions as an overarching architecture that literally keeps the narrative together. In travel blogs, instead, we witness the epicization of the narrative, that is, the predilection for the recounting of brief episodes that are chronotopically disconnected one from the other. In this case, the blog, as a medial format, does not structure the text; rather, it asks readers to perform, to various degrees, a hyper-reading that mixes paradigmatic and syntagmatic logics of apprehension of the text (and of use of the medial format). The epicization of the accounts manifests, in turn, an objectification of the "represented world" and a datafication of the whole (travel and writing) experience. In fact, travel blogs are usually conceived for a precise readership (i.e., other bloggers and/or tourists) and are filled with practical advices that sacrifice the subjective rendition of the journey.

It could be said that travel books embed comprehensive narratives that, so to speak, provide readers with a global vision of the traveler's experience in China (e.g., challenges, surprises, the confirmation of certain imaginaries, etc.). In doing so, travel books tend to fulfill the readers' desire to travel to the extent that all that has to be experienced is in the book. Travel blogs, instead, offer readers with a parceled picture of China, which is mainly composed of hints and suggestions. In this way, travel blogs nurture the desire to travel, being grounded on the (silenced) pact that "anybody can do it" and "anybody can write about it." In this regard, the following chapter will address more closely the pragmatic side of the travel writing genre, discussing, with the aid of a number of interviews, how travel authors and bloggers travel and write.

CHAPTER 3

Unpacking the Genre: In Dialogue with Travel Writers

Looking at the travel writing genre from a pragmatic perspective means to consider travelling and writing as practices that not only give birth to the literary work, but also anticipate, surround and follow it. It is, therefore, necessary to explore and unpack the interplay between these two practices, in order to overcome a purely textual approach to the travel writing genre. Methodologically speaking, the analysis provided here relies on the interviews conducted with the contemporary travel authors and travel bloggers surveyed and puts these interviews in relation with the final works of these writers. In this way, the texts enter into dialogue with the writers' voices, so that it becomes possible to highlight convergences and discrepancies between what the writers say about their activities (i.e., their ways of conceiving writing and travelling) and what the finished works effectively comprise. Specifically, the analysis: 1) delves into that grey area that precedes and follows the "landing" of travelling and writing on a particular medial format; 2) addresses the much-debated distinction between "traveller" and "tourist," on the one hand, and that between "amateur" and "professional" writers, on the other; and 3) questions and widens the interstitial border separating *in loco* and "itinerant" travel experiences, questioning the loop "home-away-home," which characterizes many definitions of leisure travels.

As mentioned in the Introduction, travel writing started to attract academic attention around the 1970s, when literary studies began to host an increasing number of theoretical interventions from a variety of other fields. Since then, travel writing has been addressed as a "politicized" (in a broad sense of the term) literary form embedding a hegemonic gaze directed toward the Other, that is, those people who were invariably silenced (and often colonized). These studies (among which, Pratt 1992; Lisle 2006; Huggan 2009; Edwards and Graulund 2011) have certainly the merit of reframing travel writing within the broader political, cultural, and ideological context that fueled them. For instance, many of these studies have correctly pointed out the extent to which contemporary travel writing depends upon and unfolds a "romanticized vision" of travelling and writing, which implies the erasure of the practical conditions that are behind the very possibility of travelling and writing. "Much of this [travel] writing," Debbie Lisle (2006: 10) notes, "would have us believe that the increase in mobility brought about by globalisation results in the equal movement of people, goods and ideas around the world. The idea that 'everybody moves freely' in a globalized world is a fallacy." Next to this inflated conception of travelling and writing, to be idealized is also the figure of the traveler, who often emerges, in contrast with the disdained figure of the tourist, as a solitary and eclectic person: "some travellers," Thompson (2011: 124) notes, "will make great show of the extent to which they journeyed 'off the beaten track', thereby avoiding tourists and the infrastructure that support them." These tendencies characterize much of 20th century travel writing. Yet, with the steady growth registered by the tourism industry since the aftermath of World War II[88], the canonical distinction between tourist and traveler has become less and less tenable. Sure, still today some travel authors (pretend to) distance themselves from mass tourists, either inflating the freedom they enjoy, stressing the search for authentic places, or recounting extremely adventurous tales. However, more and more they come to terms with tourism, by resorting to different ethical approaches. The "self-conscious engagement with global modernity," Graham Huggan (2009: 6) points out, "has resulted in several new, or at least reinvigorated, forms of travel practice. These include practices attached to specific forms of 'responsible' tourism (ecotourism, humanitarian tourism, spiritual tourism)." This means that "travel writing can no longer take refuge in the classic distinction (tourist/'native', local/foreigner, etc.) on which it previously depended" (2009: 4). These observations are certainly valuable for any serious attempt to understand contemporary mobility in relation with the travel writing genre. However, insofar as they chiefly focus on the texts as finished works, as literary artifacts, they overlook the practices that underpin the texts. By contrast, the analytical dialogue established here between the texts and the interviews aims to transcend the literary work *per se* and to explore the genesis of travel writings (plural). Kevin Hannam, Mimi Sheller and John Urry (2006: 13) explain this point well when they contend that "there is a complex relationality of places and persons connected through performances" that "need to be examined in their fluid interdependence and not in their separate spheres (such as driving, travelling virtually, writing letters, flying, and walking)." It is exactly the relationship between two of these performances – the practice of travelling, on the one hand, and the writing that derives from it, on the other – that is of interest here. Hence, the chapter will assess how travel authors and bloggers conceive of travelling and writing; or also: the motives behind their travels and the strategies behind their writings, as well as how they think of themselves in relation to both practices.

THE WRITING PROCESS

To begin with, let us consider the writing process adopted by travel authors and bloggers. This will shed some light on how these writers represent themselves in the texts as well as in the interviews, leading to an understanding of their own perception of the writing as a professional and/or amateur activity. Secondly, building on the synopses of the texts provided in the Appendix, to be addressed will be the travelling practices with the goal of investigating the reasons behind travel writers' journeys and what fuels the idea itself of travelling.

All the interviewed travel authors affirmed that they take notes *while* travelling so that they can be accurate and not forget important details. Colin Thubron, for instance,

---

[88] This growth is also signaled by the statistics of the World Tourism Organization (UNWTO), according to which in 2012, for the first time, more than one billion tourists travelled worldwide (http://media.unwto.org/en/press-release/2012-12-12/international-tourism-hits-one-billion).

stated that: "I take notes, all the time. My memory is not particularly good, and I need to take notes in order to remember."[89] At the same time, almost all the authors mentioned the need to take a rather long time to write the whole manuscript once they are back home. It usually takes "about a year" for Colin Thubron, while it can take "up to four years"[90] for Italian writer Bamboo Hirst. French author Constantin de Slizewicz, instead, adopts a rather heterogeneous strategy: "first of all comes the time during which you digest the experience and you write the book in your mind," then "because I am usually caught up in several projects I prefer to dedicate sessions, slots of time, to the writing."[91] De Slizewicz's strategy, then, implies a long gestation, but this does not require a full-time dedication to the writing. This is why, ultimately, the author does not think of himself as "a person who focuses exclusively on what I write." As for travel artist Faravelli, we have seen in the previous chapter that, despite defending the immediacy of his creations, which are depicted *in loco*, he does not disdain to work through his carnets in different phases, so that the "writing" – here in a broad sense – encompasses the artist's whole life. The only exception with regard to the need to take some time for the writing is represented by Germain-Thomas, who, concerning *La traversée*, said that he wrote it very quickly just after the journey, when "memories were still fresh in my mind."[92] Nonetheless, the French writer also mentioned that *Le Bénarès-Kyôto* demanded much more time to be completed. Overall, it could be suggested that all travel authors acknowledged, to various degrees, the importance of letting the time pass, as a gesture that allows to negotiate between the self and the experience; a mediation that, while not being technologically dependent (unless one thinks of body and memory as technologies), selects and shapes what is going to be written. This means, from a pragmatic point of view, that while their writing is certainly rooted in a precise travel experience, it nonetheless calls upon a reworking (and recollection) of this same experience, which can only be accomplished at a certain distance from the events. In this sense, Paul Fussell's argument that travel books have to make constant reference to actuality (1980: 203) can only be intended as a cross-reference to those "actual" notes that anticipate the writing and work as anchorage for it. In fact, such anchorage necessitates a reworking that is already, *per se*, a *mise en abyme* of the experience. This is even more so if considering that the recording of the events is always a subjective act that implies processes of selection as much as deletion. This also means – looking at the much-debated distinction between fact and fiction in travel writing – that it is not much a matter of exclusive options (factual travel accounts vs. fictional travel accounts) but of a whole spectrum of possibilities opening up. As Thubron acutely noted, "there are two kinds of diary: one that triggers your memory and one that almost takes the place of memory because it is extremely detailed." Put differently, there can be different degrees of accuracy and factuality, spanning from a dutifully precise travel account to one, as travel writer Bruce Chatwin (1988: introduction) famously points out, in

---

[89] Colin Thubron, interview by Stefano Calzati, May 27, 2013, in person.

[90] Bamboo Hirst, interview by Stefano Calzati, April 28, 2014, in person.

[91] Constantin de Slizewicz, interview by Stefano Calzati, July 17, 2014, Skype.

[92] Olivier Germain-Thomas, interview by Stefano Calzati, January 22, 2014, Skype.

which "the word 'story' is intended to alert the reader to the fact that, however closely the narrative may fit the facts, the fictional process has been at work."

More generally, the interviews brought to light the complexity of the temporalities of travelling and writing: far from being linear and consequential practices, their overlap and interpenetration are much thicker than a textual analysis might lead one to suppose. This interpenetration can produce as much a synergy as a mutual negation of the practices. Not only, indeed, is the passing of time a form of mediation between them, but also the choices of what to write and how are, at once, a confirmation and a negation of the experience. To a certain extent, then, the writing overwrites the travel on which it depends. This, as we will see shortly, is explained well by Italian blogger Gattosandro Viaggiatore.

The most interesting remarks about the writing process are those that pertain to travel bloggers. From the interviews, it became clear that the need to put some distance between the event and its recollection concerns travel bloggers too, despite the fact that they use a medium that favors – due to the collapsing of the publishing processes – immediate, daily-based writing. Almost all the travel bloggers interviewed said that they dedicate a discrete amount of time to rework the notes taken while on the road. Ataritouchme, for instance, argued that "After a trip, I try to get right on with [the writing], but it often takes a long time. Sometimes it's nearly a year after I've travelled. This actually works out better: things you think so important to share in the moment aren't actually that important, and you can spare them down or cut them out completely."[93] Ataritouchme suggests that the passing of time is not only important but necessary for his writing, insofar as it allows him to apply to his notes a selective process that eventually makes them worth remembering. In his case, then, the writing immediately follows the experience (or is parallel to it), but it takes some time for the notes to be uploaded online. Italian blogger Gattosandro Viaggiatore, on her part, affirmed that she writes once she has returned home for two reasons: "It takes a lot of time to be precise and include all the details for each place, the correct links, and to verify the information in order not to give incorrect advice. Moreover, writing when I am back allows me to live the journey a second time, and this is a great sensation."[94] On the one hand, the long span of time dedicated to writing is functional to the fact-checking of the information provided, so as to be as useful as possible for other bloggers and travelers. Time, rather than diluting memories, is required precisely to make them clearer and more accurate. On the other hand, it is worth noting that Gattosandro Viaggiatore conceives of the writing as a means to go back: it allows her to retrace the experience and to live it a second time. The writing is in itself a journey that, by skipping the temporal and psychological lapse separating the blogger from what-has-been, permits her to relive the experience.

The only exceptions in this respect are British bloggers Becki and Robjstaples. Having turned her whole life into an endless journey around the world, Becki is urged to regularly update her blog wherever she is, precisely because her travel experience

---

[93] Ataritouchme, interview by Stefano Calzati, July 3, 2014, email.
[94] Gattosandro Viaggiatore, interview by Stefano Calzati, July 8, 2014, email.

has neither a point of departure or end. In her case, the sole mediation between the experience and the publishing of the posts is represented by the tweets and Facebook's updates that parallel her blogging. Robjstaples, instead, is a blogger who spent a whole year teaching English in China. Then, at the end of his experience, he spent a few months travelling around the country. He is the only blogger that overtly stated he was writing while travelling, to the point that the two practices almost coalesced: "The travel blog was a new experience to go alongside that of travelling and living outside of my home country for an extended period of time. It was based on notes I made as I travelled about what I was thinking – one might think of it as photographs of my state of mind."[95] Robjstaples' words testify that the writing became part of his journey (also due to the length of the journey, which lasted about three months). Hence, similarly to Becki, he felt it "natural" to write along the road and updated the blog whenever he had time. It is also remarkable that he defined his posts as "photographs" of his mood, reasserting implicitly the idea of the epicization of the narrative discussed in the previous chapter, but also the fact that photography, by privileging a paradigmatic representation of the experience, is more akin to the thoughtless writing usually found on blogs.

With the exception of Becki and Robjstaples, by reading the interviews with travel bloggers, a legitimate question concerning the discussion about the medial chronotope of blogs arises: if, indeed, bloggers tend to write in the "old way," that is, by taking a long time before uploading their posts, does this mean that the blogs' chronotope is, in a way, bypassed? Was it not the case that the online medium impressed over the writing precise chronotopic features in terms of rhythm, syntax, style, etc.? Clarification is needed. It could be that writing in the "old way" *while* making use of the new medium constitutes a form of (conscious or unconscious) resistance to the chronotopic features of the blog as a medial format. Hence, travel bloggers would pretend to take their own time, *despite* adopting a medium that, in theory, reduces the distance between the experience and the writing. To an extent, this would constitute an opposition to the overwhelming flow of content that new media favor nowadays. At the same time, however, the very fact that posts are often very short, bare in syntax, and frequently filled with typos – that is, they manifest features that are typical of online writing, *even though* they are the result of a rather long gestation – reasserts, rather than undermines, the strength of the blog's chronotope, even beyond such hypothetical resistance. Travel blogger Becki, for instance, said that she is always very busy: "This is a full-time job and you take on every role possible – editor, writer, advertiser, sales, PR, new business pitching, photographer, etc."[96] From this testimony it becomes significant to investigate more in depth how travel bloggers and travel authors think of themselves in relation to their writing and travelling, that is, what are the reasons behind such practices and how each writer mixes these motives to shape his/her own persona.

---

[95] Robjstaples, interview by Stefano Calzati, August 28, 2013, email.
[96] Becki, interview by Stefano Calzati, April 28, 2014, email.

TRAVEL BLOGGERS AND AUTHORS' SELF-REPRESENTATION

Before calling upon the interviews, it is worth looking at the texts. In particular the analysis focuses on what constitutes the most evident element in the definition of the writers' identity: the signature. Genette's (1997) work on paratext provides again a good starting point. Genette considers the signature of the writer as a peritextual element. He notes that

> The author's name fulfils a contractual function whose importance varies greatly depending on genre: slight or non-existent in fiction, it is much greater in all kinds of referential writing, where the credibility of the testimony rests largely on the identity of the witness. The maximal degree of this involvement is obviously autobiography. (1997: 41)

According to Genette, the signature not only has the nominal function of legitimating the paternity of the work, but it also bears a role in defining the kind of genre to which the text belongs. Whenever we are in presence of "referential writing" – such as travelogues – the signature plays a determinant role in granting the text credibility in that all that is recounted is related to an identifiable authorial stance. This is why travel books usually fall under what Genette calls the case of "onymity," in which the work is signed with the author's real name. The other two cases identified by Genette are "anonymity" (when the work is not signed) and "pseudonimity" (when the author recurs to a fictitious name to hide his/her identity). If, on the one hand, all travel books analyzed represent, in fact, cases of onymity, on the other hand bloggers resort to a different strategy. With the exception of Becki, who alongside the renovation of her blog abandoned the alias "Backpacker Becki" to use her real name, all bloggers under discussion adopt aliases: we go from Robjstaples and Supermary58 – which are somewhat close to the real names of the bloggers – to Millycat, Gattosandro Viaggiatore and Curieuse Voyageuse, which have very little to do with the bloggers' real names. Online aliases can be defined as fictional identities in the spirit of pseudonyms. Yet, they also differ from these latter in some respects, if we are to follow Genette's definition of pseudonyms. Indeed, while Genette argues that the most intriguing aspect of pseudonyms is that of appearing as real names, online aliases are often easily recognizable as fictitious. As a consequence, with aliases a reversal of what Genette defines as the "pseudonym-effect" and the effect of "given pseudonym" (1997: 48) can be noted. The French scholar affirms that "the effect of a pseudonym is not in itself different from the effect of any other name" (1997: 48), meaning precisely that a pseudonym (aims to) function(s) as a real name without blatantly appearing as fictitious. On the contrary, an alias does have an effect of its own, for it is straightforwardly identified as a fictitious name. In this respect, it is argued here that if real names strengthen the credibility of what is recounted (particularly autobiographic texts), online aliases tend rather to generate a ludicization of authorship, to be intended as a form of softening of the blogger's authority within the public sphere (i.e., the blogosphere). In order to assess such assertion, this must be framed within the broader context concerning blogging practice and the nature of cyberspace.

The Web is a space that allows a wide spectrum of negotiations in terms of self-representation (Nakamura 2002). The adoption of aliases moves precisely within this spectrum of possible negotiations, as it allows bloggers to take a middle way between the need for recognizability (by other users) and the protection of sensible data. Vanessa Dennen (2009) wisely notes that aliases prove to be a double-edged sword: they are usually perceived to be reliable by other bloggers, but unprofessional by outsiders. Hence, aliases do bear "given effects" – differently from pseudonyms – because their fictionality is responsible for affecting both the self-representation of bloggers – as more reliable than anonymity but also as informal and not fully trustworthy – and the contested perceptions that outsiders can have of them. Conversely, the "pseudonym-effect" of aliases rests not so much on the pleasure to discover their fictitiousness, as noted by Genette in relation to pseudonyms, but on the consequences they bear on the text for the very reason of being fictive. In this sense, the distance marked by the travel bloggers' aliases from their real names, while perfectly conformable to the practice of blogging, weakens the bloggers' authority (compared to "classic" authors) and presents their accounts as basically amateur tales. This claim finds proof, for instance, in the introductory post to Robjstaples' blog, in which the blogger defends the unpretentiousness of his account:

> What to write? Well, let's try this for size: 1. Write to amuse myself and learn about myself. 2. Assume most things are the same everywhere. 3. Observe the differences. 4. Few if any people understand China, least of all me, and certainly not the Chinese! 5. The writer's discretion is final, always totally rational (honest) and mine alone! (Robjstaples 2005)

Robjstaples argues that his writing is fully discretional: he wants to describe how he sees China and the Chinese (rather than provide an accurate representation of the experience) and he wants to do so by amusing himself along the way. Therefore, the text should not be assessed for its accuracy, insofar as the blogger claims for himself a disengaged, unpretentious role. The adoption of an overtly fictitious alias responds to this same logic and smoothens the formal expectations of rigorousness that might be demanded of a travel account. This (to be sure) applies not only to Robjstaples, but to the greatest majority of travel bloggers analyzed. At stake, then, is not so much the assessment of the trustfulness of what is recounted, but the realization that online bloggers play with their identities in ways that challenge the relations instituted by Genette among the autobiographic genre, onymity, and the intrinsic self-referentiality (and trustworthiness) of the text. It is also significant that the decision to choose an alias is independent from the travel blog being hosted on a platform or independent. So, for instance, on platforms one finds Millycat and Robjstaples, but also bloggers who have decided to open their own spaces resort to fictitious names, such as Gattosandro Viaggiatore and Curieuse Voyageuse. The main difference between travel blogs on platforms and individual ones is in the "About" page that characterizes each blog. It is here that the travel bloggers' self-representations are played out more overtly. By analyzing the travel bloggers' personal profiles and putting them in connection with the interviews, it becomes possible to better understand how travel bloggers think of themselves in relation to their writing and travels.

As seen in Chapters 1 and 2, travel bloggers on platforms are largely dependent upon "the infrastructure behind the interface" (Uszkalo and Harkness 2012: 18). This means that the platforms both establish what kind of information the bloggers can provide about themselves (usually: their name, age, nationality, and a picture) and also decide what data about the bloggers' activity to include in the profile (which often leads to the "datafication" of the bloggers' personae). When they were asked to characterize their blogging and travels, all the bloggers on platforms confessed not to see themselves as travel writers. For them, to blog is functional to "keep record of the events"[97] and "share experiences with relative and other bloggers."[98] Emblematic, in this regard, is the position of Ataritouchme who mentioned that he does not consider himself as a "good writer in any sense except for perhaps spelling" and added that "I am, quite frankly, shocked when any post is viewed more than a few times," thus suggesting low expectations in terms of social exposure. This also shed a light onto the reasons why, as discussed in Chapter 1, the account of travel blogs on platform are usually characterized by a mono-rhythmic narrative that tends to flatten the representation of both the traveler and China: it is more a record of events with which readers are confronted and not a wholly thought-through narrative.

As far as the way of travelling is concerned, the experiences of the bloggers on platforms comply with the prototypical tourist tour, even when it is up to them to decide where to go, as in the case of Italian Supermary58 and Millycat. The former said in the interview: "To be honest, I had some problems planning the trip because China is a huge country, rich in history and landmarks. Eventually, I opted for the classic tour"; similarly, the latter writes on her blog that "having planned 6-7 itineraries, we decided to opt for the one that many tour operators call 'classic China': Beijing, Xi'an, Guilin and Shanghai"[99] (Millycat 2013; author's translation). This homogenization of the experience also triggers a clear-cut self-representation: indeed, all travel bloggers on platforms think of themselves, in the first place, as tourists, the best reworking of such category being Mathieu's definition of himself as a "curious tourist."[100] It could be argued, then, not only that travel bloggers on platforms fully embrace a touristic persona, but also that they do not feel the need to model such self-agency according to a more ethical, sensible or sustainable perspective.

Individual travel bloggers, instead, manifest more composite self-representations. To begin with, if we look at their "About" pages it is possible to find some autobiographical information that goes beyond what is found in the blog (sometimes the blogger's real name is also disclosed). This is how Gattosandro Viaggiatore and Curieuse Voyageuse present themselves:

---

[97] Emil, interview by Stefano Calzati, February 24, 2014, email.
[98] Supermary58, interview by Stefano Calzati, July 4, 2014, email.
[99] "Dopo aver fatto 6-7 itinerari possibili, ci decidiamo per quello che ricalca un po' quello che i tour-operator chiamano la "Cina classica," e cioè, Pechino, Xi'an, Guilin, Shanghai."
[100] Mathieu, interview by Stefano Calzati, July 3 2014, email.

My name is Simona. On this blog, I describe my experiences and I make available information, addresses and useful links to all those people who are about to leave. And obviously, I also provide personal advice. When I am not dedicating myself to the organization of a journey, I love drawing and gardening. I am a cashier and also work as a film operator. For those who are curious, the title of my blog is homage to the furry one of the house, super Cat Sandro [Pertini].[101] (Gattosandro Viaggiatore 2012; author's translation)

I have loved to travel since I was a child and have been writing for a few years. I share my travel writing on Curieuse Voyageuse (and sometimes something else). In March 2009, I decided to go to live in China. So, I started to share my impressions about everyday life and trips around this strange elsewhere. My passion for writing quickly equalled that for travelling.[102] (Curieuse Voyageuse 2009; author's translation)

These autobiographical notes constitute a sort of behind-the-scenes of the travel bloggers' lives. They are particularly useful in the present discussion because they reveal the motives that fuel the bloggers' writing and travels, as well as how they think of both. Gattosandro Viaggiatore acknowledges her willingness to share her experiences with other bloggers, while also providing personal tips and impressions. In this latter respect, she also pointed out in the interview that she plans her journeys autonomously, marking a certain distance from mass tourism: "I like to organise my travels completely alone: to study the destination, the itinerary, and the places to visit, be it a trip down the road or to the other side of the world." It does not come as a surprise, then, that Gattosandro Viaggiatore ended up mapping out a rather personalized itinerary in China, especially for her second journey:

It was hard, but eventually the itinerary of my second trip to China was ready! The most difficult thing was to decide the area to cover and ensure the feasibility of the transfers. The result is good, maybe a bit ambitious, but within my budget limits. Here are the legs: Guangzhou Zhangjajie, Wulingyuan, Fenghuang, Guilin, Yangshuo, Beihai, Weizhou Island, Hainan – Haikou, Hainan – Sanya, Guangzhou. (Gattosandro Viaggiatore 2013; author's translation)

---

[101] "Mi chiamo Simona. In questo blog racconto le mie esperienze in viaggio e metto a disposizione informazioni, indirizzi e link utili a chi sta per partire. Oltre a qualche consiglio assolutamente personale. Quando non sono impegnata nello studio di una meta mi piace dedicarmi al disegno e al giardinaggio. Nella vita faccio la cassiera e all'occorrenza l'operatore cinematografico. Per chi se lo stesse domandando, il titolo del mio blog è un omaggio al peloso di casa, il mio super Gatto Sandro [Pertini]."
[102] "Je suis passionnée par les voyages depuis mon enfance, et par l'écriture depuis quelques années. Je partage sur *Curieuse Voyageuse* mes récits de voyage (et parfois d'autres choses). En mars 2009, je décide de partir vivre en Chine. Je commence à partager mes récits de vie quotidienne et voyages dans cet étrange ailleurs. La passion de l'écriture égale rapidement celle du voyage."

While the very fact of taking a second trip to China signals an interest that goes beyond a mere touristic break, it is also significant that in her second experience Gattosandro Viaggiatore aimed at visiting a number of places that are quite off the most popular paths. In this sense, her approach to travel is certainly ones that requires dedication, preparation and a "deep reading" of the visited destination. On the other hand, when I asked Gattosandro Viaggiatore to characterize her online activity she revealed an ambiguous conception: "insofar as writing is a pleasure for me and not a job – although I would really like to have such a job – when I have free time I prefer to relax rather than being chased by the anxiety of updating the blog." To a certain extent, Gattosandro Viaggiatore thinks of her blogging as chiefly a leisure activity and she reasserts what we already know, notably that travelling and writing remain two separated practices also for travel bloggers. And yet, it is notable that both Gattosandro Viaggiatore's effort toward accuracy in the information provided and her hope that blogging might one day become a job testify to the blurring of any neat demarcation between amateurship and professionalism. In fact, if ever such a distinction can be traced it pertains to the economic sphere only. This resonates with José van Dijck's (2013: 32) claim that, nowadays, online bloggers "may be considered amateurs and citizens, as well as professionals and labourers," validating the contamination between amateur and professional realms.

Curieuse Voyageuse has an even more ambivalent position: on her blog, she defines writing as a passion that is equal to travelling. The two, therefore, seem entrenched passions, but once one confronts this piece of information with what the blogger said in the interview, travelling and writing are displaced onto a more professional level. Curieuse Voyageuse argued that she thinks of herself in terms of "a traveller and also a blogger in the process of becoming a writer."[103] On the one hand, this statement appears to imply a hierarchy between blogging and writing, where the former is considered as amateurish and the latter as professional. At the same time, these words reveal Curieuse Voyageuse's own awareness of the economic potentialities of her online writing in relation to her journeys (in particular around China where she lived for two years. We should also not forget that she published her first book out of her blog). In fact, she further pointed out that "blogging has become central in my life: it helped me to find my present job, it opened me the door of my publisher, it allowed me to travel and to take wonderful trips." Here, then, amateurship and professionalism are completely blurred; they are two sides that presuppose each other. Telling is also the fact that Curieuse Voyageuse manifests constant effort in keeping a dialogue with readers, both through the blog and through other social networks that are integrated into it: "The social, interactive and communitarian aspects," she noted, "are very important in my blog. These aspects are almost non-existent when it comes to a book: once the author has finished it, it does not interact with the readers, apart from some meetings, but only very few readers meet all the authors they have read, while my blog's readers can directly interact with me." In other words, Curieuse Voyageuse shows a good degree of expertise in the

---

[103] Curieuse Voyageuse, interview by Stefano Calzati, July 28, 2014, email.

managing of the virtual relations that online social networks strongly enhance and demand from writers who have crossed the line of professionalism.

In terms of self-representation – and here the circle closes – the most radical position is certainly Becki's. For her, not only is blogging a professional activity but travelling has become a commoditized practice:

> I'm Becki and I'm a British Travel Press award winning writer and avid explorer. This website first came about over two years ago when I quit and sold everything (yes, that familiar story) to leave for what was meant to be an initial 18 month adventure around the world. My passion for insightful travel, combined with my inherent love for English literature, history and sociology, alongside the skills harnessed from my 10 year PR career, led me to setting up the blog "Backpacker Becki" and growing it as a go-to resource for those wanting to travel in a similar way. (Becki 2014)

This passage, found on the "About" page, testifies the extent to which for Becki blogging has turned from a passion into a profession. This position was made even clearer in the interview, where she argued that "We just happen to be the information providers. Our profession is slowly becoming more well-known and is growing rapidly." In this case, the traveler persona, despite the blogger's statement in the interview that she likes "to go with the flow" without planning the journey too much, loses its romantic aura and is fully inscribed into a business-minded framework that stresses the commodification of mobility. As a consequence, the blog also changes its *raison d'être*: rather than simply recounting a journey or giving tips, it aims at "talking about travel with a social conscience and understanding places that are misunderstood. It's from a personal account but not written like an on-going diary," if we are to rely on Becki's (2014) own words on her site. This means that the ideas of travel-as-leisure and traveler-as-tourist, which characterize the majority of travel blogs, thicken and take on a social/ethical connotation in the spirit of that found in travel books. Furthermore, Becki is well aware that having the ability to manage an individual space grants her greater control over what she publishes and how she presents it: "Your website is your open book, so you have full editorial control." Interestingly, the comparison she makes is not between her travel site and those blogs hosted on platforms but between her online space and other social networks: "Currently, Twitter and Instagram are not that limited, but Facebook is enforcing a lot of control in regard to who sees your updates, in the hope that people will pay more to promote posts." From such a statement, it is possible to argue that Becki aims not only at being in control of all that she writes but also at getting the most out of her blogging activity in terms of social exposure and economic compensation.

***

The analysis moves on now to discuss the travel authors' self-representation and how they think of their writing and travels. To begin with, it is worth noting that in all the travel books selected the authors' signatures not only appear on the front covers and title pages, but also on the back cover (an occurrence apparently overlooked by Genette in his study). What is remarkable is the fact that such signatures go beyond a mere nominal referentiality and they rather take the form of brief paragraphs, which are similar to the "About" page on travel blogs (or vice versa). Reading these, one is introduced to some biographical information concerning the authors. For instance, one learns that:

> Clara Arnaud was born in 1986. She studied Mandarin and geography while travelling in Central Asia. Then, some missions to Africa brought her to Senegal, Benin and Ghana, before reaching Congo. Settled in Kinshasa, she worked there for two years leading a few projects of international development.[104] (Arnaud 2010; author's translation)

Or also:

> Sergio Ramazzotti was born in Milan in 1965 and works as a freelancer for various magazines, among which *Lo Specchio della Stampa* and *D* by *la Repubblica*. Feltrinelli Traveller has published his works *Vado verso il Capo* (1996) and *Carne Verde* (1999).[105] (Ramazzotti 2002; author's translation)

These peritextual pieces of information have at least three consequences for: 1) the self-representation of the authors beyond the text *per se*; 2) the perception that the readers get of them; 3) the (perceived) literary form of the text itself. Knowing, for instance, that Ramazzotti has already written other travelogues confers upon his persona an expertise that surpasses that of the occasional traveler or writer. This, in turn, is likely to shape the reader's perception of him, possibly in the direction of higher credibility. Moreover, the fact that Ramazzotti is defined as a freelance journalist can variously steer, confirm or even dismiss some considerations made by the reader about the author's style and the literary form of the book (e.g., a commercial autobiographic book, but also one with political conscience). Lastly, any reader sufficiently acquainted with the Italian press can recognize *Lo Specchio della Stampa* and *D la Repubblica* as two weekly magazines that enjoy a wide distribution but that nonetheless limit the presence of in-depth analyses, usually preferring to focus on light/popular contributions (hence, Ramazzotti's writing may be expected to fit within the editorial guidelines of these magazines).

Similarly, reading that Clara Arnaud has studied Mandarin and voyaged around central Asia projects over her persona the allure of the navigated traveler when it

---

[104] "Clara Arnaud est née en 1986. Elle étudie le chinois et la géographie, tout en voyageant en Asie centrale. Ses premières missions en Afrique l'amènent au Sénégal, au Bénin et au Ghana, avant la République Démocratique du Congo. Basée à Kinshasa, elle y travaille durant deux ans sur des projets de développement international."

[105] "Sergio Ramazzotti è nato a Milano e lavora come freelance per diverse riviste, tra cui 'Lo Specchio della Stampa' e 'D di Repubblica'. Di Ramazzotti, Feltrinelli Traveller ha pubblicato *Vado Verso il Capo* (1996) e *Carne Verde. La straordinaria storia del peyote, dio del Texas* (1999)."

comes to China (i.e., an insider). Besides, her interests in Africa and her commitment to humanitarian and developmental projects further broaden her self-representation as not simply a traveler and writer, but also a politically engaged person, usually toward countries that are not at the center of tourism fluxes.

A radically different self-representation from both Arnaud and Ramazzotti's is Thubron's. His persona adheres monolithically to that of

> An acknowledged master in travel writing. His first books were about the Middle East. In 1982 he travelled in the Soviet Union, pursued by the KGB. From these early experiences developed his great travel books on the land mass that takes up Russia and Asia. He has won many awards. (Thubron 2006)

Thubron appears as the "classic" traveler and adventurer; one whose literary talent has been widely acknowledged worldwide. This, in turn, steers the expectations that the readership projects onto his work – as eminently literary, in the British tradition of travel writing – and his own persona – as an erudite and mannered middle-aged man – to the point that readers fairly acquainted with the travel writing genre in English could be led to associate Thubron with another great travel writer, Peter Fleming. More broadly, all these brief biographical notes, apart from extending Genette's discussion on the signature of the work beyond the mere signature, testify to the extent to which authors provide a self-representation that enriches the one emerging from the book (of course, it is not a matter of who wrote these excerpts, but the effects they produce).

When it comes to the interviews, all authors showed widespread agreement in defining themselves as writers and travelers. To a certain extent, this complies with the idea that having published a book constitutes a form of official sanctioning of their status. For instance, Clara Arnaud thinks of herself as a "writing traveler," while French author Luc Richard argued that: "I'm a bit all of these: an author, a journalist, a traveller." At the same time, under the umbrella of "travel writer," some differences can be retrieved. Legerton and Rawson, for example, amended such definition by seeing themselves as experts of China, but also as amateur writers, insofar as they had never published a book before *Invisible China.* "We were always very cognizant of the fact," they said, "that we were very fortunate to be able to make this journey. Travelling took a large chunk of time, and a lot of places were not particularly easy to reach."[106] In a way, then, Legerton and Rawson undermine the romantic traveler persona by acknowledging the material conditions that made their journey possible. To this, they added that "We were both novice writers, so writing was definitely a learning process for us." On his part, Germain-Thomas rejected any formalization of his writing activity, claiming that "writing is a vocation. I do not see it as a profession because I have never really lived out of it. I do it as a pleasure." This latter case, while drawing back on to a romantic idea of writing as an unbound activity, testifies

---

[106] Colin Legerton and Jacob Rawson, interview by Stefano Calzati, November 4, 2013, email.

paradoxically to the reversal of Becki's position, who moved from the amateur realm toward the professional one. Overall, Germain-Thomas's words remain as an admonishment of the intrinsic instability of all forms of writing, even those that managed to eventually get published: to appear on the shelves of bookstores does not necessarily imply a change in the (material) conditions of the writer. Lastly, Italian author Ramazzotti unfolds a rather controversial self-representation. In the interview, he overtly declared the professional purposes of his journeys: "When I travel, I try to make the most out of this investment, not so much economically speaking but in terms of personal experiences."[107] Hence, Ramazzotti is willing to offer of himself a professional portrayal – the term "investment" is emblematic – of which the traveler-facet is only one minor aspect. Reinforcing this, he added: "sometimes, I must respect precise deadlines for the reportage to be delivered, so I usually rely on an interpreter or, more generally, a fixer: a local person who can help you solve bureaucratic issues better and faster." In Ramazzotti, the emphasis on the professionalization of the practices of travelling and writing is very strong, but the consequence of this is that he cannot help but draw back, eventually, on rigid distinctions between amateur/professional and local/foreigner: the two worlds – of the traveler and the fixer – meet for the time of the experience, but then return to be fully independent. At the same time, while Ramazzotti rejected the romantic idea of travel, by negating the possibility, nowadays, of "leaving all behind and travelling," he nonetheless confessed to dislike "to plan all the details of the journey in advance because I believe that the component of the unexpected – what English people call 'serendipity' – is essential to the trip, to preserve its allure." Here we find a controversial approach to travel, considered as both a practice out of which the most has to be taken, but also one to be accomplished unconditionally. This controversy entails, in turn, a double articulation of Ramazzotti's self-representation: on the one hand, as a reporter, he admits to resorting to locals' help; on the other hand, he pretends to be perceived as a traveler who has the needed freedom to make of the journey something unique. In fact, Ramazzotti's polarized strategy seems to epitomize Alex Gillespie's (2006: 362) claim about travelers' self-perception: "[they] usually claim, at a discursive level, a position that is superior to that of the 'average tourist' or 'typical tourist'." However, their actions are likely to run counter to these claim" (as seen in Chapter 1, both Ramazzotti's short stay in Shaoshan and his disdaining attitude toward Celia support such a claim).

To conclude this section, it is remarkable that none of the authors and bloggers framed their travels and writings within a gender perspective. As for the travel, China appears as a safe place to go, which does not solicit any concerns in terms of security, while the writing seems disjoined from any manifest gender-related awareness in terms of potential access to publication. In other words, the texts under examination – both travel accounts and interviews – largely overlook such gender-related themes. Two cases are very useful to show the apparent retreat of the gender issue into the background. Blogger Becki rejects any clear-cut gendered self-representation: she

---

[107] Sergio Ramazzotti, interview by Stefano Calzati, September 18, 2013, Skype.

wants to appear neither as an empowered woman nor as one who took over a male role. In this respect, while on her old blog she overtly negated a possible gendered interpretation of her adventures – "I'm not just another solo female traveller, but a curator of great travel tales," it could be read on the old "About" page (2012) – on her new blog she describes herself as "a British Travel Press award winning writer and avid explorer," a definition that erases any possible gendered framing. Similarly, travel author Clara Arnaud, who travelled alone to the Western regions of China, affirmed in the interview that her journey was "also shaped by the Chinese authorities who did not allow me to go wherever I wanted."[108] When asked to further elaborate on that, she did not hint at the fact that these issues had something to do with her being a woman: "I have found that Chinese people are much funnier and more sympathetic than we think in Europe. Some labourers even hosted me when travelling in Tibet." Hence, it seems that her female persona has not been subjected to any specific form of attention, despite the fact that her way of travelling was rather perilous, having walked hundreds of kilometers on foot and ridden horses up to Tibet. More generally, it can be remarked that, if the adoption online of aliases hinders a clear-cut genderization of the writing, also in printed travelogues gender issues are backgrounded in favor of the emergence of travel writers' personae that focus on other issues and identity facets.[109]

TRAVELLING AND MOVING WHILE DWELLING: "HOME" AND "AWAY" RECONSIDERED

The last aspect to be discussed concerns the difference, if any, between *in loco* and itinerant experiences, as well as the kind of representations of China that these experiences can provide. Underpinning such discussion is the idea that travelling is as much a moving as a sedentary practice. James Clifford (1997) is of great help to further disentangle this point: "When borders gain a paradoxical centrality," he contends, "margins, edges, and lines of communication emerge as complex maps and histories" (7), so that "practices of displacement might emerge as *constitutive* of cultural meanings rather than as their simple transfer or extension [italics in original]" (3). This chapter aims precisely to understand what it means – for Self and Other, for the representation of the traveler and China – that travel and dwelling are not exclusive terms, but mutually interdependent, and it aims to do so by interrogating the solidity of the conceptual borders separating "home" and "away," "dwelling" and "being on the move."

Although all the texts analyzed here refer to actual journeys, it does not mean that the dwelling within the country did not play a role in them. It is the case, for instance, that some of the travel writers surveyed were living in China at the time of the journey, or also that some of them decided to focus on specific places rather than wandering around the whole country. These occurrences demand to unpack the

---

[108] Clara Arnaud, interview by Stefano Calzati, January 22, 2015, email.
[109] This argument will be also tackled in the next chapter dedicated to "older" travel writing about China.

125

relations between travelling and dwelling, as well as writing while on the road, or once the journey is over (which, as seen, is what many travel writers do). Consequently, this leads to question the practical validity of the loop "home-away-home" that characterizes the imaginary of travel *per se* and, for sure, many definitions of touristic travel. What the analysis will show is that, despite theoretically constituting the two extremes of any travel experience, the concepts of "home" and "away" are, in fact, constantly worked through by the practices of moving, dwelling, and writing.

For many travel writers the above-attested need for writing after the return seems to imply a sharp distinction between "home" and "away." Epitomizing this is the position of Gattosandro Viaggiatore who, in the interview, explicated that the kind of distance that she requires for writing is not only a temporal distance but also a spatial/cultural one (she has to be back at home in order to recollect the journey). In this regard, Robyn Davidson (2001: 2) interestingly contends that it is contemporary travel writing that "create[s] the illusion that there is still an uncontaminated Elsewhere to discover," which one opposes to the security of a familiar environment. And yet, there remains, undisputable, the need for the majority of travel writers to "recollect memories in tranquillity" as William Wordsworth would put it. That being the case, in order to effectively investigate the conceptual validity of the terms "home" and "away," the question becomes: what *kinds* of "home" and "away" are at stake here? For some authors and bloggers – such as Richard, Thubron, Ramazzotti, Hirst, Flavia, Supermary58 – home is, no doubt, identified as their homeland: a precisely locatable place that, temporally and spatially, frames the greatest part of their daily lives. For these writers, travelling can have an infinity of reasons – curiosity, profession, desire, even necessity – but the horizon that frames such practice is well-defined: they travel to (more or less) distant lands for a certain amount of time *and* they come back to tell their stories. Tzvetan Todorov (1995: 68) can be of help in explicating this point: "a true travel narrative," he claims, "recounts the discovery of others, either savagery of faraway lands or the representatives of non-European civilizations." This characterization of travel rests upon a conception of space as an ontological dimension: a Cartesian space that can easily function as the ground for the encounter/clash between the traveler and the Other. I have criticized this vision and the consequences it has on the analysis of travel writing elsewhere (Calzati 2015a); yet, here Todorov's words serve well the purpose of exemplifying the paradigm "home-away-home" that is at the base of many travels accomplished by the writers discussed here. At the same time, there are some travel writers for whom home comes to represent more an imaginative space: a space of security and isolation, in which the writing can be done without interferences. Most importantly, this space does not have to coincide with the writers' physical home or with a single place. Rather, the spatial coordinates of home sublimate to the point of becoming either ephemeral or multiple. It is in this regard that to investigate the pragmatics of travel (and writing) helps to deconstruct the loop "home-away-home." So, for instance, the artist Faravelli spreads the "writing" across different locations: *in loco* during the journey, but also in his artistic studio, in his house, or open air when the journey is over and he is back in Italy. On the other hand, it can happen that the writing, although coming after a certain time, is accomplished in a place that is still part of the "visited" country, such as the cases of Curieuse Voyageuse and de Slizewicz. The implications are not only nominal – what to call home – but epistemological and cultural. Regardless of whether these writers are long-term residents or temporary visitors in the visited country, theirs represents an in-between condition that differs from both the self-enclosed travel experience, in which the traveler goes to a place and then comes back, and the so-called "home travels" or "domestic travels," in which the travel writer wanders around and reports about his/her own country of origin.[110] As we will see, such in-between positioning has also consequences for the kind of gaze projected over the visited destination.

Globalization and the exponential development of human mobility have challenged any neat definition of what travel is and who travelers are. In fact, there have been many efforts within and outside academia to characterize both. Very often, the principles at the base of these attempts are spatial, temporal, or a combination of the two. For instance, the World Tourism Organization of the United Nations (UNWTO) broadly defines tourism as

> the activities of persons travelling to and staying in places outside their usual environment for less than a year, for any main purpose (leisure, business or other personal purpose) other than to be employed by a resident entity in the country or place visited. (UNWTO 2013)

In other words, tourism is conceived as a displacement over a limited span of time to places that are beyond the everyday context. Next to that, the UNWTO outlines a series of sub-classes of tourism: "domestic tourism, inbound tourism, and outbound tourism. These can be combined in various ways to derive the following additional forms of tourism: internal tourism, national tourism and international tourism" (UNWTO 2013). The purpose of this classification is clearly to outline a space-time based taxonomy that helps to distinguish tourism from other forms of contemporary mobility (commuting, migrations, exile, etc.). However, in doing so, the definition advanced by the UNWTO works via criteria of negation, that is, it deduces what tourism is by excluding other forms of mobility, rather than by defining it *per se*. In contrast to that, a definition via positive criteria is that advanced by Francesca Battisti and Alessandro Portelli (1994), according to whom tourism and exile are considered as two extremes of a spectrum of mobility forms, of which migration represents a sort of in-between. Along this same line, Allan Williams and Colin Hall (2000) come to consider tourism as strictly interwoven with migration: "Many forms of migration generate tourism flows. Migrants may become poles of tourist flows, while they themselves become tourists in returning to visit friends and relations in their areas of origin. Tourism may also generate migration flows. Most obviously, this is through

---

[110] To this latter occurrence is dedicated Chapter 5 that focuses on contemporary Chinese-authored travel books and blogs about China. This will allow an understanding of how Chinese people think of and represent their own country, rearticulating the concept itself of "home" and China in a plurality of perspectives.

the demand generated for labour which, if it cannot be met locally, will stimulate labour migration" (8). However deep and varied the analysis of (the relation between) tourism and migration may be, the main problem with these definitions is that they rest upon a binary distinction between mobility and settlement, movement and dwelling (although William and Hall's characterization highlights at least how mobility cannot be easily defined in a univocal way). Such a distinction, while being useful for mapping and disentangling the differences between one form of mobility and the other, is based on rigid space-time coordinates that are of problematic applicability when it comes to investigating the functioning of tourism and travel as social practices. It is in this spirit that Adrian Franklin's (2012: 45) warning about the urgent need to rethink the dominant paradigm within tourism studies has to be intended: "we should begin to view modern tourism," he writes, "not as based on basic binaries such as ordinary/extraordinary or home/away, but as something that had to be made to happen, that belongs to a story of becoming." By exploring how travel writers think of travelling and writing as practices, this is precisely the line followed here, so that it will be possible to understand how the detailed taxonomy elaborated by the UNWTO is culturally, politically and ideologically charged. What globalization has brought about is the intensification of travel (and, along the way, of writing). However, this intensification cannot be solely seen as a quantitative increase: it also needs to be explored qualitatively. Not only have we seen that the idea that "everyone moves freely" is a fetish idealization (Lisle 2006), but the soaring in travels goes hand in hand with a hybridization of its forms: from the all-inclusive tourist experience to the ongoing travel experience, passing through the journeys accomplished by temporary dwellers or permanent residents. In this respect, a mere taxonomical approach to travel fails to discuss its cultural and ideological implications, which are of interest here. By contrast, establishing a dialogue between texts and travelers can help develop worthy reflections from a different angle.

According to French author de Slizewicz, a travelogue is worth publishing if it matches at least one of the following three conditions: "you can accomplish an extraordinary journey"; you can have "a great literary and descriptive talent"; and "the third possibility is that you are so immersed in a local culture that you have the chance, so to speak, to write about it from the inside, unfolding a more critical perspective," which is, indeed, his case. In de Slizewicz's opinion, the particular knowledge that a travel writer acquires by settling and travelling around is what grants him/her sufficient credit for writing about the place. De Slizewicz goes on to contend that "unfortunately, many contemporary travel writers do not have the necessary cultural background for describing what they see, differently from 19th century travellers, who usually departed after having acquired the knowledge needed. The majority of contemporary travellers are empty: they usually go abroad and stop at the surface of things, judging everything as more beautiful than at home and stupidly criticizing the Western culture." Here, an overt critique of a certain widespread way of travelling – possibly touristic, but surely superficial – is advanced. In so doing, the spatial and temporal coordinates of travel are qualitatively charged and evaluated. It is not simply a matter of going elsewhere and/or staying somewhere for a specific period that are sufficient for writing a good travelogue. Rather, it is important to give substance and weight to the experience. According to de Slizewicz, the knowledge of a place anticipates as much as derives from the journey; in other words, differentiating a superficial travel writer – as a mere "spectator," in de Slizewicz's own words – from a proper traveler writer – who becomes an "actor" – is not as much down to the temporal duration of the travel experience but to the critical stance that the writer (and secondly the reader) is able to bear in the face of the other-culture. De Slizewicz's position echoes Butor's idea that to travel in a certain way means, first of all, to be able to "read" the Other. It is only when one can do so that travelling bears a transformative power (for the traveler, the Other and the reader). For this reason, de Slizewicz's argument is radically different from the idea of travel as a form of evasion (as suggested, for instance, by Bourdieu, see the Introduction). As a matter of fact, for de Slizewicz it is precisely the plunging into a culture that allows the writer to deconstruct that undifferentiated background – that banal gaze – which, according to him, characterizes much contemporary travel writing. What is important to stress, at the same time, is the quality of such plunging: for de Slizewicz, being immersed into a culture is not synonymous with dwelling; again, it is not a matter of duration, but of learning to understand the Other, constantly testing oneself through cultural negotiation. The author made this point clear when he said, with regard to his life in Yunnan, that: "I am a Westerner. I know that every day is a fight: I am not at home, every day I have to re-negotiate the pact of coexistence with them [Tibetans]." Such an idea further articulates home not so much as the place where one has past roots, but as a dynamic space of interaction that is projected onto the future as a "becoming-home." Sara Ahmed's (1999: 332) words are illuminating here: "home is indeed elsewhere, but it is also where the self is going: home becomes the impossibility and necessity of the subject's future (one never gets there, but is always getting there), rather than the past which binds the self to a given place." In this way, de Slizewicz's stance comes to represent an implicit critique of those paradigmatic positions, as seen above, that consider a "true travel" only that accomplished in remote places. It is not geographic distances (or duration *per se*) that can define travel as such, if ever a definition of "true travel" can exist. Rather, it is the way in which each traveler models his relations with the place s/he visits. Specifically concerning Yunnan, where he has been living for years now, de Slizewicz affirmed that he chose this province for precise reasons:

> I arrived in Beijing when I was 19, and in the beginning I loved in particular the optimism of Chinese people. After some time, however, the eastern part of China – that is, the most developed one – has started to deceive me more and more, and it is for this reason that I left Beijing and moved inland, towards the world of minorities. In a certain way, through my ten years in China, I have witnessed the progressive inscription of the country into the global world.

From this passage, it is possible to better understand that the terms "home" and "away" acquire for de Slizewicz very precise ideological connotations. The French travel author identifies home with all those communities within China's borders (communities that are increasingly segregated and menaced) that have not been Westernized (yet). Hence, one could say that home, for him, is a "negative" concept in that it is derived as a subtraction from all that is not capitalist China. More than a physical place, home is a space of resistance. Quite telling are his words: "I fight in order to preserve the Tibetan culture. You know, we have to face a force that destroys everything." Here, the main point arises: de Slizewicz certainly considers himself as an insider, in terms of his involvement with the Tibetan cause; yet, his (Western) cultural roots will never put him on the same level as the local people. To be more precise, it is these roots that allow him to constantly look at Tibetan people with a critical gaze and one that promotes a different image of Tibet from that generally constructed by Westerners. In fact, with *Ivre de Chine* (2010) his goal is to "desacralize Tibetan people. Let's be clear: I love them, I live with them every day, but I also deemed necessary to represent them for what they are, that is, beyond all mystifications." The turning of home into a space of resistance has the effect of reframing its relation with all that is "away" within a broader picture, in which traditional cultures (plural) are opposed against the modern society (singular), found both within and outside of China. This is why de Slizewicz, far from defining himself as a European or a French person, thinks of himself as a Westerner. "Westerner" is a concept that, however anchored to a geopolitical location, has increasingly come to identify a precise neo-capitalist way of interpreting and living contemporaneity: that same way against which he strives to protect Tibetan regions.

Concerning the need to dwell in a place in order to fully understand it, a rather different perspective from de Slizewicz's is that taken by Nathan Gray. In his 2000 journey, Gray walked the whole length of the Great Wall together with four other companions, and once he concluded the walk he wrote *First Pass under Heaven* (2006). Because this is a walk that no one had ever done before (or at least recorded) Gray's text matches the first condition mentioned by de Slizewicz in regard to the publishability of a travel book: namely, the accomplishment of a unique endeavor. At the beginning of the book, Gray fully embraces the perspective of the whole group:

> Kitted out in our matching-red jackets, the Great Wall team stands proudly near the base of the flagpole – a horde of Chinese tourists lining up to get their photos taken. I imagine our faces spreading like the diaspora, adorning dusty mantelpieces throughout the continent. Yet, how will our young faces look at the end of 4,000 kilometres? What in the world will we all be thinking? (Gray: 39)

Soon after the departure, the group splits due to unfavorable travel conditions and Gray remains alone. This event contributes to kindling a shift in perspective, passing from a Western-centripetal focus – the group of walkers as conquerors of the Great Wall – toward the author's subjective interiority (and his Maori background):

> The race is solely with myself. And like a baby who falls flat on his face when learning to walk, the most important thing is to get back up and try again. The Maori – a warrior race renowned for never giving up have a

similar saying: *Whitu ki raro, waro ki runga. Seven times down, eight times up*. (Gray: 212)

Concerning the type of journey, Gray's experience is similar to Arnaud's, who also walked in remote regions of China. At the same time, Gray's shift in perspective mirrors Luc Richard's experience, narrated in his *Voyage à travers la Chine interdite* (2003). Richard was dragged onto a car journey from Beijing to Tibet by his friend Constantin de Slizewicz (it must be specified that their two tales recount different journeys) and two other companions. In the beginning of the book, Richard warns readers that "I didn't know anything about it [China], but he [de Slizewicz] had mentioned these things so many times to me"[111] (8; author's translation). This implies that Richard's persona initially revolves around a fully Western-centered stance, and in the text, it comes often to coincide with a plural "We" that includes all the members of the expedition. Yet, almost at the end of the journey the group needs to split for logistic reasons (Lao Shi, Xia Jia Xia and de Slizewicz have to wait for some components of the car to be replaced) and Richard remains alone travelling through the western region of China, up to Kashgar. It is at this time that he is compelled (similarly to Gray) to become the real protagonist of his own account: "Leaving Xia Jia and Constantin in the station hall, I had the impression of starting a journey within the journey. I knew that this time, if anything happened to me, I could only rely on myself"[112] (188; author's translation).

Finally, coming back to Gray, his experience can be seen as a metaphor of de Slizewicz's escape from a too Westernized China toward what is perceived as a more authentic way of living. Both Gray and de Slizewicz spent quite a long time in the Middle Kingdom and, to an extent, Gray shares de Slizewicz's argument about the necessity to plunge into a country in order to fully appreciate it. Gray arrived to contend in the interview that "some expatriates may live in a country for years, but be so sheltered from its actual realities they don't actually have a clue as to what is really going on." This implies, again, a qualification of the dwelling as not a temporal matter but the ability and will "'to become' someone else's culture"[113] in Gray's own words. The point on which de Slizewicz and Gray's perspectives diverge is in the epistemological value they project onto their travelling experiences. Initially, Gray's intention was to walk the 4,000 kilometers in one go, but he soon realized that the plan was so demanding that he had to stop, take a rather long break (he went back to New Zealand, where he lives, and also accomplished other trips around Asia) and then go back to China to complete the walk. It is because of that that Gray was able to shift from a Western-centripetal stance to a more personal one. What is most remarkable is that, according to Gray, the breaking up of the experience helped him to understand China and Chinese better once he was back in the Middle Kingdom. These

[111] "Je n'en connaissais rien, mais il m'en avait tellement parlé."
[112] "En laissant Xia Jia et Constantin dans le hall de la gare, j'avais l'impression d'entreprendre un voyage dans le voyage. Je savais que cette fois, s'il m'arrivait quelque chose, je ne pourrais compter que sur moi-même."
[113] Nathan Gray, interview by Stefano Calzati, September 30, 2013, email.

were his words in the interview: "I realized how much more I had learnt going back to places after a few months' break, having explored places like Cambodia, Laos, Thailand and India during those breaks, which gave me a far greater awareness of the context China is set in, in Asia in general." Here Gray suggests that it was thanks to the decision to let some time pass and distance separate himself from China that he was later able to "read" the country and its people more clearly. Of course, this might be also symptomatic of Gray's attempt to find legitimization for his need to interrupt the walk (an attempt he shares with other travel writers, as we will see). However, the crucial point to stress is that Gray's vision is rather different from de Slizewicz's, in that for the latter it is only by remaining in the hosting culture and negotiating every day the struggle that diversity entails, that one can really understand the Other. By contrast, Gray supports the need to find the "right distance" from oneself and the other-culture so that one can put judgments into focus. Eventually, for Gray understanding a country seems, above all, a matter of individual disposition; one that, by being based on spiritual connections among the people, is able to overcome any cultural gap (reason why his Maori background becomes central to the travelogue). "Home," then, intended as a space of familiarity, is anywhere the traveler is able to empathize with the others around him and feel accepted. It is no coincidence that Gray reminded me in the interview that, before going to China, he "had already travelled through nearly 50 countries, most times solo, and knew how to survive in a context where I was going from one place to the next in a nomadic day-to-day fashion." In this way, he not only stressed his ability to establish (social and empathic) connections wherever he goes, but also projected onto himself the aura of the "eternal traveller." Lastly, he overtly declared how he achieved getting in contact with locals when walking the Great Wall: "my interactions were hugely inspired by my Maori side, which encourages loving others and being appreciative at all costs." Hence, the extent to which Gray's conception of the contact with the other and the plunging into the hosting culture is a matter, above all, of spirituality and intimacy becomes clearer: to understand China and the Chinese is not, in the first place, a question of acquiring a certain amount of knowledge, but to open oneself to the people, communicate with them, listen to them. It is through such un-mediated exchange that the spiritual ethos of the journey can be fully realized, breaking down all the cultural or ideological paradigms that could constrain the experience.

Finally, Sergio Ramazzotti's position deserves to be discussed, as he unfolds a quite unique conception of the travel experience and its cultural value. In the interview, Ramazzotti argued that "very often, it is not necessary to visit a country in its wholeness in order to understand it; on the contrary, it is sometimes sufficient – and this holds true in particular for China, which is a huge country – to identify a place or a person that is paradigmatic of the country." The Italian author rejects the idea that being a long-term resident in a place is necessary in order to fully appreciate it and he also criticizes those writers who travel everywhere because they want to "see it all." Rather, Ramazzotti defends the potentiality of a short, sedentary travel experience, in comparison to an itinerant one. In doing so, he subverts the assumption at the base of travelling as a moving practice by claiming that it is when one stays still in one place that s/he can really grasp its *modus cogitandi*.[114] Surely, this attests (as in Gray's case) to Ramazzotti's need to find coherent legitimization for his (professional) choices. After all, Ramazzotti is a journalist who writes short reportages on assignment: hence his way of conceiving of travels and writing is very much driven by the material conditions at the base of such practices. It should not surprise that he specified: "I am well aware that this kind of journalism on assignment is the negation of the romantic idea of travel. For me, it is also a matter of time and economic resources." Here, then, Ramazzotti overtly demystifies a certain idealized idea of travelling and writing and acknowledges that nowadays one needs to find a compromise between time and money. Of course, this way of thinking of travel has consequences on its outcomes. When asked whether he felt he had grasped something relevant of the cultural, historical, and political momentum of China, Ramazzotti answered in the affirmative:

> I can say that that particular journey was illuminating; it showed me emblematic aspects of China's present and of its imminent future; this, despite the fact, as you mentioned, that I only visited Shaoshan. I am rather confident of this because the journey of which I speak in *La birra di Shaoshan* was not the first trip I made to China; I had already been there, and this allowed me to realize the rapid cultural and economic development of the country. In this respect, Shaoshan was surely a case in point, as in it you could find all the contradictions of Chinese society: passion and longing for the past, disillusion for the new socialism way, and all the factors that are nurturing even today its economic and cultural revolution: discipline, entrepreneurship, creativity, resilience, etc.

This passage is significant for two reasons. Firstly, Ramazzotti reveals that the journey he recounts in *La birra di Shaoshan* was not the first trip he had taken to China. In other words, he could be defined as a "returning traveller" and certainly one for whom China was not a complete novelty. At the same time, there is no mention in the text of any antecedent experience, nor comparisons between the different experiences (but this is possibly one reason why he keeps a demiurgic position within the text, as seen in Chapter 1). Secondly, the statement above is quite surprising when compared to various passages in the text, in which the author confesses to Celia his difficulty in understanding China (see Chapter 1). One could say that the incompatibility between what Ramazzotti told me in the interview and what is in the text is chiefly due to his willingness to inflate the positive outcomes of his experience. But to a certain extent it is also possible to argue that both positions are valid. On the one hand, Ramazzotti feels unable to understand China when he faces a Chinese person; on the other hand, he suggests to his readership that such a difficulty is

---

[114] This, as we will see in Chapter 5, also characterizes the approach of some Chinese travel writers and gets close to a critical practice that is referred to in academia as "psychogeography."

precisely the emblem of contemporary China. [115] When talking to Celia, then, Ramazzotti is clinging (consciously or unconsciously) to the border that separates the urgency to know from an effective understanding of China; encountering the other, after all, does not straightforwardly mean to be able to read it. When talking to his readers, by contrast, the author draws back on secure cultural values that leads him to reframe the representation of China as a whole against what is perceived as familiar (i.e., the West, in particular Italy). It is not by chance that China is defined as a "mystery," a country which is unknowable; unknowable, of course, for all those who look at it from the outside. At this point, the question becomes: to what extent is this difficulty in understanding China related to the kind of travel experience accomplished? Or also: could a longer travel experience, or one that involved residing in the country, have modified this (Western-derived) perception? A univocal answer is certainly unwise. However, by comparing Ramazzotti's travelogue with others, one can draw some reflections. We have seen in Chapter 1 that Rob Gifford is rather willing to represent China according to a macro geopolitical confrontation with the West. This is so, despite the fact that he lived in China for many years, working as a journalist. Similarly, Thubron, who stayed in the country longer than Ramazzotti, still frames his experience within a West-East opposition. Escaping the alluring temptation to make sense of otherness by comparing it to what is already known seems, then, rather difficult (the writers who escape this tendency the most are Colin Legerton and Jacob Rawson). One possible explanation is that for travel authors their readership is very important because they know that they have to sell their stories at home. There is, therefore, out of necessity, a reassertion of precise ideological and cultural borders that distinguish home and away, insofar as the authors' main goal is to be understood and appreciated in their home countries. [116] It is worth noting, however, that Thubron reversed the relation West-China arguing that, despite all economic changes, "the character of the people has not changed. It is a much slower process; you do not change a culture by changing its economy. In fact, I think that China has been less Westernized than it has Chinatized the West." Thubron is the only writer among those interviewed who mentioned the possibility not only of a mutual influence between China and the West, but of a dominant position of the former over the latter. He did not develop this argument any further. Yet, even so its relevance is high because it implies the subversion of the relation of power between the two spheres, at least as they are represented by the majority of contemporary travel authors. In Gifford's opinion, for instance, it is the East that has to catch up with the West (xix); de Slizewicz, in turn, thinks of the Tibetan regions as a space of resistance, if not retreat, against the capitalist forces that have gradually affected China but whose origins remain in the West. Luc Richard also agreed with this: "the 'divide' [between the East and West of China], as you say in English, will increase, mainly from a social point of

---

[115] The analysis in the following chapter will show that this is a very common trope also in older travelogues about China.
[116] In this respect, Ramazzotti is, again, controversial. While in the text he manifests the awareness of writing for a precise target of readers (Italians), when questioned on this topic, he mentioned that "I do not think of the reader when I write."

view and in terms of quality of life"; then "there will be a new process of assimilation, of Tibet in particular, but more in general of all the ethnic minorities that populate the borderlands of China."[117] Richard's core idea is that, soon or later, all the regions of China will follow the way to Westernization. While there cannot be a univocal answer to that, it is significant that Richard's response to such a prediction rests on the (possibly consolatory) reaffirmation that in today's China there are still forbidden, inaccessible places (from which the title of the book derives): "The forbidden China I speak about is the one that foreigners cannot access. But 'forbidden' has also a metaphorical meaning. I mainly refer to the China that is usually not shown, the one that you do not want to see or visit." The main problem is that Richard's stance still coincides monolithically with that of a Western subject, so that China remains an object to look at from the outside, even when traversing it. More generally, none of the writers (with the partial exception of Legerton and Rawson) has granted an agency to China's cultural and ethnical diversities in their own right, nor envisioned the possibility of a mutual influence and interdependence between China and the West (apart from Thubron). This pattern is telling of the (re-)emergence, despite and beyond all discourses informing globalization and global mobility, of precise cultural and ideological boundaries when it comes to the (Western-inspired) representation of China. The Middle Kingdom, in fact, is still widely considered as the "Elsewhere"[118] against which to assess the West's state of (negative or positive) advancement, in order to supply the background for the confirmation/critique of all that is familiar to (many) of these authors surveyed (and their readers). In so doing, to China is denied an active role on the global stage and/or the possibility to trace its own destiny independently from the West.

***

To conclude, the analysis is complemented with the investigation of how travel bloggers rearticulate their concepts of "home" and "away" and their sense of belonging or alienation in relation to China. Again, the distinction between travel bloggers on platforms and individual ones brings with itself substantial nuances. It suffices to refer to the Appendix to realize that the greatest majority of travel bloggers on platforms conceive of their trips as "escapes" from the daily routine. As such, the journeys are usually brief and well defined in both space and time. The main purpose is to live and taste something different from what can be found at home – fulfilling the desire of exoticism that tourism fuels – and then go back to all that is familiar – and recount the experience. The main exception within this scenario is Ataritouchme (who has been living in China for years now) and it is from him that it is worth starting the discussion. Ataritouchme seems to embody de Slizewicz's specular positioning, insofar as he affirmed the following:

---

[117] Luc Richard, interview by Stefano Calzati, December 5, 2014, Skype.
[118] A concept that will also return in the travel writers of the first half of the 20th century, who will be analyzed in the following chapter.

I live in China. What it comes down to now is: "where have I not yet been in China? Is there anything – even third, fourth or fifth tier – that I would like to see there?" Keeping the "travel gaze" is a bit difficult, for sure; almost every city in China looks the same (that is, like my home city here). But the food is always different, the language (at least slightly) different, the people often nicer (I live in the northeast, famous for brusque personalities).

On the one hand, Ataritouchme argues in favor of a loss of surprise when travelling around China – a country he knows very well by now; on the other hand, however, it is precisely this condition of permanency in China that allows him, as a resident-traveler, to notice those subtle differences that can still astonish the acquainted eye. The passing of time, then, acquires an ambivalent role: it dilutes the impact that otherness has on the traveler and also forces the traveler to seek different destination and kinds of otherness. Time thickens China, which is not, then, something given but is always reconfigured by the traveler's gaze, as if, after all, differences were nothing but what one considers – i.e. is able to see – as such. It is for this reason that the blogger usually feels the need to postpone the writing much later than the return: at stake, again, is not the mere quantitative passing of time but the qualitative effect that time has on memories. Similarly, this leads to a distinction between the inbound traveler, whose experience is chronotopically well defined, and the resident-traveler, who, having more expertise and competences at his/her disposal, learns to identify those small details that occasional travelers cannot perceive. On this issue, Ataritouchme specified the following:

> My idea of China now is probably far too complex for me to voice in words – thousands and thousands of words wouldn't do it – but I can say that travelling has certainly shaped it. In general, though, most visitors to China are really missing out if they don't go west. Many only make it to Xi'an and, while different, it's not really enough.

If one unpacks Ataritouchme's statement, it is possible to reflect on the blogger's idea of travel, as well as on his perception of China. To begin with, Ataritouchme affirms that it was his various travels around China that made him perceive the country as extremely complex. Therefore, travels do have for Ataritouchme epistemological value, although what they do is to put the traveler in contact with something that is almost impossible to describe in its complexity. The apparent paradox is that this is a similar conclusion that other travel authors, as seen above, also reach. However, it would not be wise to equate all positions. While the representation of China as an impenetrable world, which authors such as Ramazzotti, Thubron, or Gifford provide, rests on the ultimate resistance to thinking of the Middle Kingdom in isolation, thus beyond a macro cultural opposition, Ataritouchme favors an immanent representation: one that strives not to transcend China's borders. In this sense, similarly to de Slizewicz, Ataritouchme marks a cultural, internal distinction between East and West of China, which goes hand in hand with a historical and economical divide. Regions and cities on the coast are much more developed than those inland. According to

Ataritouchme, however, this tendency has not (yet) affected China's cultural diversity, so, while his home city is certainly the same as many others around the country, there is still a heterogeneous cultural background, in terms of language, food and traditions, to be explored. This is where de Slizewicz's heavily politicized vision – Westernized China as opposed to minority cultures – is deconstructed from the inside by Ataritouchme, for whom otherness and differences can still be retraced everywhere in China, as long as one is able to decipher it. Home for Ataritouchme is the security of everything that is equal to itself; yet, it is enough to go beyond one's hometown to disrupt such homogeneity and feel to be in another place. Lastly, in the passage above, the blogger indirectly distinguishes himself from those one-time visitors, whose travel itineraries are usually confined to the well-beaten path on the east side of China. By contrast, he not only explored the Western regions but also went there many times, learning, on each occasion, to appreciate the diversity that China has to offer. Here, at last, Ataritouchme moves a silent critique against the commoditized contemporary way of travelling, to which he prefers one that is more independent and unbound.

As for individual travel bloggers, we can see that Curieuse Voyageuse unfolds a controversial positioning in relation to the condition of travelling and writing. Concerning the difference between travelling as a resident and doing it as a traveler, she said: "It changes completely: when you travel for a day or a week, you do not have time to really get to know the country or develop relationships with the local population. By contrast, when you live in one place, you have all the time to do that!" Despite the fact that she dwelled in China for two years and she blogged about it, Curieuse Voyageuse seems to return to a structuralist conception of travel. Indeed, she distinguishes the travel experience from the resident one based upon a temporal and spatial fracture: travel is shorter and it is such only to faraway places. On the "About" page on her blog (2009), however, she does defend the possibility of keeping a "travel gaze" also when in the country of permanent residence (which at present is France). This contradiction was not disentangled in the interview, where she remained quite vague on the possibility that a sedentary experience would be more productive than an itinerant one for reading otherness. An answer, however, can be detected on her blog. After having travelled widely in China, it is only when she settled down in Shanghai that the blogger opened a section on her blog called "Portrait de Chine" (trans. "Portrait of China"), in which she posted interviews with Chinese friends or with people she met during her daily life in China. It could be said, then, that Curieuse Voyageuse began to really "see" Shanghai and its citizens – and them to see her – only once the blogger moved and settled there. So, the question becomes: to what extent is Shanghai really perceived as home? On the occasion of her return to France, Curieuse Voyageuse wrote a post titled "Comment garde-t-on un oeil voyageur dans son propre pays?" in which she felt the need to explore the possibility of keeping a travel gaze once one is back in his/her country of origin. It is remarkable that such questioning came at the very moment of leaving Shanghai, so that any straightforward definition of Shanghai as the blogger's home should be, at least, suspended. Indeed, what this self-reflection reveals is that it is France that is (still) perceived as home: this country is so familiar to the blogger that she wonders whether she can live in and blog about it with sufficiently attentive eyes. By contrast,

China, despite having been the blogger's home for some years, is still conceived as another-place. It is also notable that a year later Curieuse Voyageuse wrote another post in which she affirms that it is, in fact, possible to keep a travel gaze also at home (i.e., in Paris). The writing, then, disjoins from the effective accomplishment of a journey. While probably constituting an attempt to legitimize her blogging also after the return and the settling in Europe, such claim also proves the extent to which the blogger's permanence in China has affected her perception of France as home; or also, as a country (still or again) able to entice surprise and fascination.

Finally, Becki is the blogger in whom the interplay between travelling and writing reaches a conflating point. All boundaries between physical or imaginative concepts of home, between journeys as a resident or as a *stricto sensu* traveler, and between sedentary or itinerant experiences are blurred. As seen, Becki is an ongoing traveler who has been journeying continuously around the world over the last few years. It could be said that Becki appears as much a "global soul" (Iyer 2000) as a nomad soul: that is, a subject who does not anchor herself to any precise location. As a consequence, she is an ongoing writer as well and certainly one of the few to write *while* travelling. This is so precisely because her being constantly on the road erases any possibility of electing a specific place in which to accomplish the writing. "I update Facebook, Twitter and Instagram daily and post at least one article on my blog per week. I always try to find my own unique story when I am there," she said in the interview. "There" stands, of course, for anywhere she fancies going; the idea of uniqueness, then, applies not only to the writing (as discussed in the previous chapters), but also to her travel's flexibility, as well as to the places she reaches (for instance in 2015 she managed to go to North Korea). Through this statement, one also understands the crucial aspect of Becki's travel blogging. Her being an eternal traveler and writer seems to have triggered a paradox: far from freeing Becki from temporal and spatial constraints, these two statuses have serialized the practices of travelling and writing. In other words, it is precisely at the moment in which travelling and writing become the travel blogger's life that they ask to be strictly organized, if not drained out of that serendipitous sense that runs through others' amateur blogs and fuels others' travelers' personae.

CONCLUSION

In this chapter, many of the texts considered in this volume were connected with the interviews conducted with the writers. The aim was to address the pragmatic features of the travel writing genre by investigating the interplay between travelling and writing as practices, thus unveiling the conditions and reasons that guide them. Concerning the writing, authors and bloggers manifested the need to accomplish it a certain time after the experience. This is particularly surprising in the case of travel bloggers, insofar as the medial format they use invites almost immediate writing. The discussion on the writing also led to question the distinction between amateur and professional writers. From the interviews, it emerged that the great majority of authors think of themselves as travel writers (or journalists). Concerning bloggers, instead, the picture is more ambivalent. While those hosted on platforms have trouble defining themselves as writers – due to the fact that their blogging is usually functional to simply keep memory of the events – each individual blogger builds a self-representation that is a negotiation, rather than an exclusive choice, between the amateur and professional realms. This also destabilizes those assumptions about blogging as a chiefly amateur practice, which derive from early studies on blogs (as seen in the Introduction).[119] Epitomizing in this regard is the case of blogger Becki who abandoned her alias in favor of her real name when she launched her new blog, ultimately sanctioning the passage from an amateur to a professional conception of her online activity. More generally, while bloggers on platforms perceive their writing as amateur – an aspect that also explains the flatness of their accounts, as witnessed in Chapters 1 and 2 – individual bloggers put a great effort into their writing and strive to professionalize it, even when this remains unpaid.

Concerning the travelling practice, the comparison among and between travel blogs and travel books shed a light onto how travel writers think of (and plan) their journeys. On the one hand, this involved assessing how writers see themselves along the spectrum traveler-tourist. As remarked by previous studies on tourism and travel writing, a neat distinction between these two terms is by now untenable. Yet, it is possible to see a polarization between authors and bloggers: the former (still) attach their own personae to the "traveller" label, while the latter manifest more ambivalent positions. While bloggers on platforms straightforwardly define themselves as tourists – and do not feel urged to qualify their being tourists in any respect – individual travel bloggers tend to bridge the gap (if any) that separates the tourist from the traveler, by unfolding hybrid positions and self-representations. On the other hand, the discussion on travelling as a practice compelled to unpack the conceptual validity of the loop "home-away-home" that usually characterizes travel in its abstract form. The analysis showed that such a loop, far from identifying a recursive pattern, is practically remodeled in various ways. Each travel writer positions him/herself in relation to at least three coordinates: 1) the possibility to travel either for a short period (Ramazzotti and many travel bloggers) or a long one (Thubron, Legerton and Rawson, de Slizewicz, Robjstaples, Becki); 2) being residents in China (Legerton and Rawson, de Slizewicz, Robjstaples, Ataritouchme, etc.) or travelers *stricto sensu* (Thubron, Ramazzotti, Supermary58, Mathieu, Gattosandro Viaggiatore, etc.); and 3) the favoring of sedentary experiences (Ramazzotti and partially Curieuse Voyageuse) or itinerant ones (the majority of the travel writers). Aside from the number of options, what is most important to note is that each author charges the notions of "home" and "away" with precise cultural and ideological values, thus resisting any attempt to

---

[119] In the 2003 Nieman report it is also possible to read that "many traditional journalists are dismissive of bloggers, describing them as self-interested or unskilled amateurs. Conversely, many bloggers look upon mainstream media as an arrogant, elitist club that puts its own version of self-interest and economic survival above the societal responsibility of a free press." Here, a sharp distinction between professionals and amateurs is openly asserted: under the latter term are subsumed features of honesty and independence, as much as incompetence and approximation, while the former is synonymous with quality, precision and accuracy but also limited freedom. This vision has become largely unsustainable nowadays, insofar as the blurring between online blogs and traditional media is much more accentuated than a decade ago and traditional journalists and native bloggers have deeply influenced each other.

classify their experiences according to a taxonomic classification of travels that draws upon fixed space-time coordinates. This also highlighted the rhetorical strategies to which authors resort when trying to make sense of the experience (of the Other) in terms of what is known and familiar. Interestingly, there is widespread compliance with the framing of China and the Chinese within a Western-inspired and Western-oriented perspective, even when the writer has lived in China at length. The majority of these writers cannot help but look at China from "home," be it a real or putative place, and not rarely do they come to perceive the Middle Kingdom as a "mystery" and an impenetrable country.

The following chapter will assess how "older" travel writings about China coincide with and differ from contemporary ones, particularly in terms of the representation of the country and the travelers.

CHAPTER 4

Looking Back at "Classic" Western Travel Writing

In this chapter, the synchronic trajectory that has hitherto guided the transmedial analysis of contemporary travel books and travel blogs is abandoned. The purpose is to adopt a diachronic perspective that will allow us to explore the historical evolution of Western-authored travel books about China. Nonetheless, the analysis will draw upon the theoretical tenets that have been developed in the first part of the work, particularly with regard to: 1) the narrative discourse and its ideological implications; 2) the hypertextual and peritextual features of texts; and 3) the chronotope of photography. The aim is, on the one hand, to assess if travel writing has undergone substantial changes in terms of its generic/rhetorical features, and, on the other hand, to understand if the representation that Western travelers provide of themselves, as well as of China, has changed over time.

The analysis refers to a dozen travelogues in English, French, and Italian covering a period of roughly a century: from the 1890s to the 1980s. Isabella Bird's *The Yangtze Valley and Beyond* (1899)[120] constitutes the oldest referenced text, while Luigi Malerba's *Cina Cina* (1985)[121] is the most recent one. The boundaries of this temporal framework are not arbitrary, but respond to precise historical factors. As briefly mentioned in Chapter 1, it is at the end of the 19th century that China became a tourist destination, attracting Westerners who wanted to enjoy the country's imperial allure and witness its socio-political changes. At the other end of the spectrum, it is in the late 1980s and early 1990s that China put an end to its geopolitical self-closure and returned to be the target of an increasing number of tourists. Moreover, the choice to extend the analysis to the 1980s is motivated by the fact that the "oldest"

---

[120] Isabella Bishop Bird (1831-1904) was a British novelist and travel writer, also known for her journeys in Australia, the US, and Japan. In this travel book, enriched with several pictures taken by the author, she recounts her long journey in the Middle Kingdom, in particular along the east coast and following the Yangtze River from east toward the Tibetan plateau. The journey was accomplished in 1896-7 and the book represents Bird's last major travelogue.

[121] Luigi Malerba (1927-2008) was an Italian poet and novelist. He wrote the travelogue *Cina Cina* (trans. *China China*), published in 1985. The book derives from the journey that Malerba made to the post-Mao China in 1980, together with other Italian writers, including Vittorio Sereni and Alberto Arbasino. By reading *Cina Cina* it is difficult to retrace precisely the itinerary followed by the Italian delegation, because Malerba writes very short chapters about small details of Chinese daily life. Among the titles of the pieces that compose the travelogue we find "Le diecimila cose" (trans. "The Ten Thousand Things"), "Tempo circolare" (trans. "Circular time"), and "Il piacere della ripetizione" (trans. "The pleasure of Repetition"). It is ascertained that Malerba visited Beijing, Hangzhou, Shanghai, and Suzhou, thus largely complying with the itineraries that the Chinese authorities prescribed to foreign visitors. The book does not contain any pictures.

travelogue analyzed in the first part of this work – Colin Thubron's *Behind the Wall* – dates back to 1987: hence, the historical overview provided here eventually catches up with the temporal outer limits of what have hitherto been characterized as "contemporary travelogues." Overall, the temporal frame surveyed can be divided into two segments: the years from 1899 to 1949 mark a period of political turmoil in China, with the fall of the last imperial dynasty and the birth of the Republic, but also the wars against Japan and the fight between Communists and Nationalists, which ended with the victory of the former and the rise to power of Mao Zedong. To this first segment belong texts such as *Westward to the Far East* (1900)[122] by US-American Eliza Scidmore, *A Woman in China* (1914)[123] by Australian Mary Gaunt, *Peking Dust* (1919)[124] by US-American Ellen LaMotte, *Voyage d'une parisienne à Lhassa* ([1927] 2008)[125] by Belgian-French Alexandra David-Neel, *Forbidden Journey: From Peking to Kashmir* ([1937] 2003)[126] by Swiss Ella Maillart, *Travels in Tartary: One's Company and News from Tartary* (1941),[127] two travelogues by British Peter Fleming, and *Shark's Fins and Millet* (1944)[128] by Polish-born writer Ilona Sues. After that, the proclamation of the People's Republic of China (PRC) in 1949 paved the way to almost four decades of isolation of the country, especially with

---

[122] Eliza Scidmore (1856-1928) was a journalist and writer. This travelogue, a sort of travel guide, was first released in 1892 but it became so popular that it was reprinted several times (the edition referred to here dates 1900). Many drawings are interpolated into the text.

[123] Mary Gaunt (1861-1942) travelled in China in 1913-4. At that time the Boxer Rebellion and the fall of the Qing Dynasty had just occurred, leaving the country in a state of profound instability. Gaunt (also a novelist) is well known for her travelogues about the West Indies and West Africa. Many pictures accompany the text.

[124] US-American journalist and author Ellen LaMotte (1873-1961) stayed in Beijing for a few months in 1919, dwelling within the delegation quarter. She also travelled to the southern regions of China for a few weeks. In this book, the author shows some political concern about China's political situation, but overall her stay is presented as a leisure experience.

[125] The book also appeared in English in 1927 with the title *My Journey to Lhasa*. Alexandra David-Neel (1868-1969), an explorer and writer, narrates her endeavor to reach and access the city of Lhasa, which at that time was forbidden to foreigners. She accomplished the journey together with her adopted son Yongden, who was a lama. This chapter refers to both the 2008 French edition and the 2005 English edition: the former comes without pictures, while the latter has illustrations in it. Moreover, the two texts present different versions of the introduction.

[126] Ella Maillart (1903-1997) was an explorer and journalist. In *Forbidden Journey* she recounts the crossing of Tartary that she accomplished in 1935 together with British journalist Peter Fleming. At that time several conflicts among Chinese warlords affected the whole region. The 2003 edition of the book referred to here comes without illustrations (it is ascertained, however, that Maillart took pictures along the road).

[127] Peter Fleming (1907-1971) was a journalist and a writer. The book *Travels in Tartary* collects two different travel accounts: the first one – *One's Company* – recounts the journey that Fleming made in China in 1933, which led him to witness the fights between the Nationalists and the Communists; the second one – *News from Tartary* – was accomplished in 1935. On this second occasion Fleming travelled together with Maillart toward Xinjiang region, until reaching India. The 1941 edition of *Travels in Tartary* is a monomodal book.

[128] Ilona Sues reached China in 1936 as a freelance reporter. At that time, the Japanese invasion of China was looming. Sues, also an expert on the issue of the opium trade, visited the frontline of both the Nationalists and the Communists and hoped for a joint collaboration against the Japanese. Many pictures inserted in the middle of the book document Sues's acquaintance with Generals from both sides.

regard to Western countries. Accessing the Middle Kingdom during these years meant either being invited by the Chinese government, or relying upon the China Tourism Agency, which arranged the whole stay. The texts analyzed here referring to the period 1949-1985 – second segment – all bear, to various degrees, the mark of the impossibility of freely moving around the country. Apart from Malerba's *Cina Cina*, the analysis focuses on: *Io in Russia e in Cina* (1958)[129] by Italian Curzio Malaparte, *Cara Cina* ([1966] 1972)[130] by Italian Goffredo Parise, and *Travels in China* (2012)[131] by French Roland Barthes. The selection of the texts is by no means exhaustive, but it ideally covers each decade of the whole temporal frame and it takes into account texts in the three languages surveyed.

***

When it comes to the investigation of pre-modern and modern Western-authored travelogues about China, the corpus of studies is substantial. Concerning the study of late 19th and early 20th century travel writings, Kerr and Kuehn (2007: 6) discern two main axes of research: "one field [of enquiry] asks 'literary' questions about form, genre and tradition, (narrative) voice and modality, and fictionality. Another field focuses on the 'factual' and discursive side of the travel text." However blurred such distinction might be, the bridging of these two fields is, in fact, one of the aims of the first part of the present study, as well as of this chapter. To be sure, focusing on the "represented" China – that is, the written China of travelers – does not mean exclusively embracing a discursive perspective that denies the existence of a "real" China: a China that was physically there and constituted, over time, the reference point for the travelers. Hayot, Saussy, and Yao (2007: viii) are right when they warn that "the intricacies of the relationship between various written Chinas – the texts –

---

[129] Curzio Malaparte (1898-1957), an Italian journalist and novelist, wrote the book *Io in Russia e in Cina* (trans. *Me in Russia and China*), which was published posthumously in 1958. In this travel reportage Malaparte recounts the journey he made in 1957 to Russia and China, which had just witnessed the birth of the People's Republic. He was invited to China for the commemoration of the writer Lu Xun. He visited the main cities and archaeological sites around the country. At the core of Malaparte's account is the encounter he had with Chairman Mao Zedong, whose veracity remains, however, unsure.

[130] Goffredo Parise (1929-1986) was an Italian journalist and writer. In 1966 Parise went to China and published a series of articles for the newspaper *Corriere della Sera* which were later collected in a book titled *Cara Cina* (trans. *Dear China*. The edition to which this work refers is the one released in 1972 by Einaudi). Parise reached China when the Cultural Revolution was at full steam. Although Parise rejected Communism altogether, he remained fascinated by China's history and culture. Parise is one of the few Italian writers of the period who went to China alone, relying for his trip on the China Travel Agency. He visited the major and most developed cities: Guangdong, Beijing, Nanjing, Hong Kong. The book does not include any pictures or illustrations.

[131] Roland Barthes (1915-1980) filled three carnets on the occasion of his journey to China, from the 11th of April to the 4th of May 1974. *Carnets du voyage en Chine* (released in France in 2009 and translated into English by Andrew Brown in 2012 with the title *Travels in China*) gathers all of Barthes's travel notes. The French philosopher was part of a delegation composed of Philippe Sollers, Julia Kristeva, Marcelin Pleynet, and François Wahl. It is uncertain whether Barthes had planned to publish his *Carnets* as they are: indeed, they largely constitute a set of short comments and sketches, in the spirit of a private diary. They have been released without any editorial adjustments.

and the nation/culture known simply as 'China' – their main shared context – are so complex as to be nearly unspeakable. China is spoken in many idioms at times overlapping and at times mutually hostile ones." In order not to privilege one side – the textual over the other – the geo-cultural – it is necessary to look at what is (or is not) in the texts (for example, notations of historical events and autobiographical information, but also the discursive strategies adopted), as well as to contextualize each account within the cultural and historical background that surrounds it. Nicholas Clifford (2001: 2) reminds us of the importance of always bringing the ethos of the text to the surface: "that means examining not only the ways in which China was described for the readerships back home, but also the reasons why particular forms of representation were chosen and the ways in which those forms reflected changes taking place both in China itself and in the societies from which the traveller came." Put differently, each representation of China is always and necessarily the result of the interplay between the cultural, and historical conditions of the country at a given moment in time, as well as the traveler's own background and attitudes. This is why Kerr and Kuehn (2007: 5) specify that positive or negative perceptions of China cannot be uniformly applied to any specific historical period; on the contrary, they have to be inscribed into their own time (and within the author's biography) in order to be assessed and understood.

Here the attempt is to outline convergences and divergences – in terms of rhetorical and medial characteristics – among travelogues from different decades and to rescue the singularity of each work, intended as the outcome of a precise authorial vision. To be challenged is the tendency – from which Clifford's *A Truthful Impression of the Country* does not fully escape – to derive linear, homogeneous macro-trajectories of evolution specifically concerning: 1) how travel writing as a genre has evolved; 2) the way in which China has been represented; and 3) how the travelers have represented themselves. Using Peter Hulme's (1986: 12) words dedicated to the investigation of "colonial encounters," we could say that the aim and ethos of the chapter are archaeological: "no smooth history emerges, but rather a series of fragments which, read speculatively, hint at a story that can never be fully recovered." In fact, the present analysis will portray a heterogeneous textual landscape made of synchronic differences, as well as diachronic similarities; a landscape that contests any coherent reconstruction and reasserts, *a posteriori*, the irreducible uniqueness of each text.

Despite some degrees of overlap, the chapter is divided into three main sections, each of which addresses a specific theme: travel writing as a genre; the representation of Chinese history, landscape, and people; the (self)representation of the travelers. In each section, the analysis follows a chronological trajectory, starting from the oldest travelogues and moving onwards through the 20th century. In so doing, connections will be made with the contemporary travelogues previously analyzed, bringing to light the uneven (and maybe unsettling) continuity and discrepancies with older texts.

HAS THE TRAVEL WRITING GENRE EVOLVED?

The first issue concerns the generic features of the selected travel books. More precisely, this section offers a survey of the texts, focusing on their literary elements, how the narrative discourse is shaped, and the effects it produces. Even a cursory reading of the travelogues reveals that their literary form is often a combination of sub-genres, styles, and discourses. In this sense, similarly to contemporary authors, late 19th and early 20th century travel writers draw upon a variety of registers to give shape to their accounts. For example, Ellen LaMotte's *Peking Dust* and Ilona Sues's *Shark's Fins and Millet* present a heterogeneous collage of newspaper articles, private letters, and quotations from other texts. Sues, in particular, acknowledges this by warning the reader that the book is "a medley of everything, as unorthodox as life itself" (1944: 6). On the same lines, Isabella Bird's *The Yangtze Valley and Beyond* is, in the words of the author, a set of materials "consist[ing] of journal letters, photographs and notes from a brief diary" (1899: vii). Another example comes from David-Neel's *My Journey to Lhasa* (2005). In the opening pages, which serve as a historical framework to motivate the author's decision to enter the forbidden city of Lhasa, David-Neel enriches the text with quotes from a variety of texts, such as the work of the English monk Edmund Candler, who remembers that the capital "has not always been closed to strangers. Until the end of the 18th century, only physical obstacles stood in the way of an entry to the capital"[132] (David-Neel 2005: xxxiv). These examples demonstrate that these texts are the result of substantial research (which either anticipates or follows the journey); most importantly, they reveal the intrinsic hypertextuality of the accounts in that the mix of registers and sources is overtly acknowledged. This means not only, as already argued, that hypertextuality does go beyond a mere matter of medium, but that it cannot be confined to contemporary publications either.

Secondly, one understands from the authors' own voices that their texts underwent a radical rewriting and/or editing process, in order to arrange all the materials at disposal. It suffices to compare, for instance, Bird's minimal diary notes, which she sometimes included in her book as a form of self-quotation, with the final version of what is recounted. Below is how she recounts the arrival at a dormitory:

> My door was broken down with much noise and yells of "Foreign devil!" "Horse-racer!" "Child-eater!" but an official, arriving in the nick of time, prevented further damage. He ought to have appeared an hour and a half before. The entry in my diary for that evening was, "Wretched evening; riotous crowd; everything anxious and odious; noises; too cold to sleep." My lamp sputtered and went out, and my matches were too damp to strike. It is objectionable to be in the dark, you know not where, with walls absolutely precarious, and in the midst of the coarse shouts of rough men to hear a feeble accompaniment of rats eating one's few things. (Bird: 246)

---

[132] In the English edition this excerpt is fully contained in a footnote, while in the French edition Edmund Candler's words are reported in the text and then the reference to his book is given in a footnote.

This quotation attests to Bird's reworking of her notes and the inclusion in the text of personal (fictionalized) anecdotes that go well beyond what was contained in her diary. Overall, however, the first-person stance from which the account is narrated is counterbalanced by Bird's effort to deliver a "truthful impression of the country" (viii), which translates into an objectification of the account. For instance, in the first chapter one finds detailed notations regarding the characteristics of the Yangtze basin:

> Geographically the Yangtze Valley, or drainage area, may be taken as extending from the 90th to the 122nd meridian of east longitude and as including all or most of the most important provinces of SZE CHUAN, HUPEII, HUNAN, KIANGSI, NGANHUI, KIANGSU and HONAN. Its area is estimated at about 650,000 square miles, and its populations, one of the most peaceful and industrious on earth, at from 170,000,000 and 180,000,000. (Bird: 1)

The portrayal of the Yangtze valley in terms of geopolitical features is functional, not only to provide verifiable data *per se* (and implicitly reassert the author's competence over the subject), but also to clear the ground of the presence of autochthons, who are, *de facto*, turned into numbers. The Chinese people who live in the valley are barely mentioned and, when this happens, they are described as "peaceful" and "industrious," two adjectives that make of them a homogeneous mass of people and imply the relative ease of governing them. This, as we will see, responds to a specific political agenda of the author, notably the will to show that the British Empire can and should continue to have a leading role in China's affairs (the Opium Wars were still recent).

It is remarkable how those passages in Bird's text that provide accurate data about China echo vividly the many informative descriptions that characterize the seminal travelogue *The Travels of Marco Polo*. Below is a comparison of the two excerpts that Polo and Bird dedicate to today's Hangzhou (known as "Kinsay" by Polo and "Hangchow" by Bird):

> In this city, there are 12 guilds of different crafts, and each guild has 12,000 houses in the occupation of its workmen. All these craftsmen had full employment since many other cities of the kingdom are supplied by this city. Both men and women are fair and comely, and for the most part clothe themselves in silk, so vast is the supply of that material, both from the whole district of Kinsay and from the imports by traders from other provinces. All the streets of the city are paved with stone or brick, as indeed are all the highways throughout this area so that you ride and travel in every direction without inconvenience. (Polo 1958: 217)

> The "west-end" streets are, however, broad, light, well flagged, and incredibly clean for China. Hangchow impresses one with a general sense of well-being. Everything in the city and neighbourhood suggests silk. In all the adjacent country, the mulberry tree is omnipresent in expectation of a greatly

increased demand for this staple product. There are 7000 handlooms for the weaving of silk in Hangchow, employing 28,000 people. (Bird: 37)

The similarity between these two passages literally makes the time gap of more than 800 years that divides *The Travels of Marco Polo* and *The Yangtze Valley and Beyond* collapse. More specifically, these two pieces manifest the same tendency to objectify the places and people visited and show the extent to which the (Western) desire to map and commoditize China is shared between different epochs (what changes, rather, is the consequence of such desire: peer trading for Polo, colonial purposes for Bird).

In fact, Bird's goal is to make her text useful for both a popular readership at home and those people who were directly involved in the commercial exploitation of the Yangtze basin. As Susan Morgan (2007: 118) rightly points out, the Yangtze represented "an economic promise for British merchants and investors [due] to its appropriate international position." The underpinning logic of Bird's text, which reflects the historical ethos of what has been defined "the scramble for China"[133], is that China's natural resources could be, and indeed needed to be, managed by the British. The author's concluding remarks to her book are particularly telling:

> China is certainly at the dawn of a new era. Whether the twentieth century shall place her where she ought to be, in the van of Oriental nations, or whether it shall witness her disintegration and decay, depends very largely on the statesmanship and influence of Great Britain. (Bird: 544)

Here, Bird abandons any form of "detached" accounting and a patronizing tone emerges. Readers are not simply confronted with "the impressions received in fifteen months of journeyings" (Bird: 520), but with the manifest call for a major political involvement of the British Empire in China. These impressions, therefore, serve to support Bird's political agenda which is also, coincidentally, the British agenda as the dedication of the book to K. G. Marquess of Salisbury – who had been three times Prime Minister of the United Kingdom and four times Foreign Secretary – also attests.

Another example of Bird's defense of the British role in China occurs when she touches upon the delicate issue of the opium trade. Firstly, she diplomatically overlooks Britain's role: "I shall not touch on the history of the growth and use of opium in China" (497); later, she suggests that the spreading of opium was largely due to the indolence of Chinese people: "Outside of commercial pursuits an overpowering shadow of dullness rests on Chinese as upon much of Oriental life. All make the blissful dreams and the oblivion of the opium pipe greatly to be desired" (Bird: 514). Most importantly, it is by remarking the (supposed) passive attitude toward the life of the Chinese, that the author claims the necessity to intervene in the

---

[133] Following the Opium Wars and alongside the weakening of the Qing Dynasty, at the end of the 19th century. China increasingly became the target of Western powers, whose intentions were to seize its resources and control its territory. Although this "interest" never led to a proper colonization of China, it fuelled what has been named the "scramble for China." On this issue, please refer to Robert Bickers' *The Scramble for China* (2012).

country. In so doing, the interests that Bird promotes are masked, as often happens, by the allure of a *mission civilisatrice* which has moral rather than commercial motives (epitomizing this is also the author's claim that China should be considered not as an area of "control," but as one of "influence"). Such a mission, then, is subservient to restore Britain's integrity with regard to China's recent past and assign to the Western Empire a leading position in China's affairs.

To be sure, Bird was by no means the only author to betray a political agenda in her travelogue. The US-American Ellen LaMotte, for instance, defended in *Peking Dust* (1919) the US's non-intervention policy into China's affairs. Mirroring Bird's erasure of Britain's responsibilities in the opium trade, LaMotte mentioned how "the European powers just arrange it among themselves, each decides what provinces it wants, agrees not to trespass upon the sphere of influence of one another, and then notify China" (19). And yet, in her reporting of the situation LaMotte seemed to forget the US strategic role in China: the Western power had concessions in Beijing (the international legation quarter where she was staying), as well as in the International settlement in Shanghai (where the Americans remained for almost a century, from 1848 to 1945), without considering the American commercial interests in the region, which were best exposed by the "Open Door"[134] policy aimed at securing free trade in the Middle Kingdom by and among Western powers. A further attempt by LaMotte to conceal her book's political agenda can be retrieved in the opening statement concerning the generic features of her account:

> Two classes of books are written about China by two classes of people. There are books written by people who have spent the night in China, as it were, superficial and amusing, full of the tinkling of temple bells; and there are other books written by people who have spent years in China and who know it well – ponderous books, full of absolute information, heavy and unreadable. This book falls into neither of these two classes, except perhaps in the irresponsibility of its author. It is compounded of gossip – the flying gossip or dust of Peking. Take it lightly; blow off such dust as may happen to stick to you. (LaMotte: 7)

This passage strives to convey the idea of her account as a ruffled set of notes that do not aim to be accurate or precise. Put differently, LaMotte makes a plea in defense of the amateurish nature of what she writes. It is precisely such supposed unpretentiousness that projects onto the "irresponsible" LaMotte a politically disinterested allure, so that she can claim to provide readers with an honest report on China's current situation. And yet, even conceived as a report on "flying gossip," LaMotte's account manifests the fragility of its tentative impartiality whenever the author resorts overtly to a paternalistic tone, by reclaiming a sort of private ownership of China:

---

[134] See the following US-governmental online resource: https://history.state.gov/milestones/1899-1913/hay-and-china.

> That is what makes Peking so absorbing, the peculiar protective feeling that it gives one. In a way, it seems to belong to us; its interests are *our* interests; its well-being is peculiarly our concern. You wish the best to happen to China, you wish Chinese interests to have the right of way. (LaMotte: 123)

In LaMotte's case, it is not objectivity, nor the shaping of the account as a supposed "truthful" text, that guides the author's political agenda, but rather the presentation of the book as an uninterested mix of volatile and off-the-record notations; a sort of diary that has (voluntarily) transcended the borders of privacy to go commercial. In the quoted passage China and the Chinese are domesticated and considered unable to decide for themselves: we witness the flattening of any distance – physical and emotional – dividing the traveler and the Other, as if LaMotte was immersed into China and not separated from it by the walls of the international legation quarter. This sense of familiarity has the effect to undermine the potential allegations of the US having interests in China and allows for a reversal according to which it is China's destiny that comes to coincide with all that matters to the US.

A travelogue that constitutes a formal compromise between these two works is David-Neel's *My Journey to Lhasa*. The journey, we have seen, is motivated by the willingness to break the restriction on foreigners accessing Lhasa. One can say that such a goal represents a political motive. However, the endeavor is presented more as a personal achievement than as a confrontation between national interests. For example, discussing the contested involvement of Britain in Tibet, David-Neel rejects any speculation that her critique might be generalized: "before ending I wish to assure my many English friends that my criticism of the part their government has played in this situation is not the outcome of bad feelings against the English nation as a whole" (David-Neel 2005: xxxix). Hence, David-Neel thinks primarily of her journey as an individual endeavor. In this respect, it must be noted that the book, despite never falling into introspection, flirts with the canon of the initiation journey, in which the author – indeed the protagonist of the plot together with her companion Yongden – is asked to pass a series of "tests" and surmount difficulties due, not least, by the harshness of the walk. This also finds a reflection in the literary style that characterizes the text:

> Night came and snow began to fall again. The sky was pitch dark, but a dim, dull light, that made me think of Hades, seemed to ascend strangely from the white ground and issue from the snow-clad trees. White from head to foot, mind and body benumbed in that fantastic landscape, we looked like two queer ghosts *en route* to answer the call of a Tibetan wizard. (David-Neel 2005: 168)

The passage testifies to a certain tendency of the author to poeticize the narrative. In so doing, David-Neel abdicates by and large that observatory stance which, as Sara Mills (1991) notes, was expected from early 20th century female-authored travel writing. By contrast, David-Neel's account approaches those contemporary travelogues in which the tale is openly filtered through (and depends on) the traveler's persona. In fact, according to Mills (1991: 153), who focused on David-Neel's text as one of her case studies for the investigation of female travel writing, the filling of the narrative with descriptive elements that belong to the realm of the "irrational" "is enough [for some critics] to call the entire account into question." It has been argued, indeed, that the journey's political *raison d'être* – entering Lhasa – unusually mixed with fictionalized elements – which draw upon the mystic journey, the picaresque adventure, and the personal diary – is symptomatic of the fabrication of the whole experience. The unorthodoxy of the text's literary form (and the fact that it was authored by a woman) represents, then, a good counter-example of Shaping's concept – discussed in the Introduction – about the necessity for travel writing to comply with the "epistemological decorum" of its own epoch.

Continuing the survey of the travelogues from a formalistic point of view, Scidmore's *Westward to the Far East* is a text that does not respond to (or support) any stringent political agenda. In fact, its generic affiliation approaches the contemporary travel guide. Scidmore's brief book (roughly 80 pages) aims at presenting China (but also Japan and Indonesia) as a tourist destination. More specifically, the passenger traffic manager of the Canadian Pacific Railway, who wrote the introduction, states that the book wants:

> to tell the possible traveler what there is to be seen and the actual traveler how to see it. It is the result of personal observation and enquiry prompted by the desire to acquire the knowledge most useful to a tourist, and while being a trustworthy guide to those traveling in the countries referred to, will teach others a great deal about China and Japan which they cannot fail to be interested in knowing. (Scidmore: 1-2)

Such a statement could easily be found on the cover of one of today's travel guides. It is also remarkable that the author openly defines the kind of knowledge provided as specifically directed to tourists; as such, this claim positions the text differently from all the others written about China up to that point. The "I" of the writer disappears from the text together with any concrete reference to the effective unfolding of the journey, which sublimates in a rarefied experience with no temporal anchoring points. It could be advanced that the narrative of the text is very close to that found in travel blogs, but also, more radically, that the absence of a manifest subjective stance in charge of the tale pushes the text to the limit of travel writing as defined in the introduction to this volume. To the extent to which China is conceived as a tourist destination, the narrative (and ideological) discourse of the text is objective (and the representation of China objectified): no more patronizing "I"s, but suggestions on where to go, what to see, and how to move around; no more commercially driven mappings, or politically motivated seizures of lands, but leisure and entertainment. Once we accept this, however, we are confronted with a practical short circuit: in the Middle Kingdom – more radically than elsewhere – there has been a synchronic collapsing between the practice of mapping the territory for ethnographic and explorative purposes and the practice of tourism. Mike Crang (2011: 211) notes on this issue that "a destination becomes such by producing a sense of 'hereness' and becoming a place distinguished from others through its possession of some attributes. Increasingly, one might argue, the 'hereness' of destinations are socially inscribed values and meanings layered onto the landscape." No doubt, China's acquisition of social value as a tourist destination is exemplified by Scidmore's listing of the things to be seen in Beijing:

> The Summer Palace, without the walls, destroyed by the French in 1861, is now being rebuilt, and is closed to visitors. The Temple of Heaven, where the Emperor annually worships, was burned a few years since, but its ruins and the other temples within its park are interesting. The Confucian Temple, the Hall of Classics and the Examination Hall, where the students assemble every year to strive for rank and honors, are also to be seen. (Scidmore: 57)

Nonetheless, if we consider that Bird's account, which is contemporary to Scidmore's, recounts the immersion into "the beyond" – that is, the westernmost unexplored areas of the Yangtze – it is evident that also "natural/geographical" features of the country (and not only "social," as Crang calls them), had a great relevance for Western travelers, to the point that, according to Morgan (2007), Bird's final pages recount an exploration in the tradition of 19th century ethnography. This overlap of natural and social features is particularly visible when looking at the pictures that accompany Bird and Scidmore's texts (and it is remarkable that in Crang's words, a photograph "can almost stand as a marker of the tourist on occasion" [2011: 206]).

A wider discussion on the visual elements in early travelogues will be conducted later on in this chapter; here, however, one specific picture deserves to be analyzed: on page 69 of Bird's text is a picture whose caption states "street in Hangkow." This same picture appears in Scidmore's travel book on page 54, and here it stands for a "street in a Chinese city" (Figure 39). What Scidmore does is to decontextualize the picture, which, in this way, loses its geographic specificity and comes to stand for a generalized "street." In Scidmore's text, one could say, the picture functions as proof of how Chinese streets are and, most importantly, of "having been" in China. The dynamics of (re)appropriation of this image are telling not only of the social stratification of a specific place, from being geo-localizable to a mere touristic apercu, but also of the history that pertains to photographs as reproducible artifacts. In fact, the photograph was taken neither by Bird nor Scidmore, but by the eminent British photographer John Thomson, who travelled in China and collected his shots in *Straits of Malacca, Indo-China, and China* (1875). The link that this picture creates among these authors shows – more than the fact that China was already a widely photographed subject at the end of 19th century – the circulation and uses to which images of China were subjected. Clearly, the meaning of these images depends on, and influences, the kind of projects they serve, similarly to what happened with Hirst's *Il mondo oltre il fiume dei peschi in fiore* where Giorgio Lotti's photographs, which in themselves had the function of witnessing China in the 1970s when the country was closed to Westerners, in the travelogue were subservient to visualize Hirst's own memories. Moreover, in the case of Scidmore, the reappropriation of the picture via the generalization of its referent (and the lack of information about its author) flattens the internal chronotopicity of what it represents and attests to the tourism's force to erase specificity and turn places into landmarks.

Figure 39: The picture of a "street in a Chinese city" in Scidmore's *Westward to the Far East*

To conclude, one last example of the generic diversification of late 19th century-early 20th century travel writing is associated with the reportage. "By the 1930s," Clifford (2001: 6) argues, "the line between the travel account and journalism becomes less and less clear." According to Clifford, the affiliation of the travel book (about China) to journalism parallels the escalation of internal conflicts and the approaching of the second Sino-Japanese War. So the turning of travelogues into reportages reflected the changed socio-political situation in the country. However tempting such parallelism may be, it does not hold when a broader diachronic perspective is favored. Not only, as seen in Chapter 1, do contemporary travelogues also take the form of reportages, despite the current stability of the country, but in the first decades of the 20th century there were also travel writers who refrained from addressing China's stringent "actuality" (using Fussell's terminology).[135] Scidmore's guide and David-Neel's journey to Lhasa, as seen, are two examples; a third one is certainly Mary Gaunt's (1914) *A Woman in China*. When the Australian traveler and novelist travelled to China, the first Sino-Japanese War (1894–95) and the Boxer Rebellion (1900) were just over, but even more recent were the fall of the Qing Dynasty and the establishment of the Republic (1912). Despite informing China's socio-historical background of the period, these events are rarely mentioned by Gaunt in her account. Overall, the author thinks of herself as an independent traveler, affected by a wander fever that leaves no space for politics. The following passage, in the overture of the book, frames the horizon of the tale well:

> I got into the habit of gauging my chances of seeing a country by the number of books written about it. China, judged by this standard, fell naturally into the place assigned to it by my grandmother's curios; for from the days of Marco Polo men have gone up and down the land, painfully, sorrowfully, gladly, triumphantly, and at least half of them seem to have put pen to paper to describe what they have seen. Was it likely there would be anything left for me to write about? (Gaunt: 2)

The inscription of the author's desire to travel in China into a sort of familial genesis has the effect of "privatizing" the account – Gaunt does not go to China to witness what is going on as, for instance, Peter Fleming and Ella Maillart do – and impressing upon the Middle Kingdom the allure of a long-desired destination, which can be rewritten over and over. Even when Gaunt does mention important events that are more or less contemporary to her journey, she tends to seal them off from historical contingency:

> Tuan [Gaunt's coolie] had got as far as the fact that a President had taken the place of the Manchu Emperor, but I wondered very much whether the inhabitants of Tsung Hua Chou had. I meditated on my way back to "Missie's Inn" on the limitations of the practical Chinese mind that because it is practical, I suppose, cannot conceive of liberty, equality, and fraternity that a Republic denotes. The President, to the humble Chinese in the street, has just taken the place of the Emperor, he is the one who rules over them, his soldiers are withdrawn. (Gaunt: 200)

The birth of the Republic is described as an almost transcendent event, one that "just happened" and did not change at all the life of the (close-minded) Chinese. More than that, for such an event the Chinese have no responsibility: Gaunt's text exemplifies,

---

[135] The already mentioned "scramble for China" saw involved primarily Britain, France, Germany, the US, Russia, and Japan. At the same time, the instability accompanying the last decades of the Qing Dynasty led to internal instability and the rise and fall of warlords who fought among themselves for the control and partition of certain areas of the inland. This state of uncertainty spanned well over 50 years between the end of the 19th century and the first three decades of the 20th century.

once more, that China is conceived as an object of study – an object to be partitioned among foreign powers – rather than an empowered political subject which is arbiter of its own destiny.

Overall, the shaping of travel books as reportage neither is a homogeneous phenomenon, nor a historically determined one. Generic affiliation (the comparison between Bird and Marco Polo's accounts is a case in point) is largely a trans-historical issue; one in which China's actuality plays a role, together with the individual choices made by each traveler on where to go and what to tell. Similarly, Clifford's (2001: 184) argument that "as the war closed in, changing the frame through which travellers saw China, out of the faceless mass there began to come into focus at least a few individuals with recognizable features" is controversial. In this respect, the case of Peter Fleming and Ella Maillart is emblematic. Fleming was a British journalist for *The Times* and travelled to China in two occasions – 1933 and 1935 – the first one of which is recounted in *One's Company* (now collected in *Travels in Tartary*, 1941). Despite addressing the Chinese internal situation directly and witnessing the Civil War between the Nationalists and the Communists, in this book Fleming tends to look at China from a distance: "I kept major issues in the background" (xi), the author warns in the opening. In other words, Fleming reports on China's current situation, but he does so by producing a largely monological account in which the mastering "I" of the narrative is never really challenged in its underpinning assumptions. A similar approach also characterizes his second travelogue, *News from Tartary*, in which the British author recollects the journey he undertook together with the Swiss writer and journalist Maillart through the western region of Xinjiang. At that time, a series of conflicts affected Xinjiang: both Fleming and Maillart, who recounts her experience in *Forbidden Journey* ([1937] 2003), set off together to obtain a more accurate picture of the whole situation. While Fleming focuses on the progression of the journey, with an almost frantic desire to cover the region, Maillart is less obsessed with getting the news and more open to engaging with the people. Below is a comparison of two short passages that recount the same encounter with a Cantonese man:

> Kini shared the seat beside the driver with a mysterious little Cantonese, who wore spats and smoked a pipe, but spoke no word of any foreign language. He said that he was a friend of the Governor of Sinkiang and was going to fly up to Urumchi from Lanchow, then go on to Moscow and afterwards to London. At first the only question in our mind was not whether he was a secret agent or not, but whose secret agent he was; but gradually he showed himself to be such a silly, ineffectual little man that we were not in the least surprised that he never got farther than Lanchow. (Fleming 1941: 290)

> Another privileged passenger sat with the driver beside me. Wearing European clothes and smoking a little, pretty pipe, he had shining teeth and smiling eyes. He was a Cantonese, the son of a rich merchant, and he was going to see the world, just to amuse himself. "I am going to Urumchi," he said as though it were quite a simple matter. "A friend who is a general has invited me. I'll take a plane from Lanchow." "But," I protested laughing,

"the air service has stopped. You'll never get there." I was certain of my facts, but I did not disclose the secret of my own itinerary. "Haven't you heard," I enquired, "about the mortifying experience of Lo Wen-kan himself?" Lo Wen-kan was one of the Nanking ministers. Following an ill-advised order to make a landing at Urumchi, he had only been able to get back to China by going round through Siberia. My fellow-traveller began to ask questions and I told him we were going to visit the famous lamasery at Kumbum. But suddenly a terrifying idea crossed my mind – unjustified, as it proved in the event. Perhaps he had been sent to spy on us? (Maillart 2003: 30-1).

The different approaches to the travel and to the writing that Fleming and Maillart manifest are quite striking. The above passages show the extent to which Maillart tends to communicate with, and give space to, the people they meet, while Fleming embeds these encounters into the narrative. This is also reflected in the presence of dialogues in the form of direct speech in Maillart's text, while in Fleming's these take the form of reported speech. In the third section of this chapter, dedicated to the authors' self-representation, there will be a discussion of how differently Fleming and Maillart think of themselves and of the journey; here it suffices to note how different their writing is, although they relate the same experience. As a consequence, while Maillart can be said to show a certain willingness to represent the people encountered (beyond the undifferentiated mass), Fleming maintains a distanced view on the Chinese who continue to be represented as a monolithic whole (especially useful for the Western readership to which his account was directed).

Among the authors surveyed, Ilona Sues manifests the deepest involvement and engagement with China. When the Polish-born writer reaches China in 1936, the second Sino-Japanese war is looming and Communists and Nationalists are forced to collaborate in order to stop the foreign invasion. Generically speaking, it could be said that Sues's work highlights the blurring between the travel book and reportage. However, there emerge also substantial (narrative and ideological) differences with texts of the same period. Clifford suggests that, despite Sues's effort to be "the eyes and the ears of the man-in-the-street" (as she claims to be in the beginning of the book), she cannot help but linger on the portrayals of relevant figures. As an example, Clifford (2001: 248) recalls Sues's description of Mao Zedong, as a person who "combined all the characteristics of the Chinese people: their wisdom, in his high square forehead; their patient and untold sufferings in those spare, painfully knitted brows; their dreams and their keenness, their shrewdness and irony in his large black eyes." The point is that this description, which is clearly ideologically inflated, is the exception rather than the rule, and by no means does the author limit herself to the representation of Chinese leaders.

Sues's goal to "live and work with people who make history, to see their real faces undistorted, unembellished by propaganda" (10), is pursued in various ways. Although her first contacts *in loco* are usually Western people, these, rather than representing the outer horizon of the author's experience (such as in Bird, LaMotte, Gaunt), help Sues to get in contact with local people. For instance, Sues, who had been also employed at the Anti-Opium Information Bureau in Geneva, gets to work for a while for the Nationalists as a press officer. This does not stop her from also reaching the Communists' front and reporting on their military and educational actions. In this way, Sues reports on both fronts, meets a varied number of Chinese people and is able to represent them from a peer-to-peer, anthropological perspective:

> I looked into the round face of a peasant boy in uniform. "Foreign comrade," he said, "you must not say 'Down with Japan.' We have no grudge against the people of Japan. What we are fighting is Japanese militarism. Do you understand my language?" "Yes, I do. Go on and tell me – do you hate the little devils that invade your country? The soldiers, I mean?" "We do not hate them. They are forced to fight in a foreign land, far from their families. They suffer as we do. They are peasants and workers, as we are. And when they are killed, their mothers and wives and children weep as our womenfolk weep." (Sues: 234)

Sues makes a great effort to open herself toward common people, to whom she grants a voice. Moreover, in the quoted passage it is the Chinese man who provides an "illuminated" and tolerant perspective, in a way shaking Sues's own expectations about the war. The Chinese are no longer solely an object to stare at, but subjects to interact with and from which to learn. The consequence of that on the literary form of the book is that the journalistic register that characterizes the text is contaminated with elements of dramatization. It could also be suggested that the book constitutes an example *ante litteram* of the American new journalism, in which fact and fiction are invariably mixed. The following is an example in which the author recounts the raids of the Japanese resorting to a poetic description that would not be expected by the classic war reportage of that time:

> The most fascinating hours during my employment at Headquarters were watching the air raids with Donald, on a hill at the foot of Purple Mountain. The valley below and the soft contours of the surrounding hills in their rich green, which autumn was slowly splashing with flaming dabs of yellow, red and orange, made a superbly serene setting for the airfield before us and the southern wall of the city to our right. High up behind us, at a distance, cushioned in a velvety carpet, half-up Purple Mountain, the white gleaming Sun Yat-Sen Mausoleum with its dark blue roof (Sues: 144)

Sues's book was published in 1944, one year before the end of World War II and five years before the birth of the People's Republic of China. From 1949, the political situation in China stabilizes. However, far from meeting the hopes that Sues and many Western travelers had expressed, the rise to power of Mao Zedong coincides both with a (re)closure of the Middle Kingdom to the outer world, and with restrictions on mobility and civil rights for its people. Due to the historical situation, it is possible to witness not only a quantitative reduction of travelogues about China,[136] but also a reshaping of its literary form.

The four books selected for this period are the French *Travels in China* (2012) by Roland Barthes, and three Italian texts: Curzio Malaparte's (1958) *Io in Russia e in Cina*, Goffredo Parise's ([1966] 1972) *Cara Cina*, and Luigi Malerba's (1985) *Cina Cina*. The three Italian texts could all be classed as travel reportages, although some differences among them are to be found. Malaparte's is surely the most narrative one; while Parise and Malerba opt for short, self-standing thematic chapters that provide brief apercu on some aspects of China's life. As for Barthes's carnets, they adhere to the diary form, in that the French author dutifully reports the dates and hours of all visits. At the same time, his notes present neither a coherent thematic organization, nor a thread that ties them together; rather they constitute, similarly to *Cara Cina* and *Cina Cina*, a skeleton of impressions whose sole structuring principle is the chronotopic sequentiality of the stay.

One reason for the rarefication of the diegetic discourse in the texts is the control that the Chinese authorities exert on the travelers: "Who travels in China and is not a guest of the Chinese government," Parise (1972: 716) notes, "is a (paying) host of the Chinese Travel Service, the sole travel agency for the whole country. In both cases, he is a prisoner, body and soul"[137] (author's translation). This means that these writers were confronted with a one-sided, uncontested image of China – the one prefabricated by the Chinese authorities who accompanied them – which left no space for serendipitous encounters. As a consequence, all four travelers resort, to various degrees, to an imaginative, metaphorical writing. According to Parise (1972: 662), for instance, Chinese architecture comes to stand for eternal repetition (spatial and temporal), while for Barthes (2012: 27) tea functions as a metonymy of the whole country: it is as tasteless as the impression that the traveler can obtain of China. Also, Malerba (1985: 25), who went to China in 1980, writes that "every civilization, after all, is the representation of a utopia, but utopias are undecipherable for those who have not attended at their staging" (25; author's translation).[138] The apparently unavoidable tendency, common to all writers, is to present to the readers reflections and observations in which it is not the referent (China) that dominates, but the referential: the sign. Barthes is again illuminating when he denounces the "bricks," as he calls it, of the Chinese propaganda through a parallelism with language:

[1. Discourse of the signifier (writing)
2. Discourse of the signified (Bricks)
3. Interpretation. Struggles, Structures. Process.]
[Level of the signified: in other words: what bars the signifier.

---

[136] As seen, this paucity also concerns the number of studies on Western travel writing going from the birth of PRC to the death of Mao and the rise to power of Deng Xiaoping.

[137] "Chi viaggia in Cina, e non è ospite del governo, è ospite (pagante) del China Travel Service, la sola agenzia turistica cinese. In entrambi i casi è prigioniero, anima e corpo."

[138] "Ogni civiltà in fondo è la rappresentazione di un'utopia, ma le utopie sono indecifrabili per chi non ha partecipato alla loro messa in scena."

Total eviction of the signifier.] (Barthes 2012: 122)

For these travelers, China is staged; reality is there, but it is one that must be overcome; life is there, but it is still, it is a scenic view. Everything in China stands for something else and such otherness can only be metonymically implied (i.e., inferred).

Beyond the socio-historical situation of China, a second reason at the base of the texts' formal features is connected to the writers' own background. However rigid the Chinese prohibition might be, there is, as David Scott (2004: 37) puts it, "an ulterior motive shared by many western travel writers: that of escaping if only momentarily the determinism and essentialism of western linguistic and cultural Structures." Parise, Barthes, and Malerba (and partially Malaparte) were all involved in the European literary neo avant-gardes of the 1960s. These movements wanted, among other goals, to rethink the canonical use of language and the epistemological foundation of Western thought. To an extent, then, the travelogues of these writers can also be seen as *exercises de style* in which China constituted a privileged terrain of experimentation, given its resistance to being represented, and against which language required to be deconstructed. The Italian critic Romano Luperini writes in the introduction to Malerba's *Cina Cina* (1985) that

> Here, one of the themes (or rather: the theme) of Malerba's intellectual and artistic research emerges: the "indecipherability" of reality. This word refers to a universe of signs and to their alterity to the code known by the interpreter. The world is made up of words, but these are unable to communicate and even master reality.[139] (Malerba: 8; author's translation)

Hence, if it is true that in the new-born PRC "everything that these travellers are about to accomplish is established, pre-ordered since the departure" (Pellegrino 1985: 87; author's translation), it is also true that the cultural (Western) ethos to which these authors refer compels them to turn their journeys into an almost virtualized experience whose means of expression can only be, ultimately, a language that reflects upon itself. Even in Malaparte's text, which is the oldest of the four, one can attest to the sublimation of the experience, particularly in the portrayal of Mao:

> President Mao stared at me silently for a few moments. Meanwhile, I was staring at him too. The President of the People's Republic of China, the hero of the Chinese revolution, the commandant of 600 million people, is a sixtyish man, tall beyond the average, with wide shoulders, a wide face, a wide front and black, thick, soft, hair. His gaze fascinated me: a still, serene, sweet and deeply good gaze. If his prodigious life as a man of action, as a

---

[139] "Appare qui uno dei temi (anzi: non un tema tra gli altri: il tema), della ricerca intellettuale e artistica di Malerba: l' "indecifrabilità" del reale. Il termine rinvia a un universo di segni e alla loro alterità rispetto al codice dell'interprete. Il mondo è fatto di parole, ma queste sono incapaci di comunicare e anche di impadronirsi davvero della realtà."

revolutionary, is the mirror of his courage, his sense of sacrifice, his iron will, his face is the mirror of his good and generous heart.[140] (Malaparte: 121; author's translation)

This portrayal sounds almost like an elegy and, in fact, it becomes so once one acknowledges that it was written by an intellectual who had flirted with fascist ideology and was miles away from the political ideals of Mao. It could also be remarked that this description is very similar to that provided by Sues at the end of her book. However, whereas in Sues such a description functioned as a synthesis of the author's hopes about the future of China and did not prevent her from engaging with other Chinese people, in Malaparte's book Mao's description sets the tone of the whole account. Even for Malaparte, the discovery of China could only be the one prescribed by authorities and, as such, it required being imagined. The utmost paradox, in this respect, is that it is not ascertained that he really met with chairman Mao. Some critics, indeed, suggest that he fabricated the episode.[141] If this is the case, it would imply the definitive collapsing between factual and fictional modes of telling and the sublimation of the experience to such a point to become a fantasy.

Lastly, it is worth recalling that a number of contemporary travel authors, such as Thubron, Ramazzotti, Bettinelli, and Richard, also proclaim the difficulty of properly reading China, that is, of properly get acquainted with it and dispel the sense of mystery that contours every aspect of its life. This issue will be at the core of the following section.

CHINA IN SPACE, TIME AND ITS PEOPLE

In this section, it is explored more closely how travel writers from the turn of the 20th century up to the 1980s perceive and represent China as an object/subject of interest. In particular, it is possible to identify three major threads: the history of China (as a country and a civilization); the places visited and, more broadly, the space of travel; and the Chinese as peoples. Of course, the distinction among these three threads is operational: in practice, they are very much intertwined, so that the analysis does not pretend to keep them separated, and aims, in fact, at stimulating comparisons and cross-references.

---

[140] "Il presidente Mao mi ha osservato per alcuni istanti in silenzio. Anch'io l'osservavo. Il Presidente della Repubblica Popolare della Cina, l'eroe della rivoluzione cinese, il capo di un popolo di 600 milioni di abitanti, è un uomo sui sessant'anni di statura oltre la media, dalle spalle ampie, il viso largo, la fronte altissima, i capelli neri, folti e soffici. Mi affascinava il suo sguardo: che è fermo, sereno, dolce, profondamente buono. Se la sua prodigiosa vita di uomo d'azione, di rivoluzionario, è lo specchio del suo coraggio, del suo spirito di sacrificio, della sua volontà di ferro, il suo viso è lo specchio del suo animo buono, generoso."

[141] Giordano Bruno Guerri, for instance, notes in his monumental study *L'arcitaliano* (1980) dedicated to Malaparte that one needs to question any piece of information that comes from Malaparte, as he tended to mix autobiographical facts and fiction. After all, the epigraph that opens Malaparte's book – "What's the purpose of saying the whole truth?" – sounds already like a warning. See also *In Cina: Il Gran Tour degli italiani verso il centro del mondo, 1904-1999* (2010), edited by Danilo Soscia.

In the first chapter of his book, Clifford (2001) notes that late 19th century travel writers tend to conceive of China as a timeless country, or better, one whose civilization, by sinking into a remote pre-history, annihilates any possibility of historical development. This also applies to the texts discussed in this chapter. In fact, almost all authors avoid exploring the past of the country: it is not, to be sure, that China does not have a history of its own, but that such history is perceived as so "old" and overwhelming as to appear meaningless and still. In *One's Company*, for instance, Fleming stresses on various occasions the dullness of the journey, and he writes that "our progress was as uneventful as progress can be in China" (1941: 134). Of course, it is a historical and materialistic (Western) conception of progress (rather than physical) about which Fleming is talking: one that is straightforwardly negated, without even the attempt to explore China's past. Similarly to Fleming, Gaunt does not refrain from projecting onto her experience a rather trans-historical allure. Indeed, what she sees is often described as unchanged since old ages: "here come the camels from Mongolia, ragged and dusty, laden with those 'black stones' that Marco Polo noted seven hundred years ago. Here come slowly, in stately fashion, the camels, as they have come for thousands of years" (Gaunt: 44). Interestingly, this same impression of being confronted with an ageless past is also traceable in those writers who visited China after 1949. In particular, Malerba poetically writes that:

> Pagodas, Imperial Palaces, the Great Wall, the Yellow River and the Blue River, all the unavoidable places of China's history, which you cannot erase burning books, nor scraping tombstones (and not even killing literati), are the mirror of an imperial tradition that also includes inundations, famines, massacres, lice. But history jumps: The Republic, the betrayal of the Republic, the Civil War, the Long March, the Victory, the Cultural Revolution, the After-Mao are eventually mixed with monuments, sanctuaries and monsters created over four thousand years. The ancient Function becomes the modern Ornament, history vertiginously drifts away and acquires unrecognisable connotations. [142] (Malerba: 22; author's translation)

Malerba's passage exemplifies very well the travel writers' tendency to address China's history as a whole, that is, a realm in which events lose their own specificity, to the point that they can be easily interchanged, or forgotten. China's history is a hoover that absorbs everything: in it, all answers can be found, if only one were able to decipher them. A specular perception is that offered by Parise. By rhetorically

---

[142] "Le pagode, i Palazzi Imperiali, la Grande Muraglia, il Fiume Giallo e quello Azzurro, tutti i luoghi obbligati della storia cinese, che non si cancella né bruciando i libri, né raschiando le lapidi (nemmeno decapitando i letterati) sono specchio di una tradizione imperiale nella quale sono comprese anche le inondazioni, le carestie, le carneficine, i pidocchi. Ma la storia fa i suoi salti: la Repubblica, il tradimento della Repubblica, la Guerra Civile, la Lunga Marcia, la Vittoria, La Rivoluzione Culturale, il Dopo-Mao si trovano così a convivere con i monumenti, i santuari e i mostri creati in quattromila anni. La Funzione antica diventa Ornamento moderno, la storia si allontana vertiginosamente e assume connotati irriconoscibili."

asking how it was possible for emperors and dynasties to survive and succeed one after the other, he claims that this has to do:

> First of all, with the passing of centuries and then with the stronger and stronger conviction that outside or beyond that "point in infinity" [the Forbidden City] nothing existed, or, if ever anything existed, it was always as a function of that "point." In this way, for millennia China has remained the same.[143] (Parise: 662; author's translation)

Even more strongly than Malerba, Parise provides a representation of China's history as an abstracted dimension. Time becomes an indefinite coordinate, while China becomes a purely imaginary space of mirrors and returns, of enduring stillness. There are no contingency, nor immanence, but mere categories. In fact, what distinguishes the earliest travelers from those of the 1950s, 1960s, 1970s, and 1980s is that the latter tend to transfigure China into a form that transcends observation: "all these notes will probably attest to the failure, in this country, of my writing (in comparison with Japan). In fact, I can't find anything to note down, to enumerate, to classify" (2012: 73), writes Barthes disappointingly. In this respect, Steve Clark and Paul Smethurst's (2008: 32) claim that "early travellers to China did not only suffer from a 'traveling incarceration' because their own 'cultural baggage' prohibited them from seeing (understanding, appreciating) the Chinese; instead they were literally isolated, restricted and forbidden from looking beyond the city walls" needs to be contextualized. Indeed, not only were there writers such as David-Neel and Sues (and partially Maillart) who engaged with locals, but early travelers, after all, enjoyed a greater freedom than those coming after 1949.

In many of the writers surveyed here, the idea of China as an immutable country is often linked to the denouncement of the country's backwardness, an impression that is framed within a precise spatial frame: the countryside. As far as metropolises are concerned, indeed, they already bear the mark of modernity. Cities such as Beijing and Shanghai are so developed that already Isabella Bird confesses that her "chief wish on arriving at a foreign settlement or treaty port in the East is to get out of it as soon as possible" (Bird: 15). To emerge from these words is the classic trope of the escape from (Western) modernity, which fuels many modern and contemporary travelogues: an escape aimed chiefly at finding authenticity outside of what is perceived as compromised and too similar to the West. It is no coincidence that Bird defines Shanghai as a "foreign city risen on Chinese shore" (Bird: 15). Bird (who is not alone in this) wishes to plunge into that rural China which conforms to her expectations of a timeless country, as if other, more advanced realities were not Chinese enough. To witness "real" China, then, means to be able to experience a travel back in time: not much through the past of China, but through the past of the West. It is this purpose that the countryside often serves. Fleming, for example, when

---

[143] "Col passare dei secoli innanzitutto e con la convinzione sempre più profonda che, al di fuori o al di là di quel 'punto nell'infinito', non esistesse nient'altro: o che, se esisteva, esso esisteva ancora una volta come funzione di quel 'punto'. Così, per millenni, la Cina è rimasta uguale a se stessa."

travelling in Tartary, does not hesitate to straightforwardly characterize the landscape as prehistoric: "We were passing through country which, according to the learned men, is the original home of the Chinese race. There was a kind of prehistoric look about this land, through which the train snorted laboriously like an antediluvian monster" (281). Fleming's description is not necessarily inflated: Sinkiang *was* and still is an extremely inhospitable area. The point is that for him it functions surreptitiously as a mirror for attesting to how far the West (the learned men) has progressed.

By looking back at the first part of this study, it is notable that the city/countryside dichotomy, defined in terms of progress vs. backwardness, is still present in today's travelogues, such as those by Gifford and de Slizewicz. Similarly, it should not be surprising that both today's and early travelogues share common descriptions of the advancement of the journey, perceived as exhausting, tedious, and full of inconveniences as soon as the "civilized" city is left behind. From Bird and Maillart to Richard, from Gaunt and Fleming to Thubron, almost all travel writers represent the journey through the West of China as a tiring experience, due to the bad conditions of roads and transports and the lack of commodities. It is, rather, on the cultural and ideological plan that differences among these writers play out. So, if for Bird and LaMotte the backwardness of the countryside is an implicit motivation for the intervention of Western powers, for Fleming it is proof of the harshness of his endeavor. In turn, while de Slizewicz favors the countryside over the city, because he perceives the former as a place of resistance against the process of modernization that has already affected the eastern region of the country, Gifford fills the timelessly poor countryside with the anonymity proper to the "old one hundred names" (the common Chinese) he wants to meet. Each author, then, pours into what he observes a whole set of values that, while being kindled by the material socio-historical conditions of the country, belongs to his/her own vision of the country (and the experience), as well as to the kind of text s/he wants to produce.

The desire to leave the metropolis and visit the countryside also has consequences for how the travelers perceive themselves. Indeed, it is only when they go to the outback that they lose their privileges and become the Other to be stared at. This happens unevenly to a number of travelers from all decades. In one of the early quoted passages in this chapter, taken from Bird's travelogue, the British traveler is addressed by local people as "Foreign devil!" "Horse-racer!" "Child-eater!" (246). In a similar tone, Gaunt reports on her excursion out of Beijing as follows:

> The people came and looked at me, and they were invariably courteous and polite, with an old-world courtesy that must have come down to them through the ages. It was just as well to make the most of a show, because their lives were uneventful, that was all. (Gaunt: 178)

For these authors, the longing to explore China's inland goes hand in hand, willingly or not, with the fact of being perceived as different. It seems as if travelling in China acquires the seal of authenticity only once the traveler finds him/herself in the situation of being othered by local people.

On this point, the main exception among the early 20th century authors surveyed is David-Neel. This happens for a specific motive: in the first pages David-Neel confesses that her biggest concern all along the journey is to disappear among other pilgrims, so as not to be identified (as a Western woman). In David-Neel's case, then, to experience China, means, above all, not being othered, in order to be able to accomplish her endeavor: "I had decided to disguise as an *ardjopa* [pilgrims on foot] because this was the best way for me to wander without raising suspects" (David-Neel 2005: 17). The paradox is that, in order to "disappear" among locals, David-Neel has to know how to deal with people; she has to know, in other words, how to go unnoticed. Hence, she learns the Tibetan language, as well as the Tibetan costumes and manners. The following passage, which occurs when the author has already reached Lhasa, is a case in point:

> I was wandering in the market when a policeman stopped and gazed at me intently. Why? Perhaps he only wondered from what part of Tibet I might hail, but it was better to be prepared for the worst. I chose, amongst the things for sale, an aluminium saucepan, and began to bargain for it with that ridiculous obstinacy shown by people of the half-wild tribes to the borderland. People around the booths began to laugh and exchange jokes about me. The cowmen and women of the northern solitudes are a habitual subject of mockery for the more civilized people of Lhasa. "Ah!" said the merchant, laughing, and yet irritated by my continuous twaddle, "you are a true *dokpa*, there can be no doubt of that!" And all present ridiculed the stupid woman who knew nothing besides her cattle and the grass of the desert. The policeman passed on, amused like everybody else. (David-Neel 2005: 277-8)

In this passage, we find a number of elements that characterize the whole travelogue. First of all, the author is constantly inclined to reflect upon her persona and on how she is perceived by others. In this respect, it is not rare to find direct questions, in the form of free indirect speech, which are not only openly directed to the people she and Yongden meet, but also to the author herself, as a form of self-doubting. Secondly, the author demonstrates knowing the Tibetan language and also its minor dialects. This is, in fact, what allows David-Neel to smoothly mix with locals. Such linguistic knowledge is reasserted in the text in two ways. On the one hand, the author inserts a variety of Tibetan words and phrases (usually in italics) that bring to the surface of the text the heteroglossic nature of the narrative discourse. On the other hand, she reports dialogues in the form of direct speech, thus stressing the contact with the other. In so doing, David-Neel manages to appear to the readers as an insider in Tibet: it could also be said that the often-claimed willingness of travelers to go native finds here – out of necessity – a concrete realization.

The practice of being othered almost disappears in the travelogues of the in-between generation (1950s, 1960s, 1970s, 1980s). The Chinese people whom Malaparte, Parise, Barthes, and Malerba met were most of the time well-chosen figures, who were used to meeting foreigners. Parise explains the pre-arrangement of every encounter noting that "between the man and the object, or the variety of objects, that he, as an inexhaustible traveller, wants to know, does not open the abyss of the unknown (always fascinating), but the plain way (always boring) of conventionality" [144] (717; author's translation). Barthes, however, reports some occurrences in which he and his companions are stared at: "[Yesterday Opera: We are *sacred*: people come up in crowds to stare at us, they move aside as not to touch us]"[145] (2012: 113). In this example, the French delegation is vividly perceived by the Chinese as different. In contrast with what happens to many travelers of previous and following epochs, however, the othering process to which the French are subjected puts them in a privileged position, to the point that Barthes suggests the idea of being worshipped (rather than being despised).

Lastly, the thrill of being perceived as different also emerges in contemporary travelogues, as a consequence of China's opening to the world. The following is a telling passage from Thubron's *Behind the Wall* (but occurrences are also found in Gray's *First Pass under Heaven*):

> His son emerged from indoors with a bird-like wife and child. As the little boy saw me he stopped dead with a breathy squeak, and rushed against his mother. "Don't be afraid." The woman turned the child's face towards me. "It's only a foreign devil." (Thubron 1987: 164)

This episode vividly echoes the one quoted above by Bird. Moreover, it is most surprising that this episode in Thubron's journey happens when he is in the area surrounding Hangzhou, which is one of the biggest and most prosperous cities on the east coast. Such example further testifies to the recurrence of certain episodes and tropes over the centuries that seem to be rooted into the relationship West-China beyond the contingency of history.

One further tile can be added to the analysis of the temporal and spatial representation of China by discussing one aspect that is usually overlooked by critique and scholarly works. The idea that the Middle Kingdom is a timeless country is complemented by a symmetrical and paradoxical conception: China as being constantly on the verge of change. In the previous section of this chapter, two excerpts were provided in which, respectively, Bird affirmed that "China is certainly at the dawn of a new era" (544), while Sues was sure that to be in China in the 1930s meant, above all, "to live and work with people who make history" (10). Their standpoints are different: one is supporting Britain's intervention, the other celebrating the Chinese resistance against the Japanese. However, they both claim that China has reached a historical turning point and action must be taken. Remarkably, this same idea runs throughout the whole century. At the beginning of the 21st century, Gifford

---

[144] "Tra l'uomo e l'oggetto, o la varietà di oggetti che egli, viaggiatore inesausto, vuole conoscere, non si apre più l'abisso dell'ignoto (sempre affascinante) ma la strada piana e sempre noiosa della convenzione."
[145] "Hier Opéra: nous sommes sacrés: on s'approche en masse pour nous regarder, on s'écarte pour ne pas nous toucher."

is convinced that "there could well be a crunch coming in China. There is one big question in my own mind: which is it going to be for China, greatness or implosion?" (xix–xxi) The recourse to this image is functional to ground Gifford's claims that, still a century after Bird, "the West needs to pay more attention to China's problems" (xix).

The difficulty of finding a coherent solution to the conflicting views of an immutable China and a rampant China is possibly one of the reasons why many authors from all periods tend to think of the Middle Kingdom as incomprehensible and inaccessible. This idea can be disentangled either as a physical-political impossibility of entering certain regions, or as a more metaphorical impossibility of knowing, which results in China being represented as a mystery. To the first group belong, among others, David-Neel, whose journey is a challenge to Tibet's closure; Maillart and Richard, the titles of whose travelogues are exemplary, and all the travelers of the in-between generation, insofar as, being obliged to follow predetermined itineraries, they were confronted with the phantom of a China that had not to be seen. In the second group are contemporary authors such as Thubron and Ramazzotti: the former confessed his difficulty in understanding China in the interview; the latter admits to Celia to not understanding China (although he argued in the interview that his experience helped him grasp the country's spirit). Moreover (again) within this group are travel writers from the 1950s, 1960s, 1970s, and 1980s. Malerba is exemplary when he suggests at the very beginning of his work that "to orient oneself in this universe of mad signs and gentle metaphors is a desperate endeavour"[146] (9; author's translation). At the same time, this idea of a metaphorical inaccessibility is also present in the writings that belong to the earliest temporal frame discussed here. Authors such as Bird, Gaunt, and LaMotte all manifest to various degrees a sense of alienation and disorientation. Bird (1899: 12) confesses at the beginning of her book that "the human product of Chinese civilization, religion, government, is to me the greatest of all enigmas, and so it remains to those who know him best." Beyond the objectification to which both China and the Chinese are subjected – they are defined as a product – it is notable that, according to Bird, the country and its people remain incomprehensible also to those Westerners who have studied them, so that the unintelligibility of China almost becomes a given. Gaunt, for her part, acknowledges many times in the text that she has trouble interpreting certain customs or situations, marking an incommensurable distance between her and the people she deals with (e.g., Gaunt: 285-6; 347; 445). The main point to highlight is that even when these authors declare that they have trouble understanding China, early 20th century travelers only seldom question their role and position within the Middle Kingdom. The very possibilities of travelling, writing and learning about (and from) the Chinese go undisputed. In other words, however difficult it might appear to understand China, the fact of being there proves sufficient for being entitled to provide an accurate portrayal of the country. Fleming, for instance, at the end of his first journey to the south of China where the Communists where fighting, remarked –

---

[146] "Orizzontarsi in questo universo di segni pazzi e metafore gentili è un'impresa disperatissima"

to his (self-flattering) surprise – that he had become one of the "Greatest Living Authorities" on the Communist areas (236). Such a claim, which overlooks a discussion of the practical conditions underpinning his travels and writing, makes it appear as if it is enough for the traveler to be there in order to be able to competently report on China. Expertise and ignorance are not the two extremes of a spectrum of possibilities, but rather two mutually exclusive conditions.

Of course, not all authors follow this trend. Travel writers such as Sues and David-Neel resist the temptation to reduce China to a matter of incomprehensibility. Specifically, they do so either by granting to the Chinese a well-rounded representation (see the previous quoted dialogue between Sues and a Chinese soldier), or by reflecting on their own persona. For example, David-Neel shows herself on various occasions questioning the solidity of her stance and competences. Similarly, David-Neel demonstrates on various occurrences questioning the solidity of her stance and competences. It is true that David-Neel sometimes tends to secure for herself a position of superiority, for instance when she mocks Yongden's superstition by comparing it to the more trustworthy western knowledge:

> While we were busy, a few blackbirds alighted on some branches and appeared to follow our doings with a mocking interest, moving their heads and uttering chirps like laughter. Their noise was unpleasant and Yongden grew angry. "These little black fellows," he told me, "do not seem to be natural birds. They must be some mischievous *mi ma yin* who play tricks at night with fire and music to delay us on the road, and have now taken another shape." I smiled at his imagination. (David-Neel 2005: 22)

Yet, the author also mentions a number of circumstances in which it is Yongden who plays a leading role, and certainly he emerges, with the passing of time, as the one on whom a greater responsibility is placed, either when it comes to dealing with locals, or for the solution of ordinary needs:

> As we were in a hamlet and night protected us, Yongden thought he might well take the opportunity to purchase some food. I wrapped myself in the thick dress according to the manner of the poor Tibetans, and made a pretence of sleeping to avoid useless talk if, by any chance, someone passed near me, while my companion went toward the houses. The first one he entered happened to be that of the lama in charge of the Lhakang-ra shrine. He was welcomed on his two-fold title of colleague and buyer. (David-Neel 2005: 37)

These are just two examples that attest to the rather balanced relation between David-Neel and Yongden. Albeit showing a good dose of self-confidence, the author is able, whenever necessary, to set herself aside and let Yongden take the lead. More generally, both Sues and David-Neel show awareness of the not-so-granitic position they occupy. It is precisely because they strive to take an insider perspective that they are capable of deconstructing that superior, uncontested position occupied by other travellers.

After having discussed how travellers perceive and represent China according to time and space coordinates – that is, lack of history vs. imminent change; city vs. countryside – at this point it remains to discuss more closely the representation of Chinese people, although some notes have already been provided.

***

The people of the Middle Kingdom are approached from different perspectives not only within the same epoch, but sometimes even within the same text. It is in these latter cases (Sues, Gray, and Legerton and Rawson are good examples) that the travel experience sets in motion an epistemological path that is both self-reflective and open to the Other. Conversely, there are texts whose horizon of knowledge remains largely unaltered from the beginning to the end, and in these travel books, more than elsewhere, one can detect the tendency to conceive of the Chinese as an indistinct mass. As seen in Chapter 1, contemporary authors such as Gifford and Bettinelli manifest this to various degrees, but the same happens with Bird, LaMotte, Gaunt, and the travelers of the in-between generation, for whom the homogenization of the Chinese betrays the unwillingness or difficulty to engage with them. For instance, when LaMotte lingers on political gossip, she often avoids mentioning the source from which she got the information, nor does she report dialogues. Hence, the Chinese (and the foreigners) become two wholly separated groups; two entities with no face or individuality:

> There is no special feeling for the Central powers any more than there is for the Entente Allies. We have gathered these impressions from many talks with the Chinese. Also we have talked with many foreigners who have lived in China for a long time, who have many Chinese friends and acquaintances, and understand the Chinese point of view. (LaMotte: 37-8)

Talks, rumors, superficial information: in short, it is a dusty, ephemeral China that LaMotte portrays. Voices are impersonal, opinions do not belong to anyone, the degree of generalization is maximum. As for the travelers from the '50s toward the late '70s, a vivid example comes from Parise who, at the beginning of his diary decides to list

> the characteristics of the Chinese crowds that strike the eye. These characteristics are an almost morbose shyness, their blushing, their fickle and cheeping lightness, who leads women, apart from dressing like soldier and men, to resemble with canaries or other tiny, happy birds; their sudden seriousness, which is attentive and full of calm; the candour of their faces and eyes, which sometimes are traversed by such big astonishments that they

become a bit cross-eyed; lastly, in a single word, the purity of their life.[147]
(Parise: 664; author's translation)

The deep estheticization of the Chinese with which this description is imbued is only the secondary effect of the preliminary reduction of the Chinese to a uniformed mass; one to which the general characteristics that Parise identifies can be attached without the risk of being contradicted. Even when people are granted a space and a voice, such as in Barthes's text, these people speak through a fully objectified language; they are dispossessed from their own words:

> 9h. Small hall of the hotel. Answers to the questions we filed in yesterday. Five young people, among which a woman. Futan University. 2) Our question: Lin Piao and the parallelism with Confucius? Scrums of Confucianism in today's traditions? It's the boyish philosopher (pretty sexy) who answers (look at the former drawing). Lin Piao: right-wing in essence; left-wing in appearance. Lin Piao and "restraining oneself and going back to rituals," the "Right Place." These precepts by Confucius: in fact, they are political precepts for going back to enslavement. (Barthes 2012: 64)

The French delegation arrives in China when the campaign against Confucius and Ling Piao is at operating speed. For this reason, they meet a number of people – from University professors, to teachers or factory managers – who explain to them the core ideas of the campaign. What is striking is the dryness of Barthes's notes, even when dialogues with these people are reported: it is a dryness, in fact, that mirrors the impossibility to know and understand, but also one that questions – implicitly – the extent to which the Chinese too can understand the indoctrination conducted by the Communist Party. Indeed, in another circumstance Barthes reports the words of the manager of the Agency (through which they have organized the journey) saying: "We realize that you do not understand wholly. We neither: [the campaign] is a movement that begins in depth" (Barthes 2009: 65; author's translation).[148]

***

Concerning the representation of people, the role of photography in the travel books under analysis acquires particular relevance. To begin with, there are travelers for whom photography has a chiefly documentary function. Pictures have to attest to what the traveler saw, or the places s/he went to. This is the case with Bird, who

---

[147] "Le caratteristiche della folla cinese che saltano agli occhi. Queste caratteristiche sono la timidezza quasi morbosa, i rossori, la leggerezza mobile e pigolante dei modi che fa assomigliare le donne, nonchè traverstite da soldatesse e da uomo, a canarini o altri uccelli minuscoli e felici, la serietà improvvisa, attenta e piena di calma, il candor infantile dei tratti del volto e degli occhi che ogni tanto si spalancano in stupefazioni che li rendono perfino un poco strabici e infine, in una sola parola, la purezza della loro vita."

[148] "Nous comprenons que vous ne compreniez pas tout. Nous non plus: mouvement qui commence en profondeur."

actually "had taken a course in developing and printing her own films before leaving England" (xix). This piece of information by Pat Barr, who wrote the introduction to the book, while enhancing the ethnographic and explorative motives of Bird's travel, projects onto her persona a professionalism that is at odds with her opening claim that the journey to China was "undertaken for recreation and interest solely" (preface). After all, being able to develop and print films is not something that was expected, at that time, from an amateur traveler (and even less so by a woman). It can also be advanced that Bird represents an early case in which the two pairs of concepts professional-amateur and traveler-tourist are very much blurred, signaling that their overlap could be a trans-historical trait (although more evidence would be needed).

Overall, Bird's book is enriched with 116 visual elements – photographs and drawings – out of 545 pages. One year after *The Yangtze Valley and Beyond*, Bird published *Chinese Pictures* (1900) that contains a selection of 60 photographs taken during the journey. According to the captions that accompany each image in *The Yangtze Valley and Beyond*, the great majority of Bird's pictures portray sceneries or visited places, while only a few of them focus on the people encountered along the journey or those who accompanied her (Figure 40). The paucity of photographs representing people is symptomatic of that domestication of the space of China witnessed in the opening of this chapter, where it was discussed how the Chinese are either overlooked, or defined as peaceful and industrious. In fact, Figure 40, which portrays the author's truckers, is a good example of how Bird's photography tends to typify the people who surround her journey (and make it possible). The point of view from which this picture is taken (as almost all Bird's pictures) is frontal, a perspective that calls for an engagement between the viewer and the represented subject (Kress and van Leeuwen 1996). In this way, Bird (attempts to) show(s) matter-of-factly who her Chinese crew is and how her truckers behave (i.e., in a very docile way, being all gathered together on the sampan). At the same time, these people are photographed from afar, a choice that makes them emerge as a whole; the details of their faces are sacrificed in favor of an overall seizure of the group (this is also due to the rudimental nature of the medium). Such distance reflects the one that separates the author and the staring viewer from the truckers, thus reasserting a clear division of roles and spaces. It is in this respect that Rosalind Morris (2009: 8), introducing a collective work on photography in (and about) East Asia, argues that photography, rather than a technology, constitutes the "discursive elaboration of a technologized relation to difference; a discourse, that is, that formalizes and reproduces difference, either social, racial or cultural.[149] To this, one must add that the caption of Bird's picture – "author's truckers at dinner" – definitely relegates the subjects to their function only: as Morgan (2007: 117) acutely notes "Bird repeatedly presents and names the people she photographs as representative types. Together, these types add up to one great prototype which would be named 'The Chinese'." This aspect is reinforced by the presence of drawings in the text, which usually integrate pictures whenever the author

---

[149] Similarly, by studying John Thomson's work about China, from which, we have seen, Bird took the picture "a street in Hangkow," Thomas Prasch (2007) contends that Thomson's work "reveals the ways in which Victorian photography was employed to define, delimit, and categorize groups" (53).

writes about something that she did not witness directly (it is the case, for instance, with the Chinese's fishing technique represented in Figure 41). These drawings, by reducing the saturation of details (even more than old pictures) and by being in black and white, strengthen the effect of typologization of Bird's photography and they come to metonymically stand for the generic ensemble (of people or a region) to which they point.

To conclude, beyond places and people there is one picture in Bird's text that deserves to be mentioned: a self-portrait of the author in a Manchu dress (Figure 42, staged once Bird was back in England). This is the sole picture in the whole book that portrays Bird, attesting to the author's tendency to move the attention away from her and toward what she witnesses. Again, the photograph is taken from a frontal perspective and the subject is photographed at a sufficient distance to be fully framed within the picture. In her *A Traveller in Skirts: Quest and Conquest in the Travel Narratives of Isabella Bird,* Evelyn Bach (1995: 593) affirms that Bird, by performing "an ongoing literary cross-dressing and re-dressing" allows "the narrative to escape a fixed gender category as Bird contrives to carve out an unsteady niche for herself." Bach is exclusively referring to Bird's shift in her writing from an authoritative masculine stance toward a more "poetic" and "rapturous" feminine stance, as she defines it. What is remarkable is that these same cross-dressing and re-dressing occur – literally and metaphorically – also in the picture. Indeed, by dressing up in a Manchu dress – a characteristic chinoiserie that reinforces the Western imaginary of China – Bird crosses and blurs the boundaries of a clearly gendered persona, whose traits are smoothed by both the distant perspective from which the picture is taken and by the pompous outfit she wears.

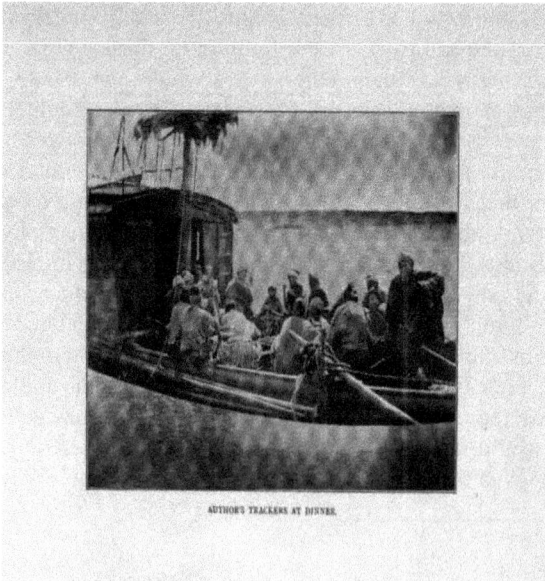

Figure 40: A photograph of Bird's truckers inserted in *The Yangtze Valley and Beyond*

Figure 41: One of the drawings in Bird's travelogue

Figure 42: Isabella Bird's self-portrait in Manchu dress

Overall, Bird's conception of travel writing's photography follows the ethos of the Royal Geographical Society to which she – one of the first women – belonged. According to Morgan (2007: 117), at that time "the view of photography as providing objective data, a scientific record, was already well entrenched at the Royal Geographical Society." In fact, the pictures that Bird includes in the book have the function of presenting the reader with the referent of her writing – however biased such an idea might be, as discussed in Chapter 2 – and visually proving where she went. In this respect, Bird's pictures tend escape the "tourist chronotope" not only in that the author is reluctant to appear in them – as a form of double sanctioning of her "having been there" – but also because she resorts to photography primarily as a tool for mapping those inland areas of the Yangtze that were still unseized by Western powers (the majority of pictures of landscapes come from the Yangtze's inland). In these cases, then, photography works more as a mapping of the "natural" rather than a stratification of the "social," that is, of China as a tourist-destination.

The underpinning logic of representation of Bird's pictures can be retrieved also in Gaunt's, at least to the extent they pretend to prove that what is recounted is credible. Again, places and broad views (Figure 43) are favored over people and details, although the ratio between pictures representing sceneries, on the one hand, and people, on the other, is more balanced than in Bird's text.

INSIDE THE CURTAIN WALL OF THE CHIEN MEN.

CAMELS OUTSIDE SOUTH-WESTERN WALL, PEKING.

Figure 43: Two pictures in Gaunt's *A Woman in China*

These representational choices reassert the idea of China as an object of interest – a place to be observed rather than one into which to delve or with which to actively engage. At the same time, Gaunt's case is worth discussing, because the book is introduced by a self-portrait of the author taken together with the truckers (Figure 44), an occurrence that seems to go in an opposite direction from what has been said so far.

Figure 44: The picture that opens the book *A Woman in China*

The travelogue opens with a detailed table of contents and a list of all the photographs included. Yet, the photograph of the author reproduced above is not mentioned, despite being not *a* picture among the others, but *the one* that occupies the frontispiece. The picture, it is suggested, takes on an exemplary significance because it signals what the reader will find in the text. Unlike Bird, Gaunt is here shown among local people. In a way, then, the distance between the traveler and the Chinese is zeroed. Yet, the power relations and roles between them remain very much unbalanced and separated. Gaunt is photographed while seated on her sedan chair and placed at the center of the frame; the coolies, instead, sustain her at both sides. Furthermore, while the author is staring at the camera, none of the truckers is, each of them looking in a different direction or keeping the gaze down. This leads to contend that, despite being included within the photograph, the Chinese maintain a subaltern position with respect to the author and they only exist as far as their function is concerned. In this respect, it is also notable that the caption, which reads "the author at the Ming tombs," makes no reference to the people surrounding Gaunt, as if they were merely an unavoidable part of the context. More than that, Gaunt fails to acknowledge the author of the picture, whose identity is unmentioned in the book. For all these considerations, we enter the realm of photography intended as a social performance: as Larsen (2006: 250) points out: "the camerawork is concerned not only with consuming places, but also with producing social relations." It could be advanced, therefore, that the picture exemplifies, *ex principio*, the disparity between Gaunt and the people with whom she travels, and, more generally, the stance maintained by the author throughout the whole text: one of privileged mobility – at least for that time – and imbued with a good dose of paternalism for all the people she encounters.

Continuing to follow a chronological path, a third example for the discussion of photography is LaMotte's *Peking Dust*. The analysis has already shown that the American author manifests in her writing the tendency to deny the Chinese an active agency concerning their own destiny. On the contrary, the pictures, which were taken by Warren R. Austin, F. C. Hitchcock, Margaret Frieder, T. Severin, and Rachel Snow, as LaMotte acknowledges at the beginning of her work, convey a different attitude.

Figure 45: A photograph of a "fruit stall in the bazaar" inserted in LaMotte's *Peking Dust*

Figure 46: The photograph of a "village outside walls of Peking" in LaMotte's travelogue

Figure 47: The picture of a "fortune teller"

First of all, LaMotte never appears in the pictures. This means that China and the Chinese are the sole subjects in focus (Figures 45, 46, 47 are examples). Specifically, the majority of pictures portray people rather than places, a feature that distances these images from both Bird and Gaunt's. Moreover, the mode of representation that characterizes the photographs in LaMotte's text is different from what we have hitherto seen: by getting closer to the subject, these pictures break away from the afar views favored in *The Yangtze River and Beyond* and *A Woman in China*, preferring to take a closer look at the subjects portrayed. It is true, as the captions of the Figures 45 and 47 above testify, that the Chinese are still represented according to their activity. Yet, the proximity of the photographers to their subjects allows pictures to become less typological: people's roundness thickens; life in its serendipitous manifestation begins to fill the frame. What Morris (2009: 3) characterizes as the "self-disclosing and static quality of the Asian images," that is, the intentional staging of the subject to be photographed, loses in these pictures part of its strength. China, in other words, begins to be perceived in its plurality, as an ensemble of subjects with whom to get in contact. Hence, the engagement between Westerners and the Chinese, which in LaMotte's written text is largely unmentioned, finds a form of mediation (if not a full realization) in and through photography.

Scidmore's *Westward to the Far East* is a case in itself. It was already noted that, at the level of writing, the book approaches closely the tourist guide in that the representation of China is reduced to a mono-dimensional tourist set. Visual elements follow the text along the same line, but they also bring to light some interesting frictions. The text presents both pictures and drawings: most remarkable is that these elements are rarely consonant with the written text, despite the fact that they are mingled into it. Put differently, words and images follow different representational paths. This discordance is strengthened by the fact that drawings and pictures show types, rather than the precise subjects or places described: "a pagoda," "a sampan," "a Chinese street" (Figures 48, 49 below, and Figure 39 above). In this same respect, captions do not help much in contextualizing what we see, leaving the impression of being confronted with a sort of visual catalogue, rather than with a representation of precise subjects and places. The sense of uprootedness of the images is also conveyed by their inevitable poor quality that tends to de-materialize the referent, which is frequently projected onto an indefinite background. From these considerations, it would be hazardous to claim that the illustrations inserted in Scidmore's book embed a tourist chronotope; rather, they seem to function primarily as a visual typologization of China; a typologization whose goal, if any, is to kindle the readers' imagination and his desire to reach the destination, while self-referentially celebrating the potentiality of the "new" medium.

Figure 48: A pagoda in Scidmore's text

SAMPAN AND FLOWER BOAT, CANTON.

Figure 49: A sampan

With the passing of time, one can observe an improvement in the pictures' quality – photographs become neater due to improved technology – as well as a reworking of the modes of representation. Sues is a case in point. The pictures that are inserted in her travelogue mimic the author's attempt to become "the man in the street" (Sues: 9). First of all, almost all the illustrations portray people: not only famous political leaders, but also common soldiers and locals. Sceneries and landmarks are almost completely eschewed. Photography acquires an eminently social and reportage-like connotation: it does not pretend to show how China is; rather, it compels readers to become aware of the internal conflicts and the political tensions that affect the country. Pictures give faces – suffering but smiling faces – to both Nationalists and Communists. Besides, the predominant point of view is the close-up, a choice that, together with the improvement in photographic films and developing processes, gives a higher-quality definition to the subjects portrayed. Captions finally report the names of the people shown, going beyond their mere roles or functions. Most importantly, Sues becomes herself part of the visually represented world and she does so by engaging *intra pares* among the Chinese, be they military authorities or humble people (see Figure 50).

With Commander Chu Teh, father of China's guerillas

Farewell, Shansi: P'eng Teh-hwai (*background*), K'ang
Keh-chin and Chu Teh (*front*)

Figure 50: Ilona Sues portrayed with commander Chu Teh and soldiers

More generally, early travel writers refrain from entering the scene of photography. It is only from the 1930s that we witness a turn of the camera toward the traveler. Moreover, the comparison between photographs from different epochs shows that pictures bring with(in) them, beyond the chronotope of the "represented world," the historicized "chronos" of their mode of representation – that is, photography as a technology – attesting to the evolution and improvement of the medium, of its techniques, and of the abilities of its users.

***

Lastly, the analysis addresses a few examples of monomodal travelogues. As it was for the contemporary travel writers analyzed in the first part of this work, the absence of pictures can be symptomatic of a number of reasons, such as editorial choices or the political implications (i.e., censorship) that photography brings with itself.

Pictures are absent from the chosen edition of Fleming's travel books. Fleming, however, does mention that he took some photographs during the two journeys, so the motivation for their absence shifts toward an editorial-related matter. The same logic also applies to Maillart: not only does the French edition of *Forbidden Journey* (*Oasis interdites*) include some pictures, but Maillart also published visual works – for example, *La vie immédiate* (1991, with accompanying text by Swiss traveler Nicolas Bouvier) – which are devoted to presenting the pictures she took on her journeys. This means that a thoughtful discussion on the presence/absence of illustrations from "classic" travelogues should also take into account the various editions and reprints of the "same" text, as well as the release of country-tailored publications (such as the mentioned distinction between the French and English edition of Maillart's travelogue). "Even original editions," Stacy Burton (2014: 56-7) notes on this matter, "differ in the number and placement of photographs: Fleming's *One's Company* was published with four pages of photos in Britain, twenty in the United States. Reprints typically treat visual images as ephemera akin to cover art, excising them entirely or in part without acknowledgement." This means that when it comes to investigating early 20th century travelogues as artifacts, the analysis should configure a diachronic collation among the various mediations of each genium (contemporary texts, instead, usually have one single edition). As far as the present work is concerned, however, this task would exceed its scope, so only one edition for each travelogue was taken into account.

Concerning David-Neel, the insertion of images in her text calls directly into question the political and documentary relevance of photography. The author specifies at the beginning of her *Voyage d'une parisienne à Lhassa* (French monomodal edition of her travelogue):

> It was impossible for me to include a camera in my beggar's bundles. Moreover, neither Yongden nor myself, disguised as poor pilgrims as we were, could run the risk of getting caught while taking photos. The most part of those that illustrate this book have been taken during my earlier peregrinations in Tibet.[150] (David-Neel 2008: 16; author's translation)

From this passage, we deduce that all the pictures that enrich *My Journey to Lhasa* (2005, English multimodal edition of her book) refer to experiences that are antecedent to the travel described. In this regard, some literary (but not photographic) critics[151] have attempted to prove that the pictures inserted in the books are hoaxes, which would then attest to the fact that David-Neel never reached Lhasa. However

---

[150] This passage, which concludes the introduction in the French edition of David-Neel's travelogue, has been excised from the 2005 English edition: "Il m'était impossible d'inclure un appareil photographique dans mes bagages de mendiante et, ni Yongden, ni moi, déguisés en pauvres hères ne devaient être surprise prenant des photographies. La plupart des celles qui illustrent ce livre ont été prises au cours de mes précédents pérégrinations au Thibet."

[151] Sara Mills (1991) discusses in depth Jeanne Denys's critique of David-Neel's endeavor: according to Denys, David-Neel never made it to Lhasa.

valid these arguments might be,[152] for the present discussion it is crucial to highlight once more photography's fragile relation to truthfulness, whose epistemological function can be, at once, that of documenting or challenging what words allude to. Here, again, a discussion on the chronotopic discrepancies between pictures and text (as mentioned by the author) could bring to light interesting findings concerning the precarious relation between the represented world and its modes of representation, but the analysis would exceed the limit of the present work.

It is possibly more relevant to remark, from the passage quoted above, David-Neel's awareness of the consequences that photographing might have on her goal. In other words, photography becomes a discriminating medium; one that can attract the attention of locals and authorities alike and, as such, that can spoil the author's endeavor. Quite interestingly, this statement echoes what Thubron said during the interview, namely that one of the reasons why he did not take a camera with him is the fear of seeing his freedom of mobility limited.[153] It seems as if certain restrictions in China continue to run throughout the 20th century up to the present day. On this point, it is also worth mentioning that none of the travel books from the 1950s, 1960s, 1970s, and 1980s under analysis present pictures. Be it a conscious choice by the authors or an imposition by the publishers or the Chinese authorities,[154] the absence of illustrations from these three travel books reinforces the sense of unrepresentability proper to the travelers' experiences. Among them, a quite unique case is that of Barthes. His diary does not include pictures, but here and there readers encounter small pencil sketches of the places visited, or the people encountered. These sketches are sometimes so stylized that their intelligibility can become problematic. It could also be contended that the effect they produce is to further complexify the Chinese universe – that is, the reading of what is "worth looking," according to Barthes' (2012: 79) own words – rather than clarifying some of its features. Through these sketches, the country becomes even more skeletal and phantasmal and, as soon as the bricks of propaganda are bypassed by the trait of the pencil, China appears as a signifier that has ultimately lost its referent. It could be said that China is turned into that *Empire des signes* (1970) that Barthes had sketched out of Japan just a few years before. However, while in Japan these signs, as Charles Forsdick (2006: 71) notes, "evolved from the untranslatability of his surroundings into Western terms as well as the dislocations this provoked, from China he [Barthes] returns with 'rien'."

---

[152] Refer back to Chapters 1 and 2.

[153] Colin Thubron, interview.

[154] In this respect, it must be remarked that Franco Fortini, an Italian writer who went to China in 1955, took a great number of photographs, which were later exhibited in Italy.

THE SELF-REPRESENTATION OF LATE 19TH TO 20TH CENTURY TRAVEL AUTHORS

Mirroring the analysis conducted in Chapter 3 (without however the possibility of collating the texts with the authors' own voices) this section briefly explores the way in which the travel writers under analysis think of and represent themselves.

We have seen that Bird offers to the reader a composite image of herself. On the one hand, she underlines the unpretentiousness of her journey, arguing that she travels for leisure. This is so, despite the fact that the author travelled well beyond beaten tracks and sometimes in very uncomfortable conditions. On the other hand, the kind of information she provides, together with the paternalistic, pedagogic tone that permeates the travel book, confer upon Bird a decisive authority as far as China's matters are concerned. Moreover, the accompanying of the writing with a variety of pictures that required a fair degree of expertise of the medium shows Bird's desire, *ex principio*, to go to China in order to accurately report on the country, rather than as an amateurish visitor. A similar ambivalence can be found in Fleming's persona. In the foreword to *One's Company*, Fleming warns the reader that:

> This book is a superficial account of an unsensational journey. The book describes in some detail what I saw and what I did and in considerably less detail what most other travellers have also seen and done. If it has any value at all, it is the light which it throws on the process of travel amateur travel. (Fleming: xi)

Once we add to this self-deprecating statement Fleming's disclosure that he cannot speak any Chinese, what emerges is a representation of the author as an amateur figure. Yet, as soon as one begins to read *One's Company*, one "discovers" that Fleming is a well-trained journalist and he is travelling on the premise of going into the field and getting a clearer idea about the latest updates on the "great game" in which China is caught at the turning of 1930s. In this sense, the professionalization of his persona clashes with the pretension of appearing as an amateur, either in writing or in travelling. When passing through Poland by train, he reports this telling dialogue:

> I dine with a pleasant young Englishman. He claims to know Warsaw and we embark on a markedly one-sided discussion on the Upper Silesian plebiscite of '21. My mission, when revealed, awes him. "Manchuria!" he exclaims. "But can you speak Russian, or Chinese, or Japanese?" Alas, I cannot. "Then, how will you manage?" I say I do not know. He eyes me with respect; a desperate fellow, this, he is thinking. It is clear that he finds me Ouidan. My own sense of proportion I regard as impregnably established. In the light of it, a journey to Manchuria is a perfectly normal undertaking: nothing to get excited about. But the world at large persists in maintaining a set of values the simplification of travel has rendered obsolete. (Fleming: 17)

By resorting to the transposed speech – quite rare in the text and never with Chinese people – it is possible to derive the two complementary facets of Fleming's persona. On the one side, so unprepared is he that he appears to the other's eye as a naïve traveler; on the other side, however, the bewilderment of the interlocutor once Fleming reveals his plans has the function of projecting onto the author's persona the allure of the adventurer: not only does he accomplish an uncommon journey, but he turns the "extraordinary" into the ordinary. Fleming's persona becomes even more complex when one thinks that at the end of the first book he mentions having become to the others' eyes a sort of authority on China's political matters: a professionalization of his figure that contrasts, once more, with the opening of the first book (quoted above) where the value of the information he acquired while travelling is downplayed. In the opening of the second book, however, he declares more overtly the two motives at the base of his journey: as a journalist, he aims to get a closer look at the current situation in the region; as a traveler, he wants to satisfy his selfish desire to move. More broadly, Fleming loves to let his self-representation float between an amateur traveler persona and a more professional role, as both a traveler and a writer.

For her part, Maillart does not refrain from straightforwardly presenting herself as a journalist. At the same time, it is in the different way in which she conceives the whole experience that she distances her own traveler persona from Fleming's. All along the journey, Maillart tends to linger, to take her own time, to let time flow unreservedly. As a consequence, if for Fleming the journey consists of a physical crossing to be accomplished in the fastest way possible, Maillart's experience configures a much more interiorized space-time dimension. She acknowledges this divide in various circumstances:

> United in the craving to succeed in our enterprise, we had come to a perfect understanding. Yet, we did not see things from the same angle. Every night Peter would repeat his refrain "Sixty *lis* nearer to London." He did it to annoy me and I would tell him to shut up, for I wanted to forget that we had, inevitably, to return home. I should have liked the journey to continue for the rest of my life. (Maillart: 88)

To be sure, Fleming himself is aware of the fact that he and Maillart have different horizons in sight. Indeed, he remarks in the last pages of his book that the end of the journey probably meant less to her than to him, who craved being back in London as soon as possible. Maureen Mulligan (2008), who has devoted an article on the comparison between the two texts and authors, contends that Maillart's inclination toward a more subjective, slow-paced approach to the journey reflects a broader picture in which Fleming and Maillart re-enact a traditional gender division of roles while on the road. In fact, a gendered taintedness characterizes both accounts, often in the form of an overt mirroring of Fleming and Maillart's different visions:

P. was bored by my craving to understand the thousands of diverse lives that make up humankind and bored, too, by my need to relate my own life to life in general. Peter was troubled by none of these things. (Maillart: 148)

Fleming and Maillart share the same wish to travel, but this responds to very different, if not opposite, conceptions of the experience. Fleming wants to witness and report; Maillart thinks of the journey as a diversion from Western materialism. On these premises, the journalistic facet of Maillart's persona becomes secondary in favor of a self-representation as a freed and unbound explorer. Again, it is Maillart herself who puts this in print: "what mattered was myself, I, who was living at the centre of the world – that 'I' who did not want to disappear without accomplishing something worthwhile" (268). Despite the radical differences between Fleming and Maillart, the two manage to get along quite well for the whole duration of the journey. In particular, it is Fleming who pays tribute in the book to his companion, pointing out that "I got, during our seven months together, so used to regarding Kini as an equal in most things and a superior one in some that perhaps I have paid over-few tributes to (among other things) her powers of endurance" (223). While, at the base of such praise, certainly lies a gendered representation of feminine and masculine roles, it also works as an acknowledgment of the positive outcome of their pairing along the road, notwithstanding the mutual reluctance, at the beginning, to travel together.

This same form of gender mirroring is also present in David-Neel's text. As noted, between David-Neel and Yongden there is a rather balanced division of roles and competences. It takes roughly 20 pages for David-Neel to report Yongden's own words for the first time, but from that moment on his figure becomes essential, either for the better – such as when he is the "key" to getting hospitality from other lamas – and the worse, for example when he gets injured and David-Neel is obliged to care after him. Hence, one derives a representation of the author as an intrepid (and persevering) traveler, but also one who is aware of her own constraints as a Western woman, compelling her to travel with somebody more expert than her. Such awareness finds its manifestation in the constant confrontations between the two, as if the accomplishment of the journey in a pair promoted a gendered characterization of each person's own persona as a mutual process, bringing to the surface of the text a neater distinction of roles. This does not mean, of course, that gender issues are altogether absent from texts such as those by Bird and Gaunt, nor that these authors necessarily take on a male role, but that in texts where a man and a woman are travelling together gender issues are more likely to appear. As Mills (1991: 149) correctly points out, in solo female travelogues "the narrator is a strong, determined figure who battles against extremes of hardship, rarely losing face or making reference to 'feminine' concerns." This tendency was also touched upon in the previous chapter, noting that in contemporary travel books and blogs – retrospectively, one could say *also* in contemporary travel books and blogs – female travel writers avoid explicitly defining their persona in terms of gender. Arnaud, Becki, Curieuse Voyageuse, and Gattosandro Viaggiatore rarely underline that they are women travelers, preferring to stress either the uniqueness of their journey, or their desire to write in order to share their experience. In this respect, if Thompson

(2011: 163) warns that "women have always travelled more extensively than such masculine mythology would suggest," Mills (1991) complements such a statement by arguing that travel writing appears as a predominantly male literary form because of the systematic exclusion, especially in the 18th and 19th centuries, of female voices from the publishing market. Mills' claim acquires an even greater significance when taking a transmedial perspective. Indeed, while, through the whole 20th century, the number of travel books about China authored by male writers is substantially greater than that of women-authored publications, the ratio is much more balanced when one looks at travel blogs. The online environment, in other words, seems to represent a more easily accessible (and accessed) channel for female travelers than the publishing market.

Lastly, with regard to the self-representation of the travel writers who went to China between 1949 and the early 1980s, one can observe a radical erasure of that galaxy of terms – explorer, traveler, tourist, amateur writer, journalist, novelist, etc. – that characterizes earlier and later peers. Political restrictions, on the one hand, and predetermined itineraries, on the other, are so encumbering that they turn the experience into a sort of parade, to which travelers attend powerlessly. They are not even urged to question or contextualize their roles: as Westerners, they simply are privileged subjects (i.e., delegates) whose function is to report on China, or, better, on the smooth functioning of propaganda. By being confronted with loads of "bricks," it becomes arduous for these delegations to think of themselves as travelers or even tourists; rather, they could be more properly defined as spectators: spectators of a reiterated show. This is how, mockingly, Barthes reports the question of a Chinese writer, who wants to know the perception in France of Confucius and Lin Biao: "Lin Biao Confucius in France? Up until now, confusion in France, incomprehensible. One of our tasks when we get back: make him better known and divulgate. [What did you do on this trip? We worked!]" (Barthes 2012: 48)

CONCLUSION

This chapter provided a diachronic analysis of Western travel books about China, beginning at the end of the 19th century and covering almost a century, up to the 1980s. In so doing, the survey merged with the analysis conducted in the first part of the work. The study highlighted that some of the rhetorical tropes and medial features that are characteristic of early travel books run, in fact, throughout the whole century. Authors from different epochs represent China's history, geography, and people very similarly (both verbally and visually, although as far as photography is concerned a major difference with contemporary authors is that these latter tend to appear much more often in pictures than early travelers). In particular, the idea of China as a timeless country, whose authenticity can be only found in the outback, as well as the recurrence of the travelers' dissatisfaction when it comes to understanding the Chinese, are common tropes to many of the travelogues surveyed. At the same time, it can also happen that travel writers who are contemporaneous deliver radically different accounts in form and content. It is the case, for instance, of Fleming's *News from Tartary* and Maillart's *Forbidden Journey*, but also David-Neel's *Une parisienne à Lhasa* and LaMotte's *Peking Dust*, or Scidmore's travel guide.

These contrasting trends demonstrate that the historical and cultural conditions of China played a role – as suggested by Nicholas Clifford (2001) – in dictating the travel books' agenda, but the individual attitude with which each traveler approached China is also a decisive factor. In this sense, it is argued that it would be hazardous to identify an overreaching linear evolution of the way in which China has been represented. Rather, the picture that derives from the analysis is very much fragmented.

The same also applies to the conception of travel writing as a genre. Wars and conflicts in early 20th century China attracted (and were the consequence of) the attention of Western powers and people: from popular readers, to professional reporters and political and commercial stakeholders. Nonetheless, it also emerged that a number of travel writers of that period overlooked these same events, preferring to provide a more romantic representation of the experience. Hence a univocal transition from the travel book to the travel-reportage is contested, insofar as it was ultimately the travel writer's attitude toward China to shape his/her work.

As for the self-representation of travel writers, the chapter brought to light that the blurring of concepts such as "traveller," "tourist," "resident," "amateur," and "professional" (already witnessed among contemporary travel authors and bloggers), is also indicative of early travel writers. This poses the question of whether a clear distinction among these terms has ever had any practical foundation, beyond an abstract theorization.

Lastly, the generation of Western travel writers who went to China between 1949 and the early 1980s constitutes a case in itself. The suffocating limitations on mobility imposed by the Chinese authorities, together with the following of pre-fabricated itineraries, led to a sublimated representation of China, one that often conveys to the reader a sense of powerless unintelligibility. At the same time, contributing to such a representation is also the literary credo of the surveyed authors. To a greater or lesser degree, Malaparte, Parise, Barthes, and Malerba were all influenced in their writings by the experimentations in language of the neo-avant-gardes of which they were part.

The proposed survey did not aim at being exhaustive, but hopefully it managed to show the variety of stances as well as the common (Western) imaginary through which China has been approached in printed travel writing over the 20th century. Returning to the transmedial comparison that framed the first part of the study, it could be argued that the medium plays a more relevant role in the shaping of the travel writing genre than the passing of time. This was epitomized by the striking similarity posited in the opening to this chapter between Bird and Marco Polo's descriptions of Hangzhou; a similarity that led to contend in favor of the trans-historicity of the rhetorical and medial features of the texts.

CHAPTER 5

"Heterodox" Representations in Chinese Travel Books and Blogs

This last chapter "rescues" the transmedial axis characterizing Chapters 1 to 3 and applies it to Chinese travel writing. The analysis presents an overview of six contemporary Chinese-authored travel books and three travel blogs about the Middle Kingdom. Such an overview does not pretend to be exhaustive or to counterbalance the analysis of the texts offered in the previous chapters, but rather aims to provide an exemplary choice of Chinese texts, in order to 1) understand how Chinese writers perceive and represent their own country (and the extent to which these accounts are rhetorically and medially consonant with, or differ from, those analyzed so far); and 2) investigate how Chinese writers make use of the chosen medial format (and how such use may be culturally dependent). Eventually, the chapter offers insights into both the travel writing genre and the figure of the travel writer as they are conceived and shaped in today's China. As a matter of fact, the geopolitical notion of "China" is questioned through the chosen authors and travelogues. Given that the materials were largely collected in Hong Kong, many of the texts are written by Hongkongers, whose positions toward China, as well as their own self-representations, make evident the extent to which the relations between Mainland China and the ex-UK colony (but also Taiwan and Macau) remain subjected to a latent instability.[155] Moreover, the way in which these texts are written also raises debate. Indeed, some authors, although being Chinese, resort to English as their preferred language for publication. In this regard, during the interviews with Chinese writers who made such a choice, their underpinning motives were addressed, showing that these largely relate to the fact of having a hybrid cultural background.

In practice, the chapter is structured following a gradual transition: it starts from the analysis of an English travel book written by a Chinese-born and currently UK-based author – Sun Shuyun – and concludes with Chinese travelogues and travel blogs written by Mainlanders, passing through those texts that have been authored in English and/or Chinese by Hong Kong writers. In such a transition, the analysis follows the critical path developed from Chapters 1 to 3, in terms of the texts' narrative form, their hypertextuality and paratextual elements, and the kind of

---

[155] Epitomizing is the case of the Umbrella Movement, which was also mentioned by some writers in the interviews. The Umbrella Movement was a protest held in Hong Kong for over two months at the end of 2014 against the proposed reform of the election system, which basically introduced the possibility for the Chinese Communist Party to pre-screen Hong Kong's candidates before they could take part in the electoral campaign. The protest, however, did not mange to bring any kind of amendment to the reform. At the same time, the UM raised further concerns about the way in which the coercive force of the police was put at the service of the government during the protest.

information they provide (with considerations about the chronotope of photography). Moreover, as was the case with Western writers, here too the analysis is complemented by references to the interviews with Chinese authors and bloggers.

HISTORICAL OVERVIEW

When it comes to investigating contemporary Chinese travel writing, it is necessary to draw upon two main research axes in order to contextualize the analysis. On the one hand are those studies that look at Chinese-authored travel accounts about the West. In this sense, it is essential to note a widespread tendency in Western scholarship to diminish, if not dismiss completely, the presence and impact of these accounts. For instance, in the introduction to the collection *Travel Writing and Empire: Postcolonial Theory in Transit*, Steve Clark (1999: 3) contends that "to a certain extent travel writing is inevitably one-way traffic, because the Europeans mapped the world rather than the world mapping them." Clark's claim seems to postulate a deterministic linkage between (more or less) expansionist projects by Western powers and the production of travel writing. Eventually, then, the absence of hegemonic goals by the Chinese is symmetrically tied to the lack of travel accounts. To be sure, Clark is not alone in holding such a position. James Clarke (1997: 29) argues that "on the whole the East has not approached the West with enthusiasm and curiosity, has not on its own accord welcomed Western ideas, nor used the latter to undermine its own." Clarke's core assumption about how the East – China and India in particular – has played a chiefly passive role with respect to the West is not that dissimilar to Clark's argument about the univocal mapping of the world by Westerners. The picture, however, is much more complex than that. The claims of these two scholars – which seem affected by the same ethnocentrism they aim to criticize – have been undermined by recent research on pre-modern and modern China in relation to travel. This is the case, specifically, with Xiaofei Tian's (2012) *Visionary Journeys*. By proposing a parallel between modern and medieval China, on the basis that in both epochs the contacts between the West and China were extremely frequent, Tian (2012: 2) argues that travels were also undertaken by Chinese people to the West and "not just by sailors and traders but by members of the elite who wrote accounts of their journeys for the eager consumption of a home audience." This finding is illuminating for two reasons. Firstly, it tells us that pre-modern and modern Chinese people also demonstrated an eagerness to know and explore the West. Therefore, the (supposed) passivity of the East seems chiefly the result of a Western lack of interest, at best, or of conscious erasure, at worst. Secondly, Tian makes clear that the reporting was done not only for official motives, but also for information and entertainment. Hence, it would be hazardous to univocally relate the production of travel writing to hegemonic and mapping projects.

The second research axis addresses those travel accounts written by Chinese people about the Middle Kingdom (which is of greatest interest here).[156] *Inscribed Landscapes* (1994) by Richard Strassberg is a seminal standpoint for any research that aims at exploring the evolution of the travel writing genre within China. By providing translations into English of texts authored by Chinese poets, aristocrats and scholars from the 1st century A. D. to the 19th century, Strassberg identifies the emergence of two canons. The main differences between the two have to do with the texts' purposes and their characterizing discourses: "at one pole," Strassberg (1994: 10) points out, "was the objective, moralizing perspective of historiography; at the other, a mode of expressive and aesthetic responses to the landscape derived from poetic genres that could be termed 'lyrical'." Yet, to make these canons similar is the fact that they both offer a static, immutable representation of the experience. Indeed, in the case of historiographical travel accounts, the travel experience was subservient to a portrayal and reassertion of the social, cultural, and political status quo, celebrating Confucianism and its founding precepts of waiting, detachment, and balance. Similarly, those texts that celebrated landscapes provided a "pictorial" flattened representation of China, in which the writing subject was merely a gazing "I" who did not manifest any engagement with the context or personal growth. As Strassberg (1994: 22) himself underlines, "the quest is less significant in Chinese travel writing," and therefore "whereas Western travel writing, with its novelistic orientation, emphasizes social events and portraits of noteworthy characters, the poetic underpinnings of Chinese travel writing tend to stress objects and qualities perceived in the landscape" (31). Even James Hargett (2016), albeit acutely distinguishing various phases within the Chinese travel writing's tradition, claims that "one key aspect of Chinese travel literature is its visual quality. Essentially, authors are creating cinematic-like word-pictures of places – places they want readers to 'see' by reading a text" (114).

As the analysis will show, contemporary travel books are rather distant from modern and pre-modern ones, in terms of their epistemological horizon and rhetorical features. At the same time, travel blogs do bear – somewhat paradoxically – similarities with classic printed texts.

---

[156] These texts recount journeys that go under the label of "home travels." However, given the presence of special administrative regions (such as Hong Kong), this term is contested when it comes to today's China. The analysis will bring this to light and discuss the fragmentation of the notion of "China" operated by the writers surveyed. This largely depends on the writers' biographies. In fact, some of them are Hongkongers, others are returning (Chinese or Hong Kong) expatriates, and still others are Mainlanders. While all of these writers can rely upon a deep knowledge of the language and the culture of the places they visited in China, speaking exclusively in terms of "home travels" is reductive insofar as for some of them China does represent a "different" context from Hong Kong or from the place abroad where they lived a part of their lives. Therefore, for some of these writers it is more a matter of "returning travels" and of acknowledging the differences and similarities they share with today's Mainland China.

THE LONG MARCH DECONSTRUCTED

The analysis starts from an English travelogue written by Chinese-born writer, scholar and filmmaker Sun Shuyun. After studying English literature at Beijing University, Shuyun obtained a scholarship from the University of Oxford, where she moved to complete her studies. Since then, she has been working between Beijing and London (where she currently lives). Having lived in the UK for decades, Shuyun has a privileged position from which to speak about the Middle Kingdom to both Chinese and Western audiences. In this respect, one question in the interview revolved around how she judged the Western perception and representation of China. Shuyun answered promptly that

> When you look at Western mainstream media reports on China it all revolves around very few subjects: politics, religion, environment, dissidents. But why is that so? China is much more complex. I also met personally with some foreign correspondents and I have to say that I was not impressed by their knowledge of China: it was, indeed, very superficial.[157]

With this as a departure point, it is possible to see that Shuyun's varied projects as a writer and filmmaker share the common goal of presenting a different, more composite image of China. In terms of her written works, Shuyun has published three major books: *Ten Thousand Miles Without a Cloud* (2003), *The Long March: The True History of Communist China's Founding Myth* (2006), and *A Year in Tibet* (2008). *The Long March* – which is of most interest here – recounts Shuyun's effort to re-travel the whole itinerary of the Long March and, along the way, to meet up with the few surviving veterans who accomplished that endeavor. Shuyun's goal is to understand, from direct testimonies, if what is narrated in history books is plausible. In fact, the lived reality of soldiers turns out to be much more complex and contradictory than the one construed by the Communist Party. "Genuinely, 90% of the people did not know what they were doing," Shuyun said in the interview, "if they had something to eat, it was enough for them; they were living day by day." The author's journey, then, represents the opportunity to travel around China and (try to) deconstruct the grand narrative at the base of today's China. This is what she writes in the introduction to her book:

> For us the Long March is a story on a par with Moses leading the exodus out of Egypt. We can hardly escape it. Few have ever challenged or even modestly questioned the Long March myth; it is just part of who we are. In 2004, seventy years after it began, I set out over the same route to discover as much as I could about the realities beyond the myth. I managed to find more than forty veterans, happily with their memories still fresh and their spirits

---

[157] Sun Shuyun, interview by Stefano Calzati, December 16, 2014, in person.

undiminished. Once I started talking to them, their stories poured out. (Shuyun 2006: 2-4)

From the outset, Shuyun presents her work as one grounded in the firm will to dig into the past. It could also be suggested that her purpose, rather than being instrumental to a celebrative representation of China, as was the case with historiographical classic travelogues, is to exploit the epistemological power of travel (and writing) in order to destabilize many of the commonly held assumptions about the country's recent history.

In the book, at least three discourses about the Long March intertwine: the one of the interviewed veterans, the one which belongs to Shuyun (as a representative of her generation), and the official one promoted by the Communist Party (which is variously quoted by the author throughout the text). While at the beginning Shuyun's perspective is closer to the official one, largely due to her indoctrination since primary school, with the unfolding of the journey she realizes the extent to which veterans have a different story to tell. Each of these discourses is, at the same time, collective and individual; it frames the conception that a whole society has elaborated around the Long March, as well as the individual memory(ies) – direct or indirect – from which each subject derives his/her own representation of the events. This also means that the book is structured on varying degrees of factuality – the official/collective one of the Party and the individual ones of the veterans and Shuyun herself, through the memories of her father – and it is only through an accurate collation of the three discourses that the debunking of the myth – which is by definition a-temporal – can occur. The potential discrepancy among the different discourses is overtly addressed by Shuyun while talking about veteran Huang with a government clerk:

> "He [Huang] is only a peasant. You should really talk to old Wu. He used to be the Prime Minister's bodyguard. He knows things." I knew what he thought: it was only worth talking to the heroes and the big decision-makers; but their stories are already in our history books, told and retold until they have become symbols, the eternal refrain. Perhaps to him, Huang was not enough of a committed revolutionary, but his ordinary life as a foot soldier on the march was just what I was missing. With luck it would tell me the unadorned truth. (Shuyun 2006: 28)

Notwithstanding Shuyun's optimistic faith in the possibility of uncovering an ultimate truth, what is of greatest importance here is the strategy she professes: if a reliable understanding of what happened during the Long March can ever be achieved, it will be by avoiding dominant voices and contrasting those with the testimonies that have not been heard yet. It is, in other words, a comparative-archaeological matter: one of excavation, research, collation, and assessment of the ideological charge of the sources. Shuyun explained in the interview:

> The discovery of the journey begins much earlier than the physical displacement. The joy that came to me from the reading of the books

> included in the bibliography is already part of the journey. But it was difficult because the Party controls the books published. Therefore, the journey really played a crucial role and allowed me to bring home a significantly different view from the one you can find in official documents.

Ignorance and knowledge, oblivion and re-discovery: to connect these polarized terms is travel, intended as a practice that, if mindfully performed, can bring (self)clarification. In particular, it is worth highlighting that Shuyun acknowledges the intertextual canvas that underpins her work: she read a lot before the departure and reported all the quoted documents in the bibliography. This, together with the insertion of pictures of the veterans and a map of China that signals the Red Armies' wanderings, strengthen both the text's hypertextuality and its generic hybridity, mixing features of the treatise, the collective autobiography, and the ethnography.

Looking retrospectively at Chapter 1, it could be said that *The Long March* gets close to Legerton and Rawson's *Invisible China* as far as the documentary and dialogic features of the work are concerned. At the same time, however, Shuyun's work is quite different from all the texts hitherto encountered: what makes it unique is to be found where the epistemological plan of the text intersects with the autobiographical plan of the author. In the previous chapter emerged the extent to which, beyond the fluctuating socio-historical conditions that inform each journey, the individual background and the attitude of each travel writer greatly influence how the account is shaped. Shuyun's work differs from Western ones in that it is framed within a qualitatively different horizon: her point of departure, her *modus operandi*, and, finally, her conclusion are different. Emblematic is the fact that the book opens with the author's following remembrance: "I was born to the sound of a bugle in the barracks of the People's Liberation Army where my father served; I grew up with stories of his battle" (2006: 1). Acknowledging the cultural *and* autobiographical terrain on which the whole experience rests is of primary importance here, because it is precisely on such terrain that the author builds her desire to move beyond what she has been taught about the Long March. It is, in other words, the fact of "travelling at home" that substantiates the text with a completely different ethos. The questions posed by Shuyun both to veterans and herself come from a different set of needs than those that usually inform Western travelogues. Alongside this, the more the author delves into the incongruities of the myth, the more her persona unfolds a plurality of facets and it shifts from the "travel writer" toward the ethnographer and researcher, whose basis are both autobiographical (Shuyun's memories) and professional (indeed, Shuyun was trained as an historian).

In the end, the clash/encounter between Shuyun's own memories and those of the veterans calls into question the line that separates official history and bottom-up counter-narratives; or also: the intertwinement between the desire to know, the possibility of knowing, and the contested knowledge that a journey like Shuyun's can effectively provide. A crucial episode that sums up these tensions is the recollection of the battle on the Xiang River in 1934, when the Red Army was escaping from the Nationalists. Shuyun writes:

This is the general description of it in the official history of the Long March: "The battle on the Xiang River was the longest and most heroic on the Long March. It involved the largest number of soldiers and the fiercest fighting, with the heaviest casualties for the Red Army, a loss of almost 50,000 men in five days." The official story says that the Red Army lost two-thirds of its 86,000 men, but it is implausible that they could all have died in battle. Nobody wants to admit it but the majority almost certainly deserted. As Liu [an interviewed veteran] remembered, he hardly experienced any fighting until the Xiang River; even then, his unit was mainly running rather than fighting. (Shuyun 2006: 79)

From this passage, the thickness of the propaganda's fabrication of the myth vividly emerges: a fabrication that – Shuyun notes – is sometimes based on minor adjustments, but often rests upon radical distortion or suppression of events. Eventually, then, the journey becomes a journey back in time; a rescuing endeavor for the sake of truth before the testimonies of the witnesses will be lost forever; an individually accomplished journey whose narration, informed by the voices of the unheard, aims at deconstructing the institutionalized, collective imagination.

The analysis moves on to discuss the work and activity of a Hong Kong author – Wong How Man – who, similarly to Shuyun, spent much time in the West; however, contrary to her, How Man has now returned to Hong Kong where he lives and works.

TO THE SOURCE

Wong How Man (1949-) is a Hong Kong explorer, conservationist, and journalist. Back in 1987, he founded the Chinese Exploration and Research Society (CERS), in Hong Kong, with the goal of "committing ourselves to China's remote regions and implementing projects to conserve nature and culture, in a sensitive and equitable manner."[158] How Man completed his academic studies in the West – more precisely at the University of Wisconsin – where he graduated in journalism. His experience in the US was crucial not only for his education, but also because it is from that outsider-insider standpoint that How Man has fostered his connections to, and interest in, China: "it wasn't until I entered University," he writes in the introduction to *From Manchuria to Tibet* (1998: 9), "that I began to identify deeply with China. Throughout college, I sought to understand better my heritage, avidly reading about China's geography, history, art and culture, both past and present." Then, sensing that China was a country with a huge unexploited potential for ethnographic-journalistic work, in the mid-1970s How Man decided to return to China, and officially embarked on his career as an explorer with the support of the National Geographic Society. In 1985 How Man accomplished what is possibly his major achievement: at the head of a team of Chinese geographers, he surveyed the full length of the Yangtze River, eventually claiming the discovery of an even remoter source than the one usually credited.

---

[158] http://www.cers.org.hk/index.php/en/about-cers/mission-statement.

This journey is recounted in his book *Exploring the Yangtze: China's Longest River* (1989). In all respects, this can be considered as a travelogue, because it recounts the expedition's journey from the lower reaches of the river up to the Tibetan plateau where it originates. How Man's account is largely a description of the features of the Yangtze and the difficulties that the team encountered with the progression of the mission. The text is certainly not a scientific mapping: indeed, it presents the unfolding of a narrative, which is enriched by dialogues with the local population. Nonetheless, How Man's reluctance to expound on the recounting of the events, as if unwilling to thicken the discourse with too many personal insights, is evident. Hence, the narrative takes on a rather steady and monochord rhythm in which well-rounded, subjective apercus on the experience are very limited. The following passage, taken from the beginning of the book, is a good example:

> One of our first stops was the Yangtze Valley Planning Office at Wuhan. "The Changjiang (Long River [as the Yangtze is called in China]) is treacherous and difficult to tame, both for a hydrologist and a boatman," remarked Cao L'an. His next line: "Our goal is to put the river to work for people," sounded all too familiar to China. Some hundred kilometres downstream at Xiaogu Shan, an old monk saw it differently: "The Changjiang is peaceful, like a mirror flowing by." When it is peaceful, the Yangtze serves its populace. But at other times, its ravaging water inundates thousands of kilometres and leaves devastation behind. The massive flood of 1931 menaced seven provinces, left over 140,000 people dead and made 28 million people homeless. (How Man 1989: 58)

On the one hand, How Man's commitment to interact with locals (in this case, an officer and a monk) is necessary because their knowledge can be of help to the expedition. How Man also stressed this point in the interview by calling for a coupling, instead of an opposition, between scientific and indigenous knowledge: "Science does not explain everything: this is the starting point. Many things have also to do with survival, adaptation, the ability to feel the environment around you."[159] The quoted passage is just one of the many occurrences throughout the book which testify to how the whole experience, far from being a mapping in isolation of the Yangtze River, relies on the sharing of information with the people encountered along the road. On the other hand, the author does not let these encounters take center stage. Therefore, the narrative is never really dialogic, nor is it open to self-reflectivity. In this passage, for instance, the testimonies of the officer and the monk are juxtaposed without any commentary. The argument is then complemented with statistics that recontextualize these testimonies within a historical, documented perspective. Overall, a certain formal technicality concerning not only the reporting of data, but the writing itself permeates the whole account. According to How Man, this is due to both the process of writing he adopts and the function he projects over it. With regard to the

---

[159] Wong How Man, interview by Stefano Calzati, April 11, 2015, in person.

former aspect, How Man noted in the interview that "usually, I write short pieces, which do not require a great deal of editing. Even though I miss the possibility to reflect on my reflections or to shape my writing in a literary way the writing is kindled by the immediacy of the event: there is less packaging, but more truthfulness." This point is made even clearer when he claimed to consider literariness as a form of fictionalization that weakens the accuracy of the account:

> Anytime I read travel writings – that is, non fiction stories – and I feel that writers are dramatizing it, I feel kind of cheated; I usually think: "Damn! Is it true, or are they making it up?" The more captivating it is, the more I doubt it.[160]

The effect of detachment conveyed by How Man's narrative is the result of his attempt to let the events speak for themselves, avoiding the temptation to edit them or make them more appealing. Photography, which is How Man's second occupation, responds to this same logic, as it is considered as a way of documenting what is written: "I thought since the outset that I wanted to use my photographs to illustrate what I was writing about, so even when I write something quite dramatic, the picture is there to prove it." Concerning the second point, when asked how he thinks that his studies in the US have shaped his vision of China and his writing about it, How Man answered that:

> No doubt, my writing has been affected by my studies in arts and journalism in the US, but many other factors have influenced it and still influence it: emotions, age, my leftish leaning, and also my own prejudices, which I am willing to admit, although this does not have to prevent anyone from moving on.

Through this answer, it is easier to understand How Man's predilection for delivering a kind of writing that is as reliable as possible. How Man's standpoint is not surprising when one considers that what he writes and photographs largely responds to a scientific epistemological paradigm of observation and measurement. In this respect, How Man seems keen to avoid the association of his figure with those of other commercially driven travelers and writers who publish their accounts with a well-defined readership in mind.[161] In other words, while he may well be considered a travel writer, How Man pretends to be perceived, in the first place, as an explorer and a researcher. On this issue, he remembered that:

> When I was working for National Geographic, after 2-3 assignments, they put me in the category "explorer." But it was not my aim to be an explorer.

---

[160] How Man, interview.
[161] In this regard, How Man's critique of Joseph Rock's work (he was How Man's predecessor at National Geographic) is emblematic. In a couple of articles, which he shared privately with me, How Man points out that Rock was more of "a flowery pen rather than an exacting perfectionist."

There are people who keep dreaming of becoming an explorer, but as far as I am concerned it took me a while to feel at ease in that role: I almost evolved into it by default.

Such a label finds further confirmation in a subsequent research-journey made by How Man: "during my third assignment for National Geographic, I explored the sensitive border of Manchuria and by 1983, I had visited and studied at least half of China's 55 recognized ethnic groups." This experience was later recollected in his book *From Manchuria to Tibet* (1998). Once again, the closest point of comparison that comes to mind when reading *From Manchuria to Tibet* is *Invisible China* by Legerton and Rawson. The aim of bringing to light the cultural and ethnic variety of China is the same for all three authors. At the same time, as was the case with Shuyun, How Man is able to do so in more depth and breadth by exploiting his fully insider position. On a similar note, *Exploring the Yangtze* could be said to share the adventurous ethos of Bird's *The Yangtze Valley and Beyond*. Indeed, although the mapping of the river's basin rests on two very different motives – Bird's was commercial and political, while How Man's is largely ethnographic and geographic – the desire to venture into uncharted areas is very similar. What distinguishes the two is the fact that Bird was entering what she considered as "the beyond" by maintaining a solid Western perspective, while How Man works from within a Chinese frame, and from here he manages to rewrite – ironically in English – the "history" of the Yangtze as it is known by both Chinese and Western people. Put differently, it is precisely because of his mixed cultural background and his access to both the knowledge of the scientific community, as well as that of the locals with whom he speaks, that How Man can delve into China with an ethnographic gaze.

Suspecting that such a double-sided gaze could be reflected in the use of English and/or Mandarin – for instance, *Exploring the Yangtze* and *From Manchuria to Tibet* are in English, while a book such as *Tales from Ancient Kingdom* (2009) is written both in English and Mandarin – one of the questions in the interview revolved around language. How Man interestingly remarked that "I write in Chinese when I want to be more emotional, but whenever I pretend to be analytic, I write in English." Taken in isolation, this claim is rather straightforward. However, when it is collated with How Man's view about his writing process, one can see more clearly the extent to which the objectivity he tries to attain through his writing cannot be the result of an immediate spontaneity, as he previously claimed. The choice of adopting the English language already represents a filtering of the explorer's own views and the *a priori* sheltering of his subjectivity, which is prevented from surfacing in the writing. At the same time, the Chinese is "attached" to a more personal and intimate sphere of explorations and writing, which, in turn, further blurs the generic definition of his works as travel writing. A comparison among his books, especially those in Chinese and English, would bring new insights into this issue; and yet, it is an endeavor that moves beyond the focus of the present analysis.

The next author to be analyzed is Hong Kong-born blogger and writer Jason Y Ng. With him the discussion begins to bridge the gap between print and online Chinese travel writing. At the same time, Ng still presents a hybrid cultural background: born in Hong Kong, he spent much of his youth in the US and Europe, before settling down again in Hong Kong.

HONG KONG AS A STATE OF MIND

Blogger Jason Y Ng revealed in the interview that he stumbled upon blogging after he set up his own online website to promote his career as a singer:

> I really wanted to become a professional tenor, so I hired a Web designer to build a website to promote my singing. Then, this Web designer told me: "Well, now you should put something on your website, apart from your biography. You need content, you need to blog." I didn't know exactly how to do it, or what to write, but because I have always been a politics junky, I began to blog about that: political issues in Hong Kong.[162]

Later, Ng broadened his thematic focus to culture, current events, and travel. In fact, the generic labeling of Ng's blog *Asiseeithk.com* and his books *Hong Kong State of Mind* (2011) and *No City for Slow Man* (2013) – which are the remediation of some of his blog's posts – is usually that of "writings about Hong Kong." The span of such a label is certainly wider and more heterogeneous than that of travel writing. Having said this, there are some good reasons why Ng's work is worth discussing here. A first hint comes from Ng's self-representation on his blog: he defines himself as "a globe-trotter who spent his entire adult life in Italy, the United States and Canada before returning to his birthplace to rediscover his roots. He is a full-time lawyer, a published author, a writer."[163] It is notable that Ng's first mention goes to his wanderings around the world – which also inspire a good deal of his writing – rather than to his occupation as a lawyer. The following extract from *Hong Kong State of Mind* does further justice to the author's globetrotting inclination:

> I gazed at the magnificent skyline before me. Only a handful of cities in the world rival Hong Kong as a true megalopolis: New York, London, Tokyo, Paris and Shanghai. To this biased citizen, Hong Kong is hands-down the most livable one among them. New York's infrastructure is shamefully antiquated; London is prohibitively expensive; Tokyo never stops treating you like a *gaijin* and Paris is as impenetrable as Tokyo except without the good manners. As for our old nemesis Shanghai, the city pampers and indulges until it doesn't. All hell breaks loose should anything happen and you find yourself at the mercy of the local, mostly corrupt, system. (Ng 2011: 77-78)

---

[162] Jason Y. Ng, interview by Stefano Calzati, April 19, 2015, in person.
[163] http://www.asiseeithk.com

In this excerpt, Ng takes a global perspective from which to look at Hong Kong. More precisely, the author's persona that emerges is that of a cosmopolitan subject who went to and became acquainted with a number of diverse contexts, before resettling in Hong Kong. Most remarkable is the fact that from this cosmopolitan standpoint Ng is able to launch a camouflaged critique of Mainland China, epitomized by Shanghai's faulty system. One of the questions in the interview aimed at understanding the author's own experiences when travelling to China; Ng's reply is condensed into an anecdote:

> I was in Beijing a month ago to participate in the Beijing Literary Festival. In one panel I spoke exclusively of Occupy Central [Umbrella Movement]. You know, it is very rare for someone to speak openly of political movements in Hong Kong when on China's soil... so I felt a little nervous. At the end of the panel, the festival organizers came to me and said: "Oh, congratulations Jason, we didn't know you were so popular." I thanked them, believing they were trying to flatter me, but then they specified: "Have you seen all the police officers at the back?!" This is how things go: authorities are sent to venues where political issues are treated, in order to pick out too sensible things.

However marginal such an episode may appear, it is telling of the bumpy relations that still endure between Hong Kong and China, in particular after the Umbrella movement (see footnote at the beginning of the chapter). At the same time, this episode signals the incongruence of Ng's global persona: for all his experiences around the world, he still perceives Mainland China – de facto his homeland – as an alienating place to be, either culturally, politically, or socially.

In terms of his writing process, the most evident sign of Ng's cosmopolitanism is his deliberate use of the English language to talk about Hong Kong. This is Ng's own opinion on the point: "My luck was that there are really few commentators on the Web that write about Hong Kong in English, so this gave me a rather unique angle." Insofar as blogging (in order to be successful) requires the identification of a unique niche, Ng has decided to give voice to his cosmopolitan persona through not only the perspective he unfolds as a returning expat but also the linguistic channel to which he resorts. If How Man saw the English language as a privileged tool for achieving clarity and objectivity, Ng thinks of it as his characterizing blueprint. It could also be suggested that Ng's resorting to English represents a way for distinguishing himself and resisting the impact on Hong Kong of Mainland China. On this point, it must be noted that both Ng's blog and his books are banned in Mainland China[164], while a few editors repeatedly asked him to write in Cantonese, as he revealed in the interview. Through the use of English, then, Ng's hybrid cultural background finds an ultimate terrain of performativity that becomes the *raison d'être* of his writing, even though

---

[164] However, the rigidity of this ban remains contentious, considering that he was invited to Beijing's literary festival (2015).

this has consequences for how he is perceived both in Mainland China and in Hong Kong.

Another reason for including Ng's work in the present analysis is that on his blog (and in the last section of his *Hong Kong State of Mind*) he dwells in more detail upon some travels he has taken over the years to Hong Kong's neighboring countries. In so doing, he reflects on both Hong Kong and Asia as travel destinations and/or as places where to live. Ng explained: "the reason why I created the third section about the journeys I took out of Hong Kong, it's because this section *is* about Hong Kong: it gives you a more objective perception of what is going on here." "Here" stands, of course, for Hong Kong, but it also suggests the role of the city within the continent. The most relevant piece, in this regard, concerns Ng's reflections about Macau and Shenzhen:

> Shenzhen, Macau and Hong Kong are three sisters separated in childhood. Tucked away in the Pearl River Delta, they might have been mistaken for triplets if it weren't for the vicissitudes of history that put them on such different paths. Good or bad, Shenzhen was the only sister of the three spared from colonial rule. While Hong Kong thrived under British rule and Portuguese Macau carved a niche for itself as Asia's Sin City, Shenzhen didn't begin to come of age until 1980 when Deng Xiaoping handpicked her to be China's first Special Economic Zone. In the late 1990s, China celebrated the homecoming of Hong Kong and Macau, only to find the abductees emotionally attached to the kidnappers in a textbook case of Stockholm Syndrome. The two sisters bade a tearful farewell to the European colonizers who modernized them and returned to a family they barely recognized. Decolonization had never been so sullen. Economically inferior and culturally worlds apart, Shenzhen looked on as the Westernized sisters came home, suddenly conscious of her own Chineseness. (Ng 2011: 160-61)

To begin with, Ng inscribes his piece into a historical narrative that owes much to a univocal way of conceiving progress. Indeed, to argue that Shenzhen, Macau, and Hong Kong were sisters separated in childhood not only flattens the three different histories of these cities, but also puts them into a linear representation of history according to which all that comes before Western colonization is to be regarded as backward, if not pre-historical. Secondly, the comparison established by Ng is valid from a geographical point of view – insofar as the three cities are all in proximity to the Pearl River Delta – but it does not hold when a political angle is favored. As Ng himself specifies, Hong Kong and Macau had to deal with colonial powers, while Shenzhen did not. The point is that the trilateral parallelism built by Ng responds to a more subtle logic, namely to show the extent to which Hong Kong *is* different from Mainland China (of which Shenzhen represents the urban prototype). This idea finds its most vivid example in the conclusion of the passage when Ng remarks that, despite all efforts, Shenzhen remains unmistakably Chinese. Lastly, the divide between Hong Kong and Mainland China is reasserted through a dramatized representation of the island's handover: an event that, according to Ng, sparked feelings of resentment and frustration. At stake is not so much the assessment of the truth of such a claim, but rather the acknowledgement that Ng poured into it his own experience as a self-imposed expat to the US. In fact, Ng's biography inscribes into the diaspora of all those Hongkongers who left the island before 1997, fearing the consequences of the imminent return of Hong Kong to China's jurisdiction. In hypostasizing the clash between Hong Kong and Mainland China, however, Ng overlooks those individual and collective nuances – for example, the imagined and real expectations of the handover – that his position as an insider and outsider in Hong Kong could have helped to disentangle. More generally, it can be suggested that, against his cosmopolitan self-representation, Ng opts by and large for unfolding a macro-opposition – cultural, ideological, individual – between the West and Hong Kong and between Hong Kong and Mainland China (eventually making his approach close to that of many contemporary Western travel writers).

The last factor that makes Ng's work relevant here has to do with the remediation process undergone by his blog. The episode that Ng recounts in the introduction to *Hong Kong State of Mind* is illuminating:

> When I first told him [Ng's brother] the idea of turning my blog into a book, Kelvin, true to form, served up a dose of reality. "Who would want to read about stuff they already know?" he asked rather rhetorically. "And you don't even write in Chinese!" Kelvin continued his bubble-bursting routine. But he does have a point. Even though every Hongkonger grows up speaking Cantonese (the city's *lingua franca*) at home and learning English at school, the latter remains ever elusive, ever feared. But if two wrongs make a right, then this book is it. When the stories we know are told in a different language even the familiar and the mundane can spring to life. (Ng 2011: 11)

Through his brother's words, Ng is prompted to reflect on the risk of transposing the posts of the blog – which anyone can read online for free – into a book. His answer is rather acute: whatever one may claim to know, as soon as things are told in a different language (i.e., English) and, we could add, through a different medium, then what is familiar is cast in a new light. By subverting the factors at the base of travel writing, it is as if the process of remediation comes to constitute a "travel of the writing": a mediated process that projects onto the "déjà-dit" the aura of novelty. As seen in the previous chapters, for this to be really the case, the "new" text has to exploit the specific affordances of the target medium. In this sense, two main features differentiate Ng's blog from his book. The pictures that enrich the posts on the blog have been substituted with drawings made by his father. This choice, as Ng stated in the interview, is mainly due to the fact that the pictures that appear on the blog are usually taken from the Web, and sometimes he has to remove them due to copyright infringement. Hence, by opting to include his father's drawings, Ng managed, at once, to circumvent copyrights negotiations and to turn the book into a more personalized artefact. Overall, when comparing the online and printed versions of the posts, it is evident that they are fundamentally the same. At the same time, the posts that have

Heterodox" Representations in Chinese Travel Books and Blogs

been included in *Hong Kong State of Mind* are now only partially accessible on the blog: indeed, it is possible to read only the first few paragraphs, after which readers are invited to buy the book. Without doubt, this represents an original solution: it strengthens the links between the online and printed versions, while keeping them fairly unique (and this solution is also an indirect response to Ng's brother's claim that nobody would read something that is already available online.)

At this point, the analysis takes into account the work of Hong Kong reporter and photographer Leong Ka Tai. In doing so, the discussion conducted in Chapter 2 about Hirst and Lotti's *Il mondo oltre il fiume dei peschi in fiore* will also be recalled.

PORTRAYING CHINA'S ORDINARINESS

Leong Ka Tai is another Hong Kong-born writer and photographer who has a globetrotting biography and a multicultural background. "The best decision I have made in my life," he writes in the "About" page on his website,

> was to quit my job as an engineer in England and move to Paris to learn photography. After three years, I returned to Hong Kong and started my own studio. The second best decision was when, after six years, I found studio work too restrictive. I stopped the studio work and turned to travelling. After a while, magazine assignments started coming in.[165]

Leong's first travel destination for his reportages was Mainland China, where he journeyed around between 1982 and 1987. These years marked a crucial epoch in contemporary China, as they witnessed Xiaoping's opening of the country to the four modernizations. These were also the same years during which Giorgio Lotti was working in China as a foreign Italian correspondent. The parallelism between Leong and Lotti, in fact, does not stop there, but involves a similar conception of photography, which will be explored shortly.

One of the projects that Leong developed from his travelling experience around China is the photo-book *On China: One to Twenty Four* (1988) which collects a selection of 24 pictures taken while on the road. Each photograph is accompanied by a poem written in Chinese by writer Leung Ping Kwan and then translated into English by Leong himself. The two versions are juxtaposed on the page. One of the questions in the interview concerned the work of translation, in order to understand how the passing from Mandarin to English has affected the meaning of the poems or their relations with the pictures:

> The translation is very important, but I do not think that the passing from Mandarin to English adds anything to the images. The Chinese text, on the contrary, I believe that it adds a new dimension to the images. There is one photo, in particular, taken in the early evening: a man is standing on a

---

[165] http://www.camera22.com/about/p01.html

balcony of a building painted in yellow and the sky is deep blue. In his poem Kwan says something about the sound of the Yellow River, which runs near where the picture was taken. The symmetry is incredible; it creates a multimedial, multisensorial sensation.[166]

The picture (Figure 51) and poem to which Leong refers are the following:

Figure 51: One of the most significant pictures in Leong's book

The bright blue sky is boundless.
You lit a cigarette at dusk,
Looking at the yellow earth under your feet, the yellow walls.
The yellow desert is boundless too.
With bowed head, you think of the distant hills beyond the distant hills,
The ancient Yellow River meandering towards the bright blue seas. (Leong: 28).

As Leong points out, the synergy between the picture – its colors – and the words – that is, the allusion to an imagined but proximate Yellow River – creates a multisensorial experience, whose result is greater than the sum of the two modes. In fact, the verbo-visual relation between the pictures and the poems could be said to constitute the major narrative force of the whole work. Leong himself remarked that "the first photo is the portrait of a family. It is one of the first photos I took in China. But for the rest there is no story nor a precise choice behind the organization of the other images." This leads to suggest that the pictures simply follow the temporal evolution of the journey. In this respect, Leong's work offers a parallel to Hirst's *Il mondo oltre il fiume dei peschi in fiore*, in which a considerable number of

---

[166] Ka Tai Leong, interview by Stefano Calzati, April 21, 2015, in person.

photographs by Giorgio Lotti accompany the text. When it comes to assessing the role and status of photography Lotti and Leong share very similar views:

> [Lotti]: Photography is an art that requires a long period of study of the subject. A click at the right moment is not enough to get a good image; you also have to know the subject. Paradoxically, with the spreading of digital technologies and their wide commercialization, Photography with a capital P has become, or better has returned to being, an elitist art. It demands time: time for studying the subject, as well as for conceiving what you want to tell visually.[167]

> [Leong]: You could say I was just lucky [he is referring to a shot he took of a man eating his soup at dawn]... But then it's also true that I woke up at four in the morning and went out in order to witness the city's awakening... So you have to place yourself in situations in which luck can happen. Luck is letting oneself be able to take advantage of the situation. When I am alone I can spend all the time I need on a single shot. So, the overall idea is that you have to adapt to the circumstances, be they the medium or the people, in order to do your best.

Both Lotti and Leong conceive of photography as an art that requires full-time dedication. This means not only being ready for the right moment, but also getting acquainted with the subject in order to correctly interpret it. Such view has a deep assonance with Butor's idea that the proper way to travel (and to write about it) is that which implies the ability to preliminarily "read" – that is, understand – the other. Lotti further specified that: "the majority of today's photographers not only cannot properly 'read' the subject once they are in front of it, but they arrive on the spot without the necessary knowledge." The parallels between Lotti and Leong's views show the extent to which travel, writing, and photography (as well as reading) are all specular practices. Most importantly, it is only when they are supported by the necessary knowledge and expertise that they become forms of art.

Returning now to Leong's work, it is worth exploring his approach to photography, as it can provide some further insights into the discussion about the chronotope of photography developed in Chapter 2. The celebrated quality of Leong's work is to seize the subjects' intimacy, by framing it within ordinariness. Figure 53 below is the picture of the man eating his soup at dawn to which Leong referred in the interview, while Figure 54 is the second-to-last found in the book:

---

[167] Lotti, interview.

Figure 53: Soup at dawn

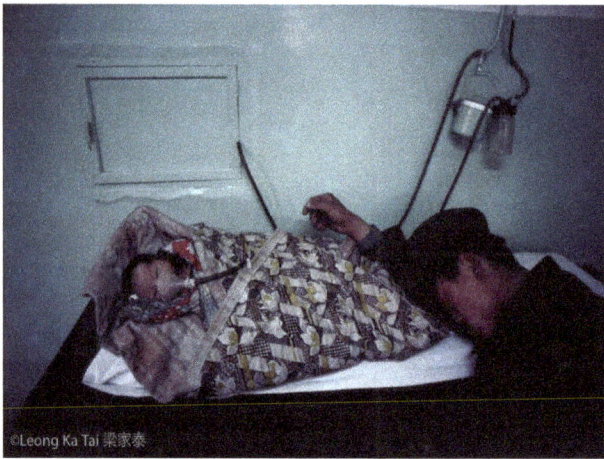

Figure 54: Child and father at Beijing's hospital

What does it mean to portray ordinariness? Why is Leong considered a master in his quest to represent people's intimacy? And how is Leong's representation of daily life different from that of tourism photography? Undoubtedly, in order to take good shots one needs to master the technique of photography, so that the camera becomes not only a means to reproduce the subject, but a vehicle to bring it to life. We have seen that the majority of travel writers – above all, bloggers – fail to pass even this preliminary stage: photography is already a commodified act.[168] Besides the technique, however, there is something else: it is also necessary to accomplish that kind of study, advocated by Leong and Lotti alike, which can eventually turn, at once, the right instant into an absolute and the subject into a story. In fact, what Leong does is to

---

[168] To be more precise, the commodification pertains in equal parts to the photographing subject, the act of photography, and the portrayed subject, which very often is a hyper-reproduced one. Of course, it is possible to photograph famous landmarks in an artistic way, but this implies an even greater ability of the photographer to look at and read the subject differently.

investigate ordinary places – such as hospitals, squares, streets – and to make ordinariness become thick, perspectival, and, possibly, moving. Leong is able to look at ordinary places unconventionally: his pictures ask to be stared at and interrogated; they are the result of a patient waiting and they embed a whole tale to be heard, if only one is able and willing to listen. Perhaps the picture of the man eating his soup at dawn could be regarded as the outcome of Leong's good timing, but in it – in the eyes of that man staring at the camera – the photographer was able to capture a whole narrative: the fatigue of early-morning Chinese workers; the longing for a bowl of rice and a better future; the pride, loneliness, and shiftiness of a gaze that encompasses a whole generation. The point, again, is not whether these interpretations are correct, but that they are possible: the photograph speaks for itself. Similarly, the picture of the young child and his sleeping father in a Beijing hospital rests on the principle of circumspection; it signals the exploration of institutional places and their metamorphosis into familial realities. Leong's picture, then, bears the mark of ordinariness precisely because they show the intimacy (differently from tourism pictures) of well-known public places. The colors of this picture are cold and the setting is inhospitable; yet the father's exhausted face, his defensive arm over his son, the multicolor blanket and the kid's open eyes above the oxygen mask all conjure up a sense of warmth and fight and longing for life. In this case, Kwan's poem further provides the reader/observer with one story:

> Children's hospital, Beijing.
> "Father is tired.
> Here the quilts are warm, the doctors are friendly
> Sleep tight, and when you'll wake up, you'll be well again!"
> "Father you are tired.
> Sleep tight and when you'll wake up, I'll tell you a story!"
> About the Monkey whose somersaults land a hundred and eight thousand
> miles away." (Leong 1988: 44)

Kwan's poem digs into the photograph's novel to such an extent that it rescues the kid's voice: the silent petition of his staring eyes is finally enunciated. Firstly, the child speaks to the reader, by recollecting the doctors' prognosis of a full recovery; then, he speaks to his father, who is sleeping and protecting him; eventually, through an epic reversal of the roles, the child promises to tell his father a story once he wakes up (thus implying a full recovery). Kwan's is just one possible tale, one interpretation, but the very fact that the picture triggered such a deep response is indicative of Leong's ability to explore the subjects' intimacy and portray them from a personal standpoint, which calls for a syntagmatic reading of the image.

Transcending the micro level of daily ordinariness, the last point addressed during the interview was Leong's perception of China as a Hongkonger who also travelled and lived in Europe:

> Before starting to travel I knew I had some notions of China, culturally speaking I know Chinese basics, I know what things mean, the meaning of

people's behaviour. But on the other hand, as soon as I went to Mainland China I realized it was a foreign country to me: the political system, the economics, the people's way of life. There was a tension between the known and the unknown. Between what I thought I knew and what travel revealed to me. Yet, I have to say that I felt and still feel different from Mainlanders.

On a cultural level, Leong's answer is close to Ng's idea of an enduring divide between Hong Kong and Mainland China. Yet, Leong adds a further layer to this feeling: it is a matter not only of knowing the other's culture but of creating a link, an empathy, between the self and the unknown. This echoes Gray's experience along the Great Wall of China, which he describes as a gradual detachment from his Western background in search of a different, possibly more instinctive, approach to the Chinese world, based upon the spiritualism of his Maori roots. Leong continued by arguing that: "This is maybe because my pictures are intimate: I strove to create a connection with my subjects, going beyond the cultural, historical differences that still endure." In this respect, photography, by showing the Other – the referent – rather than constantly postponing it as words do, is probably a favorable channel to create this link and stimulate a reaction in the observer. Lastly, when I asked Leong if and how he thinks that China has changed in these decades, his answer is dislocated on two levels:

> I think it has chiefly to do with how people perceive it from the outside: sure, materially speaking China has changed – and as far as I am concerned I do not agree with that change – but spiritually... I mean people had a great dignity even at that time... when they were poorer... and I do not think they were less happy than nowadays... The spirit of Chinese people has not changed that much, at least in certain regions of the inland.

It is again a matter of spiritualism to return. While Leong re-inscribes China's change into a Western logic of progress – the "outside" – apparently implying that there are various degrees of "outsideness" – richer and poorer regions within Mainland China, Hong Kong, Asia, the West – he espouses the idea that change is, in itself, a controversial concept, as much depends on the point of view we take to assess it. More generally, on the one hand Leong's words mirror the perspective of many Western writers, by positioning the articulation Self-Other on a macro-cultural encounter (and his years in Europe may be a reason for that). On the other hand, however, Leong manages to break such an encounter down through photography: the intimacy that emanates from his pictures tells us of Leong's ability to overcome any possible cultural divide and show humanity naked of all geopolitical and cultural labeling.

The next section moves away from Hong Kong and is dedicated to two artists who were born and currently live in Mainland China: Zhen and Qiang Gao, internationally known as the "Gao Brothers." Further on, the analysis will return to discuss the work of a Hong Kong author and blogger, Lam Fai Fred, as this will serve as a transition to the study of Chinese travel blogs.

A DAY IN BEIJING

The Gao Brothers are widely known in China and abroad for their provocative installations, sculptures, and photography often revolving around the recollection of the Cultural Revolution, which was a traumatic experience for both of them due to the imprisonment and death of their father (when they were aged 12 and 6). Apart from their artistic works, the Gao Brothers have also sporadically ventured into writing. Of particular interest here is their *One Day in Beijing* (2004, original title: 在北京一天能走多遠), in which they recount a whole day spent wandering in the capital.

The opening of the book frames the rationale of the project: "Here we are trying to capture the hustle and bustle of an urban city in China. We hope to capture the essence of time and space in a moment. This is the purpose of the volume" (1). This goal is pursued via an equal mix of words and pictures. In the interview, the Gao Brothers defined themselves as "witnesses, recorders: we tried not to think that we were working."[169] The whole book, in fact, interrogates the border that separates visibility and anonymity, transparency and engagement, the need to show and the effort not to intervene. From this premise, two main axes structure the work: one is the exploration of "authentic life," as the authors mentioned in the interview; the other has to do with the political implications of making a reportage in and about Beijing. With regard to the former, the authors adopt various strategies – verbally and visually – to appear as the casual witnesses of scenes that would unfold in the same way without their presence. Firstly, they make use of direct speech to convey a sense of closeness to the events and give voice to other people (see example further below). Secondly, as Figures 54 and 55 show, they take photographs from unusual angles in an attempt to hide their presence (see also Kress and van Leeuwen 2006) and "capture the 'authentic' expressions and moment"[170] (Gao Brothers 2004: 17).

---

[169] Gao Brothers, interview by Stefano Calzati, June 12, 2015, in person.
[170] "一天的行动，而且摄影也尽可能用偷拍 的方式完成。我们希望记录北京没有被镜头 打扰变形的真实的日常状态。"

Figure 54: Passengers on a bus photographed by the Gao Brothers

Figure 55: People queuing to get on a bus

Thirdly, the authors refrain from evaluating (in words) what they see and let the events flow, so that their engagement with the scene remains marginal. In the interview, the Gao Brothers claimed: "The book is political as far as the things we recorded are political. We wanted to record what we saw, heard and thought during one whole day in Beijing. Everything in the book responds to this." These words seem to reassert the Gao Brothers' goal to distance themselves from the scene. Yet, despite all efforts to conceal the camera and approach people discreetly, the transparency to which the authors point can only be an ideal. When we discussed if and how photography and language can represent authenticity, the Gao Brothers elaborated on their practice in a much more ambivalent way than what they state in the book:

> Neither pictures nor texts are better or worse. The authenticities of the two are relative, limited, and difficult to identify. Our task was to try our best to document the day objectively, but we did not think about how to identify authenticity. Also, we do not mind whether people believe our words or photos, as long as these can trigger their imagination.

This claim reveals the authors' awareness of the intrinsic instability of their goal to capture authenticity. Authenticity is not to be found in the portrayed subject; rather, it is a social and medial construction. The role of photography and language, then, is to kindle the feeling of authentic life, complying with the way in which society constructs authenticity. This leads the Gao Brothers to seek to neutralize the effects of photography and language as means-of-telling (quite differently from Leong and Lotti) and to convey through them a sense of non-intrusiveness and non-mediation.

The interview also revealed the extent to which the relation between photographs and words in the book is itself political. One question addressed the occasional discrepancy between text and image. The authors replied:

> We do hope the pictures can match the texts as much as possible, but due to the censorship and editing issues before publishing, some pictures and texts had to be removed. So, some pictures and texts do not really match.

It becomes clearer that the publishing process is charged here with a political burden that was absent from Western-authored contemporary travelogues. Of course, in the West the publishing process does also affect how each travelogue is formed; however, none of the contemporary texts analyzed was subjected to overt censorship. The Gao Brothers' claim sheds light on the varying degrees of censorship to which Chinese authorities can resort when it comes to sensible content: it is a matter of neither completely silencing dissidents' voices nor of promoting outspoken propaganda, but of an ongoing and ever-changing compromise.[171] It was not possible to find out more about the missing pictures. However, the very fact that words and illustrations are sometimes discrepant remains as a blueprint of the untold story of censorship that still looms over the book.

---

[171] On this issue, Michel Hockx (2015), in surveying erotic Chinese literature on the Internet, has noted how online censorship tends to be looser than in print. He argues that the Internet represents a space where moral and political boundaries are more easily renegotiated.

On another level, the political implications of making a reportage in Beijing are also vividly addressed in the text. Insofar as the Gao Brothers talk with people, they not only "become visible," but are sometimes rejected because of the questions they ask. The most emblematic example is the encounter in the subway with three musicians who are reluctant to speak with the Gao Brothers. This could appear as a rather common reaction between strangers. Yet, it conceals a deeper motivation. The three musicians' claim that "we just arrived in Beijing and we need to make a living. We don't want you to follow us" (2004: 106), betrays their distress as newly arrived migrants to Beijing and the fear of being discovered by authorities. This issue is unpacked by the authors when they discuss with another commuter the deficiencies of the system for regulating the flux of migrants to the capital:

> [Gao brothers]: "We are also not from Beijing. What do you think of the policy which allows migrants into Beijing?" [Commuter]: "Last time, there was a Guangzhou person who didn't have a residential permit and he got beaten to death… this makes me feel really sad. I think the temporary residential permit has its pros and cons." [Gao brothers]: "Do you think they should cancel this system?" [Commuter]: "Yes, but they should have a registration system for the flow of incoming migrants for regulation. During the SARS period, if there wasn't a registration system to control the flow of migrants, it would have been disastrous."[172] (Gao Brothers 2004: 73-75)

This passage addresses the social stratification of Beijing's society and the inequalities that divide urban residents from (Chinese) internal migrants. Through it, the Gao Brothers give voice to the multitude of workers and people who fuel the wealth of the city, but are obliged to live at its margins for fear of being expelled (if not killed).[173] On the one hand, these dialogues are a good example of the Gao Brothers' effort to let the "political" rise effortlessly to the surface of the text, without commenting on it. On the other hand, however, they epitomize the ultimate impossibility of delivering a transparent reportage, which was the preliminary intention of the authors.

The last issue to be discussed points to the Gao Brothers' personae as "explorers" of what constitutes for them a familiar, urban dimension. More precisely, beneath their project lies a double disjuncture: familiarity/unfamiliarity on the one hand, *in loco*/itinerant travel experience, on the other. While, to a certain extent, their personae

---

[172] "问：'我们都是外地来的，你对一直让外来人 头疼的暂住证制度问题怎么看？'答：'我觉得上次广州那个因没有暂住证被打死的孙志刚事件，让人感觉很 '悲惨- - - - - 所以我觉得暂住证制度有利有弊。''问：.你觉得暂住证制度应当取消吗？''答：暂住证制度也许应当取消，但应当有一个登记制度，这样可以对外来人口有一个控制，比方前一段时期的"非典," 如果没有一个登记制度就没法控制流 动人口，出现问题很麻烦。'"

[173] The migration from the countryside toward the city began in the late 1970s alongside Deng Xiaoping's reforms of the labor market. According to the latest statistics by Chinese government (http://data.bjstats.gov.cn/2012/tbbd/201201/t20120104_218341.htm), more than 7 millions migrants currently live in Beijing, which is more than one third of the capital's whole population.

get close to the European 19th century figure of the flâneur, the Gao Brothers do not limit themselves to stare at the city, but they challenge it. After having lived in Beijing for years, the authors plan to deconstruct the city as a commoditized space and look at it with different eyes. This project echoes that of the Situationist International (SI), a French avant-garde movement born in Paris in 1957 and active until 1972. One of the goals of the SI was to perform a critique of the capitalist urban space by uncovering its tensions through the practice of the "*dérive*," a walking strategy which allows to both traverse the city serendipitously and keep a critical mind-set about the aesthetic and architectural features of the surroundings. Today, the ethos of the SI finds a reflection in the practice of psychogeography, as a way of "responding to the environment in an active rather than passive way" (Richardson 2015: 4). This is precisely what the Gao Brothers do: "we looked like wandering aimlessly on that day, but consciously we observed, experienced, and took notes. As such, we might see, feel, and think more about Beijing than those who were around." It is through this attentive disposition, which is reminiscent of Bourdieu's (1990) idea of travel, that the authors are able to arouse in themselves that magnetic interest which is usually triggered by new places rather than familiar ones. In the interview, the Gao Brothers specified that, because they started their peregrination at an unusual time for them (early morning), "the variations in the lights and sounds, or the sudden change in the size of the crowd, could render a place you are quite familiar with a strange one." For one thing, then, deconstructing familiarity is chiefly related to a matter of a change in perspective. Eventually, walking, rather than being a trivial, superficial practice, becomes an interrogative form of displacement that demands a high level of self-consciousness. But this also means that the reporting cannot be, ultimately, as neutral as the Gao Brothers pretend it to be. As never before, travelling and writing come to represent in the Gao Brothers' work two conflicting practices. Pleasures and duties, enjoyment and self-awareness: to write about one's own experience – be it *in loco* or itinerant, about familiar or unfamiliar places – is always a negotiation between what one perceives and how one thinks of oneself in relation to it.

COMMITTED TRAVEL WRITING

With Fred Fai Lam, we moved toward the blogging sphere. Lam is a Hong Kong-born (and resident) travel writer and travel blogger. At the end of 2014 his first travel book, titled *Travelling between Hope and Suffering* (original title: 旅行在希望與苦難之間), was released in Taiwan and Hong Kong (but not in Mainland China due to its political content). The book recounts the first half of Lam's world tour, which lasted almost two years and touched 40 countries. Specifically, in *Travelling between Hope and Suffering*, Lam narrates his experiences in China, Asia, and the Middle East.

Lam and his work are relevant to the present discussion for a number of reasons. First of all, Lam's book, as a cultural artefact, reflects more than any other some of the features that characterize Chinese contemporary travel writing. In terms of multimodality, one can note the presence of a great number of color pictures – usually one per page – which attests to the tendency of Chinese travel writers to build a balanced relation between words and illustrations. To this, one could add that the Chinese characters, as pictorial ideograms, impress upon the writing a visual complexity that forces – if not transcends – the threshold of paravisuality (as discussed in Chapter 2). This means that, however standardized it might be, the printing of Chinese characters, as signifiers, does bring a visual component that further crams the page's appearance. In terms of paratextuality, when one looks at the structure of Lam's book, it is notable that the narration *per se* is introduced by not just one, but five forewords: three of these are written by Lam's fellow writers, one is a collection of short reviews – very similar to the endorsement found on the back covers of Western books – and the last one is Lam's own introduction. Therefore, the readers face a proliferation of peritextual elements that relate to multiple authors. This, in turn, fragments the book's single authorship and opens the book to a complex hypertextual dialogism made up of both internal cross-references and quotations from other oeuvres.

Beyond these notations, what makes this work worth analyzing is the way in which the author represents himself and how he conceives of travelling and writing. Lam is the Chinese author who, more than anyone else (among those surveyed), stresses his being a traveler *and* a writer. These are his words in the introduction:

> When I was applying for my border pass [to get into Tibet as a Hongkonger] I was wondering whether to write 'traveler' or 'writer' in the occupation column. I suddenly realized that I had two identities and both of them were equally romantic. Being a traveler and a writer enables me to go on trips, to record my experiences, and then share them with an audience. This, in turn, helps pay for my travels.[174] (Lam 2014: 16)

Unlike the Chinese writers analyzed so far, who tended to present multifaceted personae, Lam is keen to claim for himself the clear-cut label of travel writer. At the same time, however, he makes sure to deconstruct the romanticism that contours such a label, by specifying that it is possible for him to travel only because he regularly publishes articles in a variety of magazines. He explained this more in depth in the interview: "while I was travelling I was already writing for some magazines and newspapers and I got some articles published. It's actually how I supported my travels." Overall, the book shifts between these two poles: a certain predilection toward idealism and idealization, on the one hand, and an honest and politically committed pragmatism, on the other hand. The author addresses this polarity in the introduction to the book: "Though this book is a 'travel documentary'," he writes, "the topics touched upon bear a certain gravity. I have tried to interweave 'travel' and 'the suffering of mankind'." (Lam 2014: 16) The (political) commitment of the work is, indeed, a major trait. Wei Ba, who wrote the first foreword to the book, remarks that:

---

[174] "記得出發不久，在某國邊境辦入境手續，表格上有著「職業」一欄，我在想：我該寫 Traveller (旅行者)，還是 Writer (寫作人)呢？突然發現，原來我同時擁有了兩種相當浪漫的身分，浪漫得甚至有點虛幻——可以將旅行的見聞寫成文字與讀者分享，並透過寫作賺取旅費，讓我可以持續旅行下去。"

Being a "responsible traveler" who aims to change the living conditions of people in the world, his travel account doesn't only contain records of his travel experiences. The account also contains notes on cultural differences and his reflections on these lifestyle differences.[175] (Lam 2014: 4)

While in the West, the idea of a "responsible traveller" (or ethical traveler) is usually linked with a rejection of the massified, socially exploitative, and ecologically harmful tourist practice, from the Chinese perspective "responsibility" is chiefly related with the need to denounce injustices and political misdeeds, both at home (such as in the case of the Gao Brothers) and internationally. In China, much more than in the West – and contrary to Strassberg's findings concerning pre-modern and modern travelogues – travelling and writing are considered as privileged practices for criticizing the political status quo within and outside the country.

The politicization of Lam's book is evidently a reaction against the authoritarianism that still affects some regions of China and aspects of its life. It is again Wei Ba who touches upon this point by remembering that, as a Tibetan, he is not granted the same freedom of movement as Lam:

> This year is the Year of the Horse. According to the Tibetan tradition, it is the year for taking a pilgrimage to the most respectable mountain – Mount Kailash. To visit Mount Kailash, one must have a border pass to access China. But the government is not willing to grant this pass to Tibetans, but only to the Chinese.[176] (Lam 2014: 4)

Besides, the book's politicization reflects Lam's worldwide activism. In fact, Lam is concerned with a number of political and civil causes around the world. Zhang Cui Rong, author of the second foreword to the book, remembers that in 2009 "a foreign group who protested against the bombings of Gaza by Israel invited me to go for a talk in Hong Kong: Lam was amongst them" (Lam 2014: 8). Zhang's words impress upon Lam's figure a global political commitment that is eventually stronger than that of any other Chinese author analyzed so far. The (ironic) paradox is that when Lam reached the Tibetan plateau to begin his journey, according to the bureaucratic language of the Chinese government, he fell under the category of simply "tourist." Indeed, Lam points out in the interview that "as a Hongkonger I am considered [in Mainland China] as an outsider and, for instance, I cannot stay in 'normal' hostels, but I have to go to specific ones that have the license to host outside tourists."[177] From activist to tourist – or rather, accepting being a tourist in order to be politically active – Lam blends his longing for travelling and writing – his

---

[175] "正如林輝在遊歷了許多地方之後發現，世界的苦難太多 。好在，仍然見到希望」。履行責任旅遊理念，並對公民社會的建設傾注心力、希望人人生活有所改變乃至世界得以改變。"
[176] " 緣於依西藏傳統，今年即馬年，為西藏神山之尊——岡仁波齊的朝 聖之年，對於虔信佛教的藏人屬必修功課。然而去轉山朝聖必須辦「邊境通行證」，但當局偏 偏不給藏人辦此證，卻給中國各地旅遊者開方便門。"
[177] This also applies to international visitors.

being a travel writer – and turns it into a critical stance through which to denounce sorrow as well as exalt hopes.

Finally, Lam represents a fruitful case study in that he is the co-founder of Ironshoetravel.com, a Hong Kong-based blog platform entirely dedicated to travel. This is how Lam described the project in the interview:

> We wanted to create a website that included mainly travel blogs and also some news about travel, but not guide-related information such as transport costs or accommodation. We want to provide stories: good articles, literarily speaking; in-depth analysis or inside stories.[178]

Lam also specified that each new blog must be approved by the platform's staff – composed of him and two colleagues – before going online. The screening, he mentioned, is meant to assess the literary quality of the work, and yet it also represents a way to avoid potential censorship in Mainland China, where the platform is currently accessible.

Beyond that, it is remarkable how Lam's predilection for quality over quantity and literariness over information represents a countertrend in the blogosphere, at least as far as the present analysis is concerned: after all, a gatekeeping process contrasts with the idea(l) of the Web as a free space where anyone can publish at will. This process, in turn, redefines Ironshoetravel.com as a hybrid between a platform and an individually managed blog, blurring the distinction between the two categories. It is no coincidence that the layout of Ironeshoetravel.com gets closer to that of the typical blog, rather than that of a multi-service platform (Figure 56):

Figure 56: The home page of *Ironeshoetravel.com*

---

[178] Fred Fai Lam, interview by Stefano Calzati, April 18, 2015, in person.

The home page presents the heading at the center, two navigational bars – one above and one below the title – and then the latest updates directly below (in the form of a slideshow). Moreover, apart from two advertisements in the right column, the page is polished, which means that the peritextual elements are limited in number and chiefly organized around the posts. Thirdly, by reading the labels of the major navigational bar below the title – "Latest News," "Walker Mood," "Local Riders," "On Travel," "Top Travellers" – it is evident that the platform revolves around travel and travelers, marginalizing other informative, commercial, and data-related aspects. For these reasons, the platform turns out to be rather distant from those analyzed so far (with the exception, perhaps, of Blogdiviaggi.it).

At this point, it is worth understanding the extent to which such diversity is also reflected by what is published in the blogs. In order to do this, the case of travel blogger and author Kong Pazu – an old, good friend with Lam – is examined.

CHINESE TRAVEL BLOGS

Kong Pazu is a Hong Kong-born travel writer and blogger. In 2010, he published his first travel book, *Spinning in Tibet – Selling Coffee in Lhasa* (original title: 風轉西藏 -我在拉薩賣咖啡), in which the author recounts his six-month bike tour from Thailand to Tibet. The title also refers to the coffee shop that Pazu opened in Lhasa once he reached his destination: "I settled down [in Lhasa] because I liked it very much," he explained in the interview, "and I have launched this coffee shop, which stays open half a year."[179] He then lives six months in Tibet and six months in Hong Kong (or travelling around the world).

Similarly to Lam, while he was travelling Pazu financed his biking adventure by publishing columns in magazines and newspapers. To these, he also added the regular posting of "articles" – as he classed them in the interview – on his website[180] and Facebook page.[181] Considering the medial variety of his activities, Pazu is a travel writer very aware of the channels at his disposal for promoting his pieces and wanderings. In this regard, he revealed in the interview how he also learnt to adapt his writing:

> Online is kind of more spontaneous. I can touch upon a lot of different topics, without going into depth or worrying about the coherence of what I write. It is maybe more superficial, but wider in scope. When I wrote the book I had to plan the writing more carefully. For the same reason, whenever I have to do some research, let's say for a destination, I prefer to read a book, rather than going online. I think printed publications are more accurate.

Pazu shares his view on the formal features of online writing with many other travel writers encountered. Yet, to that, he adds a reflection about the content of the articles:

---

[179] Kong Pazu, interview by Stefano Calzati, May 14, 2015, in person.
[180] http://www.pazu.com.
[181] https://www.facebook.com/pazu88?ref=ts&fref=ts.

when he is online he feels free to cut across subjects and topics independently from their overall coherence. This statement supports the analysis conducted in Chapters 1 and 2 by stressing, respectively, the looseness of travel blogs' boundaries, the tendency online to "epicize" the narrative, and the book's imposition upon the narrative of an overreaching coherence.

Pazu's posts published on Ironshoetravel.com coherently follow the blogger's view. When we met in May 2015, the platform had just been launched and Pazu had published only a few posts: they go from one dedicated to his acclimatization in Tibet – *My Sharing on How Breathing Keeps Me Warm in Lhasa* – to his ironic confession to no longer using shampoo in order to save some space in his backpack – *In the Past 12 Months, I Used No Shampoo or Shower Gel* – passing through a post in which he gives some suggestions on how to keep fit: *In the Past 6 Months, I Spent 7 Minutes Doing One Exercise Every Day*. The pieces provide the reader with insights into the behind-the-scenes of Pazu's long experience as a traveler. The major point to stress is that the articles are rhetorically ruffish, very short, and usually touch upon light topics, as admitted by Pazu himself in the interview.[182] The following is an example:

> Why can't some people stand cold weather while others can? I read a book called *Becoming the Iceman*. The author claimed that we have been taught to keep warm because the cold is bad for us. Yet we should learn to accept the cold through training, for example, by taking cold showers or cold baths. When being exposed to the cold, it is all about concentration on breathing and meditation. Since this summer, I have been taking cold showers nearly every day, wearing thin clothes, shorts, and sandals. My friends wondered if I could live with this outfit till winter. Now, winter has arrived. The outside temperature is only –3 °C and I have proved this outfit works well for me. When I am walking on the street, people are surprised and say to me: "Wow, aren't you cold?"; "No" is always my reply. I actually don't feel the cold. Precisely, I put my feeling aside. I'm no longer afraid of the cold.[183] (Pazu 2015)

---

[182] This could also be due to the fact that the platform had just been launched and needed some content to get promoted.

[183] " 為甚麼有些人怕冷，有些人耐冷？今年自身的生活習慣改變挺大，例如減了十公斤（Insanity Workout）也重新審視一下怕凍這個問題。[...] 讀了《Becoming the Iceman》（變成雪撈人），書中提及荷蘭人 Wim Hof，穿著短褲跑上珠峰 7000 尺。作者說我們從小到大都注重保暖，總覺寒冷是害，但其實我們應該學習接受冷感。其中一些訓練，洗冷水澡，洗冰塊浴，遇冷時注意呼吸頻率，冥想等。[...] 今年在拉薩，夏季到冬日，幾乎每天也用冷水洗澡，穿件單薄上衣、短褲加涼鞋。有朋友一直都懷疑，這身衣服，能否支持到冬天。現在冬天了，有時外邊攝氏零下 3 度，我還是這身打扮。走到街上，總有陌生的藏族人驚訝地叫：「Aw, ke-gi min-du-geh?」（哎，不冷嗎？）我總說：「Ke-gi min-du!」（不冷！）其實也不是完全不冷，更準確來說，我儘量把感覺抽離，我知道這叫冷感，但已不再害怕。"

This quote represents roughly half of the whole post. The first reflection that comes to mind is formalistic: the style is not too different from that of other blogs previously analyzed.[184] In terms of content, this post testifies to Pazu's own acquaintance with Tibetan life, which is perceived as much different from how the blogger lives in Hong Kong. In this respect, it could be suggested that also for Pazu as for many Westerners Tibet represents an "elsewhere" where the traveler is asked to negotiate his attitudes, behaviors and beliefs. The peculiar trait of Pazu's experience is that his journeys to Tibet have by now turned into a sort of extreme commuting practice, as he claimed in the interview: "I usually spend six months in Lhasa and then I split the other half of the year between travelling and staying in Hong Kong." This situation is different from both the travel experiences of inbound visitors to China and the journeys accomplished by China's residents, either foreigners or Chinese. In Pazu's case, dwelling takes prominence over mobility, but the former is always temporary, precarious, further attesting to the unstable distinction between roots and the road, as discussed in Chapter 3.

A similar schism also affects the writing: although it is evident that the chronotope of the blog tends to dry the narrative skeleton of the posts, Pazu manages not to flatten completely the writing on a monochord rhythm, for instance by enriching the pieces with references to other readings, or by letting Tibetans enter the narrative via direct speech. On the one hand, these features suggest that Pazu's blog is similar to individual ones, despite being currently hosted on a platform. On the other hand, Pazu's traveler persona seems torn between the slow plunging into the Tibetan culture and the restless desire to move.

When I asked Pazu about his perception of Mainland China and Tibet as a Hongkonger, his reply firstly stressed similarities and differences (in the same spirit as Leong): "I found many resonances with what we have to study in school. We share a good deal of cultural background. But, at the same time, the way of thinking, the people, their behaviours are different." Beyond that, Pazu turned his attention to the political implications of being a Hongkonger in Tibet:

> When I went to Iran I felt free to write whatever crossed my mind without worrying about the possibility of hurting or disappointing people I knew. In Tibet, on the contrary, I am part of the society and I have to be more careful and responsible for the people that surround me: for example, because I am the Hongkonger that has lived the longest in Tibet, it has occurred to me to see that my words about Tibet are sometimes reported or quoted matter-of-factly. I am considered a kind of expert, so I have to be aware of this exposure.

---

[184] This, in turn, would lead to an interrogation of the consistency of the quest for literariness at the base of the platform, but in order to do so the analysis should be extended to other blogs.

This last passage unpacks the contradictions of Pazu's persona as both an insider *and* an outsider in Tibet. Because Pazu shares with (or has acquired from) Tibet what he perceives as a partially common background, the blogger is able to delve into the region and write about it with a good degree of accuracy. In so doing, however, Pazu finds himself in a delicate position, insofar as the things he writes are re-circulated among Chinese people, Hongkongers, as well as those Tibetans who are the focus of his attention. Hence, he must be able to keep a detached perspective in order to be not only sensible toward locals, but also attentive to how his pieces are received outside of Tibet. Paradoxically, while the conception of travel writing as a form of ethical commitment returns here, it is precisely Pazu's deep involvement in Tibet that compels him to favor light topics over more political ones, so as not to displease the people among whom he lives, or risk the banning of the posts.

***

Remaining focused on blogs, it is worth proposing finally a brief analysis of the major Chinese travel blog platform: Travel.sina.com.cn. Sina.com.cn is the main online service provider for the Chinese-speaking world. Its section dedicated to travel is rich in a varied array of information, similar to what can be witnessed on Western platforms (Figure 57):

Figure 57: The homepage of the blog platform *Travel.sina.com.cn.*

The main bar at the top contains the following links: "Top," "Destination," "Theme Breaks," "Travel Raiders," "Pictures," "Air Tickets," "Hotels," "Blog." Blogging is only one aspect of the whole website and travelling constitutes a mere section within the broader conception of mobility as entertainment (as other Western platforms). Below the bar one finds an advertisement and, further below, a patchwork of recent, popular posts. What is striking is the predominance of pictures over words, a feature that follows and reinforces a tendency already highlighted in travel books. Moreover, the layout of the page is structured horizontally rather than vertically and is composed of squares and rectangles of varied dimensions. This way of organizing the content is quite different from the prototypical structure of the websites encountered so far (with the sole exception of Becki's newer blog). The favoring of a horizontal layout helps fill the screen "above the fold" (Nielsen and Tahir 2002: 23) with more content, thus reducing the need to scroll down the page. In this particular case, the horizontality of the layout is expanded beyond the lateral borders of the page through the insertion of two arrows at the sides, which enable scrolling from left to right and vice versa.

From a paratextual point of view, the elements found on the home page are of the same kind (e.g., advertisements) and distributed in the same way (e.g., they tend to invade the space of the text) as those appearing on Western platforms. More radically from what happens on Western platforms, however, on Travel.sina.com.cn we witness the proliferation of animations, pop-ups, and interactive content (which a static image as Figure 57 cannot convey). All these elements impress upon the whole website a dynamic that demands a complex form of enaction in order for the users to discern what is relevant for them from what is not and orient their browsing accordingly.[185]

In order to investigate what is written in the travel blogs hosted on Travel.sina.com.ch, two cases are taken into account. The first one[186] is dedicated to Kunming, the capital of Yunnan province in the Southwest of China. The author of the blog is Viagra8868 (偉哥 8868). Overall, the journey comprises four stages: the top central part of the page is occupied by a large slideshow of pictures that pertain to the first of the four stages (Figure 58). The others, instead, are accessible by clicking on a narrow column on the left, which remains constantly visible as the page scrolls down. By accessing stages 2, 3, and 4, one sees that the content is organized in the same way as on the first page: a big slideshow of pictures occupies the central part of the screen and is accompanied by a few lines of text on the right.

Figure 58: The homepage of the Viagra8868's blog

The primary position of the pictures and the fact that they are of a very good

---

[185] The Western travel blog platform that comes closest to Travel.sina.com.ch is Turistipercaso.it, which as seen in Chapter 1 is the one where the platform's agents manifest their presence on the page the most.
[186] http://i.travel.sina.com.cn/qcyn/kunming/321.html

quality reassert a decisive supremacy of images over words. In fact, the blogger, who defines himself as a lover of "microblogging, photography, cars and sports" (Viagra 8868: 2015), writes just below the slideshow that the best thing to do in Kunming in the autumn season is to look at its colors: a claim that points to a chiefly visual experience. Also, the pictures of this first stage are accompanied by the following words:

> Wake up in the early morning and go out in a hurry if you want to arrive at Dongchuan before sunrise, so as to witness the magnificent beauty of the sun rising slowly above the horizon and shining on the red land. Around the time of sunrise, standing at a high slope along the roadside overlooking the village of Da Ma Kan, it is possible to see that the village is surrounded by red fields which are filled with smoke from kitchen chimneys, while the poplars around the village are glowing with the oblique sunbeam of the morning sun, which constitutes a touching tranquil rural scene. If we are lucky, we can enjoy the fantastic sunrise and the rosy clouds of dawn.[187] (Viagra8868: 2015)

The paragraph shows a decisive estheticization and poeticization of the travel experience in which the landscape is regarded as a vector of pleasure and emotions. Although by now Kunming has become a rather popular touristic hub (for then reaching the Tibetan plateau), the blogger is able to look at its surroundings from an unusual perspective, that is, through the colors of autumn.

More specifically, the discourse draws upon a poetic use of words,[188] which resonates with Strassberg's argument that pre-modern and modern travel writing favored "being in a place" and the "quality" of the landscape, over the diegetic development of the journey and the "formation" of the subject. More than that, the traveler's persona is almost elided from the text: the narrator's "I" disappears behind a gazing stance that interrogates neither the landscape nor himself. Even when the blogger, in the third stage of the journey, visits the Red Army Memorial in the village of Ke Du he largely focuses the post on nature and contemplation, avoiding providing comments on the historical relevance of the site. Hence, while visually speaking Viagra8868 is able to look at Kunming from a unique angle, when it comes to the writing, aestheticism outweighs historicism and observation takes critical reflection over.

The second blog, by blogger Yǒu Gè A (Pinyin of the untranslatable 有个啊), recounts a five-day visit to Suzhou and presents many similar features to the previous

---

[187] "要进行云南寻'色'之旅，无论如何是不能少了东川红土地的。早上早早的起床出了门，紧赶慢赶，希望在日出之前赶到东川，这样就可以目睹到太阳从地平线慢慢升起照耀红土地的壮阔美景。打马坎是一个村子的名字，早晨日出前后在公路边的高坡上俯瞰打马坎村，红土围绕的村子里炊烟缭绕，村子四周杨树在朝阳斜射下泛着光辉，一派宁静动人的田园风光。运气好的时候可以欣赏到梦幻般的日出和朝霞。"

[188] Bakhtin contrasted poetry with novel on the basis that in the former the whole burden of signification rested on and emanated from words, while in the novel the meaning is derived relationally as the intertwining of different registers.

blog.[189] Posts are largely constituted by descriptions of the places visited. The following excerpt comes from the first post, dedicated to the Humble Administrator Garden:

> The entrance to the park is located at the southern end, after passing through Lan Xue Tang (Orchid and Snow Parlour) via the porch and the front courtyard. On the east side, there is a lawn with a wide open area, and the Western side of the lawn is surrounded by the earth-piled hill on which there is a wooden pavilion, surrounded by running water, with the drooping willows along the river bank, with the stone breakwater and erected hill in between, and with the waterside pavilion and bridge near the water. On the northwest side of the hill, where black pines form a grove, there is a tearoom. Further to the west, there is a double corridor along the wall, and on this a series of decorated windows and a number of artistic doors allow the viewer to look at the central area of the garden. I sighed: if only people could live in this park for their whole life, there would be no need to try to be immortal! Then, after several minutes, the crowd increased. Well, in order to enjoy the Humble Administrator Garden you must come early.[190] (Yǒu Gè A 2015)

The main goal of the blogger is to provide a precise (spatial) representation of the place. It is no coincidence that it is only in the last two lines that his persona surfaces in the narrative through a comment. In terms of style, while Viagra8868 opted for embellished writing, here readers face a milder, paler vocabulary: accuracy is favored over lyricism. At the same time, however, both blogs give a strong sense of dealing with a static experience: one that has no internal motion. The performative force of travelling and writing is annihilated, and an attitude guided primarily by sight and contemplation prevails. A very similar approach also characterizes the third part of the account, which describes a visit to the so-called Lion Grove, and provides a chiefly informative note:

> Lion Grove was built in the Yuan Dynasty. Originally, it was a temple, which was converted to a private garden later in the Qing Dynasty. Because in the park there are tens of thousands of bamboo in the grove, and there are many strange stones under the bamboo, in the shape of Suan Ni (lion), the name "Lion Grove" was adopted.[191] (Yǒu Gè A 2015)

---

[189] http://i.travel.sina.com.cn/js/suzhou/498.html.

[190] "园的入口设在南端，经门廊、前院、过兰雪堂，即进入园内。东侧为面积旷阔的草坪，草坪西面堆土山，上有木构亭，四周萦绕流水，岸柳低垂，间以石矶、立峰，临水建有水榭、曲桥。西北土阜上密植黑松枫杨成林，林西为秫香馆（茶室）。再西有一道依墙的复廊，上有漏窗透景，又以洞门数处与中区相通。然后朝右走向一个亭子。几分钟后，我感叹：在这个园子里活一辈子，神仙也不用做了！又过了几分钟，人群奔涌而至……唉，看拙政园，必须来得早。"

[191] "狮子林建于元代，原为寺庙，后清朝才转为私家园林。[...] 因园内"林有竹万，竹下多怪石，状如狻猊（狮子）者"，又因天如禅师维则得法于浙江天目山狮子岩普应国师中峰，为纪念佛徒衣钵、

The representation of the legs of the journey as idyllic, self-standing episodes or aperçus complies with the epicization of the discourse that also characterizes Western travel blogs. However, two main differences are identifiable. Firstly, the writing of Chinese travel blogs is less objectified: it is very descriptive, but this feature is subservient to the fostering of a contemplative *regard* that eventually downplays any stringently functional purpose of the blog (e.g., touristic information; in Chinese blogs tips and info about tickets/accommodations/attractions are largely absent). Secondly, the way in which Western and Chinese travel bloggers travel is different: the former often follow well-beaten tracks; the latter are more prone either to go to places that are usually overlooked by tourists – such as the visit to the Lion Grove in Suzhou – or to shape the experience depending on a particular point of view, as is the case with the appreciation of Kunming's autumn colors.

CONCLUSION

This chapter revived the transmedial approach that characterizes Chapters 1 to 3 and projected the analysis on to contemporary Chinese-authored travel books and blogs, in order to reverse the Western perspective of the analysis. When compared to both Western travelogues and Chinese blogs, Chinese travel books manifest a stronger political connotation. This, however, happens on varying levels: some authors, such as Shuyun, address the legitimacy of China's current political system; others look critically at the relations between Mainland China, Hong Kong and Taiwan, or inscribe China into a global discourse of inequalities, injustices, and fights for rights (e.g., Ng, Lam). Nuances are also at stake: works by How Man and Leong, for instance, do carry a political meaning, but they tend to filter it, either through focusing closer on everyday life, or by favoring an academic, scientific stance.

Beyond these differences, it emerged that contemporary Chinese travel writers distance themselves quite radically from the tradition of pre-modern and modern Chinese travel writing – as investigated by Richard Strassberg – in that they refuse to resort to the genre as a vehicle for celebrating the country or its landscape. On the contrary, this latter tendency reappears in Chinese travel blogs. Here, the hegemony of visual elements, together with the fact that posts are chiefly descriptive, conjures up an estheticization of China that turns the country into a place to be looked at, rather than experienced or lived (and political issues are overlooked).

Once one compares Chinese travel blogs to Western ones, both similarities and divergences come to the surface. In terms of layout, the Chinese blog platform Travel.sina.cn is richer in interactive and multimodal content than Western ones. What is mostly remarkable is that the distinction between platforms and individual blogs is less clear-cut when it comes to the Chinese blogosphere, as Ironshoetravel.com attests (although this claim would require a greater number of case studies in order to be confirmed). In terms of what is recounted, Chinese

师承关系，取佛经中狮子座之意，故名"狮子林"。另外在北京圆明园、承德避暑山庄中则各有一处仿建。"

bloggers – either on platforms or as individuals – manage to avoid by and large a touristic stance by looking at their destination(s) from angles that are usually different from those taken by (Western) tourists. This is so because Chinese travel bloggers occupy an insider position within China and this implies certain advantages in terms of linguistic and cultural knowledge. Hence, Chinese travel bloggers are able to re-imagine China from the inside: they move beyond the homogenizing tourist gaze and break down the country's space into a multiplicity of places and experiences. At the same time, however, it was highlighted that the treating in blogs of "light" themes over sensible ones might indicate a form of self-censorship of the bloggers, who do not want their posts to be removed (hence, the insider position also has disadvantages).

Although the sample of texts is not wide enough to draw any generalization, it could be suggested that both Chinese travel authors and bloggers are more inclined when compared with Western peers to look at China "heterodoxically." This term does not suggest that Chinese writers write against a supposed doxa – a dogmatic representation of China – but rather that they manage to build a composite picture. Heterodox, then, has to be intended, in the spirit of Bakhtin's notion of "heteroglossia," as those representations that are informed by a variety of perspectives (or voices), be they touristic, political, ethnographic, artistic, or focused either on ordinariness or on global issues. This is reflected, ultimately, in the self-representation of Chinese travel writers. Apart from Lam, who defends his being a travel writer, the figure of the travel writer is fragmented into a plurality of personae, attitudes, and professions that resist an easy aggregation around a coherent and unique self-representation. We encountered, indeed, not only photographers and journalists, but ethnographers, historians, artists and many of them – if not all – claimed for themselves a hybrid cultural background as a mix of Chinese, Hong Kong, and Western culture.

Afterword

These concluding remarks are divided into two brief sections. The first one will provide some broader reflections and possible future developments concerning the analysis accomplished; the second will be devoted to the discussion of the fieldwork and its outcomes.

Three axes of enquiry underpinned the whole work. The most important was the transmedial comparison between contemporary travel books and blogs. The study showed the extent to which printed and digital travelogues, despite sharing basic generic features, respond ultimately to different expectations and are shaped by different logics of production. Firstly, travel books and blogs, as geniums, promote two kinds of writing: the former chiefly novelistic, the latter predominantly informative. The main consequence is that in travel books it is easier to identify a precise vision of China, usually one based upon an overreaching narrative in which the journey is represented as a gradual process of discovery. Travel bloggers, by contrast, tend to deliver factual, fragmented accounts, which are addressed to a precise readership: other tourists/bloggers. Secondly, the authors of books and blogs do not travel in the same way. The former plan personalized (longer) experiences, the latter usually follow well-beaten paths, even when they travel independently. Hence, the answer to one of the main research questions of this work, that is, if travel blogs as forms of digital storytelling could represent an alternative channel to mainstream media for getting an updated representation of China, tends to be in the negative: travel blogs are framed within a horizon of leisure that leaves little space for an in-depth investigation of the country or the encounter with the host culture. To be sure, this scenario pertains by and large to Western texts, to which greater attention was dedicated. Concerning Chinese authors and bloggers, the situation is more complex. On the one hand, it is certainly possible to notice a medial and rhetorical divide between Chinese-authored books and blogs (as is the case with Western works). Printed texts are very much politicized, while digital ones favor a contemplative representation of the country along the line of classic Chinese travel books. On the other hand, however, Chinese bloggers too manage to provide readers with unusual *regards*, even when they travel to touristic places. Despite the small corpus of texts studied, it was argued that both Chinese authors and bloggers are able to approach China heterodoxically, making its representation more articulated and varied. In the case of Chinese writers, then, what is at stake is the very possibility, as cultural and linguistic insiders, of drawing upon a deeper and broader knowledge of the country and, from this standpoint, of deconstructing its monolithic conception as a travel destination.

This leads to the second axis of the research: the cross-cultural confrontation between Western and Chinese writers. In this regard, the analysis made clear that the cultural background does influence the way of conceiving and shaping printed and digital travelogues. So, for instance, Western travel books and Chinese travel books are rather different geniums, despite the fact that they share the same medial format.

Similarly, Western and Chinese travel blogs are framed by, and inform, precise cultural and literary expectations, which find a reflection in how the medial format is eventually used (e.g., Chinese blogs are visually richer than Western ones). This also led us to suggest that blogs, albeit constituting a major sphere within the global medium *par excellence*, that is, the Web, also present features that are affected by the context of production and reception. In other words, blogs (too) respond to precise cultural and epistemological expectations. One essential point to note is that among Western blogs it was possible to detect a clear distinction between accounts hosted on platforms and individual ones. This divide implies, to various degrees, a greater commitment of individual bloggers, who, in turn, challenge through their activities any clear distinction between amateur and professional writers. When it came to explore the Chinese blogosphere, however, the gap between platforms and individual blogs was more blurred. Moreover, it was rather difficult to identify for both Chinese bloggers and authors a coherent self-representation that could go under the label "travel writer" (although these findings would need a more conspicuous archive to be confirmed).

Thirdly, by collating Chapters 4 and 5, it is possible to draw some conclusions about the third axis of the research, namely the historical evolution of Western- and Chinese-authored travel writing about the Middle Kingdom. The survey of Western travel writing from the end of the 19th century to the 1980s highlighted the difficulty of clearly tracing a linear genealogy of the genre, in terms of both rhetorical and medial features. Rather, it emerged that the writing (and reading) of any text is always a negotiation of socio-cultural factors *and* individual attitudes. *A posteriori*, it could be argued that Western travel authors, as a whole, share a communal ethos in the way in which they travel to, and write about, China. This, however, should refrain from drawing broader inferences about the homogeneity of the tropes found in the texts. In fact, one of the outcomes of the present work was precisely to highlight the literary and medial specificity of each genium.

From the last chapter, a substantial difference between contemporary and older Chinese travel writing emerged. While pre-modern and modern travel authors up to the 19th century usually resorted to the genre to deliver a celebratory representation of the cultural and political situation of the country, contemporary authors mainly "use" travel writing as a means for criticizing China's current status quo. Again, however, it is necessary to avoid generalizations: such commitment, indeed, presents varying nuances depending on the authors' own biographies. Moreover, it must also be taken into account that the analysis largely drew on texts published by Hong Kong writers, who enjoy a greater freedom than Mainlanders. In this respect, Lam's words come to mind here, when he noted during the interview that considerable differences can be found in travelogues written by Taiwanese, Hongkongers, and Mainlanders. According to him, authors from Hong Kong tend to focus on the practical unfolding of their experience, while Taiwanese authors usually exploit the journey as a pretext to elaborate deep reflections. This also happens with Mainlanders, although they primarily write about China, as their access to foreign countries is rather limited.

This work offered a comparative reading of roughly 50 texts. It is important to reassert this in order to say that conclusions drawn here could and should be tested further. This applies in particular to Chinese travel writing. Specifically, it would be beneficial not only to dedicate greater attention to the blogosphere, but also to (re)engage with the historical evolution of the travel writing genre in China in light of the analysis provided here of contemporary texts. This kind of investigation could open the way to a different and more accurate understanding of China's past (and its engagement with the West) and of the diverse historical and literary trajectories in Hong Kong, Taiwan, Macau, and Mainland China. At the same time, given that – according to the UNWTO – China has by now become the greatest source of outbound travelers, it might be also interesting to investigate how today's Chinese travelers represent the West in print and online. Similarly, the specific study of the Chinese blogosphere could delineate more clearly how the use of social media is nowadays culturally (and politically) affected within the country.

Another line of enquiry is one that starts from within the blogosphere – either in China or in the West – and moves toward the realm of Social Networking Sites (SNSs). As discussed in the Introduction, blogging is certainly the oldest and most stable form of social writing on the Web. However, the proliferation of SNSs has begun to challenge the hegemony of blogs. Separating blogs from SNSs is not only a temporal span, but a qualitative leap: however minimal the writing on blogs may be, posts on Facebook, Twitter, or Weibo (the Chinese version of Twitter) radicalize blogs' minimalism and witness a proliferation of paratextual elements that further threaten the existence of the text. More generally, travel narratives on SNSs – if it is ever possible to retrace a proper narrative on these platforms (see, Simanowski 2017) – further accelerate and fragment the posting, which loses even its epic form in favor of a purely topological orientation (such as when users geolocalize themselves in a place without providing any further details). In this sense, the datafied and quantified self-representation increasingly promoted by SNSs and apps constitute a strong trend: one that demands to be further investigated, especially in relation to what happens to the "I" of the writer/user and the Other represented (and to the experience of their mutual encounter) when they are reduced to a mere set of data. Eventually, the consequences that such phenomena (and the loss of our ability to narrate, substituted by a pervasive self-tracking objectivization of our subjectivities) have on the way in which we think of ourselves, interpret our "real" experiences, and write about them online still constitute a largely uncharted field of enquiry: a field that looks extremely promising, but also problematic when considering the speed of evolution (and weak regulation) of the Web and its agents. Undoubtedly, it is necessary to do research on these topics by further favoring an ethnographic approach alongside text analysis, especially in light of the political and economic value that personal information is acquiring in today's globalized society, even beyond or against users' own will and awareness.

From here, we arrive to touch upon one last research line. It has mainly to do with a "historical gaze," back to the origins of the Web. At stake is not so much a further exploration of the effects that the passage from the Web 1.0 to the Web 2.0 (and possibly 3.0, with the birth of the semantic Web) has had (and will have) on what we publish and do online (see van Dijck 2013). Rather, it is urgent to tackle the issue of the preservation of online content. Today, the Web is already more than two decades old and we can (should) start to investigate it archeologically. This, however, triggers a paradoxical condition: while the Web represents the arena where massive and increasing amount of information is endlessly shared (and exploited) by a soaring number of users and corporations, it also constitutes the archive itself of this load of information. In other words, the Web is, at once, a constantly changing stage and its own repository. The most delicate point is that the bare fact that information is stored does not mean it is accessible or easy to retrace. The reasons for that are exogenous – for instance, the speed at which technology becomes obsolete – as well as endogenous, such as the threats to which webpages are repeatedly exposed either in the form of cyber attacks or due to the internal dynamics of the Web, as a never-ending flow that swallows up and regurgitates content, that forgets and remembers, erases and overwrites. Web content is magmatic to such an extent that to find a way to selectively discern and preserve what is deemed relevant becomes crucial not only for our processes of remembrance but for the Web itself, which risks collapsing under its own weight. Studies that connect digital cultures to digital memory(ies) address these issues (see Fiormonte 2003; Numerico, Fiormonte, and Tomasi 2010), but much more needs to be done. In particular, the wish is that these studies will increasingly get involved with language programming, insofar as doing research on the Web can no longer be disjoined from the technological know-how that fuels its evolution. Again, at stake is as much an academic as a political issue, that is, the need to provide scholars and younger generations with the tools for critically understanding not only how to use new technologies, but also what these technologies are doing to us, to our (analogue) abilities and competencies, and to the gaze we (were used to) project over ourselves, others, and the world.

***

I spent roughly three months in China, thanks to two grants I received from the Worldwide University Network (WUN) and the Universities' China Committee in London (UCCL). From mid-March to mid-May 2015 I was a visiting scholar at the English Department at the Chinese University of Hong Kong. After that, I spent one month in Mainland China, which I traversed by train from south to north, up to Beijing. During this period, I conducted the interviews that enrich the last chapter of this work and I also kept a blog – www.stillwandering.net - in which I wrote about my ongoing experiences in the Middle Kingdom (with the exception of a few later posts that relate to some publications derived from the fieldwork). In other words, the blog represented a way to test the analysis presented here.

While blogging I tried to avoid what I thought were the main weaknesses of the blogs I analyzed, in terms of either medial choices or the reification of certain stereotypical discourses about China. For example, I made an effort to organize paratextual elements in a polished way, through the subdivision of the blog into sub-sections and the creation of a side column where I listed references and sources to useful materials for my research. In this sense, I made the blog as hypertextual and interactive as possible: I inserted several links, both to other posts and to external websites, without, however, fragmenting the narrative flow of the text too much – at least that was the intention. Moreover, I tried to create a balance between words and visual elements, by uploading within the posts and in a dedicated section of the blog high-quality images and a few videos (I had a reflex camera with me). Lastly, I included an interactive map that could help to keep track of my wanderings. These choices required me to get a personal domain and also pay for data upload and the use of external tools. I would say that this draws me into that grey area where professionals and amateur bloggers meet.

Strictly speaking of the writing, my goal was to mix reflections and narration, in order to keep the blog appealing to the reader but also self-conscious. For instance, whenever I sensed I could not understand Chinese people – a feeling and a trope I was rather acquainted with by the time I went to China – I strove to unpack such distress and see what lay beyond it. Often, it was simply the fact that in Hong Kong life is organized differently from the UK; but this, I am sure, happens at all latitudes. At the same time, I also attempted as best as I could to let my impressions flow effortlessly on the screen: after all, I did not want the theory and my academic role to condition entirely my writing. This meant that, while on some occasions I was consciously reflecting upon my presence in China, on others I left my blogging free to linger upon diverse topics. This resonates with Pazu's idea about the heterogeneity of his writing for the Web. In particular, I noted that such heterogeneity affected the posts I published when I was settled in Hong Kong, as if dwelling in one place naturally triggered the transversal exploration of the host culture. Hence, if coherence has to be found in the blog, it lies chiefly in the chronological organization of the posts. Extracts of what I wrote also appeared on the Italian literary magazine *Le Reti di Dedalus*. In this regard, not only did the blog undergo a remediation process, but only some of its posts were selected (i.e., those less attached to the contingency of the moment) and they were partially re-edited to fit the magazine's guidelines (e.g., I removed all the passages in English). The mixing of English and Italian is another feature of the blog which had an unexpected development. In the beginning, I intended to split each post into two parts, which recounted the same episode in the two languages. Soon, however, I realized that in so doing the blog would have become boring and extremely time consuming for me. So, I let my mood and the events I was talking about decide which was, on each occasion, the most appropriate language to use. As a pattern, when I discussed academic issues I resorted to English, while I wrote in Italian when I had less time at my disposal or I wanted to speak to a precise readership in my home country.

Once I took to the road, the posts followed more closely the linearity of the journey, although it also occurred to me to plan and write posts in advance (it became more of a duty than a pleasure). This meant that the flow of the narrative did not coincide with the writing process. Quite surprisingly, I noted that my writing kept a steady pace throughout, independently from the fact that I was either in Hong Kong or travelling. In fact, when on the road, I was even able to write longer posts than those I published when I was comfortably settled in Hong Kong. Sure, I had in mind to write as regularly as possible, but I had expected that the journey would have brought with itself some impediments. On the contrary, I was always able to find time, energy, and a good Wi-Fi connection to post on the blog. Technically speaking, I only needed a VPN to bypass the "Great Firewall" and be able to share my writing online.

Overall, my blogging was a rather intense practice: roughly 60 posts, 45,000 words, and 400 pictures over a period of three months. The blog also recounts the last ten days of the journey, which I spent onboard the Trans-Siberian railway from Beijing to Moscow. The traversing of Siberia was the only time when I could not blog live, due to the lack of Wi-Fi. However, I kept writing on my carnet, and I uploaded the posts once I reached Moscow (here Gaunt's and Paul Theroux's travelogues echo). The main reason for such intensity in the writing is that I knew from the outset it was for a short period, and the experience would have been wasted if I had written sporadically and inconsistently. This demanded a greater dedication than I had planned in the beginning (usually two to three hours' work per day). In fact, I soon realized that writing good articles on a regular basis required a consistent amount of work, from the moment of creation to the editing of the text.

There is one main aspect that connects my experience to those of many others that I have read about online: the itinerary. I became conscious of that during the interview in Beijing with travel curator Zhang Mei, quoted in the first chapter. As soon as she told me that there is much else to see in China beyond the loop Guilin-Hangzhou-Shanghai-Xian-Beijing, I realized that, with minor diversions, these were also the stages of my journey. However, as Zhang Mei pointed out, "to travel differently does not mean to avoid popular places, but to look at them from a renewed perspective." I hope to have done so, at least to a certain extent, or to have developed a (self)critical gaze. Initially, I had planned to go west, as many writers suggested I visited Xinjiang and the Tibetan plateau. However, I was held back by my language skills, which I felt were not good enough to venture into these regions. Eventually, it turned out that even on the east coast very few people speak English, so I think I could have got along fine anywhere in China. After all, as I write on the "About" page on my blog, I believe that only a minor percentage of what we know passes through language: the greatest part depends on emotions, vibes, and the body. But this is another story.

Appendix

Below is the list of all the contemporary travel books and blogs analyzed, together with a brief historical and editorial contextualization for each work and writer and the itineraries followed, to give an indication of the diversity of travel experiences as well as their forms of expression.

CONTEMPORARY TRAVEL BOOKS AND BLOGS LISTED BY WRITERS

Arnaud, Clara (1986-) is a French author who wrote the travel book *Sur les chemins de Chine* (trans. *On China's Paths*). The travelogue, published in 2010, recounts the solo journey that Arnaud accomplished in 2008 in the western regions of China (i.e., Xinjiang and the Tibetan plateau). She travelled either on foot or riding two horses and the whole journey lasted a few months. This was Arnaud's first travel book: currently, she is working as a consultant in Paris and writing a novel.

Ataritouchme is a German blogger who published the English-language blog *All o'er China during Spring Festival Holiday* (2006) on the platform Travelpod.com. The blogger is currently living in China and exploits working breaks to travel around the country. On his space on the platform, Ataritouchme published 15 blogs (as of December 2015). These concern both his journeys in China and abroad. *All o'er China during Spring Festival Holiday* is the first blog he wrote and the most popular one, according to the number of visits it has received. It contains 16 posts: as the title suggests, Ataritouchme travelled around the whole country over a period of a month and a half. He visited well-known places such as Nanjing, Beijing, Xian, Chengdu, as well as other cities beyond the tourist routes: Urumqi, Nanning, Nanhai, Dalian. In the introductory post, the blogger states that he has only travelled on ground, avoiding planes. The blog contains many pictures taken by Ataritouchme's travel companion Hannah.

Becki (real name: Rebecca Enright) is a British blogger. *Backpackerbecki.com* and *Bordersofadventure.com* are two travel blogs she created individually. *Backpackerbecki.com* was active from 2012 to 2014, after which Becki decided for a radical restyling of the blog, which has become *Bordersofadventure.com* (the older version is now accessible at http://archive.org). As the titles suggest, the two blogs recount Becki's globetrotting experiences around the world. Becki went to China in 2012 for roughly two months and wrote 11 posts about this experience. The posts were published on the first version of the blog and now they appear unchanged on the new one. In China Becki visited the major touristic destinations around the country, including Beijing, Shanghai, Chengdu, and the Yangtze River.

Bettinelli, Giorgio (1955-2008) was a popular Italian travel writer. *La Cina in Vespa* (trans. *Around China on a Vespa*) was released in 2008, just months after the sudden death of the author. Bettinelli is known for having travelled around the world always riding his scooter. The journey he accomplished around China lasted several months and was divided into two stages: Bettinelli's goal was to be the first person to ride an imported vehicle in China – a practice usually forbidden by law – and visit all the 34 geographic areas of China. A dozen pictures are inserted in the middle of the book, which was released by Feltrinelli publisher in the series "Traveller."

BitByTheTravelBug is a US-American blogger (real name: Shannon) who published the blog *China 2014* (2014) on the popular platform Travelblog.org. The journey lasted two weeks – from the 17th of May to the 1st of June – and it was made together with a group of other visitors. On her space on the platform, BitByTheTravelBug published one more blog, dedicated to Thailand and Singapore.

Croiziers, Aurélie is a French author who published the travelogue *La Chine à fleur de peau* (trans. *Under the surface of China*) in 2011. Due to her job, Croiziers travelled to China many times and to different places between 2005 and 2009. In 2009, the author moved to China for good, although the relocation lasted eventually only two years: in 2011, indeed, Croiziers went back to Paris. The book is a collection of the some of the posts that Croiziers has published on her blog *Curieuse Voyageuse* since 2009 (see below), primarily focusing on her journeys around the country.

Curieuse Voyageuse (trans. Curious Traveller) is a French blogger (real name: Aurélie Croiziers) as well as the title of her individual travel blog *Curieusevoyageuse.com*. The blog was founded in 2009 when Curieuse Voyageuse moved to China (and it is still updated today). Curieuse Voyageuse has published countless of posts about China, due to the fact that she travelled there four times before settling down in Shanghai between 2009 and 2011. Since her return to Paris, she has widened the spectrum of her blog, writing about her journeys in France and abroad.

De Slizewicz, Constantin (1977-), a French writer and reporter, is the author of *Ivre de Chine: Voyages au coeur de l'Empire* (trans. *Drunk with China: Journeys to the Heart of the Empire*), published in 2010. In it, de Slizewicz recounts his journey from Beijing to the southwestern areas of China on board of a motorbike. The journey was accomplished in 2002 together with his friend Alexandre and lasted a few months. De Slizewicz arrived in China in the 1990s: after settling down in Beijing, he gradually moved westward and eventually settled down in Kunming.

Emil (real name: Kang Emil) is a US-American blogger who published his individual blog titled *Emil's Trip to China* (2006) using the CMS blogger.co.uk (*Emilstravels.blogspot.co.uk*). Emil went to China with an organized tour that lasted a couple of weeks. He was together with a group of colleagues from the US. They visited the most popular places, including Beijing, Shanghai, Guilin, and Lhasa.

Faravelli, Stefano (1959-) is an Italian artist. *Carnet di viaggio: Cina* (2005, trans. *Journey's Notebook: China*) is a travel book he completed in order to recount his journey to the Middle Kingdom. The book is, in fact, a pictorial artefact: in each page watercolors and handwritten words give life to a precise scene witnessed by Faravelli. The author went to popular destinations such as Xian, Beijing, and Hong Kong, as well as to less known areas of the west of China. Due to the dense mingling of pictorial illustration with words, the book is not only multimodal, but could be defined more precisely as "transmodal."

Flavia is an Italian blogger found on the platform Blogdiviaggi.com (trans. "Travel Blogs"). *Conoscere Pechino tra dinastie e imperatori* (2013, trans. *Getting to Know Beijing between Dynasties and Emperors*) is the heading of the first post dedicated to China by Flavia. The blogger has written a total of five posts on China and, according to the dates of the first and last posts, she spent roughly one and a half months in the Middle Kingdom, from 21st September to 5th November 2013.

Gao, Qiang (1962-) and Gao, Zhen (1956-) are two Chinese artists known worldwide as the "Gao Brothers." Much of the Gao Brothers' artistic work focuses on the critique of the Cultural Revolution, during which they lost their father. Differently from their main corpus of works, *One Day in Beijing* (original title: 在北京一天能走多遠) is a 2004 travel reportage that the Gao Brothers published to recount their one-day experience in Beijing as (unofficial) reporters. They wandered around the city, took photographs and interviewed people in order to witness a normal day in China's capital.

Gattosandro Viaggiatore (real name: Simona) is an Italian blogger who created the homonymous individual blog *Gattosandro-viaggiatore.blogspot.it*. The blogger went to China twice: the first time in August 2012 for 20 days and the second time in July-August 2013, for a month. She dedicated two blogs to these experiences: *Cina e Hong Kong* (2012, trans. China and Hong Kong) and *Cina del sud e isole* (2013, trans. *South of China and Islands*). In the first blog, she recounts her journey around the most well-known cities along China's east coast: Beijing, Shanghai, Suzhou, Hangzhou, Hong Kong. On the second occasion, she travelled to those popular destinations that had remained excluded from her previous journey – among which Guangzhou and Guilin – as well as to less renowned places such as Fenghuang, Beihai and Zhangjiajie. The first blog contains 21 posts, the second one 27. Both blogs contain a good number of pictures taken by the blogger. The whole site also includes accounts to the other journeys that Gattosandro Viaggiatore has accomplished to the "Orient," as she calls it, and to Italy, Europe, and Africa.

Germain-Thomas, Olivier (1943-) wrote two travelogues in French that focus on China: *La traversée de la Chine à la vitesse du printemps* (2003, trans. *The Traversing of China at Spring's Rhythm*) and *Le Bénarès-Kyôto* (2007, trans. *The Varanasi-Kyoto*). In the first brief travelogue Germain-Thomas narrates his journey from the south of China – at the border with Vietnam – to its capital Beijing, accompanied by the coming of spring. The book largely revolves around the author's intimate discovery of China and its philosophical and religious thoughts. The journey lasted roughly a month and was accomplished taking public transport. This text was later included with some editorial adjustments within Germain-Thomas's travel book *Le Bénarès-Kyôto*. The book reports the author's long journey from the city of Varanasi, in India, to Kyoto, in Japan, passing through China. The journey took several months and the peculiarity is that the author never took flights, but travelled remaining on ground all the time. Both books are exclusively composed of written text.

Gifford, Rob is a British journalist who published in 2007 the travelogue *China Road: A Journey into the Future of a Rising Power*. After having worked many years as correspondent for National Public Radio (NPR), Gifford was ordered by NPR to return to the UK. Before leaving China, he decided to traverse the country from east to west along the highway 312, known as the Chinese Route 66. The book presents only an introductory map that traces the trajectory of the journey from Beijing to Kashgar, after which the travelogue is entirely composed of written text.

Gray, Nathan, a New Zealand writer and reporter, authored the travel book *First Pass under Heaven: One man's 4000-Kilometre Trek along the Great Wall of China* (2006). Gray wrote this travel book to recollect his experience walking the whole length of the Great Wall of China. The book is a detailed journal that follows the walk almost day by day. Gray started this journey in 2000 together with other four companions: a Buddhist monk, an Argentinean photojournalist, an Italian freelance journalist, and a Mormon golfer. The trek turned out to be mentally and physically exhausting. Having departed from the westernmost garrison of the Great Wall in the Gobi Desert, after a few weeks the group split and Gray remained alone. When he was still at 1000 kilometers from the Pacific shores, where the Great Wall ends, Gray gave up the walk, completely worn out. He returned to the same spot three months later to conclude the journey. Some pictures are inserted in the middle of the book: some of these are taken with a camera; others come from the documentary that the group filmed during the walk.

Hirst, Bamboo (1940-) is an Italian Chinese-born author who wrote two travel books about China. The first one is *Il mondo oltre il fiume dei peschi in fiore* (1989, trans. *The World beyond the River of the Blossoming Peach Trees*); the second is *Cartoline da Pechino* (1998, trans. *Postcards from Beijing*). Hirst was born in Shanghai to an Italian diplomat and a Chinese woman. She moved to Italy (where she currently lives) when she was 13, due to China's political insecurity at that time. Hirst returned to China for the first time in 1988, just months before the events of Tiananmen Square. *Il mondo oltre il fiume dei peschi in fiore* gathers her impressions about her homeland after many years of detachment. She visited, among others, Beijing and Shanghai, Hangzhou, Qufu, Suzhou. The book is enriched with pictures taken by Italian photojournalist Giorgio Lotti, who went regularly to China in the 1970s and 1980s as a correspondent for a number of Italian magazines. *Cartoline da Pechino* narrates

Hirst's second journey to the Middle Kingdom in the mid-1990s. However, many of the episodes and places described are the same as those appearing in *Il mondo oltre il fiume dei peschi in fiore*. Differently from the first book, *Cartoline da Pechino* is a monomodal travelogue as there are no pictures included.

How Man, Wong (1949-), a Hong Kong explorer, conservationist and journalist, published a number of books centered on his several expeditions in China. *Exploring the Yangtze: China's Longest River* is a 1989 travel book that focuses on How Man's mapping of the Yangtze. At the head of a Chinese expedition, How Man followed the whole river from the east to the west, eventually discovering a newer and remoter source of the river than the one usually credited. The book, which is largely a collection of notes recounting the difficulties and the encounters experienced during the expedition, includes a variety of pictures interspersed in the text. *From Manchuria to Tibet* (1998) is a second travel book by him. Being also a photographer, How Man conceived *From Manchuria to Tibet* as a photographic book: pictures dominate the whole narrative and are accompanied by brief notations. Gathering his many experiences about and with the ethnic minorities that live along the borders of China, the book aims at doing justice to many of these groups, starting from the north-easternmost region of the country to its south-westernmost conflictive region.

Lam, Fai Fred (1979-) is a Hong Kong writer and blogger. In 2014 his travelogue *Travelling between Hope and Suffering* (original title: 旅行在 希望與苦難 之間) was released in Taiwan and Hong Kong. Lam travelled around the world for two years between 2012 and 2014: in this book, he recounts his experiences in China – in particular the south-west regions – south-east Asia, the Middle East, and Europe. The book, which is currently banned in Mainland China, contains many pictures taken by Lam himself and mingled into the text. Lam is also the founder of the Chinese travel blog platform Ironshoetravel.com, launched in 2015.

Legerton, Colin and Rawson, Jacob are two US-American writers who authored the travelogue *Invisible China: A Journey through Ethnic Borderlands* (2009). Legerton and Rawson got their Master degrees in China; they learnt Mandarin as well as the languages of two China's minorities: Korean and Uyghur. At the end of their studies they embarked on a journey to the remotest regions of China – from north to south and through the west – in order to understand more about the ethnic minorities that populate China's borderlands. The journey was divided into two stages, depending on climate conditions. The book, published in 2009, presents many pictures of the minority groups encountered by the authors.

Leong, Ka Tai is a Hong Kong photographer and reporter. *On China: One to Twenty Four* is a photo-book he published in 1988. After some years spent in Europe – first in London where he studied engineering and then Paris where he studied photography – Leong came back to Hong Kong at the end of 1970s. Here, he opened his own photographic studio, Camera 22. This, however, did not prevent him from leaving his occupation (between 1982 and 1987) for travelling around Mainland China. *On*

China: One to Twenty Four presents 24 shots taken during Leong's five years of wanderings: each one of the pictures is accompanied by a poem written in Chinese by writer Leung Ping Kwan and translated into English by Leong himself.

Mathieu (real name: Mathieu Décore) is a French blogger who posted his account titled *Un peu partout en Chine* (2007, trans. *A Bit Everywhere around China*) on the platform Top-depart.com. Mathieu went to China together with his Chinese wife and they stayed in the country for four weeks. He wrote 10 posts on his blog. The journey was the chance for Mathieu to get to know his wife's home country, by visiting the main common destinations such as Beijing, Shanghai, and Chengdu. Mathieu has published only one blog on his space on Top-depart.com.

Millycat (1966-) is an Italian blogger who published the blog *Cina: Terra di grandi contrasti* (2013, trans. *China: A Land of Big Contradictions*) on the Italian blog platform Turistipercaso.it. This is the most famous and visited Italian portal focused on tourism and travel blogs. Millycat's journey lasted roughly three weeks, during which she visited China's major tourist destinations: Beijing, Xian, Guilin, Shanghai. Millycat has uploaded another blog on her space on Turistipercaso.it, dedicated to her journey in Bretagne and Normandy.

Ng, Jason is a Hong Kong blogger, travel writer and lawyer. Ng returned to Hong Kong in 2005 after many years spent in the United States, where he studied, and Europe. His departure from Hong Kong in the 1980s was part of the Hongkongers' diaspora due to the fear for the then imminent hand over of the island to Mainland China. Since his return to Hong Kong, Ng has been blogging about his home city on his page *As I See It*. The book *Hong Kong State of Mind* (2011) is composed of a collection of the best posts that appeared online. Substituting the pictures that appear on the blog, the book is filled with drawings made by Ng's father, who is an illustrator. Although the text touches upon a variety of subjects, the last section of the book is fully dedicated to Ng's journeys to Taiwan, Macao, and China's neighboring countries.

Pazu, Kong is a Hong Kong blogger and travel writer. *My Sharing on How Breathing Keeps Me Warm in Lhasa* (original title: 從愛斯基摩到共享陽光 --- 我在拉薩用呼吸來保暖的經驗分享) is the title of the first post that Pazu published on the blog platform Ironshoetravel.com. In 2006, Pazu cycled from Bangkok to Lhasa and eventually settled down in the Tibetan city, where he opened a coffee shop. This experience is narrated in his travel book *Spinning in Tibet Selling Coffee in Lhasa* (original title: 風轉西藏 --- 我在拉薩賣咖啡), which appeared in 2010. He has also widely travelled in China, especially in the western regions.

Ramazzotti, Sergio (1965-) is an Italian photographer and freelance journalist who authored the travel reportage *La birra di Shaoshan* (trans. *A Beer in Shaoshan*). In this book, published in 2002, Ramazzotti writes about his visit to Mao Zedong's hometown – Shaoshan – where he stayed for a couple of weeks always accompanied by Celia, his Chinese guide and translator. This was Ramazzotti's second journey to the country, but the first one to find publication as a book within the "Traveller" series by Feltrinelli publisher. Despite Ramazzotti's profession, in the book there are no pictures.

Richard, Luc is a French travel writer and journalist who published in 2003 the travelogue *Voyage à travers la Chine interdite* (trans. *Journey into Forbidden China*). The journey, made by car, lasted a couple of months and led Richard to enter into Tibet, following his old friend Constantin de Slizewicz and two Chinese companions from Beijing: Lao Shi (literally: the teacher) and Xia Jia. In the last few weeks the group is obliged to split and Richard travelled alone through Xinjiang in the northeast of China. The book does not contain any illustrations, despite the fact that Richard drew also sketches and took pictures along the road, which were sometimes used to communicate with the people, as he could not speak any Mandarin at that time.

Robjstaples (real name: Robert Staples) is a British blogger who wrote the blog *Going Walkabout and Answering Some of my Questions About China... Like When I'll Win the Lottery with All These Useless Tickets They Keep Selling Me!* (2005). This blog is hosted on the blog platform Travelpod.com. Robjstaples undertook his journey at the end of his one-year stay in China, where he worked as a teacher of English. His wanderings around the Middle Kingdom lasted almost three months. Most of the places he visited and dwelled in are off the beaten track: Dongguan, Longsheng, Chengyang, Zhaoxing. Robjstaples published 11 other travel blogs on his Travelpod's space, some of which concerns China, while others recount his journeys around the world. *Going Walkabout and Answering Some of my Questions About China...* is the blog by him that has received the greatest number of visits.

Shuyun, Sun is a Chinese writer, filmmaker and scholar. After graduating in Beijing, Shuyun received a scholarship from the University of Oxford. She currently lives in London. *The Long March: The True History of Communist China's Founding Myth* is a 2006 travelogue (in English) that narrates Shuyun's effort to retrace the paths and vicissitudes of the soldiers who participated in Long March. During this journey, she interviewed some of the last few veterans still alive with the intent to deconstruct the narrative of the Long March – the founding myth of today's China – as it is presented by the Chinese Communist Party (CCP). A map of the itineraries followed by the Red Army and a few pictures of the veterans encountered are included in the book.

Supermary58 (1958-) is an Italian blogger who wrote the blog *Cina, nel regno di mezzo* (2012, trans. *China: Into the Middle Kingdom*) on the platform Turistipercaso.it. Supermary58's journey lasted two weeks during which the blogger visited the most popular tourist places in China: Beijing, Shanghai, Xian, Suzhou. The blog counts 10 posts and in none of them are included any pictures. Overall, Supermary58 has published 14 blogs on her space on the platform: *Cina, nel regno di mezzo* is the sole one dedicated to China.

Thubron, Colin (1939-), a renowned British travel writer, has published two travel books dealing with China: *Behind the Wall: A Journey through China* (1987) and *Shadow of the Silk Road* (2006). The first travelogue is entirely focused on a journey that Thubron took around the Middle Kingdom when the country had just reopened its frontiers to tourists. In order to be able to approach Chinese people, Thubron learnt some Mandarin before embarking on his journey. He spent several months in the country following a circular itinerary: firstly, he descended from north to south touching Beijing, Qufu, Nanjing, Hangzhou, Shanghai, Xiamen and Hong Kong. Then he ascended the country visiting, among others, Guangzhou, Shaoshan, Kunming, Chengdu, Xian and stretching westward as far as Jiayuguan. In *Shadow of the Silk Road*, Thubron recounts, as the title suggests, his vicissitudes along the Silk Road, from Xian, in China, to Istanbul, in Turkey. The book is particularly relevant as it offers some impressions about China, ten years after the author's first visit to the country. Apart from two maps at the beginning of each book that retrace the author's path, the two travelogues do not present any illustrations and are exclusively composed of written text.

Viagra8868 (original name: 偉哥 8868) is a Chinese blogger who wrote a blog titled *Trip around Kunming Looking for Colours* (2015; original title: 我在云南過春節游云南尋"色"滇中 昆明周邊一日游). Also, this blog is hosted on the platform Travel.sina.com.cn. The blogger dedicates this blog to his few days journey to Kunming in Autumn. The blog has four posts and is enriched with several pictures.

Yǒu Gè A (original name: 有个啊) is a Chinese blogger who published his travel blog about *Suzhou* (2015; original title: 古韵园林風--讀不完的姑苏) on the main travel blog platform in China: Travel.sina.com.cn. *Suzhou* recollects the blogger's journey to one of the most known and celebrated cities of the whole country. The blog counts five posts and contains several pictures.

REFERENCES

Adorno, Theodor. *The Culture Industry: Selected Essays on Mass Culture*. London: Routledge, 1991.

Agha, Asif. "Recombinant Selves in Mass Mediated Spacetime," *Language & Communication* 27 (2007), 320-335.

Ahmed, Sara. "Home and Away: Narratives of Migration and Estrangement," *International Journal of Cultural Studies*, 2 (1997), 329-347.

Angé, Caroline and Deseilligny, Oriane. "Le blog de voyage: Un dispositif idiorrymatique?" in *Proceedings of the International Conference Hypertextes et Hypermédias. Produits, Outils et Méthodes: Rétrospective et Perspective 1989-2009*. Paris: Hermes, 2009.

Arnaud, Clara. *Sur les chemins de Chine*. Montfort-en-Chalosse: Gaïa Editions, 2010.

Ashcroft, Bill, Griffiths, Gareth and Tiffin, Helen. *The Empire Writes Back: Theory and Practice in Post-Colonial Literatures*. London: Routledge, 1989.

Askehave, Inger, and Nielsen, Anne Ellerup. "What Are the Characteristics of Digital Genres? Genre Theory from a Multi-Modal Perspective," in *Proceedings of the 38th Hawaii International Conference on System Sciences*. Los Alamitos: IEEE Press, 2005.

Ataritouchme. "All o'er China during Spring Festival Holiday." Travelpod.com, 2006. <https://web.archive.org/web/*/http://www.travelpod.com/travelblog/ ataritouchme/china_2006/tpod.html.>

Bach, Evelyn. "A Traveller in Skirts: Quest and Conquest in the Travel Narratives of Isabella Bird," *Canadian Review of Comparative Literature/Revue Canadienne de Littérature Comparée* 22 (1995), 587-599.

Baetens, Jan. "Image and Narrative," in David Herman, Jahn Manfred, and Marie-Laure Ryan, eds., *Routledge Encyclopedia of Narrative Theory*. London: Routledge, 2005, 236-237.

Bakhtin, Mikhail. *The Dialogic Imagination: Four Essays*, ed. Michael Holquist, trans. Michael Holquist and Caryl Emerson. Austin: University of Texas Press, 1981 (1937).

Bal, Mieke. "Descrizioni, costruzione di mondi e tempo della narrazione," trans. Marco Marchetti, in Franco Moretti, ed., *Il romanzo: Le forme*. Milano: Einaudi, 2002, 191-224.

Banyai, Maria and Glover, Troy. "Evaluating Research Methods on Travel Blogs," *Journal of Travel Research* 51 (2012), 267-277.

Barthes, Roland. *L'empire des signes*. Skira: Genève, 1970.

———. *Image, Music, Text*, ed. and trans. Stephen Heath. New York: Hill and Wang, 1977.

———. *Camera Lucida: Reflections on Photography*, trans. Richard Howard. New York: Hill & Wang, 1981.

———. *Travels in China*, trans. Andrew Brown. Cambridge: Polity Press, 2012.

Bateman, John. *Multimodality and Genre: A Foundation for the Systematic Analysis of Multimodal Documents*. London: Palgrave Macmillan, 2008.

Bateman, John, Delin, Judy, and Henschel, Renate. "Multimodality and Empiricism: Preparing for a Corpus-Based Approach to the Study of Multimodal Meaning-Making," in Eija Ventola, Cassily Charles, and Martin Kaltenbacher, eds., *Perspectives on Multimodality*. Amsterdam: John Benjamins, 2004, 65-89.

Battisti, Francesca, and Portelli, Alessandra. "The Apple and the Olive Tree: Exiles, Sojourners, and Tourists in the University," in Andor Skotnes and Rina Benmayor, eds., *Migration and Identity*. Oxford: Oxford University Press, 1994, 35-51.

Baudrillard, Jean. *Simulacra and Simulations*, trans. Sheila Faria Glaser. Ann Arbor: University of Michigan Press, 1994.

Becki. *Backpacker Becki*, 2012. <https://web.archive.org/web/*/ www.backpackerbecki.com>.

——. Borders of Adventure, 2014. <http://www.bordersofadventure.com>.

Benveniste, Émile. Problems in General Linguistics, trans. Mary Elizabeth Meek. Coral Gables: University of Miami Press, 1971.

Bettinelli, Giorgio. *In Vespa. Da Roma a Saigon*. Milano: Feltrinelli, 1997.

———. *Brum Brum. 254.000 chilometri in Vespa*. Milano: Feltrinelli, 2002.

———. *La Cina in Vespa*. Milano: Feltrinelli, 2008.

Bickers, Robert. *The Scramble for China: Foreign Devils in the Qing Empire, 1832-1914*. London: Penguin, 2012.

Bird, Isabella. *The Yangtze Valley and Beyond: An Account of Journeys in China, Chiefly in the Province of Sze Chuan and among Man-Tze of the Somo Territory*. London: John Murray, 1899.

———. *Chinese Pictures: Notes on Photographs Made in China*. New York: Charles L. Bowman, 1900.

Birke Dorothee and Christ, Birte. "Paratext and Digitalized Narrative: Mapping the Field," *Narrative* 21 (2013), 65-87.

BitByTheTravelBug. "China 2014," *Travelblog.org*, 2014. <https://www.travelblog.org/Bloggers/BitByTheTravel Bug>.

Blanchot, Maurice. *The Space of Literature*, trans. Ann Smock. Lincoln: University of Nebraska Press, 1983.

Blanton, Casey. *Travel Writing: The Self and the World*. London: Routledge, 2002.

Blommaert, Jan and Verschueren, Jef. *Debating Diversity: Analysing the Discourse of Tolerance*. London: Routledge, 1998.

Bolter, Jay David and Grusin, Richard. *Remediation: Understanding New Media*. Cambridge: MIT Press, 1998.

Bonsagit, Carmela, McCabe, Scott, and Hibbert, Sally. "What Is Told in Travel Blogs? Exploring Travel Blogs for Consumer Narrative Analysis," in *Proceedings of the International Conference Information and Communication Technologies in Tourism 2009*. Amsterdam: Springer, 2009, 61-71.

Borm, Jan. "Defining Travel: On the Travel Book, Travel Writing and Terminology," in Glenn Hooper and Tim Youngs, eds., *Perspectives on Travel Writing*. Aldershot: Ashgate Publishing, 2004, 13-26.

Bourdieu, Pierre. *Photography: A Middlebrow Art*, trans. Shaun Whiteside. Stanford: Stanford University Press, 1990.

Bruner, Edward. "The Transformation of Self in Tourism," *Annals of Tourism Research* 18 (1991), 238-250.

Burton, Stacy. *Travel Narrative and the Ends of Modernity*. New York: Cambridge University Press, 2014.

Butor, Michel. "Travel and Writing," trans. John Powers and K. Lisker, in Susan. R. Roberson, ed., *Defining Travel: Diverse Visions*. Mississippi: University Press of Mississippi, 2001 (1974), 69-85.

Caldas-Coulthard, Rosa, Carmen, and Coulthard, Malcom, eds. *Texts and Practices: Readings in Critical Discourse Analysis*. London: Routledge, 1996.

Calzati, Stefano. "Alcune riflessioni critiche sul processo di rimediazione dei blog," *Bollettino '900*, 2013a. <http://www3.unibo.it/boll900/numeri/2013-i/Calzati.html/>.

———. "Intermediality, Multimodality and Medial Chronotopes: A Comparison between The Travel Book and the Travel Blog," *Caracteres* 3 (2013b), 99-113.

———. "The Privileged Case of Travel Writing: Travel Books and Travel Blogs between Performative and Possessive Knowledge," in *Proceedings of the 2014 Narrative Matters Conference*, 2014. <https://hal.archives-ouvertes.fr/hal-01077474>.

———. "Travelling and Writing and the Form of Travel Writing: Reconsidering Bill Bryson's (Supposed) Postcolonial Legacy," Journal of Postcolonial Writing 51(2015a), 422-435.

———. "Travel Writing on the Edge: An Intermedial Approach to Travel Books and Travel Blogs," *Film and Media Studies* 10 (2015b), 153-168.

Cardell, Kylie and Douglas, Kate. "Travel Blogs," in Carl Thompson, ed., *The Routledge Companion to Travel Writing*. London: Routledge, 2016, 298-307.

Carson, Dean and Schmallegger, Doris. "Blogs in Tourism: Changing Approaches to Information Exchange," *Journal of Vacation Marketing* 14 (2008), 99-110.

Chatwin, Bruce. *What am I doing here?* London: Jonathan Cape, 1988.

Clark, Steve, ed. *Travel Writing & Empire: Postcolonial Theory in Transit*. London: Zed Books, 1999.

Clark, Steve and Smethurst, Paul, eds. *Asian Crossings: Travel Writing on China, Japan and Southeast Asia*. Hong Kong: Hong Kong University Press, 2008.

Clarke, John James. *Oriental Enlightenment: The Encounter between Asian and Western Thought*. London: Routledge, 1997.

Clifford, James. *Routes: Travel and Translation in the Late Twentieth Century*. Cambridge: Harvard University Press, 1997.

Clifford, Nicholas. *A Truthful Impression of the Country: British and American Travel Writing in China, 1880-1949*. Ann Arbor: University of Michigan Press, 2001.

CNNIC. "Basic Data," 2012. <http://www1.cnnic.cn/IDR/BasicData/>.

Convertkit. "State of the Blogging Industry: 2017." *Convertkit.com*. https://convertkit.com/reports/blogging/.

Crang, Mike. "Tourist: Moving Places, Becoming Tourist, Becoming Ethnographer," in Tim Cresswell and Peter Merriman, eds., *Geographies of Mobilities: Practices, Spaces, Subjects*. Aldershot: Ashgate Publishing, 2011, 205-224.

Croiziers, Aurélie. *La Chine à fleur de peau: Journal d'une curieuse voyageuse*. La Neuville-aux-Joûtes: Jacques Flament Editions, 2011.

Curieuse Voyageuse. *Curieuse Voyageuse*, 2009. <http://www.curieusevoyageuse.com/category/voyages/asie/voyages-en-chine/>.

David-Neel, Alexandra. *My Journey to Lhasa*, 23rd edn. New York: Harper & Collins Publishers, 2005 (1927).

————. *Voyage d'une parisienne à Lhassa*. Paris: Pocket, 2008 (1927).

Davidson, Robyn. *The Picador Book of Journeys*. London: Picador, 2001.

De Slizewicz, Constantin. *Ivre de Chine: Voyages au coeur de l'Empire*. Paris: Editions Perrin, 2010.

Dennen, Vanessa. "Constructing Academic Alter-Egos: Identity Issues in a Blog-Based Community," *Identity in the Information Society* 2 (2009), 23-38.

Derrida, Jacques. *Of Grammatology*, trans. Gayatri Chakravorty Spivak. Baltimore: Johns Hopkins University Press, 1976.

————. *The Work of Mourning*, trans. Pascale-Anne Brault and Michael Naal. Chicago: University of Chicago Press, 2001.

Douglas, Christopher. *A Genealogy of Literary Multiculturalism*. New York: Cornell University Press, 2009.

Eco, Umberto. *Lector in fabula. La cooperazione interpretativa nei testi narrativi*. Milano: Bompiani, 1979.

Edwards, Justin and Graulund, Rune, eds. *Postcolonial Travel Writing: Critical Explorations*. Basingstoke: Palgrave Macmillan, 2011.

Emil. *Emil's Trip to China*, 2006. <http://emilstravels.blogspot.co.uk>.

Fairclough, Norman. *Critical Discourse Analysis*. Boston: Addison Wesley, 1995.

Fajfer, Zenon. *Liberature or Total Literature. Collected Essays 1999-2009*, ed. and trans. Katarzyna Bazarnik, Krakow: Korporacja Ha!art, 2010.

Faravelli, Stefano. *Carnet di viaggio: Cina*. Torino: EDT, 2005.

Fiormonte, Domenico. *Scrittura e filologia nell'era digitale*. Torino: Bollati Boringhieri, 2003.

Flavia. "Conoscere Pechino tra dinastie e imperatori," *Blogs di viaggi*, 2013. <http://blogdiviaggi.com/blog/2013/09/21/viaggio-a-pechino-cosa-vedere>.

Fleming, Peter. *Travels in Tartary: One's Company and News from Tartary*. London: Reprint Society, 1941.

Forsdick, Charles. "'(In)connaissance de l'Asie': Barthes and Bouvier, China and Japan," *Modern & Contemporary France* 14 (2006), 63-77.

Foucault, Michel. *The Archaeology of Knowledge and the Discourse on Language*, trans. Alan Sheridan Smith, New York: Pantheon Books, 1972.

Franklin, Adrian. "The Choreography of a Mobile World: Tourism Orderings," in René van der Dium, Carina Ren, and Gunnar Thór Jóhannesson, eds., *Actor-Network Theory and Tourism*. Routledge: London, 2012, 43-58.

Fussell, Paul. *Abroad: British Literary Travelling between the Wars*. Oxford: Oxford University Press, 1980.

Gao, Zhen and Gao, Qiang ("Gao Brothers"). *One Day in Beijing* (original title: 在北京一天能走多遠). Beijing: Beijing Guangbo Xueyuan Chubanshe, 2004.

Gattosandro Viaggiatore. "Cina e Hong Kong," *Gattosandro Viaggiatore*, 2012. <http://gattosandro-viaggiatore.blogspot.it/p/cina-e-hong-kong.html>.

————. "Cina del sud e isole," *Gattosandro Viaggiatore*, 2013. <http://gattosandro-viaggiatore.blogspot.it/p/cina-e-hong-kong.html>.

Gaunt, Mary. *A Woman in China*. London: Werner Laurie, 1914.

Genette, Gérard. *Narrative Discourse: An Essay in Method*, trans. Jane E. Lewin. Oxford: Blackwell, 1980.

—————. *Paratexts: Thresholds of Interpretation*, trans. Jane E. Lewin. Cambridge: Cambridge University Press, 1997.

Germain-Thomas, Olivier. *La traversée de la Chine à la vitesse du printemps*. Monaco: Editions du Rocher, 2003.

—————. *Le Bénarès-Kyôto*. Monaco: Editions du Rocher, 2007.

Gibson, James. "The Theory of Affordances," in Robert Shaw and John Bransford, eds., *Perceiving, Acting, and Knowing: Toward an Ecological Psychology*. London: John Wiley & Sons, 1977, 127-143.

Gifford, Rob. *China Road: A Journey into the Future of a Rising Power*. London: Random House, 2007.

Gillespie, Alan. "Tourist Photography and the Reverse Gaze," *Ethos* 34 (2006), 343-366.

Gordon Cummings, Constance. *Wanderings in China*. Edinburgh: Blackwood, 1886.

Gray, Nathan. *First Pass under Heaven: One Man's 4000-Kilometre Trek Along the Great Wall of China*. Auckland: Penguin, 2006.

Guerri, Giordano Bruno. *L'arcitaliano*. Milano: Bompiani, 1980.

Halliday, Michael. *Language as Social Semiotics: The Social Interpretation of Language and Meaning*. London: Edward Arnold, 1978.

Hannam, Kevin, Sheller Mimi, and Urry John. "Mobilities, Immobilities and Moorings," *Mobilities* 1 (2006), 1-22.

Hargett, James. "Chinese Travel Writing," in Carl Thompson, ed., *The Routledge Companion to Travel Writing*. London: Routledge, 2016, 112-124.

Hayles, Katherine. *How We Think: Digital Media and Contemporary Technogenesis*. Chicago: University of Chicago Press, 2012.

Hayot, Eric, Saussy Haun, and Yao, Steven, eds. *Sinographies: Writing China*. Minneapolis: University of Minnesota Press, 2007.

Herold, David Kurt. "Through the Looking Glass: Twenty Years of Research into the Chinese Internet," 2013. <http://repository.lib.polyu.edu.hk/jspui/bitstream/10397/5789/1/Herold_Through_Looking_Glass.pdf>.

Herring, Susan, Scheidt, Lois Ann, Kouper, Inna, and Wright, Elijah. "Longitudinal Content Analysis of Blogs: 2003-2004," in Mark Tremayne, ed., *Blogging, Citizenship, and the Future of Media*. New York: Routledge, 2007, 3-20.

Hirst, Bamboo. *Il mondo oltre il fiume dei peschi in fiore*. Milano: Mondadori, 1989.

—————. *Cartoline da Pechino*. Milano: Feltrinelli, 1998.

Hockx, Michel. *Internet Literature in China*. New York: Columbia University Press, 2015.

Hodge, Robert and Kress, Günther. *Language as Ideology*. London: Routledge, 1993.

Holland, Peter and Huggan, Graham. *Tourists with Typewriters: Critical Reflections on Contemporary Travel Writing*. Ann Arbor: University of Michigan Press, 1998.

Hooper, Glenn and Youngs, Tim, eds. *Perspectives on Travel Writing*. Aldershot: Ashgate Publishing, 2004.

How Man, Wong. *Exploring the Yangtze: China's Longest River*. San Francisco: China Books & Periodicals, 1989.

—————. *From Manchuria to Tibet*. Hong Kong: Odyssey Publishing, 1998.

—————. *Tales from Ancient Kingdom*. Taiwan: Commonwealth Publishing Group, 2009.

Huggan, Graham. Extreme *Pursuits: Travel/Writing in an Age of Globalization*. Ann Arbor: University of Michigan Press, 2009.

Hulme, Peter. *Colonial Encounters: Europe and the Native Caribbean 1492-1797*. London: Methuen, 1986.

Hulme, Peter and Youngs, Tim. *Talking about Travel Writing: A Conversation between Peter Hulme and Tim Youngs*. Leicester: English Association, 2007.

Iyer, Pico. *The Global Soul: Jet Lag, Shopping Malls, and the Search for Home*. New York: Knopf, 2000.

Jenkins, Henry. *Convergence Culture: Where Old and New Media Collide*. New York: New York University Press, 2006.

Kerr, Douglas. *Eastern Figures: Orient and the Empire in British Writing*. Hong Kong: Hong Kong University Press, 2008.

Kerr, Douglas and Julia Kuehn, eds. *A Century of Travels in China: Critical Essays on Travel Writing from the 1840s to the 1940s*. Hong Kong: Hong Kong University Press, 2007.

Knox, John. "Visual-Verbal Communication on Online Newspaper Home Pages," *Visual Communication* 6 (2007), 19-53.

Korte, Barbara. "Chrono-Types: Notes on Forms of Time in the Travelogue," in John Zilcosky, ed., *Writing Travel: The Poetics and Politics of the Modern Journey*. Toronto: University of Toronto Press, 2008, 25-53.

Kress, Günther and van Leeuwen, Theo. *Reading Images: The Grammar of Visual Design*. London: Routledge, 1996.

Kracauer, Siegfried. "Photography," trans. Thomas Y. Levin. *Critical Inquiry* 19 (1993 [1927]), 421-36.

Kuehn, Julia. "China of the Tourists: Women and the Grand Tour of the Middle Kingdom, 1878-1923," in Steve Clark and Paul Smethurst, eds., *Asian Crossings: Travel Writing on China, Japan and Southeast Asia*. Hong Kong: Hong Kong University Press, 2008, 113-130.

Lam, Fai Fred. *Travelling between Hope and Suffering* (original title: 旅行在 希望與苦難 之間). Taiwan: China Times Publishing, 2014.

LaMotte, Ellen. *Peking Dust*. New York: The Century Company, 1919.

Landow, George. *Hypertext 3.0: Critical Theory and New Media in an Era of Globalization*, 2nd edn. Baltimore: John Hopkins University Press, 2003.

Larsen, Jonas. "Geographies of Tourist Photography: Choreographies and Performances," in Jesper Falkheimer and André Jansson, eds., *Geographies of Communication: The Spatial Turn in Media Studies*. Göteborg: Nordicom, 2006, 243-260.

Legerton, Colin and Jacob Rawson. *Invisible China: A Journey through Ethnic Borderlands*. Chicago: Chicago Review Press, 2009.

Leong, Ka Tai. *On China: One to Twenty Four*. Hong Kong: Camera 22 Ltd., 1988.

Lisle, Debbie. *The Global Politics of Contemporary Travel Writing*. Cambridge: Cambridge University Press, 2006.

López-Varela, Asuncion, ed. *Cultura: International Journal of Philosophy of Culture and Axiology*, 13 (2016, forthcoming).

López-Varela, Asuncion and Sukla, Ananta Charan, eds. *The Ekphrastic Turn: Inter-Art Dialogues*. Common Ground Publishing: Champaign, 2015.

Lukács, Georg. *The Theory of the Novel: A Historico-Philosophical Essay on the Forms of Great Epic Literature*, trans. Anna Bostock. London: Merlin Press, 1977.

MacKinnon, Rebecca. *Consent of the Networked: The Worldwide Struggle for Internet Freedom*. New York: Basic Books, 2013.

Maillart, Ella. *La vie immediate*. Genève: Payot, 1991.

————. *Forbidden Journey: From Peking to Kashmir*, trans. Thomas McGreevy. Evanston: Marlboro Press, 2003 (1937).

Malaparte, Curzio. *Io in Russia e in Cina*. Firenze: Vallecchi Editore, 1958.

Malerba, Luigi. *Cina Cina*. Lecce: Manini, 1985.

Mathieu. "Un peu partout en Chine." Top-deaprt.com, 2007 <https://web.archive.org/web/*/http://matochina.top-depart.com/en/.>

McCracken, Ellen. "Expanding Genette's Epitext/Peritext Model for Transitional Electronic Literature: Centrifugal and Centripetal Vectors on Kindles and Ipads," *Narrative* 21 (2013), 105-124.

McLuhan, Marshall. *Essential McLuhan*, eds. Eric McLuhan and Frank Zingrone. New York: Basic Books, 1996 (1964).

Miller, Carolyn. "Genre as Social Action," *Quarterly Journal of Speech* 70 (1984), 151-177.

Miller, Carolyn and Shepherd, Dawn. "Blogging as Social Action: A Genre Analysis of the Weblog," 2004. <http://blog.lib.umn.edu/blogosphere/blogging_as_ social_action_a_genre_analysis_of_the_ weblog.html>.

Mills, Sara. *Discourses of Difference: An Analysis of Women's Travel Writing and Colonialism*. London: Routledge, 1991.

Millycat. "Cina: Terra di grandi contrasti," *Turistipercaso.it*, 2013. <http://turistipercaso.it/cina/68394/cina-terra-di-grandi-contrasti.html>.

Mitchell, William John. *Picture Theory: Essays on Verbal and Visual Representation*. Chicago: University of Chicago Press, 1994.

Morgan, Susan. "The 'Sphere of Interest': Framing Late Nineteenth-Century China in Words and Pictures with Isabella Bird," in Douglas Kerr and Julia Kuehn, eds., *A Century of Travels in China: Critical Essays on Travel Writing from the 1840s to the 1940s*. Hong Kong: Hong Kong University Press, 2007, 105-118.

Moroz, Grzegorz and Sztachelska, Jolanta, eds. *Metamorphoses of Travel Writing: Across Theories, Genres, Centuries and Literary Traditions*. Newcastle: Cambridge Scholars, 2010.

Morris, Rosalind, ed. *Photographies East: The Camera and Its Histories in the East and Southeast Asia*. Durham: Duke University Press, 2009.

Morrison, Aimée. "Facebook and Coaxed Affordances," in Anna Poletti and Julie Rak, eds., *Identity Technologies: Constructing the Self Online*. Madison: University of Wisconsin Press, 2014, 112-131.

Mulligan, Maureen. "Forbidden Journeys to China and Beyond with the Odd Couple: Ella Maillart and Peter Fleming," in Steve Clark and Paul Smethurst, eds., *Asian Crossings: Travel Writing on China, Japan and Southeast Asia*. Hong Kong: Hong Kong University Press, 2008, 141-148.

Nakamura, Lisa. *Cybertypes: Race, Ethnicity, and Identity on the Internet*. London: Routledge, 2002.

Nardi, Bonnie, Schiano, Diane, Gumbrecht, Michelle, and Swartz, Luke. "Why We Blog," *Communications of the ACM: The Blogosphere* 47 (2004), 41-46.

Ng, Jason Y. *Hong Kong State of Mind*. Hong Kong: Blacksmith Books, 2011.

———. *No City for Slow Man*. Hong Kong: Blacksmith Books, 2013.

Nielsen, Jakob and Tahir, Marie. *Homepage Usability: 50 Websites Deconstructed*. Indianapolis: New Riders Publishing, 2001.

Nieman Reports. *Blogs and Journalism Need Each Other*, 2003. <http://niemanreports.org/articles/blogs-and-journalism-need-each-other>.

Numerico, Teresa, Fiormonte, Domenico, and Tomasi, Francesca. *L'umanista digitale*. Bologna: Il Mulino, 2010.

Pagden, Anthony. *European Encounters with the New World: From Renaissance to Romanticism*. New Haven: Yale University Press, 1993.

Pan, Bing, MacLaurin, Tanya, and Crotts, John. "Travel Blogs and Implications for Destination Marketing," *Journal of Travel Research*, 46 (2007), 35-45.

Papacharissi, Zizi. "The Blogger Revolution? Audiences as Media Producers," in Mark Tremayne, ed., *Blogging, Citizenship, and the Future of Media*. New York: Routledge, 2007, 21-38.

Parise, Goffredo. *Cara Cina*. Torino: Einaudi, 1972 (1966).

Pazu, Kong. *Spinning in Tibet Selling Coffee in Lhasa* (original title: 風轉西藏 -我在拉薩賣咖啡). Beijing: China Renmin University Publishing, 2010.

———. "My Sharing on How Breathing Keeps Me Warm in Lhasa," *Ironshoetravel.com*, 2015. <http://ironshoetravel.com/?p=982>.

Pellegrino, Angelo, ed. *Verso Oriente. Viaggi e letteratura degli scrittori italiani nei paesi orientali (1912-1982)*. Roma: Istituto dell'Enciclopedia Treccani, 1985.

Polo, Marco. *The Travels of Marco Polo*, trans. Ronald Latham. London: Penguin, 1958.

Porter, Dennis. *Haunted Journeys: Desire and Transgression in European Travel Writing*. Princeton: Princeton University Press, 1991.

Prasch, Thomas. "Mirror Images: John Thomson's Photographs of East Asia," in Douglas Kerr and Julia Kuehn, eds., *A Century of Travels in China: Critical Essays on Travel Writing from the 1840s to the 1940s*. Hong Kong: Hong Kong University Press, 2007, 53-61.

Pratt, Mary-Louise. *Imperial Eyes: Travel Writing and Transculturation*. New York: Routledge, 1992.

Pühringer, Stefan and Taylor, Andrew. "A Practitioner's Report on Blogs as a Potential Source of Destination Marketing Intelligence," *Journal of Vacation Marketing* 14 (2008), 177-187.

Raban, Jonathan. *For Love & Money: Writing-Reading-Travelling, 1968-1987*. London: Picador, 1988.

Ramazzotti, Sergio. *Vado verso il Capo*. Milano: Feltrinelli, 1996.

—. *Carne verde*. Milano: Feltrinelli, 1999.

—. *La birra di Shaoshan*. Milano: Feltrinelli, 2002.

Rancière, Jacques. *The Future of the Image*, trans. Gregory Elliot. London: Verso Books, 2009.

Richard, Luc. *Voyage à travers la Chine interdite*. Paris: Presses de la Renaissance, 2003.

Richardson, Tina, ed. *Walking Inside Out: Contemporary British Psychogeography*. London: Rowman and Littlefield, 2015.

Roberts, John. *A History of China*. London: Palgrave MacMillan, 2011.

Ryan, Marie-Laure. "Media and Narrative," in David Herman, Jahn Manfred and Marie-Laure Ryan, eds., *Routledge Encyclopedia of Narrative Theory*. London: Routledge, 2005, 290-291.

Said, Edward. *Orientalism*. New York: Vintage, 1978.

Schriver, Karen. *Dynamics in Document Design: Creating Text for Readers*. New York: John Wiley & Sons, 1997.

Scidmore, Eliza. *Westward to the Far East: A Guide to the Principal Cities of China and Japan with a Note on Korea*, 8th edn. Toronto: The Canadian Pacific Railway Company, 1900.

Scott, David. *Semiologies of Travel: From Gautier to Baudrillard*. Cambridge: Cambridge University Press, 2004.

Shapin, Steven. *A Social History of Truth: Civility and Science in Seventeenth-Century England*. Chicago: University of Chicago Press, 1994.

Shepherd, Michael and Watters, Carolyn. "The Evolution of Cybergenres," *Proceedings of the 31st Annual Hawaii International Conference on System Sciences*. Los Alamitos: IEEE Press, 1998, 97-109.

Shuyun, Sun. *Ten Thousand Miles without a Cloud*. New York: Harper Perennial, 2003.

—. *The Long March: The True History of Communist China's Founding Myth*. New York: Anchor Books, 2006.

—. *A Year in Tibet*. London: Harper Collins, 2008.

Simanowski, Roberto. "Instant Selves: Algorithmic Autobiographies on Social Network Sites." *New German Critique* 139 (2017): 233-44.

Sontag, Susan. *On Photography*. New York: Farrar, Straus and Giroux, 1977.

Soscia, Danilo, ed. *In Cina: Il Gran Tour degli italiani verso il centro del mondo, 1904-1999*. Pisa: ETS, 2010.

Spurr, David. *The Rhetoric of Empire: Colonial Discourse in Journalism, Travel Writing, and Imperial Administration*. Durham: Duke University Press, 1993.

Strassberg, Richard. *Inscribed Landscapes: Travel Writing from Imperial China*. Berkeley: University of California Press, 1994.

Sues, Ilona. *Shark's Fins and Millet*. Boston: Little, Brown & Company, 1944.

Supermary58. "Cina, nel regno di mezzo," *Turistipercaso.it*, 2012. <http://turistipercaso.it/cina/67480/cina-nel-regno-di-mezzo.html>.

Tang, Qi and Chao, Chin-Chung. "Foreigners Archive: Contemporary China in the Blogs of American Expatriates," *Chinese Journal of Communication* 3 (2010), 384-401.

Thompson, Carl. *Travel Writing: The New Critical Idiom*. London: Routledge, 2011.

Thomson, John. *Straits of Malacca, Indo-China, and China, or, Ten Years' Travels, Adventures, and Residence Abroad*. New York: Harper, 1875.

Thubron, Colin. *Behind the Wall: A Journey through China*. London: Heinemann, 1987.

—. *Shadow of the Silk Road*. London: Chatto & Windus, 2006.

Tian, Xiaofei. *Visionary Journeys: Travel Writings from Early Medieval and Nineteenth-Century China*. Cambridge: Harvard University Asian Center, 2012.

Todorov, Tzvetan. *The Morals of History*, trans. Alyson Waters. Minneapolis: University of Minnesota Press, 1995.

UNWTO. "Understanding Tourism: Basic Glossary," *UNWTO.org*, 2013. <http://media.unwto.org/en/content/understanding-tourism-basic-glossary>.

Urry, John. *The Tourist Gaze*, 2nd edn. London: Sage, 2002 (1990).

Uszkalo, Kirsten and Harkness, Darren. "Consider the Source: Critical Considerations of the New Medium of Social Media," in Paul Bubra and Clint Burnham, eds., *From Text to Txting: New Media in the Classroom*. Bloomington: Indiana University Press, 2012, 15-42.

Vafopoulos, Michalis. "Being, Space, and Time on the Web," *Metaphilosophy* 43 (2012): 405-425.

Van Dijck, José. *The Culture of Connectivity: A Critical History of Social Media*. Oxford: Oxford University Press, 2013.

Van Lier, Henri. *Philosophy of Photography*. Leuven: Leuven University Press, 2007.

Varela, Francisco, Thompson, Evan, and Rosch, Eleanor. *The Embodied Mind: Cognitive Science and Human Experience*. Cambridge: MITT Press, 1991.

Vesterman, William. "The Death of the Scientific Author: Multiple Authorship in Scientific Papers," *Common Knowledge* 8 (2002), 439-448.

Viagra8868. "Trip Around Kunming Looking for Colours," *Travel.sina.com.ch*, 2015. <http://i.travel.sina.com.cn/qcyn/kunming/321.html>.

Walker-Rettberg, Jill. *Blogging*. Cambridge: Polity Press, 2008.

Wenger, Anita. "Analysis of Travel Bloggers' Characteristics and Their Communication About Austria as a Tourism Destination," *Journal of Vacation Marketing* 14 (2008), 169-176.

Widdowson, Henry. "Article Review: The Theory and Practice of Critical Discourse Analysis," *Applied Linguistics* 19 (1998), 136-151.

Williams, Alan M. and Hall, Colin M. "Tourism and Migration: New Relationships between Production and Consumption," *Tourism Geographies: An International Journal of Tourism Space, Place and Environment* 2 (2000), 5-27.

Wolf, Werner. "Pictorial Narrativity," in David Herman, Jahn Manfred and Marie-Laure Ryan, eds., *Routledge Encyclopedia of Narrative Theory*. London: Routledge, 2005, 431-435.

————. "The Relevance of 'Mediality' and 'Intermediality' to Academic Studies of English Literature," in Martin Heusser, Andreas Fischer and Andreas H. Jucker, eds., *Mediality/Intermediality*. Göttingen: Narr, 2008, 15-44.

Yates, JoAnne, Orlikowski, Wanda, and Okamura, Kazuo. "Explicit and Implicit Structuring of Genres in Electronic Communication: Reinforcement and Change of Social Interaction," *Organization Science* 10 (1999), 83-103.

Yǒu Gè A. "Suzhou," *Travel.sina.com.ch*, 2015. <http://i.travel.sina.com.cn/ js/suzhou/498.html>.

Youngs, Tim and Forsdick, Charles, eds. *Travel Writing: Critical Concepts in Literary and Cultural Studies*, vol. 1. London: Routledge, 2012.

Yuan, Wenli. "E-Democracy@China: Does It Work?" *Chinese Journal of Communication* 3 (2010), 488-503.